Dubious Mandate

DUBIOUS MANDATE

A Memoir of the UN in Bosnia, Summer 1995

Phillip Corwin

DUKE UNIVERSITY PRESS   *Durham and London, 1999*

© 1999 Duke University Press

All rights reserved

Printed in the United States of America on acid-free paper ∞

Typeset in Minion by Keystone Typesetting, Inc.

Library of Congress Cataloging-in-Publication Data appear

on the last printed page of this book.

Tal vez esta guerra se irá como aquellas que nos compartieron
dejándonos muertos, matándonos con los que mataron
pero el deshonor de este tiempo nos toca la frente con dedos quemantes
y quién borrará lo inflexible que tuvo la sangre inocente?

[Perhaps this war will pass like the others which divided us,
leaving us dead, killing us along with the killers
but the shame of this time puts its burning fingers to our faces.
Who will erase the ruthlessness hidden in innocent blood?]
—Pablo Neruda, *Selected Poems*

We should kill our pasts with each passing day. Blot them out, so that
they will not hurt. Each present day could thus be endured more easily,
it would not be measured against what no longer exists. As things are,
specters mix with our lives so that there is neither pure memory nor
pure life. They clash and try to strangle each other, continually.
—Mesa Selimovic, *Death and the Dervish*

Contents

Former Yugoslavia. Courtesy Harvard College Library.

During the spring and summer of 1995, I was the United Nations' (UN) chief political officer in Bosnia and Herzegovina, roughly the period between the end of the Cessation of Hostilities Agreement (COHA) between the Bosnian Serbs and the Bosnian government, which ran from 1 January through 30 April 1995, and the beginning of NATO's most intensive bombing campaign in its history, which started on 30 August and lasted until 14 September. There was war all the time I was in Bosnia.

When I arrived to take up my post in Sarajevo, the war in Bosnia had been going on for a little more than three years. There had been a few ceasefires, but during those brief periods the warring parties had simply prepared for the resumption of battle; they had not attempted to build peace. In winter, the war slowed down because the heavy snows and mountainous terrain made roads unpassable and troop movements very difficult, but once the spring emerged with its flowers and rains, the war machines came out of hibernation, and the killing began again in earnest. Those who had survived another brutal Balkan winter—often without heat, water, or light—prepared themselves for another season of terror.

What made the period that I was in Bosnia unique was that it was during this period that the UN presence in Bosnia was transformed from a peace-keeping operation into a peace-enforcement operation. Never before in history had that happened, and the implications for future UN peacekeeping operations were momentous. This book is a personal account of a critical part of that transformation.

Though I had been in Gorazde on two separate occasions in 1994, and in Sarajevo and other parts of former Yugoslavia several years before the war, nothing had prepared me for the extremes of horror and hope that I experienced during the period covered in this book.

Just before I left Sarajevo, a Bosnian government minister, who was later to become that country's prime minister, threatened my life. In a face-to-face meeting, he told me that if I didn't leave Bosnia immediately, he could not guarantee my safety. "We know where you live," he said, "and during a war, accidents can happen. We want you out of Bosnia within twenty-four hours." He also threatened to declare me persona non grata, which, he said, would mobilize the populace against me. But he never did it, and the popu-

May 1995: Front Lines.

lace never bothered me. The Bosnian people were, quite to the contrary, among the most gracious, polite, and hospitable people I have ever met. (It was the demagogic political leaders and the government-sponsored paramilitary gangs that were inhospitable.)

When I asked the minister why his government wanted me out of his country, he said, in true totalitarian fashion, that he was only delivering the message; the matter had been decided by the Department of Internal Security, and he didn't know the reason. "Perhaps something in your background," he suggested. Of course, Internal Security had never spoken with me.

The threat on my life was not unique. Two of my three predecessors had also been threatened. The Bosnian government did business that way. The head of the United Nations Protection Force (UNPROFOR), Japanese diplomat Yasushi Akashi, had already been declared persona non grata, along with a host of other international notables far more prestigious than I. If the Bosnian government suspected you were not resolutely on their side, they

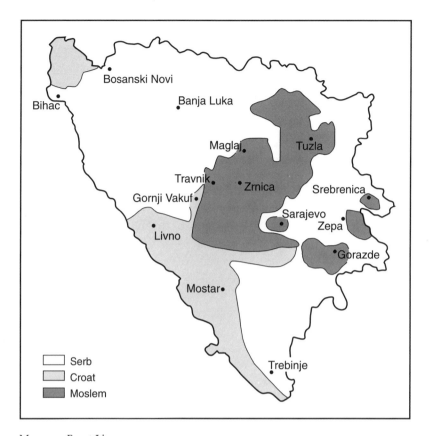

May 1995: Front Lines.

threatened to kill you, and sometimes they tried. They tried with me. They would not accept the idea of professional impartiality on the part of anyone in the international community, an extremist position that was also relentlessly promoted by the international press. This attitude, in turn, justified any behavior, including murder—even of one's own people if necessary—in the interest of what was called self-defense.

Of course, the Bosnian Serbs and Bosnian Croats were just as bad. The only difference was that the world press condemned their misbehavior, but was reluctant to condemn similar outrages perpetrated by the Bosnian government. In fact, the leaders of all the various factions in Bosnia were merely gangsters wearing coats and ties. The world community knew it, but seldom admitted it publicly. And such terroristic "statesmanship" could not be explained by a lack of education. Among the Bosnian Serbs, for example, President Radovan Karadzic was a trained psychiatrist; Vice President Nikola Koljevic had been a professor of Shakespeare and of English; and future president Biljana Plavsic was a professor of biology. They were

November 1995: Dayton Agreement. Courtesy Laura Silber and Allan Little.

highly educated persons, many of whom had studied in the West. Karadzic and Koljevic spoke fluent English. As for the Bosnian government leaders, President Alija Izetbegovic was a lawyer, and both Vice President Ejup Ganic and Prime Minister Hasan Muratovic had advanced academic degrees. They were not stupid people, but they were warriors, and war does not turn boys into men; it turns men into beasts.

I found it particularly ironic that the direct threat on my life came from Muratovic, a man reputed to be among the biggest war profiteers of all. Rumors fly, and I had no evidence of Muratovic's particular activities, nor could I rely on my own mantra that the most religious are often the most hypocritical and the most corrupt. During my stay in Bosnia, however, I heard many stories about his dealings. Once, at a farewell party for one of the international aid workers who had been solidly in the Bosnian government's camp during her tenure, Muratovic was heard boasting about how he had bargained down a carpet salesman in Istanbul by demanding a discount for paying in cash rather than charging the purchase on his American Ex-

CROATIA

REPUBLIKA SAPSKA

•Velila Kladusa

Prijedor

•Omarska   •Prnjavor   Brcko   SERBIA

•Bihac   Sanski   •Banja Luka   Doboj•   •Bijelina
             Most   Zvornik
                                                     •
Drvar•   Travnik•   •Zenica

                                          Han•   Srebrenica
                                 Visoko Pljesak•
                       Kiseljak• •Vogosca   •Zepa
      FEDERATION   Jadzici •Sarajevo
                       Tarcin• •Pale   Visegrad
CROATIA   •Livno   Igman•   •
                                           Gorazde•

                    Mostar
                    •

                              MONTENEGRO

             Ploce•
                     •Stolac
             •Neum

Adriatic Sea   Dubrovnik

November 1995: Dayton Agreement IEBL.

press Card. Several people related this story to me. Muratovic and other Bosnian government officials frequently traveled on shopping visits to other parts of Europe, and they relied on the UN, the same UN they publicly abused, to transport them out of Bosnia. They had charge cards, foreign bank accounts, and a heavy dose of righteousness. That an official like Muratovic should threaten me and other international workers was typical of the style of Balkan Communist, or former Communist, leaders. You may take the gangster out of the system, but it is more difficult to take the system out of the gangster.

What I suspect got me in trouble with the Bosnian government was my loyalty to the United Nations—my insistence that harassment and death threats to any member of the international community, military or civilian, by any of the parties to the conflict should be both opposed and exposed. I was also unsympathetic to the Bosnian government's attempts to pervert the UN's mandate so that UN forces would become the government's mercenaries. The Bosnian government, meanwhile, insisted on maintaining the moral high ground and fiercely resisted any attempt to characterize its actions as illegitimate. Government officials argued that Bosnia was *their* country (though they controlled only a minority of the territory); they were victims, and all others were aggressors, so that anything they themselves did was justified. They feared that any change in this viewpoint might weaken the base of their international support. Of course, they had a point. They *were* victims, as all the parties to the conflict were, and the Bosnian Moslems were greater victims than the others. But the Bosnian government's tactics in trying to draw NATO into the conflict often went beyond the bounds of strategy and crossed the line into provocation and reckless endangerment. I opposed such behavior, and I did not believe that refusing to accept harassment from the Bosnian government, including death threats, was tantamount to supporting the Bosnian Serbs. Neither the United Nations nor I personally ever endorsed Bosnian Serb war tactics: the shelling of civilians, ethnic cleansing, concentration camps, or the siege of Sarajevo. Indeed, we had condemned them many times.

The Bosnian government was particularly critical of the UN doctrine of impartiality, and attacked and distorted it at every opportunity. But impartiality never means moral indifference. Impartiality exists within a given mandate. It means attempting to implement that mandate in all its aspects and, at the same time, respecting the views of all the parties to a conflict. It involves maintaining the credibility of, and access to, those parties. Otherwise, one cannot be an effective interlocutor. Impartiality is never a passive doctrine. It can involve very tough talk, and it must always include the will to change the behavior of any party not complying with the mandate set forth in the appropriate resolutions of the Security Council. As Shashi Tharoor, my brilliant colleague in the department of peacekeeping operations, once said in an article in the *Christian Science Monitor* (19 January 1996): "Impartiality is the oxygen of peacekeeping." There are times when an interlocutor may have to sup with the devil, but that does not imply that the former is satanic or that he accepts the criminal behavior of the latter.

The maelstrom of contempt into which I descended when I arrived in Sarajevo is perhaps best illustrated by a passage from an article by correspondent Zlatko Dizdarevic that appeared in *Time Magazine* on 12 December 1994, less than five months earlier, commenting on a recent visit to Sarajevo by UN Secretary-General Boutros Boutros-Ghali:

> Sarajevans welcomed Boutros-Ghali on his recent visit to the city with a concert of boos and hisses the likes of which haven't been heard in this city. Two placards stood out: one, scrawled on a piece of cardboard torn from a box that once perhaps contained humanitarian aid, simply said GHALI HITLER; another said GHALI ISN'T A MAN. The first summed

up political opinion around here, namely that fascism's heavy boots have marched over the backs of Bosnian civilians to steal into Europe, aiding and abetting a new Hitlerism. The second slogan was Sarajevo's own special way of expressing its contempt for the UN. Boutros-Ghali was probably unaware that these four words dealt the lowest possible blow ever dreamed up by the legendary sports fans of Sarajevo. In former days of glory, diehard fans used to berate bumbling referees with the same slogan: "The ref isn't a man." . . . The Sarajevo diehards who chanted "The ref isn't a man" will be the same people to help the blue helmets get on their way one of these days, even though UN Commanders keep warning what a "difficult and complex operation" that will be. To leave the battlefield without having fired a shot has always been a difficult and complex operation.

In fact, the fury against Boutros-Ghali had begun two years earlier, when, during a visit to Sarajevo on 31 December 1992, the exhausted UN Secretary-General had foolishly told a group of Sarajevo journalists: "You have a situation which is better than ten other places all over the world. I can give you a list of ten places where you have more problems than in Sarajevo."

Ten? To a group of besieged media people in a beleaguered, tortured city, in the middle of winter, without fuel, adequate food, or medical supplies? The people of Sarajevo never forgot this gaffe.

Two things finally convinced me to leave Sarajevo: an action by the United Nations Security Council and my feeling that I could not be effective if I stayed. At the Bosnian government's insistence, the UN Security Council restructured the UN operation in Bosnia in 1995 and created a new post two grades above me as chief of mission, a post that assumed my main political functions and left me with little more to do than administrate. The new man sent to take over in Bosnia was Antonio Pedauye, a Spanish career diplomat and a decent and courageous man with whom I had good relations. But I felt that he would be burdened with my presence, given the Bosnian government's attitude toward me, so I decided to leave. I did not want to remain where I could not be effective, and if the Bosnian government would refuse to talk to me and would, as threatened, block me from going to Pale to talk to the Bosnian Serbs, then there was no point in my staying. But I could not leave Bosnia easily, so even after departing Sarajevo, I stayed in the mission area for several weeks, during which time I continued to follow the situation closely. On 1 September 1995, just after the bombing began, I returned to New York.

Dubious Mandate is a personal account of a tumultuous period in Bosnian history. It is sympathetic to the achievements of the United Nations and critical of those who assaulted us, whether in word or deed. It is much more than a simple diary. In fact, on some days I made no entries because I was simply too occupied, or preoccupied, to record my thoughts. Rather, it is a detailed and faithful record based on personal contact with a wide variety of international actors, a record that no one else could have written, and in that sense it should prove to be an invaluable research tool to scholars who, in the future, will undertake the more comprehensive studies of the conflict that must be done if we are ever to learn from history. This book is a source book, without which a thorough history of the civil war in Bosnia cannot be written.

The style of *Dubious Mandate* is unconventional. I have often taken facts and used them as a springboard for reflections, rather than simply stating the facts and allowing them to speak for themselves. Some reflections are part of the original notebook entries—my thoughts on events as they were happening. Some, however, I added later on as I reread what I had written and felt the need to add more details with the benefit of added perspective. I have placed brackets around these added reflections in order to set them off from material that comes from the original notebooks.

Facts (and texts) are always seen through the eyes of the beholder, as the deconstructionists are fond of telling us, and my intent in providing additional commentary has been to provoke thought more than to draw conclusions. We have all been tyrannized by the international press's distortions of the events and by the domestic political agendas of various governments. The nature of the conflict in Bosnia, and in all of former Yugoslavia, needs radical reassessment. However politically correct or incorrect my reflections may seem, they should be seen as the views of someone who was on the ground during the war, as opposed to those who were in faraway metropolitan capitals making policy. Regrettably, the distance between us was often vast. Policymakers frequently have their own career ambitions, regardless of the facts.

In sum, I hope that my experiences in Sarajevo can serve as a prism through which may be refracted and reflected the major issues of the civil war in Bosnia and in all of former Yugoslavia, both before and since I was there.

I left Yugoslavia in September 1995 emotionally exhausted and politically depressed. The emotional exhaustion stemmed from having lived under very difficult conditions for almost two years. (I had been the UN's chief political officer in Eastern Slavonia in Croatia for twenty months before coming to Bosnia.) The political depression may need some explanation. I was deeply distressed by NATO's massive military intervention against the Bosnian Serbs, an intervention not very well camouflaged under UN cover. There were those (mainly, the laptop bombadiers) who believed that NATO's bombing campaign would have the effect of maintaining or restoring UNPROFOR's integrity. I believed quite the opposite. I believed it destroyed UNPROFOR's integrity as a peacekeeping operation. If NATO wanted to declare war against one of the parties to the conflict in Bosnia, then it should have done so under a NATO flag, not under a UN flag. It was disingenuous to enter a country as a peacekeeping force and then to wage war against one of the parties. The UN should either have changed its mandate or left Bosnia before NATO began its assault.

All the righteous indignation voiced in the international community about the civil war in Bosnia ignored the simple fact that *the highest moral achievement is a durable peace.* A durable peace does not mean that one has to surrender to aggression. It means that one begins with an understanding of the origins of the conflict and attempts to redress reasonable grievances. NATO's bombing campaign against one of the warring parties shattered whatever claims to impartiality the United Nations still had in former Yugoslavia, although admittedly those claims had almost atrophied by August 1995.

In most cases, the use of force is a sign of desperation, not of determination. It signals a failure of diplomacy. If international diplomacy in Bosnia had been more effective, there might have been no need for massive bombing by NATO. Certainly, the parties to the conflict, the Serbs more than others, bore responsibility for the continuing war. But so did the members of the international community, whose stated purposes were often contradicted by their actions.

I was concerned that NATO's assault in Bosnia would injure UN peacekeeping in at least three ways. First, it would discourage major financial backers such as Japan, as well as other nations committed to nonviolent conflict resolution, from supporting a peacekeeping operation that might end in underwriting military intervention against one of the parties. Second, troop-contributing nations might be less likely to participate in a peacekeeping operation if there were the prospect that the operation might suddenly be transformed into a military confrontation between the United Nations and one of the warring parties. Such a confrontation would place their lightly armed troops at risk. (Some nations had already threatened to remove their troops from Bosnia after they had been taken hostage by the Bosnian Serbs in retaliation for the NATO bombing of Pale on 25 and 26 May.) Third, I was concerned that it would be more difficult in future to get unanimity among the five permanent members of the United Nations Security Council for undertaking and maintaining a peacekeeping operation. Russia and China were antagonistic to the NATO bombing; France and England were ambiguous about it.

Nonetheless, I remain convinced of the positive value of United Nations peacekeeping operations. Finally, no other institution can do the job.

What was often stunning about the situation in Sarajevo—and for that matter in many of the areas of former Yugoslavia—was its geographical proximity to the so-called heart of Western civilization. I recall a conversation I once had with an educated, forty-something woman whom I met at a social event in New York City. I had returned to New York briefly one spring for what is best termed personal maintenance (i.e., visits to the dentist, doctor, supermarket, and bank, not to mention family) and administrative necessities (i.e., inquiries at United Nations headquarters about the paperwork that was not going where it should have been going).

My charming companion at the party asked me where I intended to spend my summer. Never having been a member of that privileged New York set that summered in the Hamptons and wintered in Gstaad, I answered wryly: "I expect to be spending the summer in Europe."

"Oh," said she, shamelessly exposing that cultural inferiority complex that in Americans is second only to obesity as a national illness, "How nice! Southern France, perhaps?"

"Sarajevo," I replied mischievously. "And maybe a weekend or two in Vukovar."

The point is that Sarajevo—and Vukovar and Banja Luka and Srebrenica and so many other locations in former Yugoslavia that rightly summon images of horror, medieval torture, destruction, and cruelty—are only a few hours by jet plane from Paris, London, Amsterdam, Rome, Athens, and other pillars of Western culture. How near, for example, were the Louvre and the bombed-out marketplace of Sarajevo. Yet how far.

The war in Bosnia was a media war as well as a land war, and there were very few, if any, impartial commentators. Editorial writers thousands of miles away, and certainly those in the battle area, sided with one of the warring parties. In the United States, that meant to be on the side of the Bosnian government. As a corollary, it also meant that anyone who tried to be objectively analytical was considered an accomplice to the genocidal massacre of Moslems.

Many professional historians and scholars, whom one might have expected to be more objective than daily journalists, were equally galvanized by the relentless TV images of brutalized Moslem children. I personally knew academics, both those who specialized in Balkan history and those who knew nothing about the region, who would rage out of control in support of one of the warring parties. Given such fury among noncombatants an ocean away, one can begin to appreciate how difficult it was for those of us directly involved on the ground to promote a peaceful resolution to the conflict—to chart a course through the minefields of ethnic hatreds, international meddling, disinformation, and ambiguous mandates. The war in Bosnia generated deep passions.

Little consensus could be found on any aspect of the war. To begin with, there was not even solid agreement on what kind of war it was. Was it a *civil* war, plain and simple—a tripartite battle among Serbs, Croats, and Moslems? Perhaps. Yet some maintained that because Serbia assisted the Bosnian Serbs and Croatia assisted the Bosnian Croats, it was not truly a civil war, but an international war. (Assistance by Iran, Turkey, and Afghanistan to the Bosnian government was not as often mentioned.) Indeed, there were those who insisted that Serbian President Slobodan Milosevic had actually invaded Bosnia, using the Yugoslav National Army (JNA) to promote his goal of a Greater Serbia. And that in Western Bosnia, since Croatia's army (HV) assisted and fought alongside of the Bosnian Croat army (HVO), that Croatia had also invaded Bosnia. Perhaps. But no civil war these days is completely domestic. Foreign advisors—military, financial, industrial, and even propaganda specialists—are always involved in every internal conflict. Political borders have no resistance to the World Wide Web, not to mention spy satellites.

At what point does foreign involvement constitute flagrant interference, even aggression, and turn a civil war into an international conflict? There is no easy answer, particularly if one considers that until Bosnia received international recognition in April 1992, Croatia, Serbia, and Bosnia were all part of the same country, Yugoslavia. Also, one cannot make aggression retroactive. Is it possible to argue that if Serbia sent arms to the Bosnian Serbs and Croatia sent arms to the Bosnian Croats while Bosnia was still part of Yugoslavia, such acts were internal matters, but that once Bosnia's independence was recognized by the European Community (but not by rump Yugoslavia), the very same assistance constituted aggression? Even the harshest critics of Milosevic would admit that when fighting first broke out in Croatia and Bosnia, the JNA considered itself to be putting down a secessionist movement. It was trying to preserve Yugoslavia, not promote Greater Serbia. (Much of the international community, which had incipient nationalist movements in their own countries, agreed.)

In the fall of 1991, when the Bosnian government was considering declaring independence, it sent emissaries (Bosnian Moslems, to be sure) to the United Nations to ask that a peacekeeping force be stationed in Bosnia, in anticipation of Bosnia's independence, as a deterrent to anticipated Yugoslav military opposition. The United Nations of course refused because it could not justify placing a peacekeeping force within the national borders of a sovereign country, Yugoslavia, without that country's permission—especially *before* a contested, and therefore unpredictable, election were to take place. Bosnia was still a part of Yugoslavia, and Yugoslavia did not want an international peacekeeping force within its sovereign territory, encouraging and protecting a secessionist movement. (Bosnian Moslems in 1991 were not even a majority in Bosnia; they were a plurality—44 percent.) The member states of the United Nations certainly would not have wanted to set this dangerous precedent. Imagine elements in Northern Ireland (not even an outright majority) asking for international forces to be placed in that region so that certain counties in Northern Ireland might be guaranteed the right to secede from the United Kingdom *if* they chose to do so.

Disputes rage not only about what to call the war in Bosnia and about who started it but also about *when* it started. It is not unusual to hear observers, even scholars, say that the wars in Croatia and Bosnia were only the latest phase of a continuing war that has been "going on for centuries." (This is also known as the "antique hatreds" thesis.) How many centuries? Since the Holy Roman Empire divided? Since the Ottoman Empire dissolved? Since the Congress of Berlin in 1878?

My own opinion is that the murderous internecine antagonism of the 1990s in Yugoslavia had its origins only half a century earlier, in the Nazi occupation. Jasminka Udovicki and Ejub Stitkovac speak eloquently to this point in their essay "Bosnia and Herzegovina: The Second War":

> Contrary to many interpretations of pent-up ancient hatreds in Bosnia, the tightly knit multiethnic community disintegrated for the first time in World War II. The roots of the conflict rested not in a "historical predisposition" of the Bosnian population mix, but in the Nazi-inspired policies of Ante Pavelic's puppet regime [in Croatia], which controlled a good part of Bosnia. There was no historical precedent for the 1990s war. It was the very threat of disintegration—expressed through the outcome of the elections and through the demand for secession by the Muslim and Croatian legislators on October 14, 1991—that unleashed the forces of war.*

Most Western historians will choose 6 April 1992 as the date when the war in Bosnia began because that was the day when the European Community formally recognized Bosnia's independence, the day that Serbian snipers opened fire on a massive antiwar demonstration in Sarajevo, killing five people and wounding another thirty, and the day when Serbian irregulars reportedly (never confirmed by independent sources) began crossing the Drina River from Serbia and pouring into Bosnia. (Not insignificantly, 6 April was also the anniversary of Hitler's bombing of Belgrade in 1941, a

---

*Jasminka Udovicki and James Ridgeway, eds., *Burn This House* (Durham, N.C.: Duke University Press, 1997), 176–177.

coincidence that the Serbs took as yet more evidence of an international conspiracy against them.)

But there are those who will argue for other dates to mark the beginning of the Bosnian conflict. On 14 October 1991, Moslem and Croat legislators in the Bosnian Parliament insisted that they had the right to secede from Yugoslavia. Bosnian Serbs walked out of the Parliament. On 9–10 November of that year, Bosnian Serb leaders conducted a plebiscite among Bosnian Serbs and received the expected result: Bosnian Serbs did *not* want Bosnia to secede from Yugoslavia. Meanwhile, the European Community's Arbitration (Badinter) Commission declared that 24 December 1991 was the deadline for any Yugoslav republic wishing to apply for international recognition of its independence. However, the commission added, the validity of any claim to independence would depend on whether a sufficient proportion of the voters of *each of the three ethnic communities* supported that claim. Obviously, the Serbs did not support Bosnian independence. The commission also expressed its opinion that the vote in favor of Bosnian secession had been inherently destabilizing. (Many international observers believed that Bosnian Croats voted in favor of secession only as a prelude to their own secession from Bosnia in order to join with Croatia.)

There were other possible beginnings for the war in Bosnia. On 9 January 1992, Radovan Karadzic declared the existence of a Bosnian Serb Republic within Bosnia—even before Bosnia had formally voted for independence. Did the war begin on that day, with an unauthorized secession from a country that had not yet itself seceded? Or what about 29 February 1992, the actual day of the referendum for Bosnian independence? Or what about the following day, 1 March, when an unidentified sniper killed the father of the groom as a Serbian wedding procession wound through a Moslem quarter in old Sarajevo? Or what about President Izetbegovic's vision of an Islamic state in the modern world, contained in his book *Islam between East and West*, published in the United States in 1984 and then in Yugoslavia four years later after his release from prison? Or does the exact date even matter?

In his book *Origins of a Catastrophe*, Warren Zimmermann recounts a conversation he had with Croatian President Franjo Tudjman, on 14 January 1992, more than six weeks before Bosnia voted for independence and just after Karadzic had declared the intent of Bosnian Serbs to secede from Bosnia to create their own republic. The day, in Zimmermann's words, was "just a few weeks after [Tudjman's] German protectors had bullied the European Community into supporting Bosnia's independence." Mind you, this is Tudjman speaking, not Milosevic:

> The Muslims want to establish an Islamic fundamentalist state. They plan to do this by flooding Bosnia with 500,000 Turks. Izetbegovic has

also launched a demographic threat. He has a secret policy to reward large families so that in a few years the Muslims will be a majority in Bosnia [at the time they were 44 percent]. The influence of an Islamic Bosnia will then spread through the Sandzak and Kosovo [Muslim areas of Serbia] to Turkey and Libya. Izetbegovic is just a fundamentalist front man for Turkey; together they're conspiring to create a Greater Bosnia. Catholics and Orthodox alike will be eradicated.*

Perhaps the civil war in Bosnia began when political leaders in former Yugoslavia began to speak like this.

*Warren Zimmerman, *Origins of a Catastrophe* (New York: Time Books, 1996), 181–82.

Acknowledgments

The opinions in this book are mine, and I am solely responsible for them. There are those, however, whom I should like to thank for having given me the opportunity and the inspiration to write this account of a terrible period in history, even if they did not help directly with the manuscript. Kofi Annan, now Secretary-General of the United Nations, was at the time of my service in former Yugoslavia the Under-Secretary-General for Peace-Keeping Operations. He always gave me his full support and the benefit of his insights. Cedric Thornberry, the Secretary-General's first special representative in former Yugoslavia, first selected me to serve as a political officer in Eastern Slavonia in Croatia, where I was in charge until I moved to Sarajevo. He had one of the best political minds I have ever encountered, and he was very appreciative of my analyses. Yasushi Akashi, who appointed me to be the UN's chief political officer in Bosnia, had abiding confidence in me and was always eager to hear my views. His patience was inexhaustible. My deputy in Sarajevo, John Ryan, was loyal, diligent, fearless, and, unfortunately, unappreciated by many. He worked incredibly long hours, more than once risked his life, and never let career ambitions interfere with his obligations as an international peacekeeper. I shall always be grateful to Bruno Chaubert, the French warrant officer who served as my driver/bodyguard, in addition to other duties, and who had the intense courage not to be distracted when a sniper's bullet targeted him one time as we were driving over Mount Igman. Had he flinched, all four of us in the vehicle would have gone over the precipice. Dianne Fairweather, my personal assistant, both in Eastern Slavonia and in Sarajevo, was always there to provide encouragement and assistance. She had the ability to be punctual, efficient, and pleasant, even under the most difficult conditions. My thanks must also go to the support staff in New York, who gave those of us in the field hope at the very time that much of the world was cynically denouncing the United Nations. Finally, there were my editors at Duke University Press. I am indebted to Valerie Millholland, who had the fortitude to publish this book, knowing how controversial it might be. Patricia Mickelberry, my managing editor, was a delightful tyrant, always insisting on accuracy and calmly enduring my complaints.

Major Players

Aguilar, Enrique UNPROFOR chief political officer in Bosnia and Herzegovina (BIH), January–April 1995

Akashi, Yasushi Special representative of the UN Secretary-General for former Yugoslavia, December 1993–October 1995

Annan, Kofi UN Undersecretary-General for Peacekeeping Operations

Bildt, Carl Co-chair of steering committee of ICFY, 1995–97; former prime minister of Sweden

Boutros-Ghali, Boutros UN Secretary-General, 1992–96

Izetbegovic, Alija President of Bosnia and Herzegovina

Janvier, Bernard Commander of UNPROFOR forces in all of former Yugoslavia, 1995

Karadzic, Radovan President of Republika Srpska, leader of the Bosnian Serbs

Koljevic, Nikola Vice president of Republika Srpska

Menzies, John U.S. chargé d'affaires, later ambassador to Bosnia and Herzegovina, 1995

Milosevic, Slobodan President of Serbia

Mladic, Ratko Commander of Bosnian Serb army

Muratovic, Hasan BIH minister, head of committee for relations with international organizations and, later, prime minister

Sacirbey, Muhamed Foreign minister of BIH, 1995; BIH permanent representative to the United Nations, 1992–95

Smith, Rupert Commander of UNPROFOR forces in BIH, 1995

Stoltenberg, Thorvald Co-chair of steering committee of ICFY, 1993–95, and former foreign minister of Denmark

Vance, Cyrus Former U.S. secretary of state under President Jimmy Carter; personal representative of the UN Secretary-General to former Yugoslavia, 1991–92; and co-chair of ICFY steering committee, 1992–93

Acronyms and Terms

AOR	area of responsibility
BiH	Bosnia and Herzegovina
Bosniak	Bosnian Moslem
BSA	Bosnian Serb army
CAC	Civil Affairs coordinator
CAS	close air support
CL	confrontation line
COHA	Cessation of Hostilities Agreement, from 1 January to 30 April 1995
Contact Group	A negotiating group of six countries: France, Germany, Italy, Russian Federation, United Kingdom, United States
D/SRSG	delegate of the special representative of the UN Secretary-General
Federation	Croat-Moslem Federation of BiH established under Washington Accords, March 1994
FOM	freedom of movement
HV	Croatian army
HVO	Bosnian Croat army
ICFY	International Conference on the Former Yugoslavia
ICRC	International Committee of the Red Cross
IFOR	Implementation Force
ILR	Igman Logistics Route
JNA	Yugoslav National Army
MNB	multinational brigade
OP	observation post
ROM	restriction of movement
RRF	Rapid Reaction Force
RS	Republika Srpska
Safe areas	six areas in Bosnia—Bihac, Gorazde, Sarajevo, Srebrenica, Tuzla, and Zepa—that, in the words of the UN Security Council "should be free from armed attacks and from any other hostile act" (Resolution 824 of 6 May 1993)
SCS	special coordinator for the reconstruction of Sarajevo
SFOR	Stabilization Force

SOFA	Status of Forces Agreement
SRSG	special representative of the UN Secretary-General
TEZ	Total Exclusion Zone (zone within which all heavy weapons were excluded)
UNHCR	United Nations High Commissioner for Refugees
UNMO	United Nations Military Observer
UNICEF	United Nations Children's Fund
UNPF	United Nations Peace Forces
UNPROFOR	United Nations Protection Force
WCP	Weapons collection point
WHO	World Health Organization

1. Author next to armored vehicle targeted
in assassination attempt on Mount Igman road
coming into Sarajevo. (1995)

2. Merrick Fall, UNPROFOR political officer who was with author
during assassination attempt. (1995)

3. French warrant officer Bruno Chaubert, author's driver
and bodyguard, after the assassination attempt. (1995)

4. Author's office (and bedroom) in UNPROFOR barracks
in Sarajevo. (1995)

5. Author with Yasushi Akashi, chief of UNPROFOR mission
in former Yugoslavia (1994–95), and Russian general
Alexander Perelyakin in Erdut, Croatia. (1994)

6. Author with General Rupert Smith (looking down) and two other British officers in Sarajevo. (1995)

7. View from Sarajevo airport of destroyed apartment buildings. (1994)

8. UNPROFOR outpost (French company) at Veliko Polje outside Sarajevo. (1995)

9. Front view of UN barracks in Sarajevo. U.S. embassy to the left. (1997)

10. Jewish cemetery, Sarajevo—on the confrontation line, and the scene of heavy fighting between Bosnian Serbs and the Bosnian government during the war. Still mined in 1997. (1997)

11. Convoy preparing to leave Sarajevo airport for Gorazde. (1994)

12. Bosnian children in Gorazde. (1994)

13. Unexploded missile in private home in Gorazde. (1994)

14. Author beside Red Cross vehicle on outskirts of Gorazde, shortly after NATO bombing in April 1994. UNPROFOR troops believed the vehicle had been moved there after the bombing and was torched, not hit by a missile as claimed by the Serbs. (1994)

15. Author with Viktor Andreyev, on of his predecessors
as chief UN political officer in Bosnia, beside Drina River in Gorazde. (1994)

16. Author in hills above Gorazde. (1994)

17. Author's apartment in Banja Luka (Republika Srpska),
Bosnia, after having been bombed. Author was asleep
at the time. (1997)

18. Another view of author's apartment in Banja Luka
after the bombing. (1997)

19. Street in Mostar two years after the war. Few repairs had been made. (1997)

20. Street in Vukovar, Croatia. (1994)

21. Sidewalk in Sarajevo where Gavrilo Princip stood
when he assassinated the Archduke of Austria in 1914. His footprints,
once painted on the concrete, were removed by the Bosnian government
in the fall of 1997. (1997)

22. View of wall on building above where Gavrilo Princip stood when he
assassinated the Archduke of Austria in 1914. It once contained a
relief entitled "Young Bosnians," the name of the organization to
which Princip belonged. The relief was removed by the Bosnian
government in fall 1997, and the street was renamed
Green Berets Street. (1997)

23. Author briefing Cyrus Vance, the UN Secretary-General's
special representative to former Yugoslavia, at Batina Bridge in
Croatia, 1992. Batina Bridge spans the Danube River, one of the
boundaries between Serbia and Croatia. (1992)

24. Preliminary excavation of mass grave at
Ovcara, Croatia. (1992)

The Notebooks

4 May 1995

Arrived Sarajevo last night by car from Split, Croatia. Eventful journey. Couldn't fly because Sarajevo airport is closed. Came as part of a convoy. Several UN vehicles. I was in a large GMC armored car. We were four. Driver was a 20-year-old Danish soldier from Headquarters company in Sarajevo. Others: a French warrant officer, mid-thirties, who was a bodyguard/driver; and my personal assistant, Dianne Fairweather.

Shortly after passing through Kiseljak, a Croatian pocket in the federation, we came upon two men in civilian clothes walking by the side of the road and waving frantically for us to stop. We were in Bosnian government territory. The two men worked in the UNPROFOR Administrative Office in Sarajevo. One was a Filipino, the other was an East European. They had just had their car hijacked by armed men in civilian clothes. Their vehicle was a white Nissan pick-up, clearly marked with the UN logo. The Filipino was terribly upset. He said it was the second time he had been hijacked, and he had had enough of Bosnia. "They pointed guns at me and told me to get out of the car," he said. "I don't know what they were saying, but one looked drunk and was pointing his gun at me. You know, these people don't like Asians. There were four of them." His companion was silent, but he was scared too, I could tell.

We contacted UNPROFOR headquarters in Sarajevo by car radio and told them to notify the closest military unit in the area about the hijacking. We then gave both men a ride to Sarajevo. The Filipino kept swearing that he was going to leave the mission as soon as possible.

Having been threatened several times myself by drunken soldiers with guns, I know very well how the two men felt. It happens to most of us on peacekeeping missions. You try to block out such memories. Sometimes you even try to block it out while it's happening. You keep saying to yourself, *No, this can't be happening. He won't shoot me. There's no reason for him to shoot me. I'm not even a combatant, I'm an international peacekeeper.* That's what happens on peacekeeping missions. It happened to me in Afghanistan, it happened to me in Croatia, and it will probably happen to me again in Bosnia. And no matter how many times it happens, you never get used to it. And you never forget it.

What surprised me was that the hijacking happened on territory controlled by the Bosnian government, and not far outside Sarajevo. One expects hijacking in Bosnian Serb territory, or in Bosnian Croat territory. Not here. But there are gangsters everywhere in Bosnia. Not necessarily in equivalent numbers, but they are everywhere, and they *all* have armed elements that hate the UN.

Doubt if UNPROFOR will ever retrieve the hijacked vehicle. Hijackers in Bosnia are very professional. Specialists, one might say. Usually drive the hijacked vehicle immediately to a pre-arranged location, more often than not a police station, spray-paint the vehicle a different color, change the license plate, and within hours, have a new car. Sometimes they sell the car on the black market, sometimes cannibalize it for spare parts to use in other stolen cars. In any case, along with the vehicle went a Motorola car radio, on which one can listen to UNPROFOR communications. And since it's impossible for us to change our communications codes every time a car is hijacked, we have to assume that our mobile communications are monitored by all sides.

Next "event" was that we almost went off the road and over the precipice while crossing Mount Igman. The dirt road over Igman is thin and narrow, and meant for goats, not wide-bodied armored vehicles. We were delayed and pushed off to the side by a Bosnian military convoy. Military convoys always move at night. It took hours for us to cross over Igman. Dark by the time we were at the top. Our vehicle had night lights, which couldn't be seen by Serb artillery gunners, who normally target the road during the day. The road, meanwhile, has numerous switchbacks. At one point our driver, who was driving slowly, didn't turn fast enough, and suddenly we had stopped and were staring at nothingness. There was brush under our tires instead of dirt road. You could feel it. The night lights were not focusing on trees or other vehicles. They were fixed on nothingness for as far as we could see. Our driver applied the brakes, backed up slowly, and turned back onto the dirt road. The French warrant officer asked if perhaps he should drive, since he had more experience in crossing over Igman. Dianne thought that would be a good idea. I said nothing. But we didn't switch drivers, and we made it over Igman.

The two men who were hijacked will make a formal report today. Probably they will leave. Any international worker who wants to leave Bosnia can do so—a privilege resented, understandably, by local inhabitants.

Law and order (what I call law and *ordure*) in Bosnia is minimal. One expects danger on a battlefield, but off the battlefield one hopes for a minimum of law and order. No way. The local situation is close to anarchy, most of all in Bosnian Serb areas. Most trained police have been drafted into local armies. The remaining police are either poorly trained or unconcerned with anything but their own survival, including supporting their families. And everyone has guns. Finally, the international community is considered fair prey, by all sides, albeit for different reasons, so that crimes against us are not only tolerated but even encouraged. We are considered political antagonists by the Moslems and Croats because we won't take a more aggressive stance against the Serbs, and by the Serbs because we are considered partial to the Moslems and Croats. And we are rich. We have food and clothing and electronic gear. Good pickings.

One can never relax anywhere in Bosnia.

5 May 1995

Began "familiarization" tour of Bosnia today by attending a briefing at 8:00 A.M., chaired by Lieutenant General Rupert Smith, the British commander of UN military forces in Bosnia and Herzegovina. Smith holds three briefings each day: one at 8:00 A.M. for heads of all departments and agencies, civilian as well as military; a second one at 9:00 A.M. for select heads of departments, which includes mine, Civil Affairs; and a third at 6:00 P.M., to review what has gone on during the day. With few exceptions we all work seven days a week. The briefings are held in the United Nations barracks in Sarajevo.

I have just been appointed the UN's chief political officer for Bosnia and Herzegovina, and before my predecessor leaves his post, he is giving me a whirlwind, four-day tour of the Sarajevo-Pale area to meet Bosnian government and, if possible, Bosnian Serb officials, as well as the heads of international agencies. My official title reads like an overturned cup of alphabet soup, but is significant for its intentions, once deciphered. I am Civil Affairs coordinator (CAC) and delegate of the special representative of the Secretary-General (D/SRSG) for Bosnia and Herzegovina. A Civil Affairs coordinator is expected to coordinate all nonmilitary aspects of the mission. There are seven Civil Affairs coordinators throughout all of former Yugoslavia, three of whom have the heightened status of being delegates of the UN Secretary-General's special representative.

The spreadsheet reads something like this. Yasushi Akashi, a Japanese national and a UN career diplomat, is based in Zagreb, Croatia, where the headquarters of the UN's operations in former Yugoslavia is located. Akashi is the special representative of the Secretary-General (SRSG) for all of former Yugoslavia, which comprises the six republics of Bosnia and Herzegovina, Croatia, Macedonia (officially called former Yugoslav Republic of Macedonia [FYROM] because the name *Macedonia* has not yet been agreed to by Greece), Slovenia, Montenegro, and Serbia. The United Nations operation, which includes both civilian and military contingents, is known as the

United Nations Protection Force (UNPROFOR). At this point, UN troops are concentrated almost exclusively in Bosnia and Croatia, except for a few hundred in Macedonia as part of the UN's first exercise of "preventive deployment." Because Akashi can't be everywhere at once, and because certain outposts are considered more important than others, he has "delegates" to represent him in Sarajevo, Belgrade, and Skopje. I have a staff of about thirty, at various sites in Bosnia, including suboffices at Bihac, Tuzla, and Gornji Vakuf.

CACS are essentially the eyes and ears of the United Nations Secretary-General, a kind of zoom lens into the darkest corners of the peacekeeping mission. We see and tell. At the same time, we are periscopes that poke up from the depths of the daily realities of war and surface, hopefully, in the clear light of day. The words we write are eventually transformed into the ambiguous and hallowed phrases of UN Security Council resolutions, which comprise our mandate. We, the premier political officials in our areas of responsibility (AORS), are the ones who begin the information chain that climbs from local happenings, through several critics, and lastly into the Secretary-General's reports to the Security Council. And it is, in part, on the basis of the Secretary-General's reports that the Security Council makes its momentous decisions—whether to authorize the use of force in Bosnia, whether to recognize the legitimacy of Croatia's international borders, or even how much to pay people like myself. The Security Council has the ultimate authority on how to conduct a peacekeeping mission, and it draws much of what it knows from what we tell it.

How the Security Council chooses to act on the basis of our information, when balanced against other sources of information, is of course its members' prerogative and is also based on a number of factors, not just on our and others' reports. Critically, one of those factors is domestic constituencies, and although such considerations seem extraneous to us and often contrary to the situation in the field, we are always aware that the United Nations, in perhaps its most important dimension, *is* its member governments and that member governments have domestic constituencies. Such are the realities of UN peacekeeping missions.

Information from the field comes essentially in two packets: military components are expected to provide military information to UNPROFOR headquarters in Zagreb and to United Nations headquarters in New York, whereas the CACS are supposed to provide political information. But in Bosnia, for various reasons, the military has become preeminent and has virtually usurped the role of Civil Affairs. I am hoping to restore some balance to that equation, even though I suspect my best intentions will be opposed by the Bosnian government, the international press, elements of my own staff in Sarajevo, and elements of the UN military command. United Nations political officials are very unpopular in Sarajevo.

CACs also have several functions beyond political reporting, such as "coordinating" the activities of the various international agencies and assisting in bringing together the warring parties on projects of common interest. For example, I will be trying to get the Bosnian Serbs and the Bosnian government to agree on restoring utilities to Sarajevo. [Unfortunately, I was unsuccessful in that endeavor.]

Because there is war in Bosnia now, and has been for three years, it would be naïve to expect parity between the civilian and military components of UNPROFOR, especially when the military side has more than twenty-seven thousand troops in the area (prior to the arrival of the Rapid Reaction Force [RRF], which added another several thousand), whereas Civil Affairs, as stated, has less than thirty. The reason that the civilian side of the mission in Bosnia has been submerged, however, has as much to do with politics as with numbers.

The fact is that the Bosnian government (and the world press, which are virtually the Bosnian government's cheerleaders and fester with soldierly righteousness) hasn't wanted peace in Bosnia for more than a year, since the tide of the war has begun to turn in its favor. Encouraged by Washington and Bonn, the Bosnian government thinks it can achieve a military victory in the long run, and it doesn't want to settle until it can deal from a position of strength. That is perfectly understandable, but it makes the task of UN political officials very difficult. The UN operation in Bosnia is a military operation as far as the Bosnian government is concerned, and it prefers to deal with military officials rather than with civilians, especially insofar as those civilians are representatives of Yasushi Akashi, who prefers, whenever possible, patient diplomacy to military action. The Bosnian government hates him.

At the 8:30 A.M. briefing, Smith & Co. discussed the possibility of calling for the use of NATO air power in Maglai against a Bosnian Serb tank that is shelling a British position. After brief discussion, it was decided that first, letters of protest, from both the CAC and Smith, would be sent to the appropriate Serb officials, asking them to halt the shelling. Aguilar will write to political officials in Pale, and Smith will write to the Bosnian Serb military leader, General Ratko Mladic. The Serbian tank is near a school, and the use of air power may risk collateral damage.

[From the UN standpoint, two types of air power can be used: close air support (CAS) and air strikes. Close air support is used only in self-defense. Air strikes are much more wide ranging and can be used to protect designated "safe areas," of which there are six throughout Bosnia. If air power were to be employed against the Serb tank in Maglai, it would be a case of close air support.

As it turned out, the tank stopped its shelling the following day, but it would resume from time to time, unpredictably, just to let us know it was there.]

[Perhaps it is worth saying a few words about the world press here, early on, because they were such a critical factor in the Bosnian equation, as they are increasingly in most world crises. In fact, their very presence on a world scene in large numbers *makes* that scene a crisis. If it was not a crisis beforehand, it is a crisis once they have arrived, simply because they have arrived.

There are several factors to note about the international press in Bosnia. First, they were very, very talented and very, very biased in favor of the Bosnian government. There was a high level of representation at Sarajevo by all the world's major news media. Most of the reporters were experienced and brilliant; relentless, investigative news gatherers; eloquent and epigrammatic editorial commentators. They were also accompanied by agile and sensational cameramen. It was a formidable array by anyone's standards. At one time or another during the war in Bosnia, all the media superstars, as well as a few world-class intellectuals, took the stage in Sarajevo, and usually whatever they said had a way of resonating.

The second factor about the press in Sarajevo, a corollary to the first, was that they knew so damned much, more than most of us. They had access to most of the major players; they had networks that fed them news and background from the metropolitan capitals, and they had firsthand experience on the ground. They knew the locals; they traveled throughout the government-controlled areas of Bosnia and in the other republics of former Yugoslavia, wherever their corporations or their inquiring imagination sent them; and they gathered an extensive portfolio of facts. Sometimes they distorted those facts, and more often they ignored other facts, but all the best ones did their homework before filing.

A third factor, and perhaps the most important one from my standpoint, was that the press were intractably critical of the United Nations. In short, they blamed us for not being tougher with the Bosnian Serbs, whom they deemed the unofficially convicted demons in the Bosnian drama. And because the press had such influence, such knowledge, and such talent, we were clearly overmatched. They were our most potent adversaries.

Moreover, their lack of objectivity created problems greater than that of undermining the UN's credibility. By taking the side of the Bosnian government, they actually undermined the peace process. They inflamed public opinion and kept it in a state of high tension. Moreover, they failed to see that there were more than two sides to the conflict. It was not simply the Bosnian government against the Bosnian Serbs. The war in Bosnia was a polyhedron made up of Serbs, Croats, Moslems, the UN, NATO, the United States, and the Russian Federation, to name only the major players. The oversimplified view of the Bosnian civil war by the press actually undermined the peace process by attempting to interpret every development in terms of what significance it had for the Bosnian government, rather than what significance it had for a durable peace.

But we had to live with the press, and we did, as much in fear as in awe and as much with admiration as with anger.]

Following the two morning briefings at headquarters, Enrique Aguilar (my predecessor as CAC and D/SRSG) and I went to visit the American chargé d'affaires, John Menzies, who told us that negotiations between the six-nation Contact Group (Germany, France, England, Italy, the Russian Federation, and the United States) and Serbian President Slobodan Milosevic on the Contact Group Plan for ending the war in Bosnia has been 50 percent successful to this point. The Contact Group Plan will give 51 percent of Bosnia to the Federation of Bosnia and Herzegovina (mainly Moslems and Croats, but officially those who favor a unified, multiethnic Bosnia), and 49 percent to the Bosnian Serbs, who now control about 70 percent of Bosnia. There are three elements to the discussion in Belgrade, Menzies told us: rump Yugoslavia's (Serbia and Montenegro) recognizing Bosnia's international borders, sealing the border between Bosnia and Yugoslavia, and removing economic sanctions against Yugoslavia.

[As it turned out, the package did not go through. My information, gathered from reliable diplomatic sources in Sarajevo, was that the main obstacle, as it had been for more than a year, was the position of the United States. All the other members of the Contact Group were willing to make the deal. But at the last minute, the United States (with support from Germany) insisted only on suspending, not lifting, the sanctions against Yugoslavia, and the U.S. ambassador to Croatia, Peter Galbraith, reportedly protested that Serbia should also recognize Croatia before the sanctions could be lifted; he wanted the lifting of sanctions against Serbia to be tied to the Croatian issue as well as to the Bosnian problem. He and his supporters in Washington got their way. The result was that Washington won, everybody else lost, and agreement on the Contact Group Plan was deferred. The argument against lifting the sanctions on Yugoslavia was that once they were lifted, it would be much more difficult to reimpose them because that reimposition would take the approval of all five permanent members of the

Security Council, including Russia, but Russia, which had gone along the first time, would be unlikely to go along the second time. It would use its veto power. Hence, suspension only, the United States insisted.

This analysis was to be confirmed in David Owen's *Balkan Odyssey*, published later in 1995, in which Owen would recount, albeit two weeks after my meeting with Menzies, that "the deal (for ending the war in Bosnia) fell apart because the US would not accept reimposition (of the sanctions against Yugoslavia) being dependent on the UN Secretary-General (which they would be if the Security Council relinquished its authority). In effect the US had insisted on being able to reimpose sanctions themselves, which was a position that Milosevic was never likely to accept. To cover their tracks the US publicly blamed Milosevic; this he took uncomplainingly, and did not in public reveal the details of the package."*]

My first impressions of Lieutenant General Rupert Smith are quite favorable. He is tall, slim, dark haired, and pensive, in his early fifties, and the obvious possessor of an inspired and inspiring devotion to duty. As generals go, he seems more left of center politically than most, though certainly not radical, and he is clearly the darling of the international press.

[Though I came to have serious political disagreements with some of Smith's policies and tactics, I always admired him. To his credit, he never discouraged frank discussion or a difference of opinion. In fact, one of the reasons we got on so well, I suspect, was that I was always open in expressing my views. Like any good leader, he did not want to be surrounded by "yes men."

As one might expect, Smith was a devotee of military history, and I can still remember discussions we had about the Union's military tactics during the American Civil War. While at Sandhurst, he had studied the campaigns of that war. "It set the style for American military tactics ever since," he told me. "The Union set out to destroy the *war-making capacity* of the Confederacy, not just to defeat their armies. And they have done that in every war since then, including the Gulf War" (in which Smith had participated).

To his credit, Smith also had an inveterate distrust of class distinctions. Actually, he was an incorrigible democrat. In any case, he was an intelligent man with a broad vision and varied interests. One of his pleasures was to read regularly from an edition of the collected poems of Rudyard Kipling, from which, I soon found out, he could quote extensively from memory. Concerning myself, once he heard that I had been appointed, the first question that Smith posed to a mutual friend of ours was: "Does he have shit in his tank?" In other words, would I stand up to pressure, or would I roll over?

*David Owen, *Balkan Odyssey* (New York: Harcourt Brace & Co., 1995), 322–23.

The general was assured that I would fight the good fight; after all, I had *volunteered* to come to Sarajevo.]

Our next meeting this morning was with a group of representatives from international agencies that are coordinating humanitarian aid for Sarajevo. The meeting was a classic example of how a CAC exercised his coordinating functions. Aguilar chaired the meeting and turned it over to the representatives of the various agencies to discuss their problems, which are numerous.

Western Slavonia, formerly a Serb-controlled area in Croatia, was recently overrun by the Croatian army, and Serbian refugees are crossing the border into Bosnian Serb territory inside of Bosnia. They are heading for Banja Luka, a Serb stronghold in northwest Bosnia, and there is concern that Bosnian Croat forces will block relief aid from reaching the Serb refugees.

Meanwhile, in the Serb-controlled areas of Bosnia, the Serbs are hijacking UN vehicles and breaking into houses, looting and expelling non-Serbs, partly in anger for the expulsion of Serbs from Western Slavonia and partly to make room for incoming Serbian refugees. The Serbs blame the UN for not having prevented Croatia's military takeover of Western Slavonia. (Of course, the UN does not have the military strength to resist any of the warring parties in the former Yugoslavia, and it was not sent here for that purpose. It is a peacekeeping force, lightly armed and using white vehicles. It is not prepared to fight a sustained war. None of the warring parties accept this explanation, however. The weaker side always wants us to be their mercenaries and are furious when we are not. As long as the Croats and the Bosniaks are losing, they want UNPROFOR to protect them, but when the tide of battle begins to turn, they want us out of the way, and it is the Serbs who ask for our protection. In fact, UNPROFOR is misnamed: it should be called a *deterrent* force because it is not capable of being a protection force.)

The conversation then turned to Sarajevo, where only a fifteen-day supply of food is left. The airport has been closed, and donor nations are showing signs of fatigue. Because the cease-fire agreement expired at the end of April, the delivery of humanitarian supplies to Sarajevo and other areas of Bosnia has again become increasingly difficult, and donor countries are sending their aid elsewhere in the world, places where it has a better chance of getting through.

The World Health Organization (WHO) reports that fifty thousand German marks were stolen at gunpoint at a Bosnian Serb checkpoint the previous weekend. The thieves were obviously Bosnian Serbs because nobody else could work effectively inside of Serb territory. As usual, however, Bosnian Serb officials deny responsibility, claiming that the theft was carried out by "rogue elements" contrary to official policy.

A representative from the office of the Special Coordinator for the Reconstruction of Sarajevo (SCS) reported that the Bosnian government wants the
SCS office to help it pay for additional natural gas that will be piped into
Bosnia from Russia. (Yes, the Russian Federation supplied gas to the Bosnian
government during the war because business is business in the Balkans,
politics notwithstanding.) The Bosnian government is alleging that the Bosnian Serbs are now using 70 percent of the natural gas in Bosnia. The office
of the SCS, quite to the contrary, estimates that the Bosnian government is
using 70 percent of the country's natural gas at this point.

[As I was to find out soon enough, the Bosnian government was no better
than any other side in former Yugoslavia when it came to truth telling.
Moreover, like everyone else, it treated the United Nations and all the international agencies as a cow to be milked for all it could get. Bosnian government officials hated the United Nations, slandered it constantly, and encouraged their citizens to do the same. They wanted the United Nations to be
their military mercenaries and economic underwriters, and anything less
invited their recrimination, condemnation, and constant harassment.

In fact, all the warring parties in former Yugoslavia were antagonistic to
the United Nations at some point, but that was to be expected because being
a scapegoat was endemic to being an international peacekeeping force. This
attitude was particularly outrageous in Bosnia, however, because the Bosnian government had official recognition and was a member state of the
United Nations. This status entitled it to certain privileges, not the least of
which was the use of NATO air power, economic embargoes against its enemies, and loans from the international banking community. Privileges of
recognition normally carry with them the responsibilities of accepted international behavior, yet during the time I was in Bosnia, the United Nations
was seldom treated with respect by the Bosnian government. It is not enough
to say that the Bosnian government was desperate—which it was—and that
the other warring parties in Bosnia also abused the United Nations—which
they did. The privileges of international recognition entail heavy responsibility, and the Bosnian government frequently ignored that responsibility
after 1994.]

6 May 1995

At the 9:00 A.M. briefing in General Smith's office, we spoke about the
Bosnian government's harassment of locally recruited staff. Four of our local
staff have been arrested in Sarajevo. (According to a signed agreement between UNPROFOR and the Bosnian government—referred to as the Status of
Forces Agreement [SOFA]—*all* local employees working for UNPROFOR are
not to be taxed, drafted, or limited in their freedom of movement as long as

they are performing their duties. The Bosnian government, however, blatantly refuses to observe the agreement when it does not suit its purposes and has even written letters to the UN Secretary-General informing him it does not intend to observe certain provisions of the SOFA. Forty percent of our local staff is Serb, and the Bosnian government is particularly nasty to them—restricting their movement, impressing them into military service, and even harassing their families. UNPROFOR's protests to the Sarajevo government have been continuously ignored. And, of course, the international press also ignores this issue.)

Among the points Smith made this morning were that the eastern enclaves (Srebrenica, Zepa, and Gorazde) are being squeezed more and more by the Serbs. It is increasingly difficult to get humanitarian aid convoys into them, and military activity inside and around them is escalating. Bosnian government forces inside the enclaves are stepping up their forays into surrounding Serb villages, and Serb troops are determined to secure their positions. We should be making plans for possible military incursions there by the Serbs, Smith urged. [In fact, all four eastern enclaves—Srebrenica, Zepa, Gorazde, and Sarajevo, which had been declared "safe areas" by the UN Security Council—were a thorn in the back of General Ratko Mladic, the Bosnian Serb military commander, because the Bosnian Serbs controlled all of eastern Bosnia except for those enclaves.]

The representative of the International Committee of the Red Cross (ICRC) noted that the obstruction of humanitarian aid is, in fact, a violation of the Geneva conventions (which forms the basis for the behavior of combatants and others in time of war). That argument, she suggested, might be used when trying to convince the Bosnian Serbs to cease obstructing the delivery of humanitarian aid to the enclaves, including Sarajevo.

The carrot for the Bosnian Serbs in this case is that if they are serious about achieving international recognition, then they will have to abide by the norms of international behavior, such as the Geneva conventions.

Under Article 4 of Protocol 2 of the Geneva conventions, collective punishment is prohibited, and it can be argued that denial of food to the entire population of Sarajevo is a form of collective punishment. Such arguments, the ICRC representative continued, although seemingly marginal, help to build a continuing case against the Bosnian Serbs in the field of international law. It is not enough simply to brand them "outlaws." Violations of the Geneva conventions provide specific examples of their lawlessness.

7 May 1995

Today I made the decision to return to Erdut, Croatia, as soon as possible in order to pack my personal belongings and take them to Zagreb, and from there to move them to Sarajevo after I return from my planned leave in New York.

Such personal decisions may sound extraneous to this narrative, but in fact they are not because they say something about life in UNPROFOR. Many of us in the mission area have suitcases, laundry, clothes, and other personal effects in several different places at once. Some have even abandoned their dwellings in their home countries and placed their belongings in warehouses so that they will not have to pay rent back home while they are in former Yugoslavia. I myself at this point have two cartons of winter wear at a warehouse in Zagreb, unpacked belongings at an apartment in Erdut, one suitcase and some unwashed laundry in Sarajevo, as well as an apartment in New York City, where my son is living.

My decision to return to Erdut in order to pack for my leave in New York is based partly on the security situation in Erdut, which recently has deteriorated so dramatically that I fear if I do not move my personal effects to Zagreb *before* I go to New York, I may not be able to do so after I return. Either they might be looted, or I might not be able to get clearance to enter Erdut for a long while.

I also considered postponing my scheduled flight to New York in case, having got into Erdut, I cannot get out. The area has been sealed off by the Serbs since the Croatian takeover of Western Slavonia. I need special clearance to be allowed to enter the Erdut area, but it will be difficult to know what day, what time, and in what vehicle I will be traveling (all of which information is required in advance by local officials) because I cannot even be sure when I will be able to leave Sarajevo (the airport is closed) or if, having escaped Sarajevo and coming from Zagreb, I will be able to pass through Western Slavonia (now in Croatian hands) on my way to Erdut in Eastern Slavonia. Meanwhile, UN cars are being hijacked every day in the Serb-controlled areas in retaliation against the UN for not having prevented the Croatian takeover of Western Slavonia, so it is quite possible that I may be granted permission to cross into Eastern Slavonia (or Sector East, as it is called), but be hijacked before I reach my destination. In a telephone conversation this morning with a colleague who is in Erdut, I learned that five UN cars were hijacked yesterday, and that the situation on the ground is extremely tense. Many of the staff are sleeping on the floors in their offices because they are afraid to drive home to the villages where they live. Any UN car on the road is considered a fair target. I will therefore have to arrange for an escort to meet me at the checkpoint when I enter Sector East, to accompany me to my residence, and then to assist me in leaving the sector.

When one goes on mission in a war zone, one of the biggest adjustments to be made concerns the loss of personal comfort. Those of us not stationed in Zagreb are continually threatened with a loss of public utilities, have very little social life, and suffer major restrictions on our freedom of movement. At various times we are blockaded, harassed, arrested, threatened, and shot at. Soldiers tend to adjust to such treatment more readily because they are trained to deal with it, but civilians are not so easily adaptable.

On the other hand, I never plead for pity on this score. Quite the contrary. As I frequently tell anyone who will listen, including the military, those who complain about the living conditions—or about the security—should never come on a peacekeeping mission and should leave as soon as possible. In most cases we *volunteer* for this duty, and it is disingenuous to complain that conditions are not what they were back home when nobody forced us to come here. We signed on for any number of reasons—adventure, money, career advancement, family situation—and some of us even harbor the hope that we might be able to relieve the suffering of innocent people and help to bring peace to a beautiful country that was devouring itself. If the going was tough, so be it.

Finally, because the Sarajevo airport was recently closed, I realize I will have to exit Sarajevo by armored car and drive though Kiseljak (which means going through four Bosnian Serb checkpoints), from where I will then board a UN helicopter to Zagreb in order to obtain a car to drive to Erdut, from where, having packed, I can begin my journey: Erdut, Zagreb, New York, Zagreb, Sarajevo. Great fun.

The news from Bosnia today is gloomy. Fighting has intensified since the end of the cease-fire agreement a week ago, on 1 May, and snipers are picking away at UNPROFOR. The Bosnian Serbs can easily target the road over Mount Igman into Sarajevo and are harassing any traffic that tries to use that road without their permission. A mortar attack against Bosnians trying to move across Mount Igman today killed ten military and civilian persons and wounded thirty.

20 May 1995

Met this week in New York with Kofi Annan, Undersecretary-General for peacekeeping operations. (During the past couple of years, when I have not been in former Yugoslavia, I have worked for Kofi at UN headquarters in New York. He is an incredibly charming and congenial man, and has a talent for earning your respect almost from the moment you meet him. He has that uncanny ability to make you feel he is always being sincere, perhaps because he listens closely to what you say. He is humble, with a deep sense of dignity, and has an almost boyish sense of humor. And he works eight days a week; I have rarely seen anyone work harder. Not the least of his attractions, from my point of view, is that he seems to have no private political agenda. It is quite common for any person with power in a political organization to have a personal agenda, but Kofi has none. He seems to thrive on the challenge of his work and bears his responsibilities with a disarming ease. I have never seen him angry, I have never seen him disrespectful, and I have never seen him at a loss for what to say. He also has a very strong presence. He is not aggressive, but he is able to focus on the issue at hand and go straight at you without diminishing your dignity. He strains to understand your point of view, but he is equally tenacious in asserting his own point. Of course, he is not a saint, but he seems to be able to offend the least number of persons possible in any given situation, a talent that is unique in international politics.

In 1995, the United Nations had between eighty thousand and one hundred thousand troops under its command, all of them seconded by their various governments because the UN has no permanent army. I don't know what the ratio was in member states in 1995 between troops in the field and persons at home to process and manage those troops, but whatever it is in those states, it is considerably less at the UN. If, for example, nation X has one hundred thousand troops in the field, it probably has twenty thousand or more people at home engaged in processing those troops, a ratio of five to one. The UN's ratio can't be better than ten or twelve to one, which puts considerable strain on the managers. Kofi manages those managers with great ability, however. He is very good at delegating responsibility, and he is blessed with having a few very good people close to him, particularly Shashi Tharoor, who has been with him for a decade and is an astute political advisor in addition to being an accomplished novelist. One of Kofi's strengths is that he is able to recognize good people when he finds them and to inspire their allegiance.)

I spoke with Kofi for about fifteen minutes. He began our meeting by congratulating me on my appointment. Then he played the tape of an interview he recently gave to a Canadian broadcaster. The interview was very low-key and part of a broader interview on peacekeeping in general. Kofi is always aware of the need for rallying support—not merely financial but also political—from the member states. [I don't recall the exact content of his taped statement, but Kofi was not one to preach. He had a way of stating his case simply, going right to the core of the issue. In that sense, his style was very unlike that of many politicians, UN and otherwise, who too often sounded like crusaders, saviors, or putative heroes. Kofi was never pompous. He was not without convictions, but he was certainly without bitterness, and he rarely had a head too big for his hat.] He asked my opinion about the situation in Bosnia, and I told him that I feared for the worst, not only because the parties to the conflict still seemed so uncompromising but also because many of the international actors seemed to be pursuing private agendas that were inconsistent with the realities on the ground. Without

[16]

agreement among the warring parties inside of Bosnia, or among the major players outside of Bosnia, it would be a rough road to peace. Kofi warned me to be careful.

[In general, I found it extremely exasperating that those very countries that created our mandates would emerge from the UN Security Council chamber and almost immediately begin to undermine us politically. Criticism was to be expected, but it seemed to me beyond the bounds of reason to send troops into a war theater and then constantly undermine them. I could understand adversarial comments from the pro-Bosnian world press or from the citizens of various countries or even from countries that had opposed the Security Council's decisions. But how could governments that had voted in favor of a resolution turn around and verbally attack the troops and civilians in the field who were charged with implementing that resolution? It was disgraceful, even cowardly.

At one point while I was in New York, I spoke on the telephone to the man who was temporarily in charge in Sarajevo while I was gone, Deyan Mihov. The UN Civil Affairs press officer, Alex Ivanko, a Serb-bashing Russian who exudes political correctness, had recently used insulting language when referring to Serbian President Milosevic. Concern had been expressed at UN headquarters in New York that such language might make it more difficult for the international community to work with Milosevic, who is nobody's favorite political leader. I relayed that concern to Mihov over the telephone. Ivanko happened to be sitting in the room with Mihov at the time, but Mihov didn't tell me that then. He was adamant that their condemnation of Milosevic was justified and that it strengthened the international community's position by placing the blame where it belongs. He said the statement was approved by General Rupert Smith, the British commander in Sarajevo. I said that Ivanko is supposed to be working for UN Civil Affairs, not for the British army, and that such statements are not politically constructive because, like it or not, we have to deal with Milosevic. I suggested that I might have to hold my own press conferences if my own press officer feels he is more beholden to the British army than to UN Civil Affairs. Mihov accused me of trying to divide UNPROFOR. Ivanko, meanwhile, wrote a memo to Akashi's spokesman in Zagreb asking him, in effect, to advise Akashi not to appoint me because I would be divisive. Ivanko shrewdly put the issue in terms of a "turf battle"—that I was attempting to usurp the powers and privileges of the Sarajevo spokesman, who, because of official policy, was responsible to the chief spokesman in Zagreb rather than to the political chief in Sarajevo. Of course, Ivanko's objective was political, not procedural. He wanted carte blanche to assault the Serbs however and whenever he chose to do so. From the standpoint of protocol alone, such behavior was incredible. Here was a mission appointee, not even a permanent member of the UN staff, at least three grades below me, in effect urging the head of the mission not to appoint me because I might not be a guaranteed Serb basher. In any case, Akashi ignored him. I myself didn't find out about Ivanko's memo until later, but I already realized at that point that my stay in Bosnia would not be easy. It appeared I would not even have the support of my own staff.]

27 May 1995

While I was in New York, NATO war planes conducted air strikes on ammunition bunkers in Pale, the Bosnian Serb capital. It is the first time that NATO has brought the war to Bosnian Serb territory. The strikes were on 25 and 26 May. In response, the Bosnian Serbs took UN soldiers as hostages in order to prevent further air strikes.

I was terribly upset by the news, though I knew Smith had been pressing for such action, and I knew the Bosnian Serbs provoked it. I fear it is the beginning of the end of any chance for the UN to be an effective mediator.

[In his report of 30 May 1995, the Secretary-General described the events that led up to the NATO bombing in this manner:

> The Sarajevo Agreement of February 1994 and the related exclusion zone and weapons collection points facilitated the removal or placement under United Nations control of heavy weapons. . . .
>
> On 22 May 1995, Bosnian Serb forces removed two heavy weapons from a weapons collection point. On 24 May 1995, fighting erupted again, with the Serbs firing heavy weapons from within a number of weapons collection points and the government forces firing from various positions within the city. Bosnian Serb forces removed three more weapons from weapons collection points. Tanks and rocket launchers were also reported within the heavy weapons exclusion zone. Sixteen civilians and military personnel were killed and at least 60 wounded. . . . UNPROFOR decided to use all available means to restore compliance with the February 1994 agreement. (S/1995/444)

With due impartiality, UNPROFOR warned both the Bosnian Serbs and the Bosnian government that "their forces would be attacked from the air if all heavy weapons did not cease firing by 1200 hours the next day" (even though it was inconceivable that UNPROFOR would attack Bosnian government forces). The Secretary-General also took into account at the time the potential risk to UNPROFOR personnel: "When issuing this warning, UNPROFOR recognized that non-compliance would require a strong response and that a significant risk to exposed UNPROFOR personnel was likely to result."

On the advice of his advisors, however, the Secretary-General was reluctant to withdraw UNPROFOR personnel *before* air strikes because he suspected they would probably never be able to return, and without their presence there could be no international monitoring. In the words of his report:

> Large numbers of exposed personnel could not be withdrawn because of the overriding requirement to maintain observation and liaison. It would also have made little sense to conduct air strikes to achieve the return of a few heavy weapons if the United Nations had no personnel at the weapons collection points to monitor their return; nor would it have made sense to abandon the hundreds of weapons in other sites.

Weapons collection points (wcps) were not, in fact, huge storage areas to which heavy weapons had been brought. The Bosnian Serbs had no capacity, particularly no fuel, to move weapons to any central location, so, for the most part, wcps were established *where the weapons already were,* and UN monitors were placed there to make sure the weapons were not moved or used. One abandoned tank might constitute a wcp, but if unmonitored, that one tank might be used destructively.

The Secretary-General's summary of the air strikes on Pale is admirably objective:

> The first air strike took place at 1620 hours on 25 May 1995 as a result of the failure of the Bosnian Serbs to respect the deadline for the return of heavy weapons. The target, limited to two bunkers within an ammunition dump near Pale, was selected in order to make an effective strike while reducing the risk of collateral damage. After the strike, Bosnian Serb forces surrounded a number of weapons collection points. All safe areas, except Zepa, were shelled, resulting in particularly heavy casualties in Tuzla, where some 70 civilians were killed and over 130 injured. As the Serbs had again employed heavy weapons around Sarajevo and had still failed to return the missing weapons to weapons collection points, a second attack on the six remaining bunkers in the Pale ammunition dump was conducted at 1030 hours on 26 May 1995. Bosnian Serb forces reacted by surrounding additional weapons collection points, taking United Nations military observers into custody and using a number of them as human shields to deter further air attacks on potential targets, and by cutting electricity to the city.]

I was shocked, disgusted, and depressed by this news, as most of the world was. But I realized that I had a unique vantage point in that I could observe the reaction at UN headquarters and in the United States at the same time that I could well imagine the situation on the ground in Bosnia. There is, of course, anger all around me—anger at the barbarous targeting of civilians by the Bosnian Serbs, at their taking of UN hostages, at their escalation of violence, and at the breakdown of the peace process. And there is desperation. What I wonder is if and how that desperation and anger will be transformed into action. Meanwhile, as always, I believed any intelligent response would require vigorous diplomacy, whatever military choices were made. The use of force represents a failure of diplomacy, not an extension of diplomacy, and while the use of force, or the threat of force, is a necessary element in policy making, it also contains the seeds of its own destruction.

"Ah, humanity!" as Herman Melville once lamented. At times like this, I clutch at abstract thought to turn my mind from the brutality of what is happening. I think of T. S. Eliot's phrase: "After such knowledge, what forgiveness?" Though Eliot's words were framed within a Western Christian religious context, I try to relate them to what is happening in Bosnia now. How will any of the warring parties ever be able to forgive such carnage? Certainly not in less than a generation—if then.

I also think about my imminent return to Bosnia. Illogically, I am eager to get back as soon as possible. I am not vain enough to think I can alter the course of history, but I think that I may be able to work on the Bosnian Serb leadership and convince them to be more receptive to the international community's pleas, to increase dialogue, and not to shut themselves off so paranoically. All diplomacy begins with confidence building, and I am hoping that if I can gain credibility with the Serbs, I can persuade them to make small concessions. In fact, the United Nations has access to the Bosnian Serb leadership that few other international organizations have. To a great extent, the UN is the link between Pale and the outside world. Perhaps I can exploit that link.

But I am also aware that I will be taking the risk of irrevocably antagonizing the Bosnian government in my attempts to gain the confidence of the Bosnian Serbs.

2 June 1995

Here in New York I heard the news that an American pilot, Scott O'Grady, was shot down by the Bosnian Serb army (BSA) while on a NATO mission over Banja Luka, a Serb stronghold in northwest Bosnia. It is not known whether he is dead or alive.

The American public's response to O'Grady's capture has been predictable and understandable but also distressing. A great number of Americans, especially the most vocal ones, want massive and immediate retaliatory air strikes against the Serbs. ("Nuke them!" cried the bartender at my local pub.) At this point, however, the principle of the dual key—which means that both NATO and UNPROFOR have to agree to air strikes before they can be initiated—is still in effect, so that NATO cannot make a unilateral decision to wage war in Bosnia. Meanwhile, many nations, including NATO members France and the United Kingdom, both of which have troops on the ground in Serbian-held areas in Bosnia, do not want to see massive air strikes against the Bosnian Serbs, for fear the hostages from their countries might be further endangered. At this point, they prefer diplomatic pressure to air strikes. In fact, most European diplomats with whom I have spoken are certain, as I am, that UN hostages will not be harmed, and that if O'Grady is captured by the Serbs he will be released unharmed.

Although the geographical distance from the United States to Europe allows U.S. politicians the potential to be both radical and objective, usually they are the former rather than the latter. One would think that being far from the scene of battle, they might be detached and judicious, but personal ambition and political partisanship know no geographical limits, especially when the life of an American pilot is involved. The O'Grady saga has quickly become a rallying point for jingoist rhetoric.

4 June 1995

To listen to a political discussion in the United States on the subject of Bosnia is to be an eavesdropper at the Mad Hatter's tea party.

Yesterday I watched a discussion hosted by Rowland Evans and Bob Novak, two conservative columnists. Their guests were Congressman Charles Robb (D-Virginia) and Senator Mitch McConnell (R-Kentucky).

Several times, Novak mentioned the prospect, then being broached by President Clinton, of sending as many as twenty-five thousand U.S. troops into Bosnia to help with either the redeployment or the rescue of UN soldiers, but he spoke only about rescuing "European" troops. Although I didn't believe he was being consciously discriminatory against UN nonwhite, non-European troops, I had to wonder how he could be so ignorant. Finally, Evans corrected Novak: UNPROFOR troops, he said, not just European troops. (And what about UNPROFOR civilians, I thought, like me?)

Then Evans spoke about "the Bosnian crisis." Well, yes, it is a crisis, but it has been a crisis for three years. While tens of thousands of people in the former Yugoslavia are being massacred and displaced, it is newsworthy, but not a crisis. Now, one U.S. plane and pilot have been shot down, and it is officially a "crisis." Of course, national interest is a factor in any international event, and one cannot blame American leaders for calling the attention of the nation to the plight of its servicemen, but one continues to hope for more than narrow provincialism from the world's only superpower. Would it be too much, I wondered, to ask *why* U.S. planes are bombing Bosnian Serbs in the first place? Have we forgotten that during World War II the Serbs and the Jews and the Gypsies went to the concentration camps together, and that the Croats and the Bosnians, under Nazi tutelage, ran them? Such memories are not irrelevant. One should not be mired in history, but one cannot selectively ignore it either. Serb racism and Serb fascism in Bosnia are certainly to be condemned, but the anxieties that provoked them have legitimacy.

My experiences with the Serbs in the past few years have taught me that they believed Washington was more interested in Middle Eastern oil than in justice in Bosnia. In their siege mentality the Serbs believe that Moslems anywhere in the world are equated with Middle Eastern oil and that the West needs oil more than it needs Serbs. Never mind that such "logic" is illogical (or that Saudi Arabia may think the same way). Irrational anxiety is a factor in any political crisis and must be given its due.

I remain convinced that if the United States wants to see stability in Central Europe, as I believe it does, then it has to take account of the just concerns of the largest ethnic group in former Yugoslavia—namely, the Serbs. Such recognition does not imply endorsement of ethnic cleansing. It requires vision beyond the next Congressional election, however.

The Bosnian Serbs are constantly asking me why, after having been Yugoslavs for fifty years, they should suddenly, without their consent, have to become a minority in a Moslem-ruled state. When I tell them that Bosnian Moslems are neither fundamentalists nor Middle Easterners, that they eat pork and get drunk like any good European, they ask me who has the largest mission in Bosnia, who is the major arms supplier to the Bosnian government, and who extends the most financial credit to the Bosnian government. The answer to all three questions is the same: Iran. Of course, having diplomatic relations with Iran does not mean that a nation is necessarily a fundamentalist nation. Any port in a storm, so to speak. The Bosnian government goes wherever it can for aid, especially since the UN Security Council has slapped an arms embargo against all of Yugoslavia, but aid is seldom given without political strings attached. Though I never believed the Bosnian government intended to become fundamentalist, I understand why the Bosnian Serbs fear that possibility.

More to the point, I am fond of asking my European and North American (Christian and Jewish) friends who are so emotionally pro-Bosnian: if tomorrow you were told, through no decision of your own, that you were no longer a citizen of your own country, but were now a member of a minority in a Moslem country that had never before been a country, that had been a Nazi collaborator during World War II, what would you say? Without exception, they answer the equivalent of "No way!"

One can never neglect one's national interest, but one must also understand how those interests have an impact on the world situation and how the world situation has an impact on them. The present influences our understanding of the past, just as it influences our vision of the future. At the United Nations, one frequently hears talk of *interdependence*—that is, how the interests of nations are interrelated and how the different disciplines (economics, politics, human rights, and culture) are interrelated. But one might also use an aesthetic metaphor, cubism, when describing the intricacies of international politics. In cubism, the painter breaks down traditional one-point perspective and reassembles that perspective in interlocking planes. If one thinks of nationalism as a one-point perspective, then one realizes that the restrictive concept of the nation-state (each ethnic group having its own state) has been discredited since the French Revolution. It is impossible, genetically as well as economically, to have a "pure" ethnic state. In that sense, the defeat of Nazism should have been a defeat of racist nationalism (the one-point perspective). The illusion that national interests can be isolated from international life was shattered forever by the atomic bomb, and reality has been constantly reassembled since then, irreversibly interlocking the planes of all classical disciplines and regional interests. Some call this reassembly "globalism," but in fact it is simple common sense, an inevitable strategy for both cooperation and survival. We are all shards from the explosion at Hiroshima, and we are all building blocks for the future.

The good Republican senator from Kentucky spoke about asserting American "leadership"—which is generally a euphemism for "to hell with the rest of the world, we can do whatever we want." Such an attitude is usually calculated to garner political popularity, yet Senator McConnell and others like him must be made aware of the strategic risks of such an attitude: in this scenario, as in others, his concept of "leadership" (i.e., extensive air strikes or the commitment of U.S. ground troops) threatened to lead to the alienation of our European allies and to risk the lives of *their* soldiers, when those same troops might be withdrawn peacefully through proper diplomacy. Moreover, this very week, a *Time Magazine*–CNN poll found that almost two-thirds of the U.S. public is against using force to retaliate for the downing of the U.S. pilot.

It is also questionable at this point whether the United States, as a member of both NATO and the United Nations, even has the concurrence of those two groups for its policy of retaliatory air strikes or the legal basis for such an escalatory policy. On the first point, it would seem that if one is a member of a group, then one should abide by the decisions of that group or leave the group. Either the United States belongs to NATO, or it doesn't. Similarly, either the United States is a permanent member of the UN Security Council, with special responsibilities, or it isn't. Not observing the rules is not "leadership." It is arrogance.

In effect, what the laptop bombadiers are saying is to ignore the French, British, and others that have their troops in Bosnia. The United States will use force to put their soldiers (and all international civilians) at risk even if these other nations don't want it to.

As for existing Security Council resolutions regarding Bosnia, UN troops are authorized to use force primarily for self-defense. If that interpretation seems restrictive, it is only because the majority of the Security Council's members, including NATO members, want it that way. If fired upon, UN forces can return fire. But employing air strikes days after an event is not self-defense; it is retaliation. Moreover, there is serious doubt that such action is allowed under existing resolutions.

The UN may employ the use of force, beyond self-defense, on very few occasions under its current mandate in Bosnia. One such occasion was to enforce "no-fly" and exclusion zones. There has been a no-fly zone in effect over Bosnia ever since the adoption of Security Council resolution 781 on 9 October 1992. If planes from *any* of the combatants fly over Bosnia without special permission, NATO has the authority to shoot them down. In a related scenario, the Security Council has identified heavy-weapon exclusion zones around Sarajevo and Gorazde. If unauthorized weapons are discovered within those exclusion zones, then the UN can request NATO to employ air strikes to take out those weapons. Or, if declared safe areas are targeted, then NATO can use air strikes against the violators of those safe areas. In other words, there are *specific,* mandated occasions when NATO, at the request of the UN, can use air power, but NATO does not have the authority to bomb at will.

In order to expand the UN's authority to use force in Bosnia, the Security Council will either have to adopt a new resolution or "reinterpret" existing resolutions. One might argue that such official actions would only be perfunctory. If NATO wants to bomb, it will simply manipulate the Security Council and get its permission to go to war, or it will ignore the Security Council. At the same time, it must be recognized at this point that among the five permanent members of the Security Council, Britain and France are reluctant to use extensive force in Bosnia, the Russian Federation opposes the use of force against the Serbs, and China is anywhere from indifferent to against it. Moreover, if particular nations are to send in extra contingents to protect their own soldiers (contingents known as Rapid Reaction Forces), what will happen to the unified command? Will the French save only French troops and turn away Bangladeshis? Is the UN to rescue only "European" troops? And is the United States ready to employ its smart bombs, which will have the effect of drastically widening the existing war, in order to retaliate for the downing of one pilot?

The Bosnian Serbs have made two inexcusable and indefensible tactical errors: ethnic cleansing and the targeting of innocent civilians. The fact that all sides have committed these crimes does not exonerate the Bosnian Serbs, who have done it more often and more brutally. Nonetheless, one must acknowledge the legitimate anxiety of the Bosnian Serbs about having their country dismembered by the international community. They do not appreciate being told they can no longer be Yugoslavs, and that they must suddenly be ruled by a government dominated by Moslems, the descendants of those who were their enemies during World War II. *People have been known to become very angry when their country is taken away from them.* "For fifty years I was Yugoslav, and now suddenly I'm a Serb in a Moslem country," one Bosnian Serb said to me. "If Bosnia can secede from Yugoslavia, then we should be able to secede from Bosnia," Serbs say to me. What, in other words, are the limits of self-determination?

The inescapable fact is the tactics of the Bosnian Serbs are reprehensible but they do have a legitimate political concern. Had that concern been taken seriously from the start, war might have been averted; even now, taking that concern seriously might hasten an early and long-term solution. One has to distinguish causes from tactics. The Bosnian Serbs have cause to feel threatened as a minority in Bosnia.

The problem is that all throughout former Yugoslavia we have the equivalent of a kakistocracy. If, from the start, the Bosnian Serbs had had responsible leaders, those leaders would have tried to still the concerns of their people. They would have said, "Don't worry. We will have international guarantees for your rights; we will still have a major voice in the new government; we will be able to maintain our cultural institutions, our ties to Serbia. Don't panic." But instead of calming their people, the Bosnian Serb leadership inflamed them, and the leaders of other ethnic groups also inflamed their people. Historical scholars will document these inflammatory statements. They were endless, they were terribly damaging, and perhaps worst of all they obscured the legitimacy of the concerns each side had and has.

Why Germany forced recognition of the independence of the former Yugoslav republics of Slovenia and Croatia so soon will be debated for decades. Perhaps German Foreign Minister Hans-Dietrich Genscher merely wanted to flex his muscles as the premier continental power; perhaps he felt that recognition would actually *prevent* a war that seemed to be building. In any case, a Yugoslav friend once described his views on the subject to me in the following epigram: Yugoslavia never should have been divided, and Germany never should have been united.

With the secession of Croatia and Bosnia and Herzegovina from the former Yugoslavia, the Serbs in those new states moved from being a privileged plurality to becoming a threatened minority. Serbs were about 31 percent of the population in Bosnia when Bosnia was part of former Yugoslavia. They didn't mind being a minority because they were a plurality in all of Yugoslavia. (According to the 1991 census, about ten out of twenty-two million Yugoslavs were Serbs; the next largest group was Croatians, about five million.) The Serbs had political power in former Yugoslavia. They had many, but not all, of the best municipal jobs, state housing, and high posts in the military. In Bosnia, the Moslems controlled commerce in the urban centers. In general, with several exceptions, the villages and the countryside in Bosnia were Serbian, and the cities were Moslem dominated, though ethnically diverse. That distinction actually provides a partial explanation for the vehemence of the Serbian policy of ethnic cleansing. One aspect of the civil war in Bosnia is the countryside pitted against the cities (as in the French Revolution). Country people (whether they be Laotian tribes or Hatfields and McCoys) are more clannish and more brutal than urban populations, which tend to be multiethnic and more socially integrated. During the five hundred-year Turkish occupation of Bosnia, the Serbs fled to the countryside, even to the mountain tops, to escape Turkish domination. When the current Bosnian war began, they had the high ground.

At the same time, the so-called multiethnic character of Bosnia is greatly exaggerated. Except for the major cities—Sarajevo, Banja Luka, Zenica, Tuzla, and Mostar—most villages and towns are often largely occupied by one group that comprises most of the population. Moreover, in almost all the towns, and even in the cities, including Sarajevo, the separate ethnic groups live in their own neighborhoods.

Indeed, there are historic precedents for ethnic separatism in Bosnia. The American translators of Mesa Selimovic's classic novel, *Death and the Dervish,* provide the following footnote in explaining a reference by Selimovic to life in seventeenth-century Sarajevo: "Seventeenth-century Sarajevo was divided into 104 *mahals,* of which twelve were Christian, two were Jewish, and the rest Muslim."*

Having said that, one must admit that the political predominance and the accompanying privilege of the Serbs in former Yugoslavia since the end of World War II are important reasons why Croatia and Bosnia wanted to be independent. Ambitious middle-level politicians and military officers in both those countries, who were an important force for independence in each case, knew their chances for high positions were limited as long as they remained part of Yugoslavia. Those very politicians rose to power once their states became independent.

Moreover, as soon as they tasted power, those officials retaliated immediately against the Serbs—citing decades of discrimination as their justification. In both Bosnia and Croatia they began to evict Serbs from government housing, to fire them from civil service jobs, and even to "cleanse" them. In both countries, once independence was declared, anti-Serb extremists surrounded several Yugoslav National Army (JNA) barracks and shut off water and electricity. They wanted to neutralize the JNA and prevent it from intervening while extremists attacked the local Serbian population. There were even occasions when retreating JNA units were pelted by the local population as they withdrew from Bosnia.

Much has been said about the dominance of Serbs in the JNA, particularly in the officer corps. By the time war began in Bosnia, in the spring of 1992, the JNA *was* largely Serbian, but the reasons for that are seldom aired. The fact is that when Croatia and Slovenia decided to secede from Yugoslavia, they refused to allow men from their republics to be drafted into the JNA. Many of the Croatian and Slovenian officers in the JNA resigned their commissions and returned to their newly independent republics. The same happened in Bosnia. Thus, the JNA was left with an army that was mostly Serbian, about 80 percent by mid-1992. It had not been that way five years earlier.

At the same time, several months before the war started, Karadzic convinced authorities in Belgrade to reassign to Bosnia, from other parts of Yugoslavia, Serb officers who had been born in Bosnia, so that they would be

*Mesa Selimovic, *Death and the Dervish,* trans. Bogdan Rakic and Stephen M. Dickey (Evanston, Ill.: Northwestern University Press, 1996), 464.

there if a war started. Whether Karadzic's action was a response to what had happened in Croatia and Slovenia, or whether he had a more malefic intention is not known, but it was an ominous development.

There *were* occasions, particularly early in the war, notably in Zvornik and Bijelina in eastern Bosnia, when forces from Serbia intervened in the fighting. These were special police units (so-called Red Berets) from Belgrade, and paramilitary units ("Tigers," led by Arkan, alias Zeljko Raznatovic). JNA artillery from across the Drina River in Serbia also aided in the assaults on Zvornik and Bijelina. It is not clear, however, whether regular JNA units stationed in Serbia actually crossed into Bosnia. Many JNA troops were already stationed in Bosnia and in the other Yugoslav republics, as was their right, just as U.S. troops are stationed in Kansas and Oklahoma and North Carolina and most other states in the United States. Moreover, when JNA troops and weapons withdrew from Croatia after a truce was declared there, many of those same personnel and ordnance found their way into Bosnia. They had no place else to go. The problem was not that the JNA was present in Bosnia; the problem was that they had been politicized by Karadzic to give up their traditional role of maintaining order. Instead, they were used to establish Serbian autonomous areas within Bosnia. Many JNA soldiers truly believed they were fighting in Bosnia to prevent an illegal secession and to protect Serbian minorities from being persecuted. To Bosnian Moslems, of course, it didn't matter whether they were being expelled and slaughtered by regular units of the JNA or by Serbian paramilitary forces. For Serbs, meanwhile, the issue was survival of their culture, and the best way to ensure survival, they believed, was to link up all the Serbian territories in Bosnia and Croatia. If that meant "cleansing" non-Serbs, so be it. Logic was never a factor in Serb thinking at this point; anxiety and nightmares about the past were.

Imagine an Israeli being told that beginning tomorrow he would become a citizen of Egypt, or even worse, of Iraq. That is how Serbs feel about predominantly Moslem Bosnia. Please do not tell me such attitudes have no basis in fact. Irrational anxieties must be taken into account in any serious political analysis. Unfortunately, Western governments, led by the world press, simply treat this attitude as racist—as though five hundred years of Turkish occupation are irrelevant.

5 June 1995

Bosnia is still a big story here in New York, perhaps even bigger than the O. J. Simpson trial, and the media are filled with righteous indignation and speculation about unleashing the NATO juggernaut against the Bosnian Serbs.

They are condemning the UN for not bringing peace to Bosnia. Why weren't the UN peacekeepers in Bosnia, now hostages, better protected? They should never have been so vulnerable, say the pundits. (As of this date, more than 240 UN peacekeepers are being held hostage; some are chained to poles near weapons collection points in order to discourage NATO air strikes against those sites.)

In most cases, however, the questions being asked are not questions. They are homilies. And they reveal a fundamental(ist) misunderstanding about the nature of the UN mission.

To begin with, all UN resolutions under Chapter VI of the charter ("Pacific Settlement of Disputes") are based on the concurrence of the parties. Obviously, there is no concurrence on the part of the Bosnian Serbs for most of the UN resolutions regarding Bosnia. (How can one impose economic sanctions against a party and then expect concurrence from that party?) The UN Security Council may also invoke Chapter VII, which authorizes the use of force, but until now in Bosnia any recourse to Chapter VII has been interpreted to mean that force will be authorized only to protect UN troops, UN-declared safe areas, or humanitarian convoys. Turning the UN into a full combatant has not been mandated by the member states for the simple reason that the European powers *do not want* the UN to be a full combatant, and the war is in their backyard. Significantly, the United States and the Moslem countries (a strange alliance, to be sure), which want the UN to become a combatant, are non-Europeans. One must never forget that the UN is to a large extent its member governments, and if the member governments do not want the UN to be a full combatant, then it will not be.

In fact, UNPROFOR in Bosnia has been a success. It has assisted the United Nations High Commissioner for Refugees (UNHCR) as that agency has provided enormous quantities of humanitarian aid to the needy, without which starvation would have been rampant; it has *limited* the conflict through the imposition of such restraints as no-fly zones, safe areas, and exclusion zones; and it has negotiated cease-fires and constantly provided support for measures aimed at an overall political settlement. If it has not been able to enforce some of its measures, that failure has been due to the lack of agreement among the warring parties, who bear the primary responsibility for making peace, and to the conflicting aims of member governments, who bear the primary responsibility for adopting mandates. None of the warring parties in former Yugoslavia has ambitions *outside* of former Yugoslavia; they want to redivide the playing field, but they have never threatened to enlarge the playing field. The war in former Yugoslavia has always been self-contained. It is the parties *outside* former Yugoslavia that have ambitions *inside* former Yugoslavia. Those who argue that the war in former Yugoslavia may spread beyond its original borders have little to support their thesis except alarmist rhetoric. Do they really think that Serbia will invade Romania or Bulgaria? Or that Croatia will attack Italy? Or that Bosnia will attack anybody?

Moreover, the main reason that European states became interested in the civil war in former Yugoslavia was to prevent the flow of refugees into their own countries. Their interest was neither altruistic nor genuinely humanitarian. They were motivated by domestic and often racist concerns. They cared little if one million Moslems or Serbs or Croats moved from one part of former Yugoslavia to another part, no matter how cataclysmic that move might be, as long as those refugees didn't try to enter *their* countries. In that sense, the UN has achieved another success in the region. Emigration from former Yugoslavia has been drastically curtailed since UNPROFOR arrived. Ironically, one of the main dangers in the region at this point does not stem from ethnic nationalisms, but from NATO's need to establish a post–Cold War identity and to make itself a credible deterrent to any alteration in the new world order. As long as the former Soviet Union retains the nuclear capability to destroy not only the countries of Eastern Europe but also the United States, NATO feels it must remain a credible deterrent to that capability. By whacking the Serbs, it serves notice that it will "contain" the Russian Federation and, as a bonus, that it supports the "good" Moslems in the world rather than the "bad" Moslems (Iran, Iraq, Libya)—a continuation of its successful Gulf War policy. When a major military alliance has an identity crisis, the whole world is endangered.

As for the United Nations military personnel now being held hostage, their tasks are, inter alia, to patrol extensively to see that weapons exclusion zones are respected; to identify violations of those exclusion zones, which may lead to air strikes; and to protect weapons collection points. Protecting UN personnel from being taken hostage means either keeping them inside heavily guarded barracks or moving them completely out of Serb-controlled territory. In either case, they would not be able to do their jobs. They cannot patrol when restricted to barracks, nor would spy planes be able to replace them because planes cannot accompany aid convoys, guard weapons collection points, or negotiate with local officials.

Moreover, if UN personnel were removed, the Serbs would suspect that an air strike was imminent, and they would have time to prepare their defenses and to place their heavy weapons under cover. They would also cooperate even less with the UN, thus making it almost impossible to work on the principle of consent. Once UNPROFOR withdrew, it would be difficult for it to return.

8 June 1995

Left Zagreb this morning at 6:30 A.M. on a UN plane, a Russian Ilyushin designed for paratroopers, hollowed out in the center with seats along the sides. Eighty minutes to Belgrade. Very punctual. Then a four-hour drive by auto to Pale, where we had business. Couldn't fly directly to Sarajevo, which is much closer to Pale, because the Sarajevo airport is still closed. (The Serbs said they couldn't guarantee security for air traffic in and out of Sarajevo, which in effect closed the airport.) Couldn't drive from Kiseljak either, which would have been a more direct route to Pale from Zagreb, because that road has also been closed by the Serbs.

The war is in progress. Freedom of movement is severely restricted.

Our delegation was headed by UNHCR's special representative to former Yugoslavia, Anne-Willem Bijleveld, a Dutch national. UNPROFOR Legal Counsel Matthew Hodes and I went as UNPROFOR observers. We had a one-item agenda: to open a land route to Sarajevo so that food can be delivered to the civilian population. First choice is to open for UNHCR convoys the road from Kiseljak to Sarajevo, the one we were unable to take, a route known as Route Swan, which passes through what are called the Sierras. [The Sierras were so named because *sierra* is the phonetic alphabet's designation for the letter S, which also stands for *Serbs*. Traffic between Kiseljak and Sarajevo had to go through four Serb checkpoints: Sierras one, two, three, and four.]

Advance speculation in the international press on the purpose of our meeting was erroneous. Some thought the meeting was to discuss the hostage situation (approximately 125 UNPROFOR personnel are still being held hostage by the Serbs in response to NATO air strikes on Pale on 25 and 26 May; more than 100 have already been released), or to try to open the road over Mount Igman (Igman Logistics Route, or ILR), or to restore utilities to Sarajevo, or to discuss the resupply of UNPROFOR units in the designated safe areas. Only one of those items was on the agenda: UNHCR convoys from Kiseljak to Sarajevo through the Sierras. Side issue: treatment of non-Serbian minorities in Banja Luka. The priorities and previews of the press were once again inconsistent with reality and for the usual reason: they reflected what the press thought the priorities at any given moment *should* be. It was exhortation disguised as reportage.

During our talk there was never mention of the use of force by UNPROFOR if the Serbs resist, but the threat is in the background. One UNPROFOR colleague said, "We're going to feed Sarajevo one way or the other, and the Serbs know it." But the emphasis was still on consent. UNHCR does not want to be associated with the use of force, the threat of the use of force, or even the use of military personnel when civilians can be used.

We met first with Bosnian Serb Vice President Nikola Koljevic, around

12:30 P.M. He said he had to leave for a State Committee meeting at 2:00 P.M., but he talked to us briefly so that he could get an idea of what we wanted to discuss later. Bijleveld told him what we wanted. He said that as of today there is no flour in Sarajevo, no bread for the people. Distribution of flour has begun in the other enclaves, but not in Sarajevo, and there is a group of one hundred thousand people—mainly the elderly and infants—who are vulnerable, seriously endangered. UNHCR's stocks in Sarajevo are depleted, and they have nothing left in the warehouses.

"You'll get what you want," Koljevic said. Whatever the reason, the Bosnian Serbs have decided to allow resupply of Sarajevo, or they have decided they would *say* they have agreed to the resupply of Sarajevo. Both sides are very effective with propaganda. When they feel that international pressure is building against them, they will relieve the pressure by consenting to certain essential demands, but then it will take days, sometimes weeks, before those demands are actually implemented. It is an institutionalized stalling tactic. Meanwhile, what the Serbs really want is to retain control of any traffic entering Sarajevo; they want the power to turn on and off the feeding of Sarajevo. That is why they are offering transit through the Sierra checkpoints from Kiseljak—to discourage forcing open the ILR. They can harass traffic on the Igman road by shelling, but they cannot set up checkpoints there, and they cannot prevent night traffic. Most of the supplies and people who enter and leave Sarajevo do so by dark over the ILR.

We agreed to return and negotiate at 5:00 P.M. Originally, the Serbs had refused to see us at all; they said their entire day would be taken up with a State Committee meeting. Then they changed their mind, and last night at around 6:00 P.M., they said they could see us today at 2:00 P.M. Thus, we had to leave Zagreb at 6:30 A.M. this morning to fly by UN plane to Belgrade and then, under Serbian police escort, drive from there to Pale in order to have a meeting at 2:00 P.M.

While Koljevic went to attend the State Committee meeting, we went to see Radovan Karadzic, president of Republika Srpska. He looked haggard, worn, at least two decades older than his fifty years. It was the first time I have seen him in person. His English was very good. He rambled on, speaking frequently about World War II and how the Serbs had been massacred by the same forces that were oppressing them now—the Germans and the Croats and the Moslems—except that then the United States and Russia were on the side of the Serbs against the fascists. Now America has chosen to support fascism. He couldn't understand why. He constantly returned to World War II; it was an obsession with him. He spoke about it the way that Jewish people speak about the Holocaust. On the issue of road access to Sarajevo, he said he would support whatever Koljevic and the State Committee decided.

Karadzic wanted to link all the issues: release of the hostages, opening the road from Kiseljak to Sarajevo, stopping NATO bombing, opening the Sarajevo airport, and so on. It was clear he wants to end the war, but he doesn't want to give up any of the territory he already has. He wants peace on his terms. Here are some of the statements he made:

"People come to me only to express concern, never pleasure."

"The international community must change its attitude toward the Serbs. You can't cage us like beasts, bomb us, and then ask for favors."

"The Serbs in Pale are not aggressors. We have been here for centuries. The Moslems are Serbs; they are Serbian Moslems. They want to leave Yugoslavia; okay, we want to leave Bosnia."

"I cannot sell the idea of cooperation with UNPROFOR to my people in this bloody democracy so long as we are treated by the international community as aggressors and are under double sanctions—by the Security Council and by Yugoslavia."

"If you are talking about the forcible opening of roads around Sarajevo, then there will be a bloody war."

On the situation of Croats in Banja Luka, Karadzic said it was difficult to control the anger of the Serbian refugees who had just been expelled from Western Slavonia. They wanted revenge. He would try to increase the Serbian police presence in Banja Luka, but many of the Serbian police had been mobilized and were on the front lines. They were unavailable to maintain law and order.

On the Croatian invasion of West Slavonia: "It happened so fast I didn't have time to send my army."

On NATO air strikes: "There will be retaliation by the Serbs, and each time the retaliation will be worse. We are a small nation, but we are very proud."

On control: "We are a sovereign country, and we cannot allow anyone to control our territory."

While we were talking to Karadzic, he informed us that the downed American pilot, Scott O'Grady, whose F-16 was shot down six days ago over Banja Luka, has been found by NATO. Karadzic expressed relief: "I'm glad NATO found him. What would we have done with him if we found him? It would have been a big headache." He added that he doesn't want to see any individual pilots killed. Planes, however, were something else.

[Although Karadzic seemed aware that the world was against him, he had no idea how potent that opposition was. Even though the Serbs and others wanted to see analogies to the Vietnam War, the situation was very different when the United States sought to defeat the Vietcong. As the French say, "La comparison n'a pas de raison." For one thing, the Vietcong could not be geographically separated from the South Vietnamese. They were intertwined, especially in Saigon. By contrast, one of the punishments for ethnic cleansing in former Yugoslavia was, ironically, that the Serbs, having "puri-fied" the region, could be more easily identified, isolated, and bombed. Their separation made them vulnerable. Then again, the Vietcong had support from the Soviet Union and China. The Russian Federation under Yeltsin sees its future economically and politically tied to Western interests; it defended the Serbs on territorial grounds because it did not want NATO making war in Eastern Europe, but it also did not want to see a revival of the nation-state idea. If the Russian minority within every former Republic of the Soviet Union tried to establish its own state on the ground of being ethnic Russians, there would be chaos. Finally, of course, there were no U.S. troops on the ground in Bosnia as there were in Vietnam. The American people, thank goodness, have a low tolerance for American casualties in the Balkans.

Karadzic's comment about the Moslems in Bosnia being "Serbian" Moslems was yet another salvo in the propaganda war for the minds and genes of the people of Bosnia. There are no birth records from the Ottoman Empire to confirm the ethnic origin of any Bosnian, and there was no abiding sense of nationhood among any of the constituent peoples of the former Yugoslavia until late in the nineteenth century. For centuries, rebellions in Bosnia were class based or anticolonial: peasants against landlords or subjects against foreign colonial powers. Although most of the landlords in Bosnia during the Ottoman Empire were Moslems, many of the peasants were also Moslems (as well as Croats and Serbs). When the peasants and urban dwellers weren't fighting the landlords, they were fighting Turkish colonialism or Austrian colonialism.

One of the reasons that World War II was so chaotic in the Balkans was that there were three wars going on at the same time, a war within a war within a war. At the international level, Yugoslavia was fighting the Nazis, but there was also the war between the Serbs and the other constituent peoples (Croats, Slovenes, and Moslems), and a war between Communist partisans and royalist Chetniks. The most destructive of all civil wars are those against a nation's past.

Most historians would probably agree that during the Ottoman period, a Serb in Banja Luka had no national identification with a Serb in Novi Sad or in Knin, even though they both belonged to the Eastern Orthodox Church. Allegiance was to regions or to feudal lords, not to ethnicity. Ethnic rivalry and hatred were relatively recent phenomena, fueled by the Austro-Hungarian monarchy in the nineteenth century by the Vatican and most recently by the Nazis. It is common among many commentators to say that ethnic conflicts in the Balkans have been going on for a thousand years. Nonsense. There have been wars in the Balkans for a millennium, but they have not been ethnic conflicts.

Even Warren Zimmermann, by no means a defender of Serbian nationalism, notes that "Serbs and Croats, the most antagonistic of adversaries today, had never fought each other before the twentieth century. The millennium they spent as neighbors was marked more by mutual indifference than by mutual hostility. Serbs, though demonized by many as incorrigibly xenophobic, don't fit that stereotype."*

As for Karadzic's comment about a "bloody war" around Sarajevo, it only showed that he had no idea of NATO's destructive might. He was trying to tell us that the Bosnian Serbs would be able to retaliate in kind against NATO. No way. Although it was probable at this point that NATO air power *would* eventually have its "bloody war" around Sarajevo and act as mercenaries for the Bosnian government (also, incidentally, as precinct workers for Bill Clinton's reelection campaign), it was clear that the Bosnian Serbs would not be able to resist in the same way that the Vietcong had—not from a lack of courage, but from a lack of any support in the international community and from an overestimation of their own military capability.

On Western Slavonia, Karadzic had plainly prevaricated. Republika Srpska didn't help because it couldn't. It was too stretched out already, wafer thin across thousands of kilometers of frontier with the Croats and the Bosnians.]

We resumed our meeting with Vice President Koljevic around 5:00 P.M. and continued for five hours. We were joined by Lyubisa Vladusic, the Bosnian Serb commissioner for refugees and humanitarian aid. There were practical, as well as political, problems.

Bijleveld expressed his concern that the road from Kiseljak to Sarajevo might be mined. Koljevic said he would have the Bosnian Serb army check the Serbian-controlled part of the road and demine it if necessary, but he could not guarantee that the portion running through Bosnian Croat territory would be demined. (Kiseljak was a Bosnian Croat "pocket" inside of Moslem territory.) In fact, he alleged that it is the Bosnian Croats who are preventing humanitarian aid deliveries to Sarajevo, not the Bosnian Serbs. [It was well known that the Bosnian Croats were exacting heavy bribes from private traffic that passed through Kiseljak en route to Sarajevo. In a perverse way, they had an interest in maintaining the siege of Sarajevo.]

Bijleveld then asked if UNHCR would be able to use UNPROFOR drivers and trucks to deliver the aid because UNHCR did not have enough trucks. He also wanted an UNPROFOR escort. Koljevic said there might be a problem here. What did Bijleveld mean by "escort"?

"APCs," Bijleveld replied.

Koljevic frowned. Trucks are not a problem as long as license plate num-

*Zimmerman, *Origins,* 209.

bers are submitted in advance, but UNPROFOR soldiers and UNPROFOR Armored Personnel Carriers (APCS) passing through Serbian territory might be provocative, considering the recent NATO bombing in Pale. He suspected this problem would take some time to resolve, as much as a week or two, because he would have to go back to his parliament and to the military with any proposed solution. Meanwhile, he suggested a Serbian police escort to replace the APCS.

After about an hour, Koljevic left the room for an urgent phone call. When he returned, he seemed distressed. [Whether or not he was really distressed is debatable, but he had the appearance of being distressed. In fact, I suspected we were witnessing a bit of Balkan theater, and as a student of Shakespeare, Koljevic was an accomplished performer in that art form. Theater was an element in every negotiation in this part of the world.]

"Bad news from Zepa," Koljevic said, shaking his head sadly. "Our guards have found two boxes of ammunition hidden in flour bags in a UNHCR convoy."

We could scarcely contain our skepticism. "They may have been planted by the guards at the checkpoint," I suggested.

Koljevic: "Oh, no! The bags were in the back of the truck. It would have taken hours to plant them there. They were put there long before they reached the checkpoint."

Vladusic: "Probably the ammunition was planted without the knowledge of UNHCR, by people trying to discredit UNHCR or by smugglers. But we must be more careful in the future."

Koljevic: "Let's not publicize this problem, okay? We'll try to keep it quiet."

We thanked them both for their cooperative attitude.

Koljevic: "The most important thing is to feed Sarajevo, and it would be best not to use UNPROFOR military vehicles. That would only complicate the issue."

Bijleveld: "But we need assurances that our drivers will not be taken hostage. That is why we want UNPROFOR protection."

Koljevic: "Whether we want to admit it or not, the political, humanitarian, and military aspects are all linked. UNPROFOR APCS make a military and a political statement, even if they are guarding humanitarian aid."

Bijleveld: "We need security assurances, or we will not be able to get drivers."

Koljevic: "We'll provide you with drivers and an escort."

We refused the offer of Serbian drivers.

Koljevic: "We have to build confidence between the Serbs and the international community. After the bombing, it's going to take awhile to build confidence. We can start by providing security for you with our police."

Then Matt Hodes, the UNPROFOR legal counsel, made a suggestion. I am very fond of Matt Hodes, who embodies the best qualities of a good international lawyer. He protects his client, which in this case is UNPROFOR, and he is always looking for compromise positions. "We can have an armed UNPROFOR escort *plus* Serbian police. We have to protect against rogue elements and protect our drivers. We will protect our drivers, and you will protect against rogue elements. If shelling starts, our drivers must have a safe place to hide; that's what the APCs are for."

Vladusic: "If you use UNPROFOR APCs, our people will go into the streets and block the convoys. They will lie down in the road. We won't be able to control them. But if there is no armed escort, there will be no problem."

Koljevic: "Our people will say, 'They bomb us, and then they want to start up their convoys, with military escorts, in order to feed the Moslems.' As a civilian, I cannot guarantee that our military will accept this arrangement. You don't realize the true situation. Our people are more radical then we, the leaders, are."

Hodes: "It seems we agree on the goal of feeding Sarajevo, but we disagree on the means."

Koljevic: "You people don't take the Serbs seriously. We were never even informed that you [Bijleveld] would be bringing others along today. We are willing to speak to UNHCR, but Karadzic does not want to talk to representatives of Mr. Akashi for a while. Not after this bombing." [Koljevic was referring to Hodes and me as the representatives of Mr. Akashi.]

We repeated our wish for an UNPROFOR escort. "It's perfectly within our mandate," Hodes said.

Koljevic: "If you insist on an UNPROFOR escort, then I can try to get approval, but I can't give you any guarantees, and you will undermine attempts to establish credibility. Our people are very suspicious of the Brits. We don't want to see British APCs accompanying a UNHCR convoy. We don't want a war with the Brits."

We took a break. Koljevic's tactic was familiar. If he can't have his way, he stalls and says he is having trouble with the military. It is the Good Serb, Bad Serb tactic. The civilians are moderate, but the military is rigid, Koljevic will pretend. More Balkan theater, more Balkan ballet. But inevitably the Balkan Ballet will become a war dance.

We discussed the situation among ourselves. If what we were interested in most was security, then what did it matter who provided it? We were sure that the Serbs would provide adequate security. On the other hand, would it be just one more concession we were making to the Serbs, one more retreat from our mandate, which clearly says that UNPROFOR is supposed to provide protection for humanitarian convoys? And would we ever be able to restore that right, once surrendered?

We agreed to seek compromise. We would accept Serbian security, but we didn't want to endure four checkpoints. We would accept being checked only at Sierra One, not at two, three, and four. If there were any problems with security this time, we would reserve the right to use UNPROFOR security the next time.

When we resumed our discussion, Koljevic came in with a heavy face. More ammunition had been found in the UNHCR convoy to Zepa. Ammunition boxes were hidden under the seats in one truck. "We cannot build confidence this way," Koljevic said. We said nothing. We didn't believe him.

After five hours of difficult negotiations, we agreed on a formula for restoring humanitarian aid to Sarajevo, and we issued a joint press statement, which I drafted. We thought a statement would be preferable to a written agreement. The statement said:

1. UNHCR convoys, for both sides, will resume from Metkovic via Kiseljak to Sarajevo.

2. Food will once again be supplied to Sarajevo.

3. Serbian authorities will inspect convoys only once, at checkpoint Sierra one, in order to verify their contents.

4. Serbian authorities will guarantee security for the drivers of UNHCR convoys and will escort them to Sarajevo town, Rajlovac, and Trebinja.

The Serbs are concerned that UNHCR will be supplying only the Moslem side, so Trebinja, in Herzegovina, was included in the list in order to supply Serbian DPs there.

No sooner was the deal struck, however, than the UN bashers attacked us for saying we had achieved success. [This situation was my first direct experience with the juggernaut of pro-Bosnian, anti-Serb sentiment in the international community, a juggernaut with a powerful public relations arm (a.k.a. the international press), a host of international civil servants (the Sarajevo-based staff for most of the international agencies), and elements of the British army.] I reported on our meeting to Akashi, saying we had concluded a successful agreement. As a courtesy, I showed copies of my report to the heads of other agencies.

The criticism then began. Bill Eagleton, a retired U.S. diplomat who is the SCS, insisted that our meeting was not a "success" because we let the Serbs control us and because we are still not back to where we were earlier, during the Cessation of Hostilities Agreement, *before* the access routes to Sarajevo were closed. I emphasized that our agreement was only a first step.

Though I have high regard for Bill Eagleton personally, as well as professionally, I find his political approach repugnant. His responses are always predictable. Inevitably and irrevocably, he advocates bombing the demonic

Bosnian Serbs as soon as possible. He has little patience for diplomacy in Bosnia, even though he himself is a former diplomat. Of course, he is frustrated that his reconstruction program cannot proceed as planned because the roads into Sarajevo are blocked, and he cannot bring in the materials necessary for reconstruction of the city. But what neither he nor any of the Bosnian government's other cheerleaders will state publicly is that, on occasion, the Bosnian government itself prevents the transport of building materials, as well as other assistance, from entering Sarajevo in order the maintain the "siege" mentality and the "victim" status of Sarajevans. It is necessary to maintain this image in order to perpetuate the sympathy of the international community and to increase the pressure for NATO intervention. Not coincidentally, certain Bosnian government officials are making small fortunes on the black market as long as the siege of Sarajevo continues. Yes, the Serbs are obstructive, but so is the Bosnian government.

[A few months later, General Charles G. Boyd (United States Air Force, retired), who was the deputy commander in chief, U.S. European Command, from November 1992 to July 1995, would have the following to say in a brilliant article in the September–October 1995 issue of *Foreign Affairs*:

> Some of the city's suffering has actually been imposed on it by actions of the Sarajevo government. Some were understandable policies, like the restriction on travel to prevent the depopulation of the city during those periods when movement was possible. Others were the by-product of government weakness, like relying on the Sarajevo underworld for the initial defense of the city, thereby empowering criminal elements that took their toll on the population, especially Serbs. Still others were intentional; whether out of individual greed or official policy is unclear. Government soldiers, for example, have shelled the Sarajevo airport, the city's primary lifeline for relief supplies. The press and some governments, including that of the United States, usually attribute all such fire to the Serbs, but no seasoned observer in Sarajevo doubts for a moment that Muslim forces have found it in their interest to shell friendly targets. In this case, the shelling usually closes the airport for a time, driving up the price of black-market goods that enter the city via routes controlled by Bosnian army commanders and government officials.

Of course, we were also criticized by the Bosnian government for our "deal" with war criminals. We were told that we should just shoot our way through any Serbian obstruction in order to fulfill our mandate.]

What the international community never addresses as this civil war in Bosnia proceeds are the responsibilities devolving from sovereignty and international recognition, not merely the privileges; it rarely acknowledges the constant violations of Security Council resolutions by the Bosnian and Croatian governments (not to mention the violations by foreign powers involved in arms smuggling). The privileges of international recognition are incomparable. Once a state is internationally recognized, it can do virtually anything it wants within its borders except commit massive violations of human rights. Therefore, within their recognized borders the Bosnian and Croatian governments can do whatever they want militarily and politically against Serbian rebels. Contrarily, in the eyes of the international community, the Bosnian Serbs and the Croatian Serbs have no recognized rights (except for universal human rights) because they don't officially exist as nations. Thus, the Bosnian government has the right to shell the Bosnian Serbs, even if it means breaking a truce (in fact, *especially* if it means breaking a truce) because the Bosnian government is the sovereign government within the internationally recognized borders of Bosnia and Herzegovina.

Perhaps that distinction is a just one. As often stated, the Bosnian government feels it is *their* country, and it can do whatever is necessary in order to gain control of it. Why should they accept a cease-fire and a potential settlement that will surrender large chunks of sovereign Bosnia? Sovereignty is the pillar of international relations, and the Bosnian government's attitude is consistent with accepted international behavior. The problem, however, is that unless it agrees to modify its behavior, there can be no peace.

Meanwhile, perhaps the most self-destructive of all the mistakes being made by the Bosnian and Croatian Serbs is their consistent rejection of international peace plans. By accepting to negotiate on the basis of those plans—such as the Vance-Owen Peace Plan or the Contact Group Plan—the Serbs can attain official international recognition; they can establish their legitimacy, which is the closest to sovereignty they can hope for, and this legitimacy will give them acknowledged political rights. But they are too stubborn and too paranoiac.

[Regarding the Bosnian government's provocation of conflict and obstruction of peace efforts, I shall quote here from a public document that the international press prefers not to quote. It is the UN Secretary-General's report of 30 May 1995. Paragraphs 36, 37, and 38, read as follows:

> It should be recalled that resolution 836 (1993) does not require the Government of the Republic of Bosnia and Herzegovina to withdraw its military or paramilitary units from the safe areas. However, the Council has, in presidential statements, made it clear that "provocative actions by whomsoever committed" were unacceptable. As I emphasized, the party defending a safe area must comply with certain obligations if it is to achieve the primary objective of the safe area regime,

that is, the protection of the civilian population. Unprovoked attacks launched from safe areas are inconsistent with the whole concept.

In recent months, (Bosnian) government forces have considerably increased their military activity in and around most safe areas, and many of them, including Sarajevo, Tuzla and Bihac, have been incorporated into the broader military campaigns of the government side. The headquarters and logistics installations of the Fifth Corps of the government army are located in the town of Bihac and those of the Second Corps in the town of Tuzla. The Government also maintains a substantial number of troops in Srebrenica (in this case, a violation of a demilitarization agreement), Gorazde and Zepa, while Sarajevo is the location of the General Command of the government army and other military installations. There is also an ammunition factory in Gorazde.

The Bosnian Serb forces' reaction to offensives launched by the government army from safe areas has generally been to respond against military targets within those areas, often at a disproportionate level. Notwithstanding the provocation, these acts of the Bosnian Serb forces violate the safe-area regime and other local agreements. The Serbs have also initiated unprovoked shelling of safe areas. In both cases civilian casualties have occurred. UNPROFOR's mandate to deter attacks upon the safe areas requires it to react to Serb actions, irrespective of whether the Serbs are responding to offensives launched by the other side. When they are doing so, however, the impartiality of UNPROFOR becomes difficult to maintain and the Force is seen as a party to the conflict, with resulting risks to isolated United Nations personnel.]

9 June 1995

Today Akashi and General Bernard Janvier (commander of all UN forces in former Yugoslavia) went to Split, Croatia, to speak with General Smith. [I was not invited and, in fact, was quite annoyed about it, even though the snub was not personal. It was one more example that the mission in Bosnia was a military one and that the political, diplomatic side was marginal.]

The meeting in Split is a strategy session, no doubt a step in the run-up to massive NATO intervention. There is a divergence of views between Janvier and Smith, exploited by the international press in its role as the Bosnian's government's information mercenaries and played down by the United Nations. Janvier, understandably, has to be concerned with how action in Bosnia will impact on all other areas of former Yugoslavia, specifically Croatia. Smith, on the other hand, is concerned solely with Bosnia. I myself have no problem with different views being aired in a strategy session, as long as the conclusion is respected by both sides. [As it turned out, Janvier won the battle but lost the war. Smith had NATO and the international press in his corner.]

Janvier still wants to operate on the principle of consent, whereas Smith wants to use limited force in order to retrieve what the UN has lost in the past few weeks (mainly, freedom of movement). Both agree the situation has deteriorated and that UNPROFOR's credibility needs a boost. Specifically, Smith argues that force is needed in order to implement Security Council resolution 836, which charges UNPROFOR to assist in the delivery of humanitarian aid. Once this task is achieved, the UN can work on the principle of consent. As of now, however, UNPROFOR is being blocked by the Serbs from fulfilling its mandate in Bosnia.

Janvier argues that there are still UN soldiers at risk in Serb-controlled territory, and we have to be concerned about retaliation against them. Also, the use of force by the UN in one part of the theater will impact on the UN's role in other parts of the theater (specifically, in Croatia) and make a comprehensive peace more difficult to achieve. When Croatia recently overran Western Slavonia and used military force against UN positions, there was no military response by the UN, even though it had the right to use self-defense, including the use of close air support. UN force in Bosnia against only one party to the conflict would damage even further the ability of the UN to act as an impartial interlocutor and might widen the war, Janvier maintains.

Smith's view is that of the field commander. He is looking at the situation from Bosnia—more specifically, from Sarajevo—not from Zagreb or New York. As far as he is concerned, he is being obstructed by the Bosnian Serbs from carrying out his mandate, his troops are under attack, and he wants to respond "robustly" if he is to have any credibility as a soldier, and if he is to maintain the morale of his troops.

In fact, Smith is the best general that the Bosnian government has, and they know it, although they are not what is driving him. He is motivated mainly by a great and sincere sense of duty, and he is even driving policy in London, not vice versa as is the usual scenario.

Meanwhile, there is no denying the frenetic, almost apocalyptic atmosphere of the international community in Sarajevo, inflamed each day by the international press in its determination to bring NATO into the conflict in a big way, and to use all necessary force against the Bosnian Serbs. Smith is buoyed up by this wave of emotional support. He does not pander to it and does not consciously contribute to it, but he is aware of it, and he summons it in his policy differences with Janvier, with UNPROFOR headquarters in Zagreb, and with UN headquarters in New York. He also exploits it to gain the confidences of Bosnian government officials in Sarajevo, who for the most part refuse to deal with civilian officials like me. Yes, the Bosnian government has its general, and they are not about to talk to civilians—whether those civilians be internationally appointed negotiators such as Thorvald Stoltenberg (co-chair of International Conference on the Former Yugoslavia [ICFY] and former foreign minister of Norway), Carl Bildt (the other co-chair of ICFY and former Swedish prime minister), United Nations Secretary-General Boutros Boutros-Ghali, Yasushi Akashi, or a star of a lesser magnitude, such as Phillip Corwin.

Although Smith frequently complains about having to spend too much of his day on political matters, he loves it and seldom discourages it. What he wants is relief from the paperwork that goes with being a political official, but he cherishes and encourages political contacts.

[To many of us in UNPROFOR, whatever the public perception was, it was clear that the Bosnian government did not want peace on any terms less than those of the current Contact Group Plan, and it was even doubtful they wanted peace at all at this point. They had numerical superiority, they had virtual military parity by the summer of 1995, and the tide of the war had turned in their favor. Understandably, the Bosnian government did not want to accept a partition of their country. What Bosnian politicians wanted was a NATO mercenary force to replace UNPROFOR, and, accordingly, they discredited UNPROFOR whenever they could, usually slanderously. If they could not have NATO, their first choice, then they would try to turn UNPROFOR into their armed mercenaries. Both options were, of course, understandable from the Bosnian government's point of view, and the clarity of their goals was one of the reasons they would ultimately be successful. Equally important, the Bosnian government's legitimate concerns once again called into question the role of international peacekeeping: the need to adhere to a weak mandate, the responsibilities of the host country for respecting UN troops, and the distinction between peacekeeping and peacemaking. For the international community, these questions were part of an ongoing intellectual debate, but for the Bosnian government and its people, the abstractness of these issues was eclipsed by a desperate need to survive. They had no patience with intellectual debate.]

Smith has a cogent legislative argument for the use of limited force, or what he terms "robust response," against the Bosnian Serbs. Sarajevo is a designated safe area, and under Security Council resolution 836, adopted on 4 June 1993, UNPROFOR is authorized "to deter attacks against the safe areas, . . . to promote the withdrawal of military or paramilitary units other than those of the Government of the Republic of Bosnia and Herzegovina and to occupy some key points on the ground, in addition to participating in the delivery of humanitarian relief to the population." Smith is being prevented from implementing that mandate. [The fact that that mandate was unrealistic, given the lack of military resources and the conflicting attitudes of the European community, were beside the point. Smith had a mandate to fulfill, and he couldn't do it without using force, he argued.]

Moreover, resolution 836 authorizes Smith to use limited force. In paragraph 9 of that document, the Security Council authorizes UNPROFOR, "acting in self-defence, to take the necessary measures, *including the use of force, in reply to bombardments against the safe areas by any of the parties or to armed incursion into them or in the event of any deliberate obstruction in or around those areas to the freedom of movement of* UNPROFOR *or of protected humanitarian convoys*" (emphasis mine). UNPROFOR has no freedom of movement. Not only can it not bring in humanitarian convoys, but it cannot even resupply its own forces—a condition that makes it part of the problem rather than part of the solution (except that the Bosnian government also obstructs UN convoys, but is rarely criticized for it).

In paragraph 10 of that same resolution, the Security Council states that member states, "acting nationally or through regional organizations or arrangements, may take, under the authority of the Security Council and subject to close coordination with the Secretary-General and UNPROFOR, all necessary measures, through the use of air power, in and around the safe areas in the Republic of Bosnia and Herzegovinia, to support UNPROFOR in the performance of its mandate." "Regional organizations" means NATO. "Close coordination" means the dual key concept, by which both NATO and UNPROFOR have to agree to the use of air power or it cannot be employed.

[The dual key concept was, in fact, so successful that NATO, Washington, and Bonn brought it under constant attack. What it meant was that when a request for the use of air power came from a field commander, such as Smith, that request had to be approved both by NATO (which always said *yes* when asked to bomb the demonic Serbs) and by the head of the UNPROFOR mission, Yasushi Akashi. In practice, when requests came for the use of air power against the Serbs, Akashi would huddle with his military and political advisors before making a decision. He never made those decisions in isolation. He consulted as widely and as expeditiously as possible. On at least eleven occasions he agreed to the use of air power against the Serbs. Most NATO officials, however, felt that the UN did not use air power enough, so in the summer of 1995 responsibility for the dual key was taken from the civilian head of UNPROFOR, Akashi, and passed to the force commander, General Janvier. Akashi was still consulted, but he was relieved, in more ways than one, of the responsibility for sanctioning NATO's adventurism and its search for a post–Cold War identity.]

I have come to develop great respect for Yasushi Akashi over the years. In fact, I have worked for him, on and off, for almost two decades, much of that time at UN headquarters in New York, in the Department of Public Information. In some ways he fits the stereotypical image Americans have of Japanese. He is relentlessly energetic, a workaholic, a high achiever, ambitious, and very conscious of image; at the same time, he is extremely polite, secretive, and actually quite shy. What I have come to admire most about Akashi is his infinite patience, his tenacity, and his assiduity.

Akashi sees the conflict in former Yugoslavia as a challenge. Following his success in heading up the UN peacekeeping operation in Cambodia, he itched for another challenge. In his early sixties—and very fit both physically and mentally—he is not about to sit back and write books. He is an activist.

Cambodia was different than Yugoslavia for many reasons, however, at least two of which are crucial. First, in Cambodia the United Nations had the nominal cooperation of the powers at the top, even though the Khmer Rouge was obstructive. This condition has never been true in former Yugoslavia, where the United Nations does not have cooperation at the top and, in fact, has imposed sanctions and is taking military action against one of the parties to the conflict. In other words, it is in the difficult position of having to ask cooperation from a party it is punishing. From the start, the United Nations has not been seen as being impartial, a perception that imposes severe limitations on Akashi's role as an interlocutor. It is almost impossible to be impartial when your mandate is not impartial, and if your mandate is not impartial then your credibility is suspect.

Second, in Cambodia the United Nations held several portfolios, including that of information, in the interim government. The information portfolio was critical because the United Nations could put out "official" information about its role in the peace process. In former Yugoslavia, the United Nations is certainly not part of any government, and it has very little control over the reams of misinformation that come out against it from all sides, including from those very member governments that have given it its mandate.

In Croatia, the government conducts a semiofficial campaign of slander against the United Nations and refuses to give air time to UN radio programs even though it has obligated itself to do so in an agreement with the United Nations. For at least one year prior to the Croatian military action against Western Slavonia there had not been one single favorable story about the United Nations in the Croatian media. This approach was no accident; it was policy. Croatia's intent was either to expel the United Nations and bring in NATO as a replacement force, or to take military action against the Serbian minority once the UN was out of the way and expect the West to turn a blind eye. Needless to say, the Croatian government was successful in its campaign.

In Bosnia, the international press is so pro-Bosnian and anti-United Nations that there is no need for official government censorship. The UN holds its daily press briefings, but it is understood that criticism by UNPROFOR of the Bosnian government is prohibited. In short, there is a huge difference between the way the UN operated in Cambodia and the way it operates in former Yugoslavia.

Akashi never relents in his attempts to charm the press, however. Every morning that he is in Zagreb, he emerges at 8:00 A.M. from his suite at the Intercontinental Hotel, and the press is waiting for him. He answers their questions dutifully and politely; nevertheless, he and UNPROFOR are continuously vilified in the local press.

[Meanwhile, in Bosnia during the summer of 1995, Minister Hasan Muratovic told the Bosnian press, "Akashi is dead!" He pronounced him persona non grata. Later, responding to international pressure, Muratovic told me that it was the city of Sarajevo, not the government of Bosnia and Herzegovina, that had declared Akashi persona non grata. But the distinction was disingenuous and irrelevant. The Bosnian government basically refused to see Akashi any more by the summer of 1995, about the time I arrived on the scene. The fact that I am his personal representative contributed to my difficulties.]

Akashi has amazing patience. I remember once this summer when he traveled to Osijek, at the edge of Eastern Slavonia, just after the Croatian army had conquered the Krajina and was talking about invading Eastern Slavonia, the last remaining area of Croatia still occupied by the Serbs. He went to visit a notorious Croatian nationalist, Branimir Glavas, *zupan* (governor) of the region, to make an assessment of the situation and to express his hope for a peaceful solution to the problem. There were demonstrations outside Glavas's office, and Akashi was shoved and pushed and verbally abused on his way in. Following the meeting, he asked to leave by a back exit in order to avoid the hostile crowd still waiting outside, and he was told that the back door was locked and the key *had been lost*. (Give me a break!) So he went out the front door, and he was besieged again. He had to be literally lifted by his bodyguards and carried toward the car. When I saw him in Zagreb a few days later, I offered my condolences for the way Glavas had treated him, suggesting that it was Glavas himself who had organized the demonstration. "Oh, no," Akashi said. "Everything is all right now. Glavas apologized to me five times. Five times!" At that point, I couldn't tell if Akashi was serious or if he was joking (probably serious, because the Japanese take apologies very seriously). But the point is that he seldom loses control. Although there are politicians he doesn't like, he rarely says so. He is extremely well disciplined.

I have said Akashi is a workaholic. He works at least six days a week. At first, he also worked on Sundays. Now he occasionally takes Sundays off. He rarely goes on vacation, and he expects his immediate staff to work the same way. They usually do.

Akashi is shy but not indecisive. He certainly does not like personal confrontations, either with his staff or with governments, and avoids them whenever possible. Thus, it is particularly difficult for him to deal with Bosnian and Croatian officials, who, excepting President Izetbegovic, frequently shout at him and utter the most disgraceful lies and racist slurs against UNPROFOR. The Serbs shout at him, too, but less often; they treat him with more respect.

As for his personal convictions, Akashi believes first and foremost in the need for patient diplomacy. He is against the use of force whenever possible. When force is unavoidable, he believes, it should be used to the least degree possible, and even then, it should be accompanied by diplomacy. I share every one of those beliefs myself.

Akashi's dislike of violence is a part of his personality and a part of his culture. His is the generation victimized by the atomic bomb. For the last several years of his career, in fact, prior to his appointment in Cambodia, he was in charge of the Department for Disarmament at the United Nations, a position not inconsistent with his personal beliefs. Of course there are elements of Japanese culture that are violent, but Akashi embodied other aspects of Japanese culture, its love of peace and tranquility, its stance against nuclear weapons, and its quiet diplomacy.

Carl Bildt, a Swedish diplomat and former prime minister, has been asked to replace Lord David Owen as representative of the European Union (EU) to ICFY and has been given a six-week "window" to find a way to resolve the crisis in Bosnia. He is expected to tour the area imminently. The early word is that if he fails to make significant progress, NATO will find a reason to initiate military action against the Bosnian Serbs. But there is no way Bildt or anyone else will be able to negotiate a peace settlement within six weeks, all of which makes one wonder whether Bildt's mission does not have some ulterior, unstated purpose. Is it an ultimatum?

It may be worth noting at this point that this peacekeeping mission is the first ever in UN history in which the UN is involved but does not have both military and political responsibilities. In previous situations, the UN has always had both. It has provided the troops *and* the negotiating mechanism. On this occasion, however, ICFY has been charged with the responsibility for negotiating a comprehensive settlement in the region, and the United Nations, through its member states, has been asked to provide the military forces. Perhaps this divided approach is one of the reasons the mission has had less success than it might have had.

Random thoughts:

Karadzic is reeling. Military defeats, even more than economic depressions, are the bane of political leadership. In our meeting Karadzic's statements about "this bloody democracy" refer to internal opposition forces within the ruling political party that are trying to seize power from him. Of course, there is no democracy in Republika Srpska, or for that matter in any of the republics or would-be republics in former Yugoslavia, nor was there ever any democracy of note in the former Yugoslavia. For all the bombast about "new democracies" or "restoring" democracy or "building" democracy, there is no democracy anywhere in the theater—including or especially in Sarajevo, where one-party government is ruthless, totalitarian, and corrupt. Throughout the former Yugoslavia we are dealing with gangs, organized and disorganized, official and unofficial. Perhaps Lebanon, prior to the Syrian takeover, is the best analogy to the situation in former Yugoslavia. The West keeps talking about legitimate governments in former Yugoslavia. It should be talking about legitimized gangs.

The loss of Western Slavonia was a military defeat for Karadzic in the sense that he had promised solidarity with the Croatian Serbs, and he didn't produce. The air strikes on Pale were also a loss for him because he had to resort to desperate measures (taking UN hostages) that were condemned by the entire international community. He is on a downtrend.

On the other hand, the international community is still myopic in its policies toward former Yugoslavia. If war is the continuation of political relations by other means (as von Klausewitz suggested), then in order to end war one should reexamine the political and diplomatic mistakes that brought about that war. Instead, war preparations are being increased. When there is a ditch in the road, one should repair the ditch, not buy more medicine to treat the wounded. We are putting bandaids on corpses. It is time for UNPROFOR to withdraw from Bosnia, the sooner the better, before UN peacekeeping is completely discredited by NATO's war to establish its own credibility. I am sure it would not be necessary to bring in fifty thousand troops to "rescue" UN peacekeepers. This is the land of the deal. It would be cheaper and safer to *buy* the withdrawal of UN peacekeepers: simply pay the warring parties to allow UN peacekeepers to withdraw. Then let the local armies get on with their war until they tire. More wars end from fatigue than from conquest.

NATO strategists are underestimating the difficulty of a hostile retreat from Bosnia. I am not even referring to what would have to be done with equipment, including the hundreds and hundreds of containers that would have to be disassembled and packed, or left behind, at great expense to the UN. I am referring simply to the roads that run through mountain tunnels and over bridges, any or all of which might be mined. And what of the people who might lie down on the road, the women and children who do not want UNPROFOR to leave?

It is inevitably less expensive to pay with hard currency than with lives. In May 1995, the French government paid ten thousand German Marks per head for five members of Pharmaciens Sans Frontières (four Frenchmen and one American), who had been detained by the Bosnian Serbs and accused of espionage. All the posturing and hectoring by various governments was useless; finally, cold cash did the trick. I was there.

The exchange took place at the Sarajevo airport. The French ambassador, who arrived crouched low in his unmarked car so as not be seen by the watchful press, brought with him a suitcase full of German Marks and presented it to the Bosnian Serb representative who went into another room to count the money. Within minutes the Serb returned. "No, we want *new* German Marks," he said.

The shrewd (or thoughtless) French had offered fifty thousand *old* German Marks, which were due to be replaced within months by new German Marks. Of course, the Serbs would have found a way to exchange the old German Marks on the black market, but it might have cost them a commission, and they didn't want the hassle, so the search began for new German Marks. It was late afternoon, and the exchange had already been postponed once or twice. The predatory press had been alerted. What to do? My predecessor, Enrique Aguilar, a truly resourceful diplomat, made an urgent call to a key finance officer in one of UNPROFOR's military contingents, asking if he might empty his coffers so that we could complete the deal. The Serbs had set a deadline and would take the hostages back with them if we did not come up with the cash within hours. To make the story short, we came up with the new German Marks, largely through Aguilar's intercession, and the hostages were released. The press was happy, the French and U.S. governments were happy, the Bosnian Serbs were happy, and—oh yes—the five hostages were also happy.

The point is that what the Serbs are interested in is hard currency, so why not give it to them, to all of them—Bosniaks and Croats, as well as Serbs? Let them have the money and withdraw UN troops from Bosnia peacefully.

If NATO is to declare war against the Bosnian Serbs, which seems inevitable, then UN forces should first be withdrawn, and the way to do that should be with money, not by force of arms. UN troops can return once the war is over, with a more reasonable mandate.

In point of fact, many of us, including me, believe that the ultimate release of UN hostages in May was paid for by Western governments. Milosevic's ability to convince the Bosnian Serbs to give up UN hostages was paid for in cash and weapons, and because Milosevic had no cash, that cash was provided by Western governments. Thus, the West got its hostages back, Milosevic gained prestige as a mediator, and the Bosnian Serbs got their cash and weapons.

11 June 1995

In reports to United Nations Peace Forces (UNPF) headquarters in Zagreb, I have been expressing my concern about the creation of an RRF, which is being vigorously promoted by Smith, among others. It will comprise one French brigade, one British brigade, and one multinational brigade (MNB), a total of about ten thousand combat troops. The multinational brigade will have two battalions: one British and one French. There will also be Dutch and Belgian elements in the MNB, along with U.S. intelligence support. It is clear to me that these contingents will not be neutral, and it is clear they will not be peacekeepers. They will be combat troops sent to attack the Bosnian Serbs. And it is likely they will take their orders from Paris and London and Washington, not from UN headquarters in Zagreb or New York. They will not be wearing blue helmets or driving white vehicles. Their presence will mean the transition from peacekeeping to peace enforcement—without the consent of the soldiers on the ground, and without the approval of several of the governments that had signed on to UNPROFOR thinking they were on a peacekeeping mission.

In a report in January 1995, the Secretary-General wrote:

> Nothing is more dangerous for a peace-keeping operation than to ask it to use force when its existing composition, armament, logistic support and deployment deny it the capacity to do so. The logic of peace-keeping flows from political and military premises that are quite distinct from those of enforcement; and the dynamics of the latter are incompatible with the political process that peace-keeping is intended to facilitate. To blur the distinction between the two can undermine the viability of the peace-keeping operation and endanger its personnel. . . . Peace-keeping and the use of force (other than in self-defence) should be seen as alternative techniques and not as adjacent points on a continuum, permitting easy transition from one to the other. (S/1995/1)

But the Smith Brothers (General Rupert Smith in Sarajevo and Admiral Leighton Smith, NATO's commander in Italy responsible for central Europe—I call them the Cough Drop Consortium) will have their way. They are preparing their own transition to peace enforcement, damn the consequences.

I have not raised the issue of moral or political correctness in my faxes—that is, whether the Bosnian Serbs *deserve* to be bashed, or even whether the RRF is *necessary* in order to implement the resolutions of the Security Council. I am concerned about credibility and practicality. Can the United Nations be an effective interlocutor when preparing for war with one of the parties to the conflict? And can the RRF function effectively without the cooperation of *any* of the parties—because the Croats and the Moslems do not want the RRF either.

I am also concerned that with the arrival of the RRF the Bosnian government will increase its propaganda campaign against UNPROFOR, supported by the technical expertise of the world press and with a view to expelling UNPROFOR so that NATO may replace us and get on with the mission of being the Bosnian government's mercenaries. British General Sir Michael Rose, Rupert Smith's predecessor, incurred the wrath of the international community by once saying publicly that the Bosnian government wanted UNPROFOR to be its mercenaries. He implied that we would not do that. He was correct on the first point, but wrong on the second. The Bosnian government *does* want UNPROFOR to become its mercenaries, and it *will*. The RRF is a giant step in that direction.

Moreover, President Clinton has already committed himself to sending twenty-five thousand U.S. troops to be part of a fifty thousand–member NATO force, to assist in rescuing UNPROFOR if it were to withdraw. Fifty thousand! About twice the number of troops already on the ground in Bosnia—at an enormous risk and cost. Clearly, the "rescuers," especially the Americans, will not be coming to direct traffic. They will be coming to "kick ass"—that is, to attack the Serbs if a peace treaty does not precede their arrival. They will hit the turf shooting. Whoo-eee! Be the first on your block to kill a Serb and help Bill Clinton be reelected.

There is no doubt that Clinton has a political interest in dispatching the non-American RRF to Bosnia to prevent an UNPROFOR withdrawal that would necessitate the presence of U.S. troops on the ground, and the U.S. Congress will never object to risking non-American lives to prevent American troops from having to risk *their* lives.

Although the political situation at this point is fragile, the possibilities for peace are better than they have been for a long time. The Bosnian Serbs, who are extended across a long frontier they can barely defend, are being weakened more and more each day by international sanctions and by sanctions from Yugoslavia. They have peaked militarily. They have no way to go but down, and it would be in their interest to make a peace settlement as soon as possible.

The Bosnian government understandably does not want to agree to giving up 49 percent of its sovereign territory, which it would have to do under the Contact Group Plan. Besides, the Bosnian government infantry is making gains in the field, and it has the active support of Washington and Bonn for its policies. Why should it settle for less than total victory? However, there are also reasons that this might be an optimum time for the Bosnian government to come to the peace table.

First, the Bosnian government is at a moral peak and is in danger of slipping. Despite the quiet conspiracy not to criticize it publicly, information is beginning to leak about its abuses against the United Nations, about its refusals to honor international agreements, and about its persecution of Serb and Croat minorities. Second, its alliance with the Bosnian Croats is insecure, and if that cooperation unravels, it will have less and less military and political leverage. In addition, the European troop contributors to UN-PROFOR are ready for peace, and so is Milosevic, the erstwhile patron saint of the Bosnian Serbs. It seems that only Bob Dole and Bill Clinton—in their bid for the U.S. presidency—and Iran and Saudi Arabia are not ready for peace. They want more. They want to deal from strength, and they feel that Bosnian government forces will be able to make significant military gains if the war continues awhile longer.

Meanwhile, what the Bosnian Serbs object to in the Contact Group Plan (which would give 51 percent of the territory to the Federation and 49 percent to the Bosnian Serbs) is that it was based on prewar demographic maps and censuses, rather than on economic viability. They complain that most of the industrial, communications, and transportation assets under the plan will go to the federation. The Serbs are willing, they tell me, to divide territory on a 49–51 basis, but they want an equal division of *economic* assets. Understandably, the Bosnian government wants it all.

[The Contact Group, incidentally, was so named because Washington and Moscow were originally left out of the negotiations between the Europeans and the warring parties. On several occasions, when the Europeans had reached a tentative agreement with the parties, Washington and to a lesser extent Moscow would barge in and say they could not support the agreement, so the original European Union representatives made "contact" with the United States and the Russian Federation to form the Contact Group.]

The Croatian government continues to support the Bosnian Croats, but it is assuming a low profile at this point. Its primary concern for the moment is to recover the Serbian-occupied enclaves in Croatia and then to link western Bosnia to Croatia. Western Bosnia, which is contiguous to Croatia, has for centuries been dominated by Croatians, and the Bosnian Croats want no part of being a minority in a Moslem state. They are as adamantly opposed to that prospect as the Serbs are.

Throughout the entire war in Bosnia, in fact, Croatia's political aims have never varied. Washington devised the Federation, an alliance between Bosnian Moslems and Bosnian Croats, for military and political purposes. Militarily, Croatian artillery and air power complement Bosnian government infantry; and politically, because since no single ethnic group in Bosnia has a clear majority, the federation, as a political coalition, would have a majority over the Serbs in any new Bosnian government. But the Croatians do not see the alliance in these terms. They see the federation as a vehicle for ensuring protection for Croats in Moslem-dominated areas, for creating conditions that will lead to an eventual annexation of western Bosnia by Croatia, for weakening the Serbs militarily so that Croatia may regain from them certain areas in northern Bosnia, and for allowing Croatia and the Bosnian Croats to benefit from (i.e., siphon off) clandestine arms supplies to Bosnia that must transit through Croatia. (Meanwhile, arms embargoes to Bosnia and Croatia, in accordance with UN Security Council resolutions that the United States signed on to, are being systematically violated by Washington.)

Milosevic, whose primary goal is to have the international sanctions against Yugoslavia lifted, supports the Contact Group Plan and is constantly trying to undermine Karadzic. Those who support Milosevic say he has had the strength to change, to admit his past mistakes, and to realize there can be no Greater Serbia. Those who oppose Milosevic say he is merely an opportunist trying to maintain power. In particular, the Serbs who oppose Milosevic say he is a traitor to their cause. All of them are right.

Talked recently with several British military officers about proposals for lifting the arms embargo against the Bosnian government at this point. It seems there may be several problems, including "technical" ones.

1. Weapons now being used by Bosnian government forces are, for the most part, Soviet made. One cannot simply supply shells made in the West to fit Soviet weapons. Therefore, entire weapons systems will have to be replaced. Although that may be good business for the arms manufacturers, it will take time and money.

2. One would have to transport weapons to and within Bosnia, which would mean forcing open and keeping open several land routes, a procedure that would require the use of force. One would also have to build storage depots for weapons and ammunition, and be prepared to defend them with air defense systems.

3. The users would have to be trained. Weapons today are high tech. Users would need to have some basic knowledge of physics, math, and, most

important, the English language. Once again, this procedure would take time and money.

4. It would be unrealistic to expect the Bosnian Serbs to sit idly by while this process is going on. How to restrain them? Either with air strikes or a diversionary land war—or accept a Bosnian Serb offensive. None of these prospects is pleasant. The war would widen.

5. European allies of the United States would be resentful. All UNPROFOR troops, as well as civilians, throughout the entire mission area, including the Serb-occupied regions within Croatia, would be at risk.

Moreover, the Croatians don't want to see Bosnian government forces armed, because it would mean they would then have the capability to turn against the Bosnian Croats and try to regain territory from which they have been "cleansed" by the Croats. President Tudjman has consistently opposed arming Bosnian government forces. Who, then, wants to see the Bosnian government forces armed? Washington—because it thinks this move may ensure that, in the long term, U.S. troops will not have to be deployed in Bosnia.

13 June 1995

It is difficult being an American anywhere in the world. One faces envy, petty resentment, cultural condescension. In the political arena, however, it is particularly difficult because one is immediately identified with Washington's policies, whatever they are and no matter how unrealistic they may be. In Bosnia, U.S. policies are not popular with the non-Moslem international community. Washington, with no troops on the ground, is perceived as claiming the right to dictate policy, including air strikes, a policy that will endanger the lives of every soldier and civilian who actually *is* on the ground. Moreover, the United States is seen as a superpower that does not pay its dues to the UN, yet has the right of veto in the Security Council and is trying to tell those who *do* pay their dues what risks their soldiers should be subjected to. In other words, the member who won't pay and won't play wants to dictate the rules of the game.

The Brits, with the notable exception of General Smith, flaunt their anti-Americanism whenever they can. As for the French, who have the military responsibility for Sarajevo and its environs, they have brought along their endemic antagonism to everything Anglo-Saxon, American as well as British. (At the same time, on a personal basis I get on famously with the French, and, in fact, my own views of the situation in Bosnia are much closer to theirs than to the views of London or Washington. Not coincidentally, the French have taken the most casualties in Bosnia, a fact that has contributed to making their perspective the most realistic.)

There is also a strong anticivilian bias among the military. They see civilians as spoiled, undisciplined, and indecisive—"candy asses." The military identifies a goal, an objective, and goes for it. If they are blocked, they want to fight. They have little patience with negotiation. They also adapt more easily to physical discomfort. This anticivilian bias is held by members of my own civilian staff (especially within the administration) who are retired soldiers. Once a soldier, always a soldier, and former soldiers on the civilian side feel their primary allegiance is to "the commander" (i.e., General Smith), not to Civil Affairs. They scorn the civilian side. There is also a classical anti-Semitism here among the Brits, the French, the Russians, and the Ukrainians (less among the Dutch). It is in their comments, in their jokes. Most of all, I suspect it exists within the Moslem-dominated Bosnian government, and I have my doubts that in the long term any of these groups will accept a Jew (me) as the head of Civil Affairs in Bosnia. In a lesser role, perhaps, but not as the chief.

Finally, the personal ambitions of the staff, both within UN Civil Affairs and in other international organizations cause problems. Ambition and career advancement have replaced loyalty, discipline, and any form of idealism as the driving force in this operation.

I remember Akashi telling me before I left Zagreb that the situation in Sarajevo is "very sensitive." In his understated way, he was telling me that it is a snake pit.

This morning at the 8:30 A.M. briefing in Smith's office we reviewed a wide range of topics. First, the rapid reaction force. There will be practical problems in financing, in command and control, in gaining approval from the parties on whose territory the RRF will operate, and at the ideological, governmental level in deciding how to transform a peacekeeping mission into a peace-enforcement mission.

We mentioned the imminent arrival of the UN's new chief of mission in Bosnia, who will be my boss. In its wisdom, the Security Council recently decided to install three new chiefs of mission at the Assistant Secretary-General level in the three nations in former Yugoslavia where the UN has troops—in Macedonia (which we call the former Yugoslav Republic of Macedonia, or FYROM, because Greece objects to the name *Macedonia*) in Croatia, and in Bosnia. This new layer of bureaucracy, to be inserted between the CACS, such as myself and the SRSG (Akashi) in Zagreb is intended to decentralize the UN's operation and allow for a better understanding of the individual aspects of each country's problems. It also adds (my estimate) at least another two million dollars to UNPROFOR's annual budget, in staffing costs alone.

(The Bosnian government has been promoting this idea because it believes that too many political decisions concerning Bosnia are being made in faraway Zagreb in deference to global concerns, rather than in Sarajevo in deference to Bosnian concerns. They are *Bosnia*, they argue, not a part of former Yugoslavia. They have a point, although decisions concerning Bosnia *do* impact on the situation throughout all of former Yugoslavia, especially in Croatia. In fact, administrative structures matter, and there is no doubt in my mind that the new structure will increase the Bosnian government's influence in the UN's decision-making process. It will make it even easier for the international media, based in Sarajevo, to exploit the differences, real and imagined, between Smith in Sarajevo and Janvier in Zagreb. Otherwise, with regard to the new chief of mission in Sarajevo, the UN has picked a fine man: Antonio Pedauye, a Spaniard with twenty-five years experience in his foreign office, including several in New York, during which time many of the resolutions on Bosnia were debated. I get on very well with Ambassador Pedauye, an intense and serious professional, but I also realize that his appointment is the beginning of the end of my responsibilities. He will bring in some of his own people and the magnitude of my tasks will be sharply diminished.)

This morning Smith also raised the issues of restoring utilities to Sarajevo—which seemed unlikely in the near future—of resupplying UNPROFOR, of reopening the Sarajevo airport, of the Bosnian government drafting local personnel in violation of the signed agreement with the UN not to do so; of humanitarian aid convoys being blocked both by the Serbs and by the Bosnian government; and of the likelihood of UN soldiers being taken hostage in the future. These were his views:

On resupplying UNPROFOR: We are becoming part of the problem instead of part of the solution. It will be a major effort to resupply UNPROFOR, and it raises political issues. Why would we be able to resupply our own troops, but be unable to supply the people of Sarajevo? And why are we expending precious resources on ourselves instead of on the Bosnian people?

On reopening the Sarajevo airport: It is being given undue importance. Better to secure a land route, which can be defended, if necessary. The airport, once reopened, can easily be shut down again, and air freight is not sufficient anyway to bring in the amount of supplies needed for Sarajevo.

On harassment of local staff by the Bosnian government: Smith and I will approach our respective interlocutors to discuss the matter. (I noted Smith's eagerness to be involved in what is purely a civilian matter.)

On blocking convoys: Deal with each one at the local level because commanders at the national level say they have given permission to allow the passage of humanitarian convoys.

On UN *soldiers being taken hostage:* Withdraw them from Serb-controlled areas.

[I had to admire Smith. He was a hands-on manager. He faced every problem and planned several possible scenarios for each. At the same time, most of his scenarios ended with the same message: use force against the Bosnian Serbs.

I can remember many occasions when he would sit back in his chair and with those rolling Rs utter his intentions: "We have to let Brother Serb know that if he wants a fight, then he's going to get a fight. We should simply tell him that we intend to go from point A to point B, and if he doesn't let us through, then we'll fight him."]

Perhaps the primary problem in Bosnia is freedom of movement (FOM). In Smith's language, we have to be able to get from point A to point B, and until we have complete FOM, we cannot fulfill our mandate. Moreover, the size of UNPROFOR is growing, which makes it increasingly difficult to supply ourselves.

Although I agree in principle with Smith's analysis, I disagree with some aspects of it—namely, which routes we should use to supply Sarajevo and what methods we should use to obtain those routes. I have expressed my opinion to him quite clearly—outside of the meetings. I have told him that I don't believe his mandate is to engage "Brother Serb" in a fire fight. I frequently preface my remarks by telling him that I don't want to be regarded as the voice of UNPF headquarters in Zagreb whenever I express my arguments, because it is well known that Akashi and Janvier in Zagreb prefer to work on the principle of consent, rather than on that of robust response. I tell him I favor vigorous diplomacy rather than the use of force. On such occasions he replies that he agrees, for the most part, that diplomacy should never be abandoned, even when force is being applied, but he never relents on his wish to use robust response. Perhaps he is right. In any case, he always listens.

At the end of our meeting this morning, Smith expressed his serious concern for the security of his troops, which includes their replenishment. He recalled that around 17 May, almost a month ago, there was heavy fighting around Sarajevo, during which several French troops were wounded. The fighting was started by Bosnian government forces, which sought to interdict two supply routes being used by the Bosnian Serbs. After four days of artillery battles there was a slight pause, but most Bosnian Serb weapons are still within the twenty-kilometer Total Exclusion Zone (TEZ) and are not, as they should be, in WCPs under UN control.

Smith believes UNPROFOR should take a stand. It has to insist that Bosnian

Serb weapons be removed from the twenty-kilometer zone around Sarajevo in accordance with Security Council resolutions, or else Sarajevo will never be safe. Regrettably, talks with the Serbs have broken down. The Bosnian Serbs are bitter with Smith because of the air strikes on Pale 25–26 May and are refusing to speak with him. As for Bosnian government forces, they have officially agreed for the moment to cease attacks from Sarajevo against the Bosnian Serbs, but there is no telling how long they will maintain their restraint. [In fact, Bosnian forces never completely ceased their shelling from within Sarajevo against Bosnian Serb positions around Sarajevo and against Bosnian Serb villages on the outskirts of Sarajevo. The Bosnian army's shelling had two objectives: to weaken Serb defenses and to draw Serb fire into Sarajevo, the results of which would be filmed by the world press and would increase pressure to call in NATO air strikes against the Serbs.]

Smith wants assurances from the Serbs that there will be no more hostage taking and that he will have freedom of movement in order to resupply his troops. That is the message he wants to communicate to the Bosnian Serb commander, General Ratko Mladic, but Mladic will not speak to him at this point.

The essential problem facing Smith is that of having a UN operation deployed within territory where a war is ongoing. When there is peace, the UN can be deployed anywhere in the territory, but when there is war, all UN personnel, civilian as well as military, are potentially the hostages of whichever side controls the territory where they are stationed. Because most UN troops in Bosnia, including those at UNPROFOR headquarters, are deployed on territory controlled by the Bosnian government and by the Federation, then any act by UNPROFOR determined by its hosts to be hostile invites retaliation. If Smith criticizes the Bosnian government, he might suddenly find it virtually impossible to conduct his operation. We are the putative hostages of the Bosnian government, like it or not—yet another fact that never finds its way into media reports.

At the 6:00 P.M. briefing this evening we reviewed the day's developments.

A UNHCR convoy for Gorazde has been turned back by the Serbs. No reason given.

Starting tomorrow at 3:00 A.M., a French mortar platoon will be placed on the road over Mount Igman leading into Sarajevo and be prepared to return fire whenever UN vehicles are targeted. [Most of the time, when UN vehicles were targeted, it was by the Serbs, but occasionally we were shot at by Bosnian government forces.] The decision to return fire has been approved by the UNPROFOR legal office in Zagreb. Subject to numerous qualifications, it will be considered a legitimate use of self-defense. [It would also, I knew, be the first step in the UN's impending war against the Bosnian Serbs over the use of the Igman road.]

The Serbs have announced that all but fourteen of the UN hostages have been released. This figure is as yet unconfirmed by UN sources.

Meanwhile, Bosnian government forces are massing in and around Sarajevo. The streets are strangely empty at night except for soldiers, and those soldiers are not, according to the locals who work with us, local troops. They are special forces. Indeed, a major offensive against the Bosnian Serbs is imminent. We all know it. UNPROFOR headquarters in Zagreb knows it. The entire international community knows it. I wonder if our families know it.

14 June 95

I have been sleeping in my office. I use a large bed in the room where dignitaries usually sleep when they come to visit Sarajevo. The room also has a wardrobe, a round conference table that seats about eight people, and a tiny terrace overlooking the compound. When I took over the office, I had a word processor and a desk moved in. It is slightly cramped now.

I have an apartment in town, less than ten minutes' walk from the compound, but I never walk there, and I rarely go there. When I do go there, I ride in an armored car. One rarely walks in Sarajevo. Although this part of town is sniper free, artillery rounds may be lobbed in by the Serbs from the hills beyond, and one can be hit by shrapnel. If one is hit directly by an artillery round, it doesn't matter if one is walking or in an armored car. The game is over. One rides in armor mainly to be protected from snipers and shrapnel. During the day I sometimes walk in the immediate area, usually accompanied by a colleague, but we are careful to walk close to buildings and never to expose ourselves in a completely open area. At night, one drives because there are thugs, vigilantes, and shooters who may be prowling the streets.

In spite of the curfew, restaurants, discos, and occasionally movies and even live theater function in Sarajevo. Life goes on, albeit at high cost. Businessmen who stay open at night pay heavily for that privilege to the government official responsible for enforcing the curfew. Bribery, extortion, and protection rackets are a way of life. The organized killers of prewar Sarajevo are now the paramilitary enforcers of the government, as well as their personal bodyguards. Wars are fought not only on the front line. They transform and corrupt everyday life at every level and in every corner. Americans do not always appreciate this fact because they have always had (except for the Civil War) war overseas and peace at home. But when war comes to one's country, corruption, smuggling, black marketeering, and domestic violence are its inevitable companions. Nevertheless, there is a quiet determination among the people of Sarajevo. They will survive. They will prevail.

The internationals buoy up the city economy. They pay high rents and patronize the restaurants. So do the soldiers, when they get paid. It is a very strange economy. There is a tunnel under the airport big enough for people, but not for vehicles. Trucks offload there, bearing supplies for the city. Rumor has it that one of the Bosnian army generals controls the tunnel and charges several thousand German Marks per hour for people doing business there. This is how it works: a convoy from the outer world arrives and sets up shop in the tunnel; the businessman sells his goods; local merchants pay several thousand German Marks to the general or his representative, quickly buy what they need to stock their shops, and then truck the goods into Sarajevo. I have not seen these transactions firsthand (I am not allowed to), but the Sarajevans tell me—as do journalists, some UNPROFOR soldiers, and the UN civilian police—that they take place. Bribery, corruption, and intimidation are pervasive in Sarajevo, and there are numerous war profiteers. Perhaps some of those taking the bribes would prefer to maintain the siege of Sarajevo in order to continue their extortion. The war has created a desperate condition, and certain individuals are taking advantage of this condition. But most Sarajevans want the siege to end. Besides, many of the same people making high profits now would be making profits under any conditions.

My apartment is lovely. It has four bedrooms, a large living room, two baths. The owner lives in Germany. He is a refugee there, having fled about a year ago. His sister and brother-in-law, who still live in the building, act as landlords. My predecessor rented the apartment before I did. Three CACs have lived there before me. It is almost a tradition. Most of the CACs have seldom *resided* there, however. I seldom reside there.

When I first went to rent the apartment, the landlord told me the price had risen from six hundred German Marks (about four hundred dollars) per month to six hundred dollars, a 50 percent rise. "I had a long-distance call from the owner," he said. "There was a mistake in the price. It should have been six hundred dollars, not six hundred German Marks."

I said I would think about it. One learns instinctively to bargain in this part of the world, but I was torn. I was sure that locals renting a similar apartment would be paying only a fraction of what I was expected to pay (one hundred to one hundred fifty dollars perhaps). On the other hand, I knew that the people of Sarajevo are desperate and that the internationals have large amounts of money to spend. Of course, we are being overcharged, but what of it? We can afford it, and they need it. But there is another factor, too—the local people themselves. Without exception, the locals I spoke with told me not to pay the increase. They were angry, embarrassed, perhaps even jealous of their fellow citizens who were always trying to rip off the internationals. "They're desperate," I said to one of my interpreters who was working on a translation of the lease I would have to sign if I took the apartment. "I understand."

"They are thieves," she replied. "They give us a bad image. We are not all like that. Besides, he is earning enough already. You are already paying five times what he could get for that apartment from a local."

"Perhaps I'll look around and see what else is available."

"He has to rent that apartment to you. It has already been vacant a week. If it stays vacant for too long, the government will seize it and take it for themselves or give it to a refugee family. Housing is a scarce commodity in Sarajevo, and the government is ruthless. Sometimes we are more afraid of the government than of the Serbs. The Serbs are out there, but the government is here."

I took her advice and bargained. A week later I got the apartment for six hundred German Marks.

The main reason I rarely use my apartment is that there are no utilities: gas, electricity, or water. Lack of water is the worst. Once in awhile there is gas, so if I have water, I can heat it in a pot on the stove, but much of the time there is no gas either.

The people of Sarajevo generally collect water in large plastic buckets. When it rains, which is quite often, people scurry out with their buckets and fill them up. In my apartment there are two or three large buckets of water and a couple of smaller ones. The landlord usually provides them for me. My personal assistant, who also lives in my building, has to collect her own water. She is not as important as I am in the eyes of the Sarajevans. When it rains, she frequently scurries home and puts her buckets out on the terrace. Once or twice she has brought her buckets to work and filled them with water at the compound, but then it is difficult to take them back to the apartment. The roads are so terribly rutted from mortar shells that one cannot drive smoothly, and water containers inevitably spill; even soda cans spill once they have been opened. Besides, a large bucket will not fit comfortably into a jeep, and the larger vehicles are usually unavailable for personal use.

Sometimes the Sarajevans will go to an underground spring to get water, but the Serbs know the location of the springs and occasionally shell them. It is dangerous to go to the springs—safer to wait for rain.

Once in a while I go back to my apartment just for the change. In the summer one doesn't mind the lack of heat so much, although the evenings can be quite cool; there are always blankets. As for light, there are candles, and I have a flashlight. Otherwise, I can wash with cold water, or I can wait until I get to the compound and wash there. I keep a few clothes in my apartment, but I don't sleep there very often. I know I won't sleep there in winter; it will be too cold. I can only hope that visiting dignitaries will prefer to make their own arrangements for a place to spend the night. If not, I will have to give up my office and sleep in my dark apartment.

Across the corridor from my office is a bathroom. There are two toilets, a sink, and what was once a shower, in which there is now a faucet about chest high. Once, there was a hose that connected the faucet to a spout much higher up so that one could actually take a shower, but the hose broke, and the army engineer doesn't want to hook it up again because he doesn't like the idea of people taking showers in the compound anywhere else than in the designated cabins, where the water ration can be strictly controlled.

I don't argue. My deputy urges me to use the shower upstairs, which is supposed to be exclusively for General Smith's bodyguards, or to appeal to Smith to have the engineer reconnect the shower hose in the washroom across the corridor. But I am content to do with what I have, so each morning I crouch in the shower stall across the corridor and blissfully wash myself in precious hot water that seems to come only in capricious bursts and fades as suddenly as it appears. One can never be sure of how long the hot water will last, and one can rarely regulate the temperature. But it is good enough, and it is better than most of the people of Sarajevo have.

I am usually out of my shower by 6:30 A.M. I then go to the message center to collect code cables and return to my desk. I scan the cables to see if there is anything urgent. If there is, I read it; if not, I put the cables aside to read after the series of morning briefings. Then I sit at my word processor and write for the better part of an hour before going to breakfast. I write anything and everything. Thoughts on Sarajevo. Thoughts about my children. Details of my experiences. Personal letters. I force myself to write, and the curious thing is that everything is mixed up: my personal thoughts about New York with my life in Sarajevo, Bosnian politics with private ruminations about the arts, administrative matters in UNPROFOR with poetry I am writing. But, of course, that is my life, and that is the life for most of us in Sarajevo. One does not have the luxury of distinguishing between private and public life. We are in a concentration camp of the mind.

At the 8:30 A.M. briefing in the large conference room this morning, we heard again about the massing of Bosnian government troops around Sarajevo. We are all waiting for the offensive to begin. Little attempt has been made by anyone in the international community to restrain the Bosnian government.

We also expect an attack against Gorazde by Serbian forces in response to continued attacks out of that enclave by Bosnian government forces.

UNHCR convoys destined for Bihac and Srebrenica have not yet left Zagreb. The Serbs have not granted permission for them to enter Serb-controlled territory. Convoys for Gorazde and Sarajevo are also still being blocked by the Serbs.

There is no UNPROFOR presence at several of the WCPs in the Sarajevo area, including at Lukavica. UN troops there have been either taken hostage or withdrawn. Thus, we have no knowledge as to whether the Serbs have removed their heavy weapons from the WCPs, but we suspect they have, particularly with the imminent likelihood of a major Bosnian government offensive against them.

More of the hostages have been released, but Smith expressed his view that the situation is not really better. "It is just a little less bad," he said. So long as there are UN hostages, the situation is not good.

At the 9:00 A.M. briefing in his office, Smith said he wanted to know more about the status of UN military equipment. He wanted to know what happened to it when the Serbs took UN soldiers as hostages. Did they also seize UNPROFOR equipment, including APCs, vehicles, and weapons? We must demand that all equipment, as well as hostages, be released before the situation could be considered back to normal, he insisted.

Smith also wanted to know the status of the four Bosnian Serb soldiers captured by French troops during a battle on the Vrbanja Bridge in Sarajevo. On 27 May, several Bosnian Serb soldiers attacked an UNPROFOR observation post (OP) at the Vrbanja Bridge and captured some French soldiers guarding the bridge. The French counterattacked and recaptured their post, but incurred casualties of two dead and fourteen wounded. There were also Serb casualties. There are claims that the Serb soldiers were dressed in UN uniforms when they attacked, a charge the Serbs vigorously deny.

Smith also wanted clarification on who exactly is negotiating for the release of the UNPROFOR hostages. Clearly, it is not being done by those of us in Sarajevo, which is unfortunate because they are *our* soldiers. [In fact, it was being handled in Belgrade, mostly by the United States. I, too, was astonished that Smith's command in Sarajevo was not involved in this critical matter regarding the soldiers within our area of responsibility. To us in Sarajevo, it was as though our family members were being held hostage, but to Washington and the Bosnian government, it seemed primarily another opportunity to pressure Milosevic into asserting his authority over the Bosnian Serbs so that he might eventually have sanctions against Serbia lifted. Washington and Sarajevo were still refusing to deal directly with the Bosnian Serbs, and on this occasion they were also refusing to deal directly with us or even to keep us informed about a matter that involved our personnel.]

We also discussed the need to develop a strategy for providing security for Sarajevo. Following the hostage taking, it is clear that our United Nations military observers (UMNOS) will no longer be able to monitor the presence of heavy weapons within the Total Exclusion Zone. For all practical purposes, the TEZ is gone.

We also have to consider whether or not the Bosnian government army buildup around Sarajevo may not be a giant feint. Are they really planning a major offensive? Smith has his doubts. (By contrast, the French and Russian military officers with whom I have spoken are convinced there will be a major Bosnian government offensive very soon.)

Smith also noted the apparent weakening of the Bosnian Serb war machine. "I'm struck that we have not seen a Serb counterattack since December 1994. All Bosnian government gains have gone unchallenged." Perhaps, Smith continued, General Mladic does not have the manpower to free up for a major counteroffensive in central Bosnia. The only way for him to free up manpower will be to overrun the enclaves in eastern Bosnia (Srebrenica, Zepa, and Gorazde). Those enclaves are a terrible thorn in his back, but perhaps he is reluctant to overrun the enclaves because he isn't sure whether UNPROFOR will use air power to protect them. "We should maintain that doubt in his mind," Smith said.

Next, we took up the question of supplying Bihac and Sarajevo by air. Truck convoys are continually being blocked by the Bosnian Serb army. The problem with using air drops over Bihac and Sarajevo, however, is that it would necessitate the use of significant air power to take out Serb air defenses. The UN would first have to establish air superiority over those two areas, which it is not prepared to do. Hence, the problem will continue. Meanwhile, Smith would like to see a theater-wide policy in place for resupplying UNPROFOR.

UNHCR said all its convoys throughout Bosnia have been blocked.

Our intelligence sources report heavy shelling by the Serbs into the town of Gorazde. This shelling is clearly a violation of the safe area regime. It is constant.

Srebrenica is desperately in need of resupply. It has only two days of food and water remaining. Then Smith intoned his frequent prescription for dealing with restrictions of movement against UNPROFOR: "We should notify Brother Serb that we are sending a resupply convoy from point A to point B, accompanied by a Rapid Reaction Force. Either we go through, or there's a fight. In effect, either we take the risk of starting another Balkan war, or we cannot resupply our troops."

About an hour after the morning briefings, I spoke with Ambassador Henry Jacolin of France. We spoke about UNHCR's recent agreement with Pale to resume aid shipments to Sarajevo. Like most of the Bosnian government's supporters in the diplomatic community, he believes UNHCR was wrong to make an "agreement" with the Serbs as long as UN soldiers are still being held hostage. He assured me that the French government will certainly not release the four Bosnian Serbs it is holding (from the battle over Vrbanja Bridge) until all UNPROFOR troops of French nationality are released.

In spite of his assurances, several UN officials suspect that a separate deal is cooking between the French government and the Bosnian Serbs, and that once UNPROFOR hostages of French nationality are released, the four Bosnian Serbs will be returned, even if other hostages are still being held.

As for the four Bosnian Serb soldiers in French custody, there are some very complex legal questions involved. If the Serb soldiers were impersonating UN soldiers, as alleged by some, then they were, according to my lawyer friends, committing an act of "perfidy" under the Geneva conventions (Article 37 of Protocol I). They could be considered war criminals. On the other hand, the UN has no authority to detain prisoners. It is obligated to return all prisoners, unless the War Crimes Tribunal (in The Hague) finds grounds to prosecute them. Only the War Crimes Tribunal has jurisdiction in such situations. Meanwhile, the Serb prisoners are being held as bargaining chips.

Later in the day I spoke with the U.S. chargé d'affaires, John Menzies, a well-informed, cooperative, and gracious man. *And* what I called a fundamentalist—that is, a vigorous, rigorous supporter of the Bosnian government. Lift and strike, bomb and punish are his themes, though delivered in a very suave manner. When we spoke, he rattled off the whole syllabus of anti-Serb rhetoric. As with many Americans, he took the high moral ground. Each time he mentioned an American negotiator involved in the Balkans, he reassured me of two things: that the man is completely professional and that he *hates* the Serbs. When I suggested that the Serbs are *not* Nazis, he responded by asserting that the Serbs have engaged in ethnic cleansing and genocide and have run concentration camps. They have to be punished and militarily humiliated. The Bosnian government will not negotiate seriously until it has liberated Sarajevo, taken more territory in central Bosnia, and has the Serbs at its mercy. Washington, he intimated, is in no mood for peace.

I suggested that the Serbs have good reason to feel threatened by Alija Izetbegovic's government, that they have been done out of their country without their consent. As for Bosnian Serb atrocities, I agreed they have been committed and were heinous, indefensible, and barbaric, and deserved to be punished on an individual basis. But one had to distinguish between causes and tactics, I said. There is legitimate cause for Bosnian Serb anxiety about being part of a Moslem state, even though those Moslems are European Moslems rather than Middle East Moslems. The tactics are wrong, but the anxieties are legitimate. It was my standard argument, though it was the first time I tried it on a fundamentalist American diplomat.

I think Menzies was a bit shocked by my statements, but he may have put it off to the fact that I had just arrived in Sarajevo and didn't yet know the good guys from the bad guys. In any case, he has continued to be gracious and amicable toward me and I am hopeful he will soon be confirmed as ambassador to Bosnia and Herzegovina. His confirmation, along with those of other ambassadors, is currently being held up by Senator Jesse Helms, chairman of the Senate Foreign Relations Committee, as part of Helms's continuing feud with the Clinton administration. Menzies deserves better.

15 June 95

Was awakened promptly at 5:00 A.M. this morning by the crackle of small arms fire and the thump thump of artillery. There were voices in the compound. Was this the beginning of the government offensive? The prospect of renewing the war hangs over our heads like a Damoclean sword. The compound is vulnerable: the Bosnian Serb artillery knows where we are.

But a few queries suggested that this was not yet the full-scale offensive we anticipated—merely the normal exchange of fire across front lines. Or perhaps it was a probing action. Perhaps the Bosnian government wanted to test Serb defenses.

The Serbs have been on the defensive for more than a year now. They are working hard to retain the territory they have conquered. They are like a thin membrane surrounding a clenched fist. The fist is the Bosnian army, which has greater density, better leverage. But the fist is in the valley, while the membrane is in the surrounding mountains. The Serbs have the high ground, not just in Sarajevo, but in all the eastern enclaves (Gorazde, Srebrenica, Zepa), and throughout much of central Bosnia. One of the tactical goals of the war is to control roads and bridges and mountain peaks. There are no large-scale infantry battles on open fields; there are only skirmishes for strategic objectives and long-range artillery battles. In any case, it is unlikely the Serbs will mount any offensive, and it is unlikely the Bosnian forces are strong enough to win any major battles. The only thing certain is that more young men will die. There will be more funerals. There will be more desertions. There will be more retaliations.

Meanwhile, life goes on. Hoping to have a noon meeting today at the airport to talk about restoring utilities to Sarajevo. Gas, water, and electricity have been off since the NATO air strikes almost three weeks ago. Yesterday there was a rainstorm, and the people were outside their homes with buckets, collecting rainwater.

It is the Sarajevan Serbs who requested today's meeting on utilities. One section of Sarajevo, Grbavica, has about one hundred thousand Serbs. When Sarajevo suffers, the Serbs of Grbavica suffer. (There are also approximately thirty thousand Serbs among the three hundred thousand people of Sarajevo proper.) Grbavica has its own Serb mayor, Maxim Stanisic, who in the past has bitterly denounced Radovan Karadzic for his part in preventing the restoration of utilities to Sarajevo. In fact, word has it that Stanisic even presented Karadzic with a bill last year for losses incurred by Serb businesses in Grbavica during the period when utilities were shut down.

Meanwhile, as usual, there appears to be a last-minute obstacle to holding today's meeting. The Serb military, through whose checkpoints one must pass in order to travel from Grbavica to the Sarajevo airport, where today's meeting will be held, does not want to have an UNPROFOR APC come into Serb territory to pick up Serb negotiators and take them to the airport. The Serbs, however, cannot come by themselves through Bosnian government territory; they need protection.

We are hoping to reach a compromise. We will suggest meeting the Serbs at a midway point. We do not have to go all the way into Serb territory.

At the same time, I am already wondering about the timing of our meeting. If our sources are correct, then there are about ten thousand Bosnian government troops massed just outside Sarajevo, preparing for a military offensive. How can there be a restoration of utilities during a military offensive? The Bosnian Serb leadership in Pale will certainly not be in a very cooperative mood. Besides, the offensive would involve areas where repairs will have to be made if utilities are to be restored.

Even the most experienced negotiators know that there is a proper time to negotiate. Premature efforts can only result in failure and may destroy future prospects.

On the other hand, it may be better in this case to try and fail than not to try at all, if those are the two choices. This is a classic situation for UN mediation. The two sides will not talk to each other without an interlocutor, and the UN, joined by others from the international community, is ideally suited for this task. Besides, Akashi will be meeting later today with Bosnian government Minister Hasan Muratovic (who hates him), and Akashi would like to present Muratovic with some positive news. Yes, we must negotiate. No matter what the outcome, it will be good to meet with both sides on an issue that affects the living conditions of all the innocent, civilian population of Sarajevo. I am hopeful, but not optimistic.

I try to listen to the BBC World Service every morning at 5:00 A.M. This morning it reported that the Serbs have placed conditions on the release of the remaining UN hostages. They say they must be traded for the four Serb prisoners that were captured after the fire fight with French troops on the Vrbanja Bridge, but the UN is saying that any trade, any negotiation, is in fact unacceptable. These rumors are not new. I suspect that the French are, in fact, making a deal with the Serbs, but it will not undermine UN policy. The French will get what they want, and they will stay within UN policy guidelines.

8:15 A.M. Time for the morning press reading. Official business begins each morning, even before Smith's 8:30 A.M. briefing, with a reading in my office of the local press. One of our interpreters listens to the Bosnian government and Bosnian Serb radio and TV news at 11:00 P.M. every night, as well as early the next morning, and then gives us an English-language summary.

This morning Bosnian government news reported that President Izetbegovic opposes any attempt to convene a new international conference on former Yugoslavia. (The Bosnian Serbs favor an international conference. They say the situation in Bosnia has changed drastically since the last international conference. They say the Contact Group Plan is obsolete.) Last night Izetbegovic said that any new conference would only be a transparent device for attaining diplomatic recognition of the Bosnian Serbs. Let them accept the Contact Group Plan, and then there could be a conference. He added that Sarajevo could not survive another winter under siege.

Izetbegovic is both right and wrong about a new international conference. The Serbs *are* seeking international recognition, but the situation in Bosnia *has* changed since the last international conference was held. Otherwise, Izetbegovic's reference to the "siege" annoys me. Sarajevo *is* under siege, and the siege is cruel and unjust, but the Sarajevan people *can* survive another winter even if the siege remains in place. International aid will get through, and people will not starve. Izetbegovic is exaggerating. He is playing the "victim" because it keeps him in power.

The same message of imminent doom is being presented to a group of international donors in Vienna. Minister Muratovic is calling for increased contributions from the international community to help rebuild Sarajevo, which cannot survive another winter under siege, he says. (Meanwhile, many Bosnian government officials profit personally from international aid.)

Indeed, the whole business of "humanitarian aid" has to be reexamined, reevaluated. It is a very big business all the way down the line, from the donors through the distributors. It is intended to do good, and it does much good, but it also provides a political disincentive for settling the war, as well as a disincentive for self-help. And it supports a class of war profiteers.

Many of the aid workers in the field are genuinely altruistic and are driven by a desire to relieve human suffering, but they are often manipulated by ambitious politicians and exploited by gangsters. In many cases, their work undermines rather than assists the cause of peace. In the Serbian-occupied areas of Croatia, for example, millions of dollars of food aid provide a majority Serb population with food that it could easily grow itself if restrictive United Nations sanctions were lifted. Food assistance in these areas is unnecessary. In fact, most food aid would be unnecessary if economic sanctions were lifted. The international community strangles with one hand and gives charity with the other. The effect of economic sanctions has to be reexamined, reassessed. The wrong people are harmed by them. Innocent nations, trading partners of the sanctioned nation, are devastated by them, and a frightening class of smugglers, profiteers, and gangsters are nourished by them. Moreover, the gangster class does not go away when the war stops. Organized crime loves economic sanctions.

On to the Bosnian Serb news. Pale is again cautioning Belgrade against recognizing the Bosnian government, which would be an act of "treachery," according to Pale officials. The Bosnian Serbs are also complaining about Bosnian government attacks against Serb villages.

Concerning the attacks, there *are* ongoing Bosnian government assaults against Serb villages, many of them launched from UN "safe areas," Sarajevo included. After all, the war is still in progress. What do the Serbs expect? As I often tell the Bosnian Serbs when they complain that the international press never reports such attacks, it is their own fault. They refuse to allow the international press into their areas, and they take our UNMOs hostages when we are in their areas as monitors. Thus, independent confirmation of attacks against the Serbs cannot be confirmed. They should either allow international access to their areas or expect no international sympathy. They are among the most stubborn people I have ever met.

9:00 A.M. briefing in Smith's office. Smith broached again the problem of freedom of movement. Eleven Canadians and two Frenchmen are trapped at their observation posts by the Bosnian Serbs. We cannot gain access to them.

Smith repeated that he is prepared to fight a war with the Serbs if necessary. "We should notify whomever we must that aid convoys are now being run with an UNPROFOR escort and that they are not to be checked or halted; if they try to stop us, then we will fight. We have a battle group ready to fight. I don't think Mladic will fight. I have already spoken to the battle group commander and told him to prepare for a fight. This could mean a war, but I see no other way of doing it."

On his own initiative (with proper clearance from General Janvier) Smith has formed a battle group (even before the creation of the Rapid Reaction Force) that he plans to use to accompany humanitarian convoys. It is more than a simple escort.

In order of priority, Smith wants to resupply Srebrenica, Sarajevo, Zepa, and Gorazde.

[I admired Smith's courage, but I worried about a wider war. What I wanted to tell him was that the Balkans were not the Falklands. The Bosnian Serb army was not the Argentine army. The Bosnian Serbs, who had lived in Bosnia for hundreds of years, did not want to be ruled by a Moslem-dominated government, and they would fight to the death not to be, just as British subjects in the Falklands fought not to be part of Argentina. Moreover, any use of force against the Bosnian Serbs by UNPROFOR would invite retaliation against what remained of the non-Serb population in Serb-controlled areas.]

After the meeting adjourned, I expressed my doubts to Smith about pushing the Bosnian Serbs into a corner, where they have no choice but to fight. I knew very well, I told him, that no British commander wants to write a letter home to the parents of an eighteen-year-old man or woman to say that he regrets to inform them that their child just died to defend freedom of movement in the Balkans. "Yes, there's that," he said politely.

[But I knew, even before I had asked, what Smith's position was about risking a soldier's life. On a different occasion, another British general had said to me: "That's why people join the military—for adventure. They know before they join that they may place their lives in danger. If you pull back every time there's danger, then you don't have a credible military force."]

Next, we discussed our strategy for the noon meeting to be held at Sarajevo airport on the restoration of utilities to Sarajevo. The airport negotiations are intended to be purely on "technical" matters, dealing only with who will turn on what, and where and when that will happen. No politics. The agreed strategy is to stick to the issue of utilities, not to be diverted into political argumentation—to de-link the issue of utilities from the rest of the war.

I arrived at the airport at noon. Both sides came on time. We found a way to transport the Serb representatives to the airport. Each sat on one side of a long table. I sat at the head, and John Fawcett, a very able engineer working with Bill Eagleton's group on the reconstruction of Sarajevo, sat at the foot.

The Serbs were represented by a delegation from Grbavica, headed by Maxim Stanisic, the mayor of Serb Sarajevo. The Bosnian government delegation was headed by Amir Hadziomeragic, an enthusiastic and ambitious young politician in the Ministry for Cooperation with UNPROFOR. He is Muratovic's deputy.

It was clear from the start that the Bosnian government had no intention of agreeing to restore utilities to Sarajevo at this point in time. Whether it thought any agreement with the Serbs would be impossible to enforce, or it preferred to retain its "victim" status until NATO would intervene, or a bit of both, was not clear, but what was clear was that Amir was under instructions not to make a deal now.

At the start I naïvely appealed to both sides to avoid political recrimina-
tions, but the Bosnian government side would have none of that. They
immediately unleashed political diatribes and accusations. They refused to
discuss the technical issues. They had come to denounce the Serbs, and they
made no distinction between the Serbs sitting on the other side of the table—
who were still Sarajevans and not part of Republika Srpska, and who themselves hated Karadzic—and the Bosnian Serb leadership in Pale who were
responsible for having shut down the utilities.

The Serb delegation was subdued and cooperative. They were frightened.
They were in enemy territory, and their ethnic compatriots in Pale are
continuing to unleash destruction against the constituencies of the people
sitting on the other side of the table. Ironically, Stanisic and most of the
Sarajevo Serbs also passionately hate Karadzic. They don't necessarily love
the Moslem-dominated government in Sarajevo, but they despise the Bosnian Serb government in Pale. So, in effect, the negotiations became a question of anxiety versus anger: the Serbs were anxious, and the Bosnian government was angry. Utilities were not the issue.

Besides, the Bosnian government is preparing for a military offensive, and
all other matters, including utilities, are secondary.

Within moments after the meeting began, we were all shouting. It was
mayhem. Then John Fawcett intervened. He had a good idea of what he
wanted, and he convinced both sides to adjourn and reconvene in three
small working groups to discuss the separate facilities of electricity, water,
and gas—which, if agreed to, would be turned on in that order.

After some time, Fawcett and his team worked out a schedule for restoring utilities to Sarajevo. They estimated it would take at least ten days. The
Serbian side agreed to the plan, but at the last minute the Bosnian government, which had been quiet while the details were being explained, refused.
After having conceded that no political message would be incorporated into
the written text for restoring utilities to Sarajevo, the Bosnian government
now demanded that UNPROFOR take control of the main water-pumping
station at Bacevo and several gas supply points in order to ensure compliance with the agreement. As everyone knew, however, Bacevo was in Serb-
controlled territory, to which UNPROFOR had no access. The Bosnian government even tried at one point to link the restoration of utilities to the issue
of allowing food convoys into Sarajevo.

I suggested that the question of security and access are military issues to
be discussed at a higher level. First, we should try to reach agreement on
technical procedures, and then we could deal with military security.

But the Bosnian government side said that there is no point in turning on
the utilities so long as the Serbs can turn them off again whenever they want

to, which is why UNPROFOR has to control the utilities. Of course, they had a point, but they also knew that UNPROFOR does not have military control of the area in question. Why had the Bosnian government come to the meeting then, I wondered? To embarrass UNPROFOR?

We pointed out that there is already a built-in "fail-safe" mechanism. The Serbs control the water, but the Bosnian government controls the electricity for Sarajevo. If either side shuts off one utility, the other can easily retaliate. We could discuss UNPROFOR *control* of the utilities at a later date. Amir refused to give in, however. He insisted that UNPROFOR must guarantee control of the utilities. There was more shouting.

I knew that Muratovic was scheduled to meet with Akashi this afternoon in Zagreb. I approached Amir and asked if he would like to speak to Muratovic in Zagreb, perhaps to get further instructions, but Amir just looked at me, bewildered, as if to say that he already had his instructions.

When the meeting finally adjourned, I felt terribly disappointed. Curiously, it is often the mediators who feel most depressed when negotiations collapse, more depressed than any of the parties, who are charged up with the adrenaline of venom and never expect progress anyway.

[I sent my report on the meeting to UNPROFOR headquarters in Zagreb, describing how the Bosnian government had snatched defeat from the jaws of victory. Astonishingly, a few days later, I discovered that one of my staff, David Harland, who had been present at the airport meeting, had written his own summary, saying that the Serbs had been responsible for the breakdown in negotiations because they had refused to agree to UNPROFOR's control of a key water-pumping station in Bosnian Serb territory. At first, I thought Harland's report was the innocent result of a misunderstanding. CACs do not usually write their own reports, as I preferred to do, and perhaps Harland had filed his out of habit, not expecting me to do my own. Later developments during my stay in Sarajevo convinced me, however, that this incident was simply the normal treatment for anyone who dared criticize the Bosnian government. It had been bestowed with the moral high ground, and not even truth could dislodge it from that privileged position. Any attempt to blemish it had to be rebutted.

As for Harland, he was a brilliant, well-traveled, and well-educated young man who had grown up in a diplomatic family. He knew about political hierarchies, about chains of command, and about professional objectivity. When he ignored them, it was not out of ignorance or recalcitrance, but out of zeal. The fact that someone of his sophistication could be so righteously tendentious made a deep impression on me. He was a passionate pilgrim. It happened to many people. It had happened to the entire international press corps.

Bosnia, Bosnia, Bosnia. None of us who went there remained quite what we were when we had arrived.]

Later today Smith told me of a conversation about utilities he'd had with Bosnian Vice President Ejup Ganic, who said clearly that the Bosnian government has no intention of allowing utilities to be restored to the Sarajevo area because the Serbs will only use them to supply their weapons factories. In other words, the Bosnian government was never serious in its negotiations.

[Even Ganic's explanation was spurious, however. The real reason for the Bosnian government's resistance was that it was still massing troops around Sarajevo in preparation for a major offensive, and there was not enough time to restore utilities before the war started. Besides, utilities would be an early casualty in the war, so what would be the point of turning them on if they might be faced with the responsibility for turning them off again?

In this context, I must again refer to General Boyd's article in *Foreign Affairs* (September–October 1995), which talks of a different period, but describes a similar tactic:

> During the winter of 1993–94, the municipal government [of Sarajevo] helped deny water to the city's population. An American foundation had implemented an innovative scheme to pump water into the city's empty lines, only to be denied permission by the government for health reasons. The denial had less to do with water purity than with the opposition of some Sarajevo officials who were reselling UN fuel donated to help distribute water. And, of course, the sight of Sarajevans lining up at water distribution points, sometimes under mortar and sniper fire, was a poignant image.

At the same time, other benefits would accrue to the Bosnian government if it prevented the restoration of utilities to Sarajevo. First, it wanted a military solution, not a negotiated solution, to its problems, including the problem of utilities. Even *one* negotiated solution would undermine its campaign for a military victory. Second, it wanted to place the blame on UNPROFOR when utilities were not restored to Sarajevo. UNPROFOR was supposed to subdue the Serbs and normalize the situation around Sarajevo, but if UNPROFOR could not do it, then let NATO intervene.]

16 June 1995

The Bosnian government's long-anticipated offensive against Serb positions and villages surrounding Sarajevo began at 4:00 A.M. I awoke to the pounding of artillery. It was loud and continual. By 6:00 A.M., mortar and small arms were as intense, though not as loud, as the artillery fire. Both Izetbegovic and Ganic have said publicly that the Bosnian government is trying to lift the siege of Sarajevo. To the north and west of the city the assault began yesterday, around Visoko and Ilijas. The Serbs, meanwhile, are saying that they will repulse the Bosnian offensive as brutally as possible.

Ironies abound. The Bosnian government is attacking, but at the same time it is claiming to be a victim. It feels it must liberate its national territory. The country *is* a victim of a siege, but the government is also mounting its military assault from inside a UN-declared safe area (Sarajevo), and then protesting that a safe area is being attacked when the Serbs return fire. Meanwhile, the Serbs continue to target Sarajevo at the same time they are demanding an international peace conference. Perhaps the greatest irony of all, however, is the U.S. position, which supports the Bosnian government offensive, even though that offensive is breaking the cease-fire brokered by the UN and Jimmy Carter with the tacit support of the U.S. government. Clearly, there is some friction between Carter's peacemaking efforts as a private citizen and the policies of Secretary of State Warren Christopher, a former Carter appointee.

Last night at around 10:00 P.M., Ganic came to see Smith and asked for permission to take all BiH weapons out of the WCPs. [Both the Serbs and the Bosnian government had weapons under UN supervision at WCPs in and around Sarajevo.] Smith agreed to Ganic's request [he could not have used force, military or political, to prevent the Bosnian government from reclaiming its weapons] and asked only for a letter notifying him of the government's intent.

We knew yesterday that the assault would begin this morning. Our patrols reported that by early yesterday evening everyone was off the streets except for soldiers. The streets were swarming with soldiers who had already emptied most of the WCPs. As the locals told us, the soldiers inside the city came from elsewhere. They were special forces. Both the Serb and the Bosnian government forces have been trained in Soviet tactics: they usually sent special units to the front lines and then left locals units behind to defend what they had captured. Our military intelligence calculates that it will probably take some days, perhaps weeks, for the Serbs to assemble their elite units and bring them to Sarajevo, but they will most certainly counterattack, and given their firepower, it will be brutal. We are hoping they will choose not to shell Sarajevo heavily, although a few salvos are inevitable.

There are several reasons why the Serbs use artillery so relentlessly. One is that they have superiority. Most of the heavy weapons that belonged to JNA units based in Bosnia before the breakup of Yugoslavia were passed to the

Bosnian Serbs. Bosnian government forces received no such largesse. More important, the Serbs are outnumbered almost two to one in personnel by Bosnian government forces, so they prefer to shell from long range rather than to engage in infantry battles. They cannot afford to take heavy personnel losses, for military more than for humanitarian reasons.

The Serbs also control most of the high ground, partly because the mountaintop villages have traditionally been Serbian villages and partly because the high ground was the strategic objective of the Serb army in the early phases of the war when it had overwhelming superiority.

There have been very few infantry battles in this war in Bosnia. Both sides prefer to sit back and shell from long distances. Although the popular image is that the Bosnian government army is at a great disadvantage when it comes to heavy weapons, that image is not so accurate any longer. Despite the official arms embargo against all the republics of former Yugoslavia, the Bosnian government has been acquiring weapons, and by now they are approaching virtual parity with the Serbs on light weapons, whereas their disadvantage in heavy weapons is constantly narrowing. Some even say they have already achieved parity in heavy weapons. At the same time, the weapons they receive, both light and heavy, are more modern than those of the Serbs. The problem is that Bosnian government forces must be trained to use the new heavy weapons because shelling from a tank, for example, involves more than simply pushing a button. It requires knowing how to handle very sophisticated, computerized systems of surveillance, assessment, and communications.

The 8:30 A.M. briefing was interrupted periodically by the pounding of heavy artillery. Our intelligence sources have identified three pressure points around Sarajevo. The Bosnian government army is trying to keep the Bosnian Serb army busy on several fronts simultaneously, to keep them stretched out, and to interdict their resupply routes.

All food and other convoys into Sarajevo have been halted.

At Smith's 9:00 A.M. briefing, he said he expected there may be a point at which the Serbs will target the civilian population of Sarajevo. If that happens, he will ask for air strikes to protect the civilian population. Presumably, the NATO strikes will not be limited to Serb artillery positions, but will be wide ranging—against command and control centers and other strategic sites.

Once again, Smith aired his frustration and annoyance at not being able to function properly as a peacekeeping force. He complained that he has no freedom of movement and that the taking of UN hostages has severely limited his intelligence of what is happening in the field. He has no way to provide security for the safe areas or even for UNPROFOR. If we cannot have UN monitors patrolling freely, and if we cannot keep heavy weapons in the WCPS where they belong, then we cannot function as a peacekeeping force. "Give me freedom of movement and I will be impartial; restrict my freedom of movement and I won't be impartial," he said.

[I understood Smith's argument, and I supported him. At the same time, I realized that he was protesting mainly against the restrictions on movement imposed by the Serbs. When the Serbs restricted UNPROFOR's movements, he was ready to use air power, but when the Bosnian government restricted UNPROFOR's freedom of movement, he used friendly persuasion. Of course, I understood that distinction. It was politically impossible to call in air strikes against the Bosnian government—for any reason, not the least important of which was that we were putative hostages, in a way, of the Bosnian government. More than 90 percent of UNPROFOR's personnel in Bosnia was stationed on Bosnian government and on Bosnian-Croat Federation territory. Retaliation by the Bosnian government against UNPROFOR would be very easy if we used force against them. Besides, the Serbs were the main offenders against the principle of freedom of movement.

I also believed, however, that as the war intensified, the Bosnian government would become more aggressive against UNPROFOR. The question was, How would we respond to them? For my part, I felt we should go public with our protests, even though I knew we would have scant support from Washington. I was not in favor of using force against the Bosnian government, but I was in favor of using words and of soliciting political pressure by the embassies—not because of the principle of objectivity or even credibility, but because of morale. Troops in the field have to know they are being supported by their command structure whenever they are abused. Besides, objectivity and credibility begin with self-defense. If one is attacked, one should respond; one does not ask first what cause the attacker represents. Self-defense against all attackers is true impartiality.]

Smith is special. Even when I differ with him, I always admire him. Here in the midst of chaos, he is trying to find order, or, more important, trying to create order, albeit with limited resources. And he is eloquent. At the briefing, he first set priorities. War or not, the first convoy to go through, he insisted, should be the one to Srebrenica. It is being obstructed by the Serbs, and Srebrenica is desperately in need of resupply. He wants to provide protection for the convoy. "If we're stopped, then we have to be prepared to fight," he said, as he had said many times before. His determination went down well with his senior officers. At the same time, he is neither reckless nor unrealistic. He is not calling for force at this point. He has a few other methods. One will be to use up the fuel in our trucks by the time they reach Srebrenica. Then they will have to remain blocking the road until they are allowed to enter Srebrenica to refuel. Thus, the Serbs won't be able to get in and out of Srebrenica either. And he has other ideas.

This evening at the 6:00 P.M. briefing, we were told that the Bosnian government claims it has captured the road between Sarajevo and Pale. [Their claim proved to be untrue, as I was soon to discover personally.]

I will be sleeping in my office tonight. I assume I will be sleeping in my office for the next few days. Most of my staff went home to their apartments in the city, but two or three are sleeping in their offices, on cots. We are all frightened.

17 June 95

Bosnian government radio is claiming that government forces have successfully captured several features (hills) around Sarajevo. They are also claiming assistance from the Bosnian Croat army (HVO) units in the Kiseljak area. They say HVO artillery is shelling Bosnian Serb positions. Bosnian Foreign Minister Muhamed Sacirbey has gone on the radio to say that United Nations forces should be assisting Bosnian government forces, not just protecting themselves.

[Sacirbey, by the way, American-raised and educated, spent most of his time in New York, where he worked as a lawyer and sometime representative of Bosnia at the United Nations. He was a very effective lobbyist and propagandist for the Bosnian government, largely because he understood the American mentality. He was also a darling of the world press, which would never challenge his occasionally demagogic excesses.

But he was opportunistic, vain, and irritating as well. Even Richard Holbrooke, dedicated Bosnian supporter, often found Sacirbey tough to take. Holbrooke remarks at one point in his book: "It was not entirely clear what drove Sacirbey: was he trying to show his colleagues (and enemies) back home that he was a true Bosnian patriot despite having spent most of the war in New York, was he positioning Izetbegovic for the struggle back home, or was he simply freelancing for the media?"* The fact that the same description might have applied to Holbrooke himself did not diminish the relevance of the observation.]

Heavy fighting is reported in the Hadzici area of Sarajevo. Roads south of the city are also being contested, roads that link Sarajevo to Gorazde. Meanwhile, in Gorazde there is heavy fighting as Bosnian government forces attempt to take the west bank of the Drina River.

The road between Kiseljak and Tarcin, leading to Mount Igman, has been

*Holbrooke, *op. cit.*, 176.

closed by the BIH. The road over Mount Igman (the ILR) has also been closed by government forces. Understandably, the Bosnian government does not want anyone to interfere with its offensive against the Serbs, so it has completely stopped all movement in and out of Sarajevo by anyone but Bosnian military forces. We will have to sit tight for a while. Of course, no food convoys will be able to move.

At the 9:00 A.M. briefing this morning, Smith noted that the situation has changed in and around Sarajevo, so that opening the road over Mount Igman, which the Bosnian government is now seeking to do by force, may not be possible for awhile. Besides, if we are to continue at this time in our attempt to open the Igman road, it will be tantamount to siding openly with the BIH. Therefore, it may be worth considering trying to open the Kiseljak-Sarajevo route, which is more direct and which will demand cooperation from all three factions—Serbs, Croats, and government forces—each of which controls a portion of the road.

[I myself favored opening the Kiseljak-Sarajevo route, not necessarily for political reasons, but for simple logistical concerns: it was the best road. The Igman road, even if opened, would be useless during winter, when the snows were heavy, and even during spring, when rains and melting snow would cause mud and rock slides. Smith knew this fact better than I, but he was also particularly sensitive to the Bosnian government's concerns. To open the Kiseljak-Sarajevo road meant that the Bosnian government would have to cede some of its control to the UN, which would have to take over several checkpoints from the Serbs. If the Bosnian government could open and secure the ILR by itself, however, it would be able to push back the Serbs and the UN.

In any case, it was clear that no routes could be opened during the offensive. I was also highly doubtful that any route could be secured without the extensive use of force—which we were not yet prepared, and perhaps not authorized, to utilize.]

After the morning briefings, I went to see Minister Hasan Muratovic. He was down the road a few hundred meters, just past the U.S. embassy, and I preferred to walk rather than take my armored vehicle. This time I went alone because I felt he would be more forthcoming if we were alone. He spoke very good English.

[Muratovic was unusually cordial that day, and there was no doubt he could be very charming when he wished. He was a true intellectual, concerned with ideas, concepts, even the flow of history. By education, he was a technocrat; by practice, he was an entrepreneur; by background, like most former Marxists, he was a cynical exploiter of human misery. He saw no reason not to combine profiteering with liberation. And like every Balkan politician at this point, he became relentlessly dogmatic and illogical when dealing with the current situation. There were times when he would brief me on alleged "developments" in Croatia, where I had spent the previous twenty months, and where he had not been in almost four years. When I would contradict him on the basis of having seen an event with my own eyes, he would tell me that I was naïve, that I didn't understand the Balkans. Never mind that I had counted for myself fifty Serb trucks blocked at a checkpoint outside Lipovac a few weeks earlier. He assured me there had never been a single Serb truck blocked at Lipovac; it was all propaganda, and the UN was being paid by Belgrade to let the trucks through. Like a true Marxist, Muratovic eventually explained everything in terms of the profit motive.

Muratovic, like most former Communist politicians, was a master at the Big Lie technique. He worked on the principle that a lie repeated often enough will be taken as truth. He was also a moocher, constantly asking for favors, usually transport. He would ask for a UN APC to take him to Osmice at the top of Mount Igman, from where he could get a car to drive him to Croatia; or for a UN helicopter to take him to Split, Croatia; or for a UN car to take him to Mostar. And so on. He was constantly demanding services, not only for himself but also for colleagues and visitors (and their spouses or mistresses!)—services that included taking them on shopping trips and vacations. He was a great milker of the UN cow, and if we resisted, then our patrols would suddenly find themselves held at a Bosnian government checkpoint for four hours or denied access to an observation post. In fact, constant abuse of the Sarajevo airport by the Bosnian government and others was one of the factors that finally made the Bosnian Serbs effectively close the airport by refusing to guarantee security there. Under the airport agreement of 5 June 1992, the airport was to be used only for three purposes: humanitarian and resupply missions; UN and European Community missions; and "official missions." However, the airport was also being used for press conferences, arms deals, and private travel. Under the rubric of "official missions," most Bosnian government officials continued with their high lifestyles, in spite of the war and in contradiction to the misery of the people they represented. They used the UN even more than they abused it.]

Muratovic was on good behavior this morning. He began by telling me his views on the origins of the war. "Wherever there is a Serb grave, there is Serbia," he said. I had to agree that elements in the Serb leadership thought this way. General Mladic is notorious for immediately taking high-ranking foreign visitors to Serbian cemeteries in territories he controls, to prove that Serbs had always lived in those areas, that they were not invaders. Serbs even joke about this attitude among themselves. One of my interpreters once told me the following joke. A Serb, a Croat, and a Moslem were quarreling about which owned a particular piece of territory, when a second Serb arrived on the scene. The first Serb immediately shot the second Serb and declared, "Now this is Serb territory because there's a dead Serb here."

Muratovic does not consider the war in Bosnia to be a civil war, but a war for territory. Both the Serbs and the Croats want more territory; they have no intention of keeping Bosnia whole. Nor is this a religious war. Nobody in Bosnia is very religious; the Croats are the most religious of the three, he continued, but former Yugoslavia is an atheist country. "Most people in Bosnia don't even know how to pray. Only the Bosnian government, however, favors a multiethnic, multinational state," he asserted.

He said the Bosnian government is willing to grant autonomy to certain areas, but those areas cannot be independent. Wherever the Serbs go, they kill, he insisted. The Moslem people are fighting for their lives; they cannot submit to Serbian rule because it will mean submitting to murder. When Moslems surrender, they are slaughtered; they have to fight.

As for the Federation, he was not very sanguine about it. The Bosnian Croats are essentially gangsters, he remarked. They are not politicians who want to govern democratically; they are gangsters. [The unanimous opinion of those who spent any time among the Bosnian Croat leadership in southwestern Bosnia was the same as Muratovic's. Several of the international press did investigative stories about the web of gangsters in the Croatian-controlled area of Bosnia—naming names, residences, and rackets. I agreed with Muratovic's assessment.]

Muratovic said that the Contact Group Plan was the least his government could accept as a basis for ending the war.

He said he is satisfied with UNHCR, United Nations Children's Fund (UNICEF), World Health Organization (WHO), and the Office of the Special Coordinator for the Reconstruction of Sarajevo, but not with UNPROFOR and especially not with the British and the French contingents. What he wants from UNPROFOR is:

1. Genuine protection of the safe areas (Bihac, Tuzla, Sarajevo, Srebrenica, Zepa, and Gorazde) in accordance with UN Security Council resolutions, which includes NATO air strikes if the safe areas are not respected.

2. A secure supply of humanitarian aid to Bosnia.

3. Opening of the Sarajevo airport or a land route over Mount Igman in order to keep humanitarian aid flowing.

The Bosnian government, he added, will insist that all decisions on Bosnia be taken in Sarajevo—not in Zagreb, not in New York, and not anywhere else. Otherwise, the UN can leave. "What does anyone in Zagreb know about what is going on in Sarajevo?" he asked.

I sat and listened carefully, knowing that in each of these demands, Muratovic had the weight of reason on his side. If the resolutions of the Security Council are unrealistic, as I and every UN official know they are, then that is the fault of the Security Council. But a resolution is a resolution, and Muratovic has every right to demand that resolutions be implemented.

[As for the world of unreality, as fashioned by the Security Council, I can give one specific example from personal experience. When the concept of safe areas was first seriously broached in the spring of 1993, the Secretary-General was told by his military advisor that it would take about thirty-four thousand troops to implement the resolution on safe areas in the manner envisioned by the Security Council. I was present in New York during the debate. But the member states of the Security Council simply would not accept that figure. They knew they could not convince the legislatures in their countries to commit that many troops to such a dangerous military mission. Each body bag in the Balkans would lose thousands of votes at home. So when it came to putting a figure on paper, two options were offered by the UN Secretary-General: the "heavy" option of 34,000 troops, and the "light" option of 7,600 troops. The council went for the light option. Because the UN has no standing army, all its troop commitments must come from troops contributed by its member states.

Even the 7,600 figure was only a target figure, however—an amount that had been authorized, but was never realized. Two years later, in 1995, the six safe areas together still did not have the 7,600 troops authorized. In Srebrenica, there were only 300 lightly armed Dutch soldiers, when at least three times that amount, more heavily armed, were needed. In other words, the UN had received only a fraction of the original estimate of what it would take to implement the Security Council's resolution on safe areas. This problem was a classic example of how the Security Council gave orders, but not resources.

Of course, some people argued that the lack of resources on the ground would be compensated for by air power: fewer troops on the ground and the use of air strikes if that meager number of troops were threatened. It didn't work that way, however, because the use of air power brought the conflict to a higher level, undermined the role of the UN as a peacekeeper, and required the political consensus of all the members of the Security Council, which was not easily forthcoming. There was no substitute for having an adequate number of troops on the ground. During a rainstorm you can't cover the ground with tissue paper. No cogent argument would absolve member states from their ill-considered actions regarding the safe area concept, and, of course, Muratovic and other UN-bashers were quick to say the UN was not doing its job.

"The UN is its member states," I would reply when such charges were leveled at UNPROFOR. "We in the secretariat do not decide on the number of troops. The Security Council does."

"It's Akashi who calls for NATO," Muratovic or someone like him would say.

"Not just Akashi. The decision is a group decision made after consultation with military advisors."

Not to be forgotten was that the average Bosnian of any ethnicity made no intellectual distinction between those of us on the ground, military or civilian, and the member states of the Security Council meeting in faraway New York. We were all part of the same impotent machine. We were all equally culpable in their eyes.

But there is more to tell about the Security Council's abdication of responsibility, an episode in which I was personally involved while the safe area concept was being formulated in New York. I helped to draft a background paper requested from the Secretary-General, which suggested that there might be negative consequences to the safe area concept, such as the creation of Moslem ghettoes and a false sense of security. The paper was very much appreciated by those developing countries that were members of the Security Council, but it drew particularly vehement commentary from the council's president for that month, Sir David Hannay of the United Kingdom. The weekend prior to the presentation of the paper, the major industrial nations meeting in Washington had decided that the UN should declare safe areas in Bosnia, and, Hannay asserted, who the hell was the secretariat (headed by the Secretary-General) to suggest any disadvantages? A superb diplomat, but at times somewhat of a bully, Hannay even gave an interview to the *New York Times*, attacking the secretariat for attempting to undermine the Security Council.

Such was Bosnia through the looking glass.]

Muratovic then briefed me about his objections to the arrival in Bosnia of the Rapid Reaction Force (RRF), which may comprise as many as ten thousand additional, heavily armed combat troops. He demanded a clarification of their mandate. What are they supposed to do? Who will pay for their accommodation and other needs? He insisted that they are not covered by the existing SOFA. A new agreement will have to be negotiated. The Bosnian government will have to be able to control these troops.

[Among other things, Muratovic was out for more money. Strategic considerations aside, he wanted compensation—increased compensation, cash on the line. Later on, when the Secretary-General sent a note to the Bosnian government stating that on the basis of consultations with his legal counsel he had concluded that the existing SOFA covered the RRF, Muratovic stormed and screamed. He wrote a letter of protest to the Secretary-General saying he did not agree with his decision and would not observe it. That day, in my presence, he made a show of taking a copy of the Secretary-General's note and throwing it in the garbage. "Are you saying that the Bosnian government ignores the decisions of the United Nations?" I asked him. "This is not a legitimate decision," he answered.

His letter writing reminded me of when my predecessor introduced me to Muratovic during my "familiarization" tour in May. We saw Muratovic on two successive days. On the first day, at Akashi's request, we had presented Muratovic with an official letter informing him that the UN would be assisting with humanitarian evacuations from Western Slavonia, which had just been overrun by the Croatian army, and that several hundred Serbs would be crossing into Bosnia for refuge. The next day, when we returned, Muratovic presented us with a copy of a letter that *he* had just written to Akashi, bitterly protesting the fact that the Bosnian government had never been notified that hundreds of armed Serbs were crossing into the sovereign territory of Bosnia. "You are providing armed soldiers for Karadzic's army!" he said. We insisted that just the day before we had delivered a letter to him informing him of the action; besides, the refugees were not bringing heavy weapons with them, only sidearms, which were permitted under normal terms of surrender. But he ignored our protest. He was a propagandist. This was war, and the UN was either his mercenary or his enemy.]

On another topic today, Muratovic asked me what would happen to the military equipment that was seized from the UN monitors when they were taken hostage by the Bosnian Serbs. Will it be returned? He estimated the UN equipment is worth $2.5 billion. I have no idea how he arrived at his estimate. We ourselves don't have an estimate, but Smith is also deeply concerned about retrieving our equipment. He thinks that the hostage crisis cannot be considered fully resolved until we have recovered our equipment, as well as our soldiers.

Muratovic also asked why the UN hasn't fought to defend its equipment, implying there has been some kind of "deal" to turn the equipment over to the Serbs. And what about the NATO ultimatum if the Total Exclusion Zone around Sarajevo is violated? Is NATO prepared to use force to compel the Serbs to return their weapons to the WCPs? he asked.

What the Bosnian government wants is demilitarization throughout Bosnia, he said. The Serbs can keep their territory once they have demilitarized. I made no response to this last comment, which was obviously frivolous. Why should the Serbs disarm in the middle of a war, with no peace agreement and the advancing Bosnian government armies threatening to kill them? The Serbs will certainly not give up their tanks to UNPROFOR or anyone else. In fact, nobody in former Yugoslavia is prepared to disarm at this point.

A way must be found to protect the delivery of humanitarian aid, Muratovic insisted. *That* should be the task of the RRF.

Muratovic also said he would be willing to meet with Carl Bildt, the newly appointed envoy from the European Union, but only on the condition that Bildt does not visit Pale. Negotiations with the Bosnian Serbs have to go through Milosevic in Belgrade. No international mediator should visit Pale. Pale has to be isolated.

We then turned to the issue of restoring utilities to Sarajevo. Muratovic, in his incarnation as a fox, asked me to draft a simple summary of the meeting we had at the airport concerning the restoration of utilities to Sarajevo. He proposed that he and the Bosnian Serbs could then sign the minutes of the meeting, which would constitute the basis for an agreement for restoring utilities to Sarajevo. I told him I appreciated his cooperation, but that I wanted to use a different format. I suspected that if I faithfully summarized our airport meeting, then that summary would have to include the Bosnian government's demand for UNPROFOR's control of the Bacevo facility on Serb-controlled territory. It would also have to include a reference to the political attacks by the Bosnian government against Pale, which would make the Serbs unwilling to sign it. No, I didn't want an official or even an unofficial record of that meeting. Instead, I offered to draft a few paragraphs on the technical aspects of turning on the electricity, gas, and water, as engineer John Fawcett originally proposed. It would simply be a schedule of who would turn on what, where, and in which sequence. There would be no mention of UNPROFOR, no political condemnations, and nothing official. To my surprise, Muratovic said he would sign such a document immediately. I thanked him, but said I preferred to wait until I had some indication that Pale would agree, because I wanted to be certain I could get *two* signatures before I got one.

[Muratovic's cooperation was welcome, but also suspect. He wanted to sign the agreement immediately because he knew the Serbs would not. In fact, some of the facilities that had to be repaired were on the confrontation line, so it would have been impossible to repair them or to assure they remained repaired so long as there was open war. A signature from the Bosnian government would embarrass the Serbs, however; Sarajevo officials could say they were willing to normalize life in Sarajevo, for the Serbian population as well, but that Pale was resisting. As so often happened in Bosnia, one side would agree to sign mainly because it knew the other side would not.]

Throughout the whole of our talk, Muratovic expressed his deep contempt for Akashi and Janvier and everyone else at UNPROFOR headquarters in Zagreb. He repeated his demand that all decisions regarding Bosnia be taken from Sarajevo, not from Zagreb. He also suggested that his government may not agree to extending UNPROFOR's mandate after it expires in November. "If you can't feed us and you can't protect us, we don't need you," he said.

Meanwhile, back in Washington, President Clinton has made a statement over the weekend saying that if UNPROFOR were to leave Bosnia, he will ask for a unilateral lifting of the arms embargo against Bosnia. Only a few days earlier, he said he would veto a unilateral lifting of the arms embargo under present circumstances.

One of the many things that President Clinton doesn't understand about Bosnia is that the safety of UN forces on the ground, including those of our NATO allies, is not the sole issue, though it is an important one. The lives of French soldiers, after all, are as important to the French people as the lives of American soldiers are to the American people. An equally important issue, however, is that any sign of lifting the arms embargo will encourage a wider war, and a wider war will mean more refugees. The main reason the European powers are in former Yugoslavia in the first place is to prevent refugee flows to their own countries.

[Many times in my faxes to headquarters I raised the image of Janus, the Roman god with two faces, one looking toward the past and one toward the future. He was, appropriately, the god that ushered in the New Year. His name was the root for the name of the first month of our own calendar, January, and coincidentally also the root for the French word for January, *janvier*, also the name of the current UNPROFOR force commander.

So much for coincidence. One inevitable problem of all multinational peacekeeping operations was the Janus-faced nature of the governments that sponsored them. While one face of every government looked toward the problem itself and perhaps calculated the international consequences of any action, the other face looked at domestic opinion.

Clinton's scenarios on Bosnia were designed almost exclusively for national consumption. He had little concern for international opinion or for the international consequences of his actions. He was looking over his shoulder at figures such as Bob Dole, who was challenging him for the presidency, and at the resistance of the American public to having U.S. troops on the ground in Bosnia. He was, therefore, determined to do whatever he could to prevent U.S. troops from going to Bosnia until there was peace, and if that meant arming the Bosnian government, bombing the Serbs, alienating his European allies, or coddling Croatian fascism, it didn't matter. He wanted to be reelected. *That* was what mattered.]

18 June 1995

Yesterday for the first time I met Roger Cohen, the *New York Times* correspondent in Sarajevo. He is middle-aged, elegant, articulate, and British. He is normally based in Paris. Now stationed in Sarajevo, he had come to UNPROFOR headquarters to speak to our spokespersons.

Cohen is vigorously pro–Bosnian government and anti–United Nations (in that way, he epitomizes the international press in Sarajevo). He is also righteously indignant, an attitude that seems obligatory for the Sarajevo press corps. But he is extremely well-informed, perceptive, and possesses rare acumen. He is one smart cookie. He has access to everyone, and he has traveled extensively throughout Bosnia. He has been to places I have never been and spoken to people I can't reach. He has much more depth than the endless TV stars, not simply because print can afford depth, whereas TV cannot, but also because he has the intellectual capacity that is a virtual work hazard for a TV newsperson.

But perhaps because he is so smug, I couldn't resist needling him yesterday, and in doing so, I made an enemy. No doubt, I reinforced his not very hidden contempt for UN Civil Affairs, for Akashi, and for what he considers the UN's immoral attempts at impartiality.

In fact, I am one of those Americans who foams, fumes, and fulminates when he reads the *New York Times.* Even a reader detached from the event being reported can be exasperated to confront the pious hypocrisy of what has become an institution rather than a newspaper. But if one is actually *involved* in the event being reported, then reading the *Times* can be infuriating because one realizes that not only do the reporters occasionally have the facts wrong but they can also twist what facts they have in order to be politically correct. An honest error is endurable, but a sermon hiding in an alleged news story is intolerable.

As Henry Thoreau once wrote, nothing smells so bad as goodness tainted, and Roger Cohen is in the forefront of the passionate purveyors of malodorous piety when it comes to Bosnia. Chris Hedges and Mike O'Connor of the *Times* are more balanced in their approach to Bosnia.

In any case, I behaved foolishly with Cohen yesterday. [And I was to pay for it in future.]

"Oh, yes, I've read your articles," I said.

"And?"

"They're very intelligent. . . . But sometimes they enrage me."

"Why?"

"They're so one-sided. You don't even pretend to be objective."

"Oh, I've spent a lot of time in Pale," he retorted. "I've heard the Serb side."

"That's not the point. It's not a question of being on the Bosnian government side or the Serb side. Maybe there are more than two sides. Maybe the problem is a polygon, and there are many sides: the Bosnian government, the Serbs, the Croats, UNPROFOR, Washington, London, Paris, and Moscow, to begin with. And they each have different points of view. You see events only in terms of how it affects the Sarajevo government."

"The Serbs are shelling civilians. The Serbs are running death camps. How can anyone ignore that?" he said.

"Look. During the 1960s, the international press assumed that everything the U.S. government said about Vietnam was false. They were adversarial. I don't think it's right to assume that the U.S. government is *always* wrong. But you guys go the opposite way. You're cheerleaders. You're out there in front leading the charge. You're into advocacy journalism. You think it's immoral to be impartial."

"The Serbs are racists. How can you be impartial about that? Do you know that a Moslem in Tuzla can't get medical care?"

"Do you know that I can't get medical care in New York City? Doctors don't answer their phones, and the emergency rooms are packed with the homeless. You have to distinguish tactics from causes. Serb tactics are indefensible. Nobody defends the shelling of civilians, nobody supports running death camps. But the Serbs have a legitimate complaint. The international community took away their country from them, and people have been known to get very pissed off when you take away their country. Would the Israelis want to live now as a minority in Egypt or in any Arab country in the world after fifty years of independence? Would you want to live as part of a minority in a Moslem state? For example, in Bosnia?"

"Karadzic and Mladic are war criminals," he replied, avoiding my question. "They're mass murderers."

A reporter from a British daily, who was standing there, mumbled that the Tuzla example was not exactly a fair touchstone for characterizing the situation in Bosnia. Her comment came too late, however. Cohen was incensed. The conversation was over. Doubting the *New York Times* is tantamount to sacrilege.

Sent two faxes to Headquarters in Zagreb today. In the first, I reported on my meeting in Pale with Vice President Nikola Koljevic. I noted I had returned from Pale to Sarajevo that evening on the road that the Bosnian government said it has captured. It was uncratered, and except for a few shattered sandbags, it was the same as usual and still under Serb control.

Koljevic bills himself as a professor of Shakespeare. And he is. He has studied in England and taught in the United States (in Holland, Michigan). He speaks very good English. Specialized in Shakespeare studies as a student and teacher. In his late fifties, has a pot belly, and smokes and drinks heartily.

He has a bottle of scotch in the bottom drawer of his desk, with which he consults frequently. He is convivial and emotional, and like most people in former Yugoslavia, he uses every occasion to tell you his version of how the war started, who was responsible, who the real victims are, and so on. But he *does* know his Shakespeare, and he knows quite a bit about English-language poetry in general. Once, when I told him I was a poet, he asked if he might translate my poems, some of which are about the war in Yugoslavia, into Serbian. I declined. "When the war is over," I said.

Actually, I started off well with Koljevic from the very beginning. My first meeting with him was on the day I went to Pale as an observer with the UNHCR representative, Anne-Willem Bijleveld, the day we were trying to open the road from Kiseljak to Sarajevo in order to deliver aid to Sarajevo. That night we were invited to dinner, and I sat next to Koljevic. He asked me what books I had read about Yugoslavia before coming here. I said that the best book I had read had been the classic by Rebecca West, *Black Lamb and Gray Falcon.* He looked at me strangely.

"You must have heard of it," I said. He continued to stare at me.

"Did I say something wrong?"

He continued to stare. Then after some moments he said: "I translated that book into Serbian. It took me years. And now I still get royalties from it; it's my main source of income because I don't get much salary as a government official." I had hit the jackpot—but Koljevic is also a first-rate performer.

In any case, I went to Pale today to present Koljevic with the same text for restoring utilities to Sarajevo that I had already shown to Muratovic. I urged Koljevic to agree to the proposal on humanitarian grounds. It would benefit the people of Sarajevo, including the Serbian population of Grbavica, and it would improve the image of the Serbs in the international community.

Koljevic then gave me what has become almost a classic evasion tactic. He said he stands fully behind the document, but that he will have to consult a few people first—his Parliament and the BSA. He is certain the civilian side of the leadership will support the proposal. As for the military . . .

He was playing Good Serb, Bad Serb again: the civilians are accomodating, but the military is rigid and difficult.

When I left, I told him I would be in contact with him as soon as possible and again urged him to agree to the proposal.

[What I had learned was that in the Balkans there was a perennial, almost symbiotic, relationship between machination and ineptitude, between clumsiness and conspiracy. This was the land of Byzantium, where the shortest distance between two points was a parabola. The combination of bureaucracy and endemic suspicion made swift action almost impossible. In technical terms, one might say that the infrastructure didn't exist for smooth implementation of decisions taken at high levels. True enough. Most of the time the phones didn't even work. In political terms, however, the inertia was a combination of incompetence and mischievous manipulation. When Koljevic said that he needed to consult his Parliament, as well as the military, one was tempted to ask, "Who the hell is in charge?" It was not a question of the constitutional balance of power; everyone knew who was in charge: the military. It was a military dictatorship that quickly did away with anyone who did not follow orders. Clearly, General Ratko Mladic gave the orders. (Or was it Karadzic? Or Milosevic?)

At the same time, benefits could be gained from such confusion, the most obvious of which was that no single person had to take responsibility for his actions. The bottom line was that it was very, very difficult to get a decision from the Serbs (in Croatia, as well as in Bosnia), and once extracted, it was very, very difficult to implement those decisions. Moreover, all sides, well-trained in Communist duplicity, usually claimed that any persons not implementing an agreement were "rogue" elements acting without proper authorization. True perhaps, but one never knew. It was the Balkan ballet.]

I also discussed the Contact Group Plan with Koljevic. He does not like the take-it-or-leave-it aspect of the plan. The Serbs fear that if they accept the plan, they will move directly to point B from where they are now, at point A. Although the plan allows for negotiations, if the Bosnian government refuses any changes, then everyone will be stuck at point B. The Serbs will never be able to return to point A. In addition, Koljevic reiterated his basic objections to the plan: (1) the Serb side has never been consulted beforehand; (2) the plan is based on the now outdated 1990 census, which doesn't take into account the major population shifts since the war began; and (3) the plan is based on demography, not on economic viability.

Finally, Koljevic told me that Karadzic sent a letter to President Clinton earlier this week asking him to convene a "Camp David" round of peace talks, inviting all the countries of former Yugoslavia. Significantly, the Serbs want to broaden the focus of the struggle in Bosnia, whereas the Bosnian government wants to narrow it and insists that all decisions affecting Bosnia be taken in Sarajevo. The Bosnian government sees no need for another international conference. As Muratovic has told me many times: "Let the Serbs accept the Contact Group Plan and then we can have a conference." The stand-off continues.

The second fax I sent today concerns a meeting I had with Serb General Stravko Tolimir, a high-ranking advisor to Mladic. I was accompanied to the meeting by a Ukrainian staff member of mine, Victor Bezrouchenko, himself a career military officer. Our interpreter was Colonel Milenko Indjic, a Serb military officer very close to General Mladic. We met in the town of Sokolac, at a hotel, because Indjic said it was too dangerous to meet in Pale.

Although most of my discussions are with Serbian civilian officials, I want to build a bridge with the Serbian military for at least two reasons. First, they are the ones who make the decisions, and second, they will not speak to Smith at this point. Although the Serbian military is willing to speak to Janvier in Zagreb, I think we should also have some local contact with them, and I am hoping to repair relations between Smith and Mladic. It is a difficult situation because the international community is telling everyone to isolate Pale, not to deal with them, but those of us on the ground in Bosnia *have* to deal with Pale on practical matters such as freedom of movement and utilities. In any case, I checked with Smith both before and after I went to see Tolimir. I made very clear I was not trying to intrude on his turf and that I was only trying to be helpful; if he insisted, I said, I would cancel my visit. But Smith supported me completely and gave me a few messages to deliver in case I would have the chance to meet Mladic. The main message was that he wanted to meet with Mladic.

We traveled from Sarajevo by armored vehicle, and once we passed through the last Bosnian checkpoint, we headed for Lukavica barracks to pick up Colonel Indjic. En route to Lukavica, at around 12:30 P.M., at one of the Serb checkpoints, we saw being released the four Serb soldiers who had been captured during the fire fight at the Vrbanja Bridge. So they will not be tried as war criminals after all. We received confirmation late today that the remaining UN hostages have also been released. The UN maintains publicly that there was no trade involved between the four Serb prisoners and the remaining UN hostages, but rumor would have it otherwise.

[In fact, the rumor mill (and this time I believed it) said the deal had several components. One was the release of the four Serb prisoners. A second was that some Western governments actually *paid* to have the UN prisoners released. Milosevic was reported to have given either money or fuel or both to the BSA to purchase the hostages' release, and because Milosevic had no money, the money must have come from the West. In fact, there had been tremendous pressure from Western capitals for the UN to do whatever was necessary in order to secure the release of the remaining hostages. Otherwise, domestic constituencies would demand the withdrawal of all Western European troops from UNPROFOR, and the entire mission would collapse.]

In any case, once we picked up Indjic, he informed us where and with whom our meeting would be: we were going to Sokolac to meet with General Tolimir. We would not be meeting Mladic. Indjic also asked if we might give a ride to his wife, who wanted to visit her mother in a village near Sokolac. I agreed.

In the course of our brief conversation, I mentioned to Indjic that I thought it was foolish for the Serbs to shell civilians. Why did the Krajina Serbs in Croatia, for example, shell Zagreb when the Croatian army invaded

Western Slavonia? The world was sympathetic to the Serbs for one of the few times during this war, but then they sent four or five shells into Zagreb and lost that sympathy. And why do the Serbs continue to shell civilian areas in Sarajevo? I asked. It only makes the world sympathize with Bosnia.

"You say *Bosnia*," Indjic replied. "I am Bosnian. I am Sarajevan. I spent almost all of my life in Sarajevo, and now I cannot go back. When the Moslems started the war and began killing Serbs, we had to leave behind everything we had and flee to the hills. The Serbs who stayed in Sarajevo are hostages. They have no future in a Moslem state."

"But why shell cities? Why did the Serbs in Croatia shell Zagreb?" I persisted. Indjic is in his early forties. The Bosnian government hates him and considers him to be a major war criminal.

"What else can we do?" he said. "They shell our cities, and you don't report it. We have to fight back."

It was the wrong time to argue this point. I said nothing.

We met General Tolimir at a hotel in Sokolac. I was a bit carsick by the time we arrived. We had taken back roads because of the fighting, and the air conditioning in our vehicle wasn't working. The fan was feeble. It was warm, but of course one can't open the windows in an armored vehicle, so we bounced along from pothole to pothole on a humid day, through farm villages and past curious eyes, sweating. Though Indjic was with us, we were still traveling in a hated UN vehicle, and I was a bit uncomfortable about that. Actually, we were never threatened. The soldiers knew that any UN vehicle this deep behind Serb lines had clearance from the Serb military.

Tolimir talked a lot. He fancies himself to be a historian and has an interest in classical philosophy. We met at a hotel, and he offered us a meal. [It was about 4:30 P.M. I smiled to myself. The Serbs always fed you. In fact, they almost always overfed you. Koljevic used to tell me it was because they had always been poor, and they overcompensated by heaping food upon their guests. Whatever the truth, I was reminded again how important hospitality is in what the UN euphemistically called "developing" countries.

The fact was, however, that I was always in danger of being considered an ungrateful guest because I rarely drank, didn't smoke, and didn't like the fatty meat-and-potatoes menus of the Balkans. I frequently skipped meals and preferred vegetables and fruits and salads to the heavy food of the Balkans. I remember Koljevic once saying to me: "What can I give you? You don't smoke, you don't drink, and you don't eat." I replied that I would love to have some juice (in Serbian, called *sok*), whereupon he had brought to me an orange liquid that approximated soda pop. I didn't want that either, but I drank it.]

Tolimir was quite direct in his opinions and carefully phrased them in a positive manner. Rather than say he does *not* want to agree to restoring utilities, he said the Serb side would be agreeable to restoring utilities once a cease-fire has been established. Until then, it would be foolish to consider the matter. Some of the electric power lines run through or near the confrontation line, and it is impossible to work on them while the war is ongoing. Even if they can be restored, they can be destroyed the next day as long as there is no cease-fire. Moreover, there has been additional damage since the resumption of hostilities, so it would take ten days to two weeks to restore power, not the forty-eight hours originally envisioned.

He asked, meanwhile, why the world is only concerned with restoring utilities to Sarajevo. There are tens of Serbian villages that have no utilities and have not had utilities for months, even years. Why don't we go to the Serbian villages and see for ourselves what he is talking about? He doesn't trust the Moslems. Restoring utilities to Sarajevo will only help the Moslem government's war effort. He wants to get on with the war and finish it.

On the matter of convoys, he said the matter has been resolved between General Mladic and General Janvier. UNHCR convoys coming from Kiseljak through the four Sierras Serb checkpoints were delayed by the HVO because they had mined the roads outside of Kiseljak. The Serbs did not stop the convoys, he insisted. [Although it was true that the HVO had mined the roads outside of Kiseljak, it was by no means certain that the Serbs were willing to open the Sierra checkpoints.]

Tolimir also asked me why the international community has not condemned the current Moslem offensive around Sarajevo. It is clear who began the fighting, and it is evident there can be no peace talks until the offensive ceases. Even though Izetbegovic is saying publicly that he intends to continue the war, the international community continues to condemn the Serbs. Humanitarian aid helps only the Moslems. Tolimir likened peace talks at this point to the myth of Sisyphus. He is fond of classical allusions.

I told Tolimir I was not a spokesman for the international community, so I could not answer his questions. But what did I think? he persisted. Then he launched another lecture on the world's bias against the Serbs and how it is always trying to get concessions from the Serbs, but allowing the Turks (Moslems) to do whatever they want.

Once the Moslems stop their offensive, he continued, the Serb side will be willing to have peace talks. He mentioned several conditions, however:

1. The talks must be among three sides, not just two. The Bosnian Croats should be included.

2. The UN should be present at the talks. (Although the Serbs mistrust UNPROFOR, they still believe UNPROFOR is the most objective of all the international actors.)

3. The problem of who is responsible for the latest military offensive

should be addressed. (This kind of political agenda will, of course, never be agreed to by any sensible international interlocutor.)

4. The UN will have to agree not to plan the use of force against only one side to the conflict.

He also offered to have UNPROFOR establish an office at Lukavica.

On a final point, Tolimir asked if he could be provided with a report by UNPROFOR as to why the four Serb soldiers captured in the battle at the Vrbanja Bridge were turned over to Moslem police for five hours of interrogation, during which time they were physically abused. I said I would pass on his request.

We returned to Sarajevo tonight around 7:00 P.M. It was still light. Though we had come to Pale from Sarajevo by back roads, we took the regular route back, the very route that the Bosnian government claimed it had captured. When I returned to Sarajevo, I reported to Smith that the normal route had not been interdicted or captured and was functioning normally. [My findings were reported at the daily press briefing in Zagreb the following day. The Bosnian government was not happy with my report. Meanwhile, Muratovic was furious that I had established contact with the Bosnian military. No doubt, he thought I was spying for the Serbs.]

[That weekend I began a fax I never sent. It was intended to be a brief summary of my early thoughts on the situation in Bosnia. But I never finished the fax because I couldn't find the necessary time. As it was, I only had the chance to write about credibility.

I had been thinking about Jane Austen and her novel *Pride and Prejudice*, the working title of which had been *First Impressions*. I wanted to record my first impressions of the war in Bosnia before the passions and pressures of the situation on the ground caused me to respond with pride and prejudice. As it was, my views never really changed that much from my first impressions, not while I was there and not after I left. Here is what I wrote in my notebook:

1. The main problem at this point for UNPROFOR is one of credibility, which for any peacekeeping force is second in importance only to presence. At the most basic level, credibility *begins* with presence, and each time we are forced to abandon presence (not even control, but simply presence), we lose a bit of credibility.

2. Regrettably, we have lost credibility with both warring parties at this point for reasons that have been extensively discussed and go beyond the issue of presence. Most recently, air strikes around Pale have reinforced the Bosnian Serbs' belief that UNPROFOR is not impartial. As

for the Bosnian government, it has repeated that UNPROFOR is unable to protect aid convoys or the safe areas, and UNPROFOR is unable to lift the siege of Sarajevo. Nothing we do short of bombing the Bosnian government army is likely the change the attitude of the Bosnian Serbs regarding UNPROFOR, and nothing we do short of actively becoming the Bosnian government's mercenaries will change the attitude of the Bosnian government toward us.

3. Yet there is another side to the issue of credibility. The parties themselves have no credibility with us. They are both simply liars. One can take the commissar out of the system, but one cannot take the system out of the commissar. We are seeing disinformation with a vengeance. The warring parties do not trust UNPROFOR because they do not trust one another.

4. We have expended too much energy in self-examination, in wondering how we can become more credible, how we can curry favor with the parties. What we should do is to expose the disingenuous and irresponsible propaganda of the warring parties. In Orwellian doublespeak, this technique is called proactive. In American slang, it is called *telling it like it is.* We will gain credibility and self-respect, and assert our independence with this approach.

I believed at that point that UNPROFOR should leave Bosnia as soon as possible. It could still leave with its head up rather than down. Let the parties fight it out among themselves and make their own peace. I had read an essay recently that said, on the basis of a study, that two-thirds of the wars during the past century have ended in stalemate. Not in victory, but in stalemate.

I used to joke with associates that the best policy toward former Yugoslavia would be a "mined fencepost" approach. Place a fence around the country, mine the fenceposts, and let them fight it out. When the war was over, remove the mines and the fence—in other words, a kind of giant steel cage match as in professional wrestling.

But, of course, the world could not turn its back on a war of this magnitude, and Western Europe didn't want anymore Yugoslav refugees, so it had to find a way to end the conflict.]

19 June 1995

8:30 A.M. briefing. There is still skirmishing around Sarajevo, but there has been a decrease in shelling. The Bosnian government offensive seems to have been short-lived. There are numerous speculations as to why. Some of the more vocal British officers think the offensive is only a diversionary tactic, perhaps a political statement, perhaps with some other objective than liberating Sarajevo, a kind of Tet Offensive to show that the Moslems cannot be broken, will never surrender. But the French and the Russians are sure that the offensive is the real thing and that it will fail. The Serbs, meanwhile, think that U.S. political pressure has convinced the Bosnian government to halt because the offensive is undermining the possibility of peace talks. The Serbs always see conspiracy, and see the United States behind every conspiracy. Smith is reserving judgment. I suspect that Bosnian government forces have taken heavy casualties, that their own people are resentful, and that the offensive is doomed. I believe this because the Bosnian government is now refusing to allow the international organizations to enter the hospitals, which probably means that casualties are heavy and morale is low. The Bosnian government doesn't want any adverse publicity to undermine its war effort.

Smith's primary concern is still freedom of movement. Now that the hostages have been released, he wants to try immediately to bring convoys in through the Sierra checkpoints. The fact that a war is still smoldering won't deter him.

Following the morning briefings I called Akashi's office in Zagreb. I spoke with John Almstrom, a retired Canadian colonel in his early fifties, who functions as Akashi's military advisor and special assistant. [I don't know if the UN ever got more for its money than it did with Almstrom. He was a whirlwind of energy, scrupulously loyal, and a fine judge of character. He also had good military knowledge. He knew who worked and who didn't; he knew who understood the situation and who didn't. He had a boyish enthusiasm and an unflagging intensity that was infectious to anyone who worked with him. I spoke with Almstrom a few times a week to find out what was happening at the international level.] I asked him for a brief summary of Akashi's talks with Milosevic a few days earlier.

Basically, Almstrom said, Akashi brought up two subjects: there should be no more targeting of civilian areas, and humanitarian convoys should be allowed into the enclaves. Milosevic was sympathetic to Akashi's requests.

"Was the sympathy genuine?" I asked Almstrom.

"I think so. Even Milosevic is fed up with the Bosnian Serbs."

"Does Milosevic really have that much influence?"

"Nobody knows, but I think so."

"I think so, Even Milosevic is fed up with the Bosnian Serbs."

I had a call from Minister Muratovic this morning. It was the usual request, with a slight variation. He wants a ride in an UNPROFOR APC to Mostar tomorrow. He expects us to function as a taxi service for the Bosnian government, whether it is on official business or on shopping trips. I said yes.

The extent to which the international community lives off the UN's meager resources is shameful. Muratovic is among the worst, but there are ambassadors who are just as slimy. One in particular, who shall go unnamed, comes to me at least twice a week with the most outrageous requests for favors. Once he came to me with the following proposition.

"Do you ever hire part-time interpreters?" he asked.

"Rarely," I said. Good English-language interpreters were very hard to find in the Balkans, and when you found one, you hired him/her full-time.

"Well, one of your interpreters from Sector Southwest is coming to work for us, and I thought that maybe she could retain her UN identification card by saying that she still worked for you on a part-time basis. You know, she can get places with her UN ID that we can't get to otherwise. She would work full-time for us, but I promise you that whenever you needed her, you could have her to work for you. That way she could still say she was employed by the UN."

I refused, and the ambassador scowled. I refused a second time, then asked him to speak with my deputy, who was much more patient, but who gave the same reply, except that he wrapped it nicely in administrative mumbo jumbo.

I fear I have made another enemy in the diplomatic community, and this one has quite a bit of leverage.

Thoughts. Sometimes the best way to understand a situation is in terms of images. I was thinking this morning of an accordion. The Serbs squeeze Sarajevo like an accordion. They close it all the way, then reopen it a little, then close it all the way and reopen it a little less. Each time they close it, they reopen it a little less. And what will happen this winter? Will the music stop? Will Sarajevo surrender? I doubt it. The tune will only become more plaintive.

UNPROFOR has continued to withdraw its troops from the WCPs, which means it can no longer monitor the Total Exclusion Zone. Without monitors on the spot to verify that long weapons are not being reintroduced into the exclusion zone, we don't know what is happening.

Thus, the safe area concept and the TEZ have broken down. They have been effectively destroyed by the hostage taking that followed the two air strikes on Pale three weeks ago. In retrospect, one must question again the wisdom of Smith's decision to call in air strikes against Pale. There is no doubt it was an escalatory step. In Smith's own words, before one escalates, one should be prepared to deal with the consequences of that escalation. We are facing different choices now. It is no longer a matter of preserving or not preserving the TEZ. What the international community seems to be building for now is the forcible resupply of the safe areas, including Sarajevo. The perspective has changed. Though we are withdrawing our troops from the WCPS, we do not see it as withdrawing our troops from the WCPS. We see it as withdrawing our troops from Serb-controlled areas so that NATO can prepare for wide-scale bombing.

It is what Smith has wanted, and perhaps he is right. Perhaps the Serbs are beyond bargaining, and they will only respond to power. We shall see.

Meanwhile, the Rapid Reaction Force has not yet been tasked, but the pressure is building to assign them to protect aid convoys. It is certain in my mind that if they must use force, they will use it against only one party. It is also certain that in the course of events, the Bosnian government will target aid convoys, blame it on the Serbs (who will do their own targeting as well), and thus provoke a response from the RRF and NATO against the Serbs. The scenario is approaching inevitability. I have said to Smith more than once: "If you want to declare war against the Serbs, do it under the U.K. flag, not under the UN flag." He agrees that this approach would be preferable, but reminds me that he has to work with what he has. Meanwhile, he continues to press for military action against the Bosnian Serbs. Leave the business of the flags to the politicians is his attitude; he has military responsibilities.

[But Smith also played politics, in London and Washington as well as in Sarajevo. In fact, I suspected that at this point he was driving policy in London, not vice versa. Perhaps that was reasonable. At least the British foreign office had the good sense to listen to its field commander.

As Akashi told me when briefing me about Smith: "He's a very different kind of man from General Rose" (who was Smith's predecessor). Yes, indeed. The point that Smith liked to make was that the times were different, more than the personalities. While Rose was in charge, there had been some hope for peace, but with the breakdown of the cease-fire at the end of April 1995 it was clear that all sides felt the only way to resolve the situation was by war, and because UNPROFOR was smack in the middle of that war, it had to take extraordinary measures to protect itself and the people of the safe areas.]

I had planned to go to Gornji Vakuf this week to meet new staff and familiarize myself with the area, but the roads are closed. No way to go there today. Meanwhile, the new head of mission, Antonio Pedauye, a Spaniard, is scheduled to arrive this week. Not coincidentally, Spain will be chairman of the European Union for the next six months.

Muratovic told me again yesterday that he will insist that all decisions concerning Bosnia be made from Sarajevo, not from Zagreb. He wants, as a minimum condition for extending UNPROFOR's mandate in November, that the delivery of humanitarian aid be guaranteed, that the safe areas be protected, and that the TEZ around Sarajevo be enforced. Stop the strangulation of Sarajevo and the other enclaves or else get out, was his message.

At breakfast this morning, Alex Ivanko, the Civil Affairs spokesman, asked me if I would like to attend the noon press conference today. There are daily press briefings at the Sarajevo airport. UNPROFOR has one civilian spokesman, Ivanko, and one British military spokesman, Lt. Col. Gary Coward. Because I went to Pale recently, and because I am fairly new on the job, the press are interested in speaking to me. After some hesitation, I agreed to go to the press conference.

[Among ourselves, we referred to the press as reptiles. We called them the International Order of Reptiles—the IOE. In fact, there were times when it seemed one needed a Ph.D. in herpitology to deal with these self-appointed chroniclers of history.

The main problem for the UN with the press was that they hated us. The main problem for me was that I often lost patience with their hating us. Unfortunately, a strange logic prevailed when dealing with the Reptiles. If you endured their abuse, then you were "good" with the press, but if you dared to question their hegemony and misinformation, then you didn't know how to handle the press.

Smith was much better and much shrewder with the media than I was. He took them in small doses, one or two at a time, over dinner or in his office, but he never faced the wolf pack en masse, even though they liked him. I was both foolish and arrogant in thinking I could debate them, perhaps even win them over to some objectivity. No way. They were a clenched fist, always looking for new ways to pummel UNPROFOR.]

Walking into a press conference at the Sarajevo airport is like entering a kennel. Today in particular the press was legion. I have no idea what the advance word on me was, but it didn't much matter. UNPROFOR, especially Akashi and his personal representative, are considered villains and have to be excoriated at every opportunity. The facts are irrelevant, the personalities are insignificant. Nominally, my reason for being there was to speak about the prospects for restoring utilities to Sarajevo.

I made an opening statement saying that I had presented to both sides a proposal for restoring utilities to Sarajevo and that I was awaiting a response. The proposal was nonpolitical. It spoke about who would turn on what, in which order, and when.

The audience was outraged. It wasn't clear why, but they were outraged. One reporter asked how I could have dared to go to Pale to speak with the Serbs when only yesterday they had shelled Sarajevo, killing innocent people who were standing in line at a water pump. Children had been among the victims. Wasn't I rewarding terrorism by going to Pale the very next day?

I had gone to Pale only to present the Serbs with a text of the possible steps for restoring utilities to Sarajevo, I said. I repeated that the text simply said who would turn on what and where and in which order. It was purely a technical text, with no political message whatsoever. I was hopeful.

"What was the problem?" the *New York Times* reporter asked.

"There was no problem," I said. I had presented a text and was awaiting an answer. I had presented it only yesterday, so it was too soon to expect a decision.

Then a reporter from one of the American TV networks screamed (yes, screamed) at me. I wasn't quite sure what he was asking because it was more a performance than a question, but generally he was asking the same question that the previous reporter asked. How could I speak to those terrorists in Pale about restoring utilities when they had only yesterday massacred innocent children in Sarajevo, while the UN had done nothing to retaliate? If the Serbs had not turned off the water in the first place, then there wouldn't have been a line at the water pump and *innocent children* (he liked that phrase) wouldn't have been slaughtered while the UN looked on indifferently. Or something like that. The query was almost incoherent. He was so righteously indignant that he could scarcely spit out the words. Of course, what he wanted was to antagonize me in order to embarrass the UN and to get a good sound bite. Never mind that the Serbs are *not* solely responsible for turning off the water. Never mind that the UN is *not* indifferent to the slaughter of children. Never mind that the Serbs did not turn off the water *in order to kill children standing in line at a water pump*. And so forth. The facts don't matter.

But stupidly I lost my temper. Perhaps the screaming even more than the incoherence set me off. I wanted to tell him that his tone confirmed the fact that hysteria is not gender specific, but I didn't say that. What I *did* say, however, was even worse: "That question is so illogical that I won't even dignify it with an answer."

I had swallowed the bait. An audible round of "oohs" went through the kennel. A moment later, the Reuters reporter asked me a contrived question that invited me to denounce the barbaric Serbs. I smiled, having anticipated the question. [I was certainly not sympathetic to the BSA's shelling of civilian targets in Sarajevo, but I was not eager to denounce publicly, except in the most general terms, a party I was dealing with and from which I was seeking compliance. Why, I wondered, couldn't he ask an intelligent question, instead of being so predictable?] He immediately picked up on my smile and demanded to know why I was smiling. "Perhaps you can share with us why you're smiling so that you can amuse us, too. Come on, amuse us."

What I wanted to reply was that he, being past puberty, should have known by now how to amuse himself, but with great restraint, I didn't say that. Instead, I dodged the question and mumbled something about only wanting to help the people of Sarajevo by restoring utilities to the city. I was simply astonished by the personal abuse aimed at me and the institutional hatred against the UN.

The conference went on for another fifteen minutes or so, along the same confrontational lines. Once or twice our spokesmen intervened to protect me, but the judgment had already been made. The UN had been proven guilty, beyond a reasonable doubt, of not toeing the politically correct line.

I lost a key battle, and it was my fault. One cannot blame a rattlesnake for being a rattlesnake. It was my responsibility to deal intelligently with the press, and I did not.

[A few days later I received a call from New York, advising me to be more careful with the press in future. The stories about my press conference had gone out and had been monitored at UN headquarters in New York. Because I didn't see any of the reports myself, I can't say firsthand exactly how I was skewered, but I was sure the summaries were nasty.

One publication that was particularly spiteful toward the United Nations and me personally during the time I was in former Yugoslavia, in Croatia as well as in Bosnia, was the *Christian Science Monitor*. Its main reporter, David Rohde, was an ambitious, peripatetic opportunist who was passionately pro-Bosnian.

His importance to the U.S. government, incidentally, should not be underestimated. In fact, his later detention by the Bosnian Serbs became a subject for high-level discussion at the Dayton talks. Richard Holbrooke notes that the entire afternoon of 4 October 1995 at Dayton "focused on David Rohde" (*op. cit.*, 246), who at the time was being held in what Holbrooke terms "the northwest Bosnian Serb town of Bijeljina" by the BSA on charges of having illegally entered Bosnian Serb territory and having falsified his identification papers. The Serbs threatened to indict Rohde for espionage. Holbrooke then, with dripping sincerity, recounts: "Walter Andrusyzyn, an officer from the Embassy in Sarajevo, had driven one hundred miles through a brutal snowstorm and forced his way into the Bijeljina jail to see Rohde. It was the first trip by any Embassy officer deep into the Serb portion of Bosnia since the war began" (*ibid.*). (First of all, Bijeljina was not deep into the Serbian-controlled portion of Bosnia; it was just over the border from Serbia. Second, it was not in northwest Bosnia; it was in northeast Bosnia. Third, it's unlikely that Mr. Andrusyzyn even drove himself. He probably had a driver, so that he was able to sit back and plan his strategy while some poor local employee negotiated the mountain roads. But why should facts get in the way of good melodrama, especially when one is trying to spin history?) Holbrooke then recalls that he spoke with Rohde's family and two of his editors at the *Christian Science Monitor*. His conclusion was,

"The best chance for an early release was simply to hold to the line that there would be no Dayton agreements while David was being held" (*ibid.*). Such attention makes it difficult for any observer to believe that Rohde did not have a special relationship with Washington. At the same time, he was a daring, imaginative, and resourceful reporter, who eventually won a Pulitzer Prize for his book on Srebrenica and earned a job with the *New York Times.*

In contrast to the *Christian Science Monitor,* I thought that *The Washington Post* was more balanced, though certainly not sympathetic to the Serbs. Their correspondent, John Pomfret, made an effort to ferret out the complexities of the story. Of course, the *Post* followed the approved line when dealing with Bosnia, but at least Pomfret did not adhere to the ban on criticizing the Bosnian government. As for CNN's First Lady of Bosnia, Christiana Amanpur, she was even less objective than Izetbegovic, but at least she made no pretense of being objective. She was fond of telling anyone who wanted to listen that to be objective in Bosnia was to be a party to genocide. In my faxes I used to refer to CNN as Certainly Not Neutral.]

There are numerous British journalists here, and perhaps because I am English speaking, I overestimate their influence. Yet they seem to give a character to the mission. They are, with few exceptions (such as Laura Silber), highly sanctimonious and culturally condescending. They are among the most hypocritical and supercilious, and seem to assume that they were chosen by God to assist the suffering and that in some way the Americans and the French, for different reasons, are responsible for whatever ills exist in the present situation.

Naturally, one always wants to assist those who are suffering, and it is very noble to do so, but it is the attitude that they are God's agents on earth that I find so offensive.

One female journalist keeps telling me about how *we* have to promote multiethnic democracy—the most advanced form of society—how the Bosnian government is the only party pursuing that path, and how *we,* therefore, have to support them.

Wrong, I say. Former Yugoslavia was a multiethnic society before republics like Bosnia began seceding. Now none of the warring parties believes in multiethnicity.

Besides, what right does perfidious Albion have to impose its view of Western values on the people of the Balkans and to suggest they are backward if they don't see history through British eyes? This approach is the worst form of racism and not inconsistent with a certain element in British society. The sad truth is that many people in the Balkans prefer to live among their own kind. To many in the West, including myself, such provincial behavior is puzzling. Yet, it should not be considered immoral or uncivilized.

At the same time, wanting to be among your own kind does not mean you should slaughter those *not* of your kind.

Another journalist, a female in her twenties from a prominent London daily, is fond of telling me how she, having spent ten months in Sarajevo, considers herself to be a Sarajevan. "We are all Sarajevans," she insists. (*We?* The international press? Unlike me, of course, a mongrel American and a UN official.) Never mind that she can, whenever she wishes, return to London or vacation in the South Seas, an option not available to most Sarajevans, especially the refugees. But *she* is a Sarajevan. Meanwhile, in the course of her homily she asks me when I think the Americans might agree to placing troops on the ground in Bosnia. "When they go completely out of their mind," I reply.

Clearly, I am not to be trusted.

My press conference was a disaster. It left me feeling demeaned, actively disliked, and isolated. I felt like a target, a political leper. I realize this statement sounds paranoid, but even the medical books must make allowance for a condition that might be known as "realistic paranoia." The fact is that the prevailing attitudes in Sarajevo are so cliquish, so narrow, and so prescribed that any deviation from the norm or suspected deviation from the norm is severely punished.

I also felt angry. That the Bosnian government is totalitarian in the best of Communist tradition is not even questioned by its most fervent supporters, but the accepted rationalization for this attitude is that because this is wartime, there is no room for dissent; besides, the Bosnian government is allegedly multiethnic (a key buzzword), and Sarajevo is under siege because the UN refuses to liberate it.

That a government at war should promote this line of thought is perfectly understandable, but that the international community, led by the juggernaut of the press, should voluntarily accept, promote, and attempt to impose this view on others under pain of being cast into the outer darkness is something I can never accept.

To sum up: the Bosnian government, except for Hasan Muratovic, who is often hostile and irrational, avoids speaking to Civil Affairs on major issues; the British military (with the exception of Smith) belittles Civil Affairs; the press corps demeans and denounces UN civilian officials, all the way up through Akashi to Boutros-Ghali; certain members of my own staff want to disassociate themselves from Civil Affairs; and our own civilian press spokesman looks to Smith rather than to Civil Affairs for guidance.

Moreover, these internal pressures are coming against the background of a very tense external situation. The Cessation of Hostilities Agreement expired on 30 April; the blue routes (i.e., routes used only by the UN) into

Sarajevo are closed; the Sarajevo airport is closed; shelling on the road over Mount Igman has increased; the RRF is about to ensconce itself in the hills around Sarajevo and prepare to attack the Serbs; food convoys are being blocked from entering all the eastern enclaves, including Sarajevo; sniping within Sarajevo has resumed; a major government offensive in the hills around Sarajevo is in progress, and is provoking the shelling by both sides of neighborhoods within Sarajevo; and we have no utilities in the city.

We go home to our apartments at night, if we go home at all, in armored vehicles, to no water, no electricity, and no light. We are unable to receive mail for weeks at a time. We have extreme difficulty in entering or leaving the city. Some UN personnel who have finished their tours of duty are stranded in Sarajevo for days, even weeks, unable to return home.

Yet this list of painful particulars is not meant to be a lamentation. The people of Sarajevo (about 70 percent of whom by this time are displaced persons from outside of Sarajevo) live under conditions far worse than ours. These are simply the facts. And perhaps one of the salient facts is that all of us in the international community, including myself, volunteered for this duty. We have no right to complain.

21 June 1995

At the 9:00 A.M. briefing in his office this morning, Smith reiterated his concern about convoys having to take a circuitous route to reach Sarajevo. They are still being forced to come through Belgrade, which is a much longer route and therefore slower and more costly in terms of fuel. The road through the Sierra checkpoints is obstructed, and the road over Mount Igman is not secure.

[Meanwhile, even if the Igman route could be protected from mortar attacks and snipers, the road itself was not suited for heavy traffic; it needed upgrading. Many of our trucks had foundered on that road. Driving over Igman in daylight, one could see a number of buses and heavy vehicles that had tumbled over the embankment. Some were UN vehicles; most were Bosnian buses and trucks. Smith's solution was to upgrade and secure the Igman route. As stated earlier, I and a few others favored opening the Kiseljak route through the Sierras, known as Route Swan, because it was a better road, easier to defend, and more direct, but Smith wanted Igman secured because it had no Serb checkpoints, and he knew he would have no trouble with Bosnian government checkpoints. The Bosnian government wanted to secure the Igman Road because it could bring weapons and soldiers over that route, which it could not do on Route Swan.]

"Until we have freedom of movement, we will remain part of the problem instead of part of the solution," Smith repeated at the briefing. [What he meant was that UNPROFOR could not do its job properly unless it could supply its troops. As long as we had to worry about supplying our troops instead of doing our job, then we became part of the problem. There was also the continuing political embarrassment of being too concerned with supplying ourselves when we could not supply the local population.]

Smith is still ambiguous about the RRF. Although he wants its presence militarily, he realizes the logistical nightmare it will cause. "How will we feed them, and where will we put them?" he asks. Moreover, wherever they are stationed, their quarters will have to be winterized by fall, which is only a few months away. Finally, although the RRF has not even arrived yet, both the Federation and Croatia are making noises about preventing them from entering Bosnia.

Following the morning meetings, I went to see Minister Muratovic. He was in a most unaccommodating mood—"ballistic," as one of my colleagues put it. He was angry about two things. First, that I had met with General Tolimir. My function, he raved, is a civilian one. I am not supposed to meet with military officials. I should meet either with Koljevic or with the mayor of Serb Sarajevo, Maxim Stanisic. My job is to bring pressure on Pale, through Serbian civilian officials in Sarajevo, in order to restore utilities to Sarajevo. Tolimir is an obstructionist. He will only befog the issue. I should be dealing with civilians.

I made it indisputably clear that I will deal with whomsoever I choose, that it is not up to him to tell me with whom I should deal, and that I have been doing him a courtesy by reporting to him on my discussions. After more shouting, Muratovic backed off slightly. [Smith told me the next day that Muratovic raised the issue again that evening when Smith saw him at a social function (a function to which UNPROFOR civilian officials had not been invited).]

The second point Muratovic was angry about was the issue of local staff. My colleague, who accompanied me to the meeting, raised the issue, protesting that the Bosnian government has still not issued the work permits it promised. Several weeks ago, the government issued "instructions" asserting that they had the right to tax, draft, and approve or disapprove local staff working for the UN. They insisted on their right to issue work permits. [Even though UNPROFOR tacitly recognized that right, the Bosnian government did not issue permits to several non-Moslems working for UNPROFOR. It also drafted UNPROFOR local staff into the army and continued to hound others so mercilessly that we had to give refuge to some of them in the UNPROFOR compound. The government's harassment, I might add, was multiethnic. It was engaged a war, and it needed recruits.]

Under the existing Status of Forces Agreement (SOFA), which the Bosnian government had signed with the UN, the government had no right to draft or tax UN employees or to issue work permits. On a practical basis, however, it did whatever it wanted. We could only protest, which we did. Each time we protested, Muratovic went ballistic.]

Recently, the Secretary-General sent a *note verbale* to the Bosnian government's permanent representative in New York—saying, in effect, that the "instructions" his government issued in Sarajevo have no validity because they violate the SOFA. Muratovic, who had a copy of the Secretary-General's note in front of him while we spoke, made the dramatic gesture of throwing it off to the side of the table. "That is what I think of this letter," he said.

"Are you saying that you have no respect for the Secretary-General of the United Nations?" I asked.

He pondered for a moment, then dodged the question. "Your local staff lives very well. They can go wherever they want anytime they want. We don't harass them," he said. "But we don't pay attention to notes from New York. This is Sarajevo. Decisions about Sarajevo should be made here, not in New York."

22 June 1995

At the 9:00 A.M. briefing in his office Smith informed us that currently there were four planning teams in Zagreb dealing with deployment of the RRF. He believes in the usefulness of the RRF, but he is concerned about the practicalities of its deployment: where and to whom will they report, and who will feed and billet them? On another point, he said that the Bosnian government is concerned about the possible collapse of the no-fly zone. It has complained that Serbian aircraft are flying over Bosnian government positions. (These claims are a regular feature of the Bosnian government propaganda campaign. They are occasionally true, but rarely verified by independent sources.)

Smith's next point was that it had been leaked in New York or Zagreb that a recent NATO request to bomb the BSA was rejected by Janvier in Zagreb. We would probably receive some harsh questions at the noon press briefing about that. The story is true. Smith did request the use of air power against the BSA, which was shelling an UNPROFOR position, but Zagreb turned down his request.

[What Smith did *not* mention was that Janvier had every right to deny his request. Field commanders can make all the requests they want, but headquarters makes the final decision, which is neither unusual nor illogical. Janvier saw such requests for military escalation in terms of what they would mean for the entire theater. Smith, or any other field commander, made his request in terms of what it would mean for his particular portion of the theater. It was clear, however, that the international press would accuse UNPROFOR of being soft on the Serbs, of condoning ethnic cleansing, of being indifferent to the killing of Moslem innocents, and so on.

The leak itself was another matter. There was no way of stopping such leaks. Local staff in Zagreb as well as in Sarajevo were able to access all the most sensitive communications. Moreover, some of our own staff, especially civilian staff, leaked stories to the press. But such happenings didn't upset me because I believed that the UN should be transparent. It was not a secret military organization. It was not NATO, and it could not serve its member states if it kept secrets from them. I would have liked to see a situation in which there was no need for leaks.]

Someone mentioned NATO at the briefing, and one of Smith's staff remarked, "NATO goes home after it bombs, but UNPROFOR has to stay and pay the price." [What he meant was that Bosnian Serb retaliation came against UNPROFOR—whether it be by shelling, hostage taking, restricting movement, or refusing to talk—following NATO's assaults. There was an abiding groundswell of resentment to the fact that the United States had no troops on the ground and never had to deal with the consequences of its policies.]

On another point, we have had reports of continuing military activity around Mount Dinara in the Serb-controlled Krajina region of Croatia. The assaults are emanating from locations in southwest Bosnia. Croatian and Bosnian Croat forces in western Bosnia are shelling Mount Dinara as part of their continuing campaign to capture the Livno Valley and thereby to sever the Krajina's supply lines to the Serb-controlled areas of Bosnia. If the Croatians are successful, they may isolate the Krajina and recapture it. Smith is concerned because the activity is coming from Bosnia, which is his area of responsibility. He wants to watch the situation closely.

23 June 1995

The new chief of mission, Antonio Pedauye, has arrived for a familiarization visit. He carries the rank of Assistant Secretary-General. Rank has its privileges. Because Pedauye is placed above Smith on the ladder, Smith cannot ignore him. The Bosnian government cannot ignore him. And, as mentioned, Spain is about to begin a six-month stint as chairman of the European Union, a position that may give Pedauye access to intelligence information otherwise inaccessible.

At Smith's briefing in his office this morning, Pedauye sat at center stage. He paid the expected tributes to the general. Like a good diplomat, he listened. He also decided, on the advice of all, not to speak to the press for at least three months.

After the briefings, Pedauye, Smith, and I went to see President Izetbegovic, Minister Hasan Muratovic, and recently appointed Foreign Minister Muhamed Sacirbey, who came in after the meeting was in progress. Pedauye was clearly happy to see him because he had worked with him in New York for a couple of years. Sacirbey, who calls himself Sacirbegovic when he is in Bosnia, was a familiar face in a crowd of strangers. Pedauye played the scene very well. He gave Sacirbey a warm welcome, for Izetbegovic's sake as much as anybody's. In effect, Pedauye was saying, "I understand your country's plight very well. I'm part of the diplomatic community. Trust me."

The Bosnian government expressed several concerns to us this morning. The first was the old chestnut that UNPROFOR should have autonomy from Zagreb. "We don't need Akashi, and we don't need Janvier," Izetbegovic said. "There are too many steps between here and New York. We want autonomy for UNPROFOR."

Izetbegovic then went to his second concern: humanitarian aid. The people of Sarajevo and the other enclaves must be fed. It is UNPROFOR's obligation to provide humanitarian aid.

Izetbegovic then asked when the airport would be opened. He was told that discussions are continuing. [They were not. It was one of Izetbegovic's tactics to ask a question rather than to state a demand, which made UNPROFOR even more defensive. Instead of saying, "We would like to have the airport opened," he would say, "When are you planning to reopen the airport?"]

Izetbegovic also wanted to have the blue routes reopened and utilities restored to Sarajevo. (The blue routes are supposed to be exclusively for UNPROFOR, although the Bosnian government uses them also.)

Izetbegovic spoke very quietly. He measured his phrases. In his early seventies and reportedly not in good health, he is the Grand Old Man of Bosnian politics. Though he can take extreme positions, he always makes us feel he is compromising because of his soft tone and unctuous manner. Like many of his generation in the Balkans, he is a survivor. Politically, he has been everything from a Nazi sympathizer to a Communist to a fundamentalist. Whatever has worked. Tomorrow he might be an antivivisectionist if it will keep him in power.

Muratovic, on the other hand, is an aggressive, importuning liar. He is thoroughly unscrupulous, but very bright. [In UN circles, one frequently hears the phrase: "He/she is not stupid." It is usually applied in circumstances in which the person being attacked holds an unpopular opinion. The implication is that John/Jane Doe is morally corrupt or politically incorrect, but very intelligent. My own feeling is that we tend to overrate intelligence in political life. It is certainly a positive factor, but raw intelligence or high education does not presume political maturity, emotional stability, good management skills, or personal character, all of which are needed to separate the great from the average. In the case of Muratovic, he was a true intellectual, a man concerned with ideas—articulate, discriminating, and assertive—but he could be unscrupulous.]

This morning, to my surprise, Muratovic took over the briefing. After Izetbegovic spoke for a few minutes, and Sacirbey spoke very briefly, Izetbegovic asked Muratovic if he wished to say a few words. At first, Muratovic declined, but then he unloaded, speaking for longer than any of the previous speakers, a tactic that in the diplomatic community suggests a certain amount of power. Usually, the president speaks not only first but for the longest amount of time. That is protocol. When a minister takes over and becomes the keynote speaker, it means he is speaking on behalf of the government and that he is a rising star.

Muratovic, this time speaking in a gentle voice, quickly launched his attack. "There are six thousand UNPROFOR troops here in Sarajevo, and they do nothing. You know, we can't control our people forever. Our people resent them, and something unpleasant could happen if they stay." The message, not very disguised, was that our soldiers will be at risk if they stay in Sarajevo. They may be shot, terrorized, and so on. [I had difficulty in staying quiet at times like this, but I did. How could a government minister, in the presence of the president of a country that was a member state of the United Nations, threaten the lives of UN soldiers and not be called to account? The Bosnian government often threatened our lives, however, and sometimes those threats were very real. They arrested us; they sniped at us; they shelled us. But we were not allowed to criticize them publicly.]

Muratovic continued: "If you can't do your job, then why are you staying? Your soldiers are sitting around, amusing themselves. They can't stop the Serbs from taking their weapons out of the storage sites; they can't deliver food to our people; they can't open the airport. Why are they here? We don't need them. Give us the weapons, and we will defend ourselves."

I had to admit that he had a point, and I suspected that he had been tapped by Izetbegovic to deliver the message. He was the hatchet man, but they all felt the same way, all the members of the Bosnian government. They hated us, and their increasingly strident line was that we should either be their mercenaries or leave.

As we filed out of the room, Sacirbey shook my hand in the reception line and looked into my eyes. "Oh, yes," he said. "I've heard of you."

We went next to see a leading Croatian politician, Nikola Grabovac, deputy to the president of the Federation.

On the table in his office, in small stands, Grabovac has two flags: one of Bosnia and Herzegovina and one of the Federation. But he is first and foremost a Croatian. Whenever dealing with a Bosnian Croat, one never has any doubt where his allegiance lies: with Croatia. In western Bosnia, the Bosnian Croats have set up a ministate known as Herzeg-Bosna. The region has historically, for hundreds of years, been populated by ethnic Croatians. Herzeg-Bosna officials have introduced Croatian currency there and treat the entire area as a part of greater Croatia. Bosnian Croats are allowed to vote in elections in Croatia and represent a significant constituency. Significantly, not only in western Bosnia but elsewhere, whenever Federation forces capture territory from the Bosnian Serbs, there is a scramble between the Croats and the Moslems to see who will occupy the area. They do not integrate.

Grabovac began with the same demands Izetbegovic made: open the airport and the blue routes, and ensure humanitarian aid. Then he went on to Croatian concerns.

"There's a quiet ethnic cleansing going on against Croatians. When a Croatian family leaves an area, it leaves forever, never to return, but when a Bosnian family leaves an area, another Bosnian family replaces it."

Though Grabovac did not accuse the Bosnian government of being behind this "cleansing," he clearly held it responsible. He was speaking about families that leave out of despair or whatever other reason, not families directly forced out because their villages have been overrun.

Then he became humorous. "We'll never survive another winter without heat," he said. "You know, when I used to visit my mother-in-law, I used to bring her flowers. Then, because we had no fuel, I brought her books of Karl Marx to burn as fuel. Now when I go to visit her, I bring a few liters of water and some firewood. That's what life is like in Sarajevo."

We smiled. Then, in true Balkan tradition, Grabovac turned to threats. "What would happen if a group of people just started to march toward Ilidza [a Serbian area on the outskirts of Sarajevo] to protest that Sarajevo has no utilities? Would they be shot? They have nothing to lose; they can't survive another winter without heat and electricity and water. And what if CNN were there to film it?"

I took notes. Pedauye didn't reply, good diplomat that he was.

"You see, we are really afraid that here in Sarajevo we won't be able to control the people if something isn't done soon" (more threats). Grabovac then took up the line that Akashi and Janvier should be ignored. Zagreb was too far away. They didn't understand Sarajevo's problems.

Pedauye replied that UNPROFOR in Bosnia cannot be independent. It can have a greater degree of autonomy, but it cannot be independent. It has to report to Zagreb and New York, and it needs the input of Zagreb and New York because of the ripple effect on all areas of former Yugoslavia when there is a major development in any one area. Both Zagreb and New York have a wider perspective. On another matter, he assured Grabovac that he intends to maintain close cooperation between the military and civilian components of UNPROFOR.

Grabovac then turned to macabre humor again. "You know, the only time we get light in our buildings is after someone dies so that we can conduct a proper funeral. I'm thinking of killing someone so that I can have light in my building."

We smiled again. I refrained from taking notes, but filed his phrases in my memory bank. [Actually, I thought he was quite effective. Death was so much with the people of Sarajevo that they had to joke about it, but it was no joking matter.]

When we left the unlit building, I told Pedauye I thought it was good that we had seen Grabovac. Too often, international figures and UN officials visit only Moslem leaders when they come to Sarajevo.

This evening Carl Bildt and Thorvald Stoltenberg came to visit us in Sarajevo. They are two very different men, but each in his own way is impressive. They are from different generations and have different mandates and different styles of diplomacy. About the only outward similarity they have is that they are both Scandinavians in a world that seems to think Scandinavians are always neutral. (Frequently in the halls of the UN, when a top negotiator is needed for a particularly sensitive post, the cry goes out: "Let's get a good Scandinavian.")

In this case, we have two good Scandinavians. Stoltenberg is a Norwegian in his early sixties, who is the representative of the UN Secretary-General to the International Conference on Former Yugoslavia. ICFY has two co-chairs: Stoltenberg (who succeeded Cyrus Vance) and Lord David Owen of the UK, who represented the European Union. ICFY has the primary responsibility for negotiations in former Yugoslavia.

[As stated earlier, in every peacekeeping operation in its history prior to the one in former Yugoslavia, the UN had dual responsibilities: military *and* political. That combination provided consistency. In former Yugoland, however, this was not the case. The European Union (which, at the start of the war, called itself the European Community) had originally decided that the civil war in former Yugoslavia was a European problem, so the Europeans should do the political negotiating. Then, when the EU realized it needed more troops and police than it could provide, it called on the UN, which, through its member states, provided additional troops and police. Thus, the EU had political responsibilities, whereas the UN had military responsibilities. The UN, with its 185 member states, had a broader and different constituency than did the EU, with its fourteen European states.

When Stoltenberg first came to ICFY, he wore two hats: co-chair of ICFY and head of UNPROFOR. He was Akashi's predecessor. After awhile, however, he decided he didn't have time to do both jobs, that he couldn't be half the time in Zagreb (as head of UNPROFOR) and half the time in Geneva (as head of ICFY).

The distinction between the political and military functions, which was sometimes submerged in an alphabet soup of acronymns, may sound terribly bureaucratic, but was indicative of the serious cross purposes within the European Union. In effect, the negotiators (ICFY) were telling another organ (the UN) to raise troops from nations not represented in the negotiating body. Understandably, the nations that send troops would like to have a say in the negotiations. Most of the troop-contributing nations in this particular case were not even represented in the UN Security Council, which was the body that decided on the number of troops needed.

It gets worse. The muddle in the Balkans was a case of the illness overwhelming the physician. The negotiating process in the Balkans became "Balkanized." There were: ICFY, the six-nation Contact Group, the UN Security Council, which through its resolutions endorsed the Vance Plan for Croatia and the Vance-Owen Plan for Bosnia and Herzegovina, special envoys from major capitals, and the European Union—at least five "negotiators."

Most of the blame heaped upon the amorphous image of the United Nations truly belonged to the European Union, since it was represented in ICFY and in the UN Security Council. The fact was that the major players in Europe, who were responsible for diplomatic negotiations, were divided in their goals and tactics. The French and the British had disagreements and rivalries between them. The Germans were the most influential of all the European countries, but they had neither veto power in the UN Security Council nor troops on the ground in former Yugoslavia. The Russian Federation was torn by internal divisions.

Moreover, all of those interests were eclipsed by the potential military might of Washington and the juggernaut of the international press.

I myself have sat in on informal consultations of the Security Council and heard member governments ask the secretariat to confirm or deny allegations published in the *New York Times* or aired on CNN. *As if it were the task of the United Nations to verify what appeared in the U.S. media!* Certainly a case of the tail wagging the dog. Yet, the international press was an ex officio and perhaps the most powerful "member" of the UN Security Council. Regrettably, CNN was a driving force behind the Security Council's decisions on Bosnia and Herzegovina.]

I am a great admirer of Stoltenberg. He is one of the most elegant, balanced, and well-informed men I have ever met. He is tall with thinning gray hair, a large man who has a quiet voice and listens well. He emanates a sincerity that is very rare among politicians. He also speaks Serbo-Croatian from his days as his country's ambassador to Belgrade.

[One anecdote. In spring 1995, just before I left Erdut in Eastern Slavonia, where I had been for a total of almost two years on two separate occasions, Stoltenberg came to visit. I received a call on my car radio on a Saturday evening around 7:00 P.M. that Stoltenberg was in Zagreb and wanted to come to Sector East (as Eastern Slavonia was called during the UN presence there) the following day. Could I make the necessary arrangements? Of course, it was too late to set up interviews, but certainly I could drive him around and brief him.

He arrived in Erdut about 2:00 P.M., after having been delayed at the Lipovac crossing into Sector East. We talked, and he listened carefully. On one or two occasions he asked me if it was very far from Erdut to Sombor, a town just over the border in Serbia—about a forty-minute ride, eighty minutes round-trip. "Too far," he said.

"My interpreter lives in Sombor," I said.

He then called her over and spoke to her privately. Slobodanka (called Boba) was a wonderfully warm woman, about forty, with two children. Her husband, who had only recently joined her, had fought in Bosnia. Boba used to describe herself as the quintessential Yugoslav. She had been born in Croatia, gone to university in Serbia, and lived and married in Bosnia, but now her life was a mess.

In any case, she told me later what Stoltenberg had asked her. He had said that when he had been a diplomat in Belgrade, he'd had friends in Sombor, who had recently died. Would Boba be kind enough to place flowers on their graves for him? He offered her twenty deutsch Marks to buy the flowers. Boba offered to take them from her mother's garden. Stoltenberg insisted on paying for them, and I believe they settled on ten Marks. Boba was scrupulously honest.

Now, cynics may say Stoltenberg had an ulterior political motive in making this gesture. I think not. He did it privately, without any fanfare, and I must admit I was impressed because it seemed consistent with his character.]

Carl Bildt is a very different, but equally graceful and serious man. A former Swedish prime minister in his forties, tall and blond, with a military bearing, he is terribly energetic, very bright, and very demanding of his staff. He has been given six weeks by the European Union to reassess the situation in Bosnia and make some proposals. He has also been given very strict guidelines from which he cannot stray. One of these guidelines is that he is not to go to Pale; he is to negotiate with the Bosnian Serbs through Milosevic. I think this restriction is foolish and have told him so.

We had a special briefing this evening by Smith, during which he restated to Bildt and Stoltenberg most of what he has been telling us privately.

Smith made a brilliant summation of the past few months and of our position now. Following the expiration of the COHA at the end of April, the Bosnian government launched two assaults against the Bosnian Serbs, he began. Clearly, both sides used the four-month cease-fire period to prepare for the resumption of military activity.

NATO has lost its air superiority as long as UN troops in Serbian-controlled areas can be taken hostage. The TEZ around Sarajevo is no more, and the WCPS have essentially been abandoned. The UN is effectively in retreat, but there is no withdrawal strategy as yet. "We have already begun to withdraw," Smith said. The act of withdrawal has preceded the planning.

There are too many players in the game, Smith continued. Pale and Belgrade are benefiting from divisions in the international community. We are about to lose all credibility with the Bosnian government.

Smith pointed to the involvement of the Croatian army and the Bosnian Croat army in the Livno Valley in southwestern Bosnia as they advance toward Knin (in the Krajina) and Banja Luka (in northwest Bosnia). He fears the Serbs may try to use air power from Udbina (across the border in the Krajina) or from Banja Luka, either of which will be a violation of the no-fly zone, an act that will call for NATO retaliation. If NATO acts in that situation, then there will be Serb retaliation against UNPROFOR, and UNPROFOR is vulnerable, as the recent hostage crisis has shown.

General Mladic, the Bosnian Serb military commander, is in control in Republika Srpska and wants peace as soon as possible because the Bosnian Serbs are getting weaker and Bosnian government forces are getting stronger. Time is against the Serbs.

The Serbs want a permanent cease-fire because a temporary cease-fire only allows time for Bosnian government forces to strengthen themselves. The Bosnian Serb army is isolated, stubborn, and weak. They have not mounted a major counterattack for months. [The flip side of that statement is that the Bosnian government does not want peace at this time because they are getting stronger. Although I could not blame them for this attitude, in spite of the inability to liberate Sarajevo, clearly the media never described the government's position in this way. When was there ever a news story saying that the Bosnian government opposed peace? Or that the U.S. government was urging them to continue fighting?]

The Bosnian Serbs are restricting UNPROFOR's movement as retaliation for the bombing of Pale, and General Mladic refuses to talk to Smith.

Bosnian military tactics are to nibble away, Smith continued. They fight at a snail's pace: a road here, a road there, high ground here, high ground there. They also attack in several areas simultaneously in order to keep the BSA thinned out. Mladic moves his troops from one front to another under cover of dark and in deteriorating buses. The conflict line is sixteen hundred kilometers long, and the BSA has a shortage in personnel. Meanwhile, the BSA retains an advantage in heavy weapons. Bosnian government forces are reportedly effective with light infantry. Smith believes government forces may win in the long run, including in Sarajevo.

The RRF, as it stands now, is on the far side of a mountain range and cannot reach Sarajevo without flying over the mountains; often, there is fog or rain, weather not good for air transport. Therefore, a quick deployment around Sarajevo cannot be assured, and if the RRF cannot be used rapidly, then why have it? "Where am I going to put them? How am I going to feed them?" Smith asked as he has many times.

The mission is in crisis, Smith continued. "Either send your white vehicles home, and let's have a real fight, or let's leave. You have to ask yourself two questions: Do you want to use force in self-defense, and are you prepared to deal with the escalation that such force produces? If the answer to both questions is *no,* then let's leave. If the answer is *no* to either question, then let's leave. We should stay only if the answer to both questions is *yes.*"

Stoltenberg appreciated Smith's assessment. It is time either to escalate or to leave. Although there seems to be a feeling in Zagreb that a case can be made for muddling through, those of us in the field, on the ground, feel it is time for serious choice, and given the choices Smith has proposed, most of us agree it is time to leave. I certainly believe it is time to leave Bosnia.

Stoltenberg said: "I could never tell my son to risk his life in the Balkans while the men at the top can't agree." This was pure Stoltenberg—a concise and accurate analysis with a personal touch. When there is agreement at the top among the combatants, peace has a chance. But when there is no agreement at the top, there can't be an effective peacekeeping mission.

[My disagreement with Smith was that it seemed to me he favored the use of force under the UN flag. He took note of the option to withdraw completely, but clearly he did not want to go with that option. He wanted a war against the Bosnian Serbs, and he had the moral weight of the international community behind him. As for myself, I didn't want the UN to go to war with a party to the conflict. I wanted everyone to go home.

I recalled Bismarck's remark that "nothing in the Balkans is worth the bones of a single Pomeranian grenadier."

"We are living in the middle of an armed society at war with itself," Smith concluded.

I had the greatest regard for Smith. He was not some sort of Dr. Strangelove, who loved war. He had a job to do, and he believed that if he were to do his job, then he ought to be allowed to do it properly, whatever course it took. I, a civilian, was not about to second-guess the military judgment of a field commander with the awesome responsibility of protecting twenty-seven thousand troops. Smith was an honorable and responsible wartime leader.

But he was also the best general the Bosnian government had.]

24 June 1995

At the morning briefing in Smith's office we spoke about international matters more than we usually do. It was the influence of Bildt and Stoltenberg's presence.

NATO Secretary-General Willy Claes has warned against the danger of withdrawing UN peacekeepers. There are rumblings again in world capitals about our ineffectiveness and about our vulnerability in the wake of the hostage crisis. Though it has never been made public, Malaysia actually approached the UN Secretary-General once its troops were released by the Bosnian Serbs and said Malaysia wanted to withdraw its contingent from Bosnia. Malaysia has been tenderly cajoled and assured, however, that UNPROFOR will take the necessary measures in future to protect all its contingents, and Malaysia has relented. [At the time, I wondered: Could soldiers refuse to serve unless they received prior assurance there would not be any danger to them?] Other countries, particularly Moslem countries, have also been expressing concern for the safety of their troops. The Serbs are known to hate UNPROFOR's Moslem troops most of all.

Meanwhile, in a rare display of objectivity, the UN Security Council has condemned the restrictions of movement placed by *all* parties against UNPROFOR troops. Particular criticism has been leveled at the Bosnian government's restriction of the 565 Canadian troops stationed at Visoko, which is about twenty kilometers northwest of Sarajevo. My protests and those of Canadian officers in Bosnia and Zagreb apparently moved Ottawa and were finally acknowledged in New York. Because of ongoing government military operations in the area, Bosnian government forces have virtually sealed in the Canadian contingent. The Canadians are not allowed to leave their compound, and they are not allowed to have supply trucks come into the compound. Observation posts have been surrounded and rendered ineffective. The Canadians are virtual hostages. Appeals by Smith to the Bosnian government have been treated with characteristic duplicity. At first, the Bosnian government denied the restrictions placed on the Canadians. Then they said the restrictions had been lifted. Then they said there had been a delay in transmitting to local commanders the instructions to lift the restrictions. Meanwhile, the Canadians remain hostage while the Bosnian government continues its military activities.

The Bosnian government, like the Serbs and the Croats, consider all foreign troops to be spies. They believe that if the Canadians are allowed freedom of movement, they will transmit information about government military positions to the Serbs.

Finally, I assume, the Canadian government has intervened and pressured the Security Council to criticize the Bosnian government.

The next item we discussed was a recent ministorm created by an article by Roger Cohen of the *New York Times*. He had obtained access to a letter Akashi wrote to Karadzic, attempting to allay Karadzic's anxieties about the arrival of the RRF. Cohen implied Akashi is trying to undermine the RRF, that he is assuaging the Serbs when he should be denouncing them, and that he is virtually promising the Serbs that the RRF will not be used against them, when that is exactly what Cohen and the Bosnian government want the RRF to be used for. The U.S. State Department is calling once again for Akashi's resignation, and Madeleine Albright, then U.S. permanent representative to the UN, is demanding to see Akashi's letter. To his credit, however, Boutros Boutros-Ghali refuses to release the letter, and to Akashi's credit, he has remained calm and has said nothing publicly.

The fact is that Akashi's letter is perfectly understandable and reasonable. Pale is certain that the RRF is arriving to blast its way through Mount Igman. Of course, they are right, and we all knew that they are right, but there is no evidence for that, and Akashi has to promote as much calm as possible in the hope of creating a proper atmosphere for negotiations. In that spirit, he wrote a letter to Karadzic, quoting or summarizing statements *already made* by the Secretary-General and by the Security Council in its resolutions regarding the goals of the RRF. There was nothing original, controversial, or distorted in Akashi's letter. The intent was to calm down the situation, not to inflame it, in the wake of the hostage crisis and the NATO bombing in Pale less than a month ago. Besides, Karadzic contacted Akashi and asked for clarification about the intentions of the RRF. Akashi was only responding to a request from a local leader.

But Cohen and the Reptiles are on a crusade. They have a cause and are practicing advocacy journalism at its lowest. They are building a case against Akashi.

Next, we turned to Gorazde. There is still a problem getting convoys through. The BSA is blocking us, and there are still problems in bringing convoys into Sarajevo, unless we bring them through Belgrade. Karadzic's promise to us that aid convoys to Sarajevo would not be blocked has never been implemented.

Meanwhile, Bosnian government forces are now proposing that UNPROFOR should give twenty-four-hour notice to them if it wants to pass through a government checkpoint. The government will allow no freedom of movement without prior notice. Smith calls this attitude "flat noncooperation."

He says that we will have to assert ourselves. We cannot accept this idea of having to give twenty-four-hour notice.

[In effect, the Bosnian government was doing what the Serbs had been doing for months. Still, having lost of freedom of movement to the BSA, we could not afford now to lose our freedom of movement to government forces. Besides, we were preparing to use force to restore our freedom of movement in BSA territory. We would never use force against the Bosnian government.]

The worry is that government forces don't have the infrastructure to implement extensive checking, which means that delays will be very long at every checkpoint while a foot soldier attempts to get clearance from his superiors in Sarajevo. It is a mushrooming mess. On past occasions, when government officials tried these tactics, they backed down. A mixture of cajolery and threat behind the scenes usually convinced them that UN-PROFOR was their friend, even if not yet their mercenary. But their stance is hardening as UNPROFOR continues to lose credibility in their eyes. We have now withdrawn from the WCPs, have temporarily surrendered the capacity for using air power against the Bosnian Serbs, and still can't guarantee food to Sarajevo—all these factors have virtually destroyed our credibility with the Bosnian government. They are in an angry mood and have ample justification for their anger.

Next, Alex Ivanko, our civilian spokesman, intervened. He asked why the French stationed at the bottom of Mount Igman don't fire back more at the Bosnian Serbs when UNHCR convoys are fired at? What are they afraid of? Collateral damage? Nonsense.

[Imagine this! A low-ranking information officer, with no prior UN experience, showing to Bildt and Stoltenberg and any other big name that he was politically correct and could bash the Serbs and UNPROFOR as well as anybody.

Ivanko had an interesting background. His father had been a well-known Russian diplomat, and Ivanko had spent many years in Washington. He had worked for a decade as an editor for the Hearst Corporation. His English was perfect, and his feeling for sensationalism was highly developed. As a Russian citizen, he took particular pains to show he was anti-Serb in order to establish his credibility with the Bosnian government. During his tenure in Sarajevo, he consistently made inflammatory statements against the Serbs.

In contrast to Ivanko, Lt. Col. Gary Coward, spokesman for General Smith, was much more balanced, better informed, and less politicized than Ivanko, just as the British (and the French), because they had troops on the ground, were more balanced in their approach to Bosnia than the Washington cowboys. When I had a piece of news that I thought might be relevant for the daily press conference, I went to Colonel Coward, rather than to Ivanko, with it—not out of spite, but in the hope that it would be presented objectively. As I was fond of saying, John Wayne belonged in Hollywood, not in Bosnia.]

Smith acknowledged Ivanko's comments, then continued with his analysis. He was politely unflappable.

Stoltenberg left this morning, but Bildt stayed for lunch, and my next struggle turned out to be with Smith's attaché, Colonel James Baxter. He is a huge, broad-shouldered, former rugby player, a moose of a fellow, fiercely loyal to Smith, and consistently antagonistic to Civil Affairs. He doesn't take civilians seriously and seems to think it is his duty to usurp what little privilege we have.

[Once, when I was on my way to see Smith, Baxter stopped me outside of Smith's office and asked what my business was with the general; perhaps he could help me, rather than having me bother Smith. I told him, and later Smith, that I was not obligated to get anyone's permission to talk to Smith. I reminded Baxter that Smith and I were at the same level.

On another occasion, Baxter had a bitter quarrel with my predecessor, Enrique Aguilar, when Baxter tried to evict Civil Affairs from the main building and give our office space to the military. Aguilar won that one, but it was a very unpleasant experience. These matters may seem petty, but they were indicative of an attitude. UN Civil Affairs was not taken seriously by the British military. On still another occasion, when I decided to transfer one of my staff to Tuzla, Baxter intervened with John Almstrom, Akashi's military advisor in Zagreb, and tried to have the transfer reversed because the staff member was a friend of his. Baxter concocted a transparent and obviously dishonest story that the staff member was working on a project in cooperation with the military and that she should be allowed to stay for an indefinite period until the project was finished. Finally, I won, and the staff member was transferred. After the fact, Baxter and I reached an understanding in principle that he would stay out of my business. After all, I said to him, I wouldn't presume to approach Smith on matters involving Baxter's staff.

On political matters, Baxter was even worse. He considered himself a political analyst, even though he maintained officially that he had no interest in politics. One could hear him frequently expounding loudly on the telephone, to the distraction of everyone in the front office, about the latest political development in the region, about Smith's most recent contact with the Bosnian government or with London, or about why "General Rupert" should be canonized. There is no doubt that Baxter was an aggressively loyal, zealous, and diligent British officer, and for those qualities I respected him. But he was also a bully and generally antagonistic to Civil Affairs.]

Before Bildt arrived, I asked Baxter about Bildt's itinerary, for which Baxter was responsible. Could I see a copy? Sure, Baxter said (he never would have given me one if I hadn't asked), but I shouldn't worry about briefing Bildt. "He wants only a military briefing."

"Bullshit!" I said. "He's a political figure. He's been appointed by the European Union to find a political solution to the problem in Bosnia. How can he not want a political briefing?"

"Well, there's no time for a political briefing. You see, he has a tight schedule. He has to leave right after lunch."

"Who made his schedule?"

Pause. "We spoke to him in Geneva about his itinerary. He said he didn't need a political briefing. Besides, General Rupert can say a few things."

"I don't believe you. I don't believe Bildt said he didn't want a political briefing. Look, I don't want to have to discuss this matter with General Smith . . ."

"Oh, there's no need to do that."

"Good. Then I would appreciate it if you would revise the schedule to give me a few minutes, say ten."

The briefings were scheduled before lunch. Bildt had with him General Bernard de la Presle (a former UNPROFOR force commander), a British general, Christopher Elliot, and a U.S. colonel—the latter two in civilian clothes. I had never met the Brit or the American; as for de la Presle, he was one of the most astute, balanced, and elegant officers I met all the time I was in former Yugoslavia. After several military officers spoke, Smith's chief of staff, General Nikolai, a Dutch soldier and a very decent man with whom I have always had good relations, turned the floor over to me.

I made seven points very quickly, most of which I had already made in my reports to Akashi, and offered to elaborate on them later if Bildt wanted me to do so.

1. The Bosnian government want UNPROFOR either to be its mercenaries or to get out of Bosnia. In coming months, the Bosnian government would be mounting a propaganda campaign to discredit UNPROFOR in the hope that UNPROFOR would be replaced by NATO and by a commitment to arm the Bosnians.

2. The Bosnian Serbs want an international peace conference as part of a campaign to undermine the Contact Group Plan. They want to internationalize the issue, whereas the Bosnian government wants to localize the issue, to keep it at the level of Sarajevo.

3. The peace process has been Balkanized. Too many cooks, too many envoys, too many messages. There should be one organization handling the peace process.

4. Credibility. Instead of worrying about UNPROFOR's credibility, we

should realize that the warring parties themselves have no credibility. They are the ones who lie and constantly break agreements.

5. The current government offensive to capture roads and mountains will not be successful. The Bosnian government has a low threshhold for casualties. They will take heavy losses and retreat.

6. Bringing the United States on board as a part of the peace process is a problem. Washington has its own agenda. We might have had an end to the war two years earlier if the United States had not urged the Bosnian government to keep fighting.

7. Just as, militarily, the Serbs have no way to go but down, so the Bosnian government has no way to go but down because it now has the moral high ground. Seen from this perspective, now might be a favorable time to reach an accord. Both sides are at a peak. The Serbs want peace, albeit on their terms, but we have to convince the Bosnians, who are winning, slowly but surely, that it is in their interest to have peace now.

By the time I had reached point two, Bildt's party, which had put away its notebooks following the last military briefing, began to take notes again. I say that not to boast of my speaking capacities, but to emphasize that it was clear Bildt wanted a political briefing, and it appeared he had been told either that there was no time for one or that it would be largely irrelevant because Baxter & Co. would touch all the important bases.

While I was in the middle of my last point, one of the Brits intervened to say that lunch was ready, and we had to go. Bildt said quickly that he wanted to continue our discussion and asked me to sit next to him at lunch. De la Presle remarked that he was grateful someone with an American accent had said the things I said, and the American colonel, a young and very energetic man, asked me for some elaboration on my points. During lunch, Bildt asked me innumerable questions and instructed one of his staff to take notes. Meanwhile, my deputy, John Ryan, on his own initiative brought Bildt three or four of my most recent reports to Zagreb, reports that were notoriously undiplomatic and frank. Bildt was very appreciative and immediately demanded to know why he had not been given these reports beforehand. In any case, he wanted to see them in future.

We heard this morning that the Bosnian Serb leadership in Pale has refused to see Pedauye. They are still angry about Smith's bombing raids on Pale three weeks ago. As for Bildt, he doesn't have permission from the European Union to go to Pale.

In my reports to UNPROFOR headquarters in Zagreb, I have been suggesting that Bildt should go to Pale. Two hours in Pale are worth more than ten thousand Rapid Reaction Force troops, I said, an attitude that no doubt has not endeared me to either Zagreb, Brussels, or the Bosnian government, all of whom monitor whatever I or anybody else says because there are no secrets in former Yugoslavia.

"Time is the school in which we learn, / Time is the fire in which we burn," wrote Delmore Schwarz, an American poet. Time is on the side of the Bosnian Serbs in that the longer the war remains unresolved, the longer the current confrontation lines will seem to be permanent borders. But time is against the Bosnian Serbs in that the longer the conflict continues, the better the Bosnian government army gets, under American instruction, and the more stress is placed on the Bosnian Serbs. Their fuel shortages are becoming critical. Their manpower situation is becoming critical. We can learn from our experience; in that sense, time is a school. But if we do not learn from our experience, then time is the fire in which we will continue to burn.

In a few days, on 27–28 June, European foreign ministers will meet in Cannes. Stoltenberg will report to them. Bildt will report to them. The foreign ministers will probably make a recommendation on whether UNPROFOR should stay or leave. They will probably ask us to stay.

The Bosnian government believes the arms embargo will be lifted if UNPROFOR leaves, so they are going to increase their harassment of UNPROFOR personnel in order to convince them to leave. During his trip to Washington recently, Prime Minister Haris Siladzic of Bosnia was told that NATO was *not yet* ready to replace UNPROFOR. The best he can hope for now would be a lifting of the arms embargo, and that is not at all certain because it would require the compliance of France, the United Kingdom, and Russia in the UN Security Council. The Bosnian government, however, has not given up on the idea of having NATO replace UNPROFOR. They will continue to flog that issue. Meanwhile, as my old friend General Alexander Perelyakin, the Russian commander in Sector East in Croatia, used to say: "NATO is already here; they only have to change uniforms."

25 June 1995

At the 8:30 A.M. briefing, Smith expressed his concern that UNPF [UNPROFOR headquarters in Zagreb had been renamed United Nations Peace Forces under a new mandate; UNPROFOR in Bosnia remained UNPROFOR, and UNPROFOR in Croatia had been renamed UNCRO] is focusing its attention too much on Croatia in the wake of the invasion last month by Croatian government forces of the former Sector West (Western Slavonia). The refugee problem and severe human rights violations continue there, but certain problems in Bosnia will also not go away. The Bosnian government offensive has stalled, but is not over. There is war in Bosnia and it cannot be ignored.

[It was nothing short of astonishing to hear a complaint that the UN and the international community were paying too much attention to Croatia at the expense of Bosnia. In my almost two years in Croatia, I complained bitterly about the opposite. I kept insisting that Croatia was not a suburb of Bosnia and that until a settlement could be made between Serbia and Croatia, both of which had brought their war to Bosnia, there would never be peace in Bosnia. The settlement had to begin in Croatia, not in Bosnia. I still believed.]

Smith went on. There are serious problems of command and control with the RRF. Where are its orders coming from? UNPF headquarters in Zagreb? London? Paris? NATO headquarters in Brussels? Where is it going to be stationed? It had better get installed soon because its quarters will have to be winterized.

An UNPROFOR convoy is being blocked outside of Gornji Vakuf by Bosnian government forces. The Bosnian government military, which is either conducting a military operation or preparing to conduct one, want UNPROFOR to withdraw its observation posts in Sector Southwest, which is headquartered at Gorni Vakuf. Withdrawal of the OPs would allow the Bosnian government freedom of movement in the region, freedom from UNPROFOR eyes. But we cannot agree to that, Smith said. What to do? We will have to come up with a plan. First off, Smith will talk to Bosnian Vice President Eyup Ganic; Smith will appeal through the usual channels, but we doubt that the appeals will work. The Bosnian government will either deny that any restriction of movement exists, or say that instructions have already been given to lift it or that a local commander misunderstood the policy, and so on.

In the Balkans there is a symbiotic relationship between ineptitude and machination, between byzantine bureaucracy and pernicious plotting. One never knows if something doesn't get done because the people in charge are simply incompetent or because it is part of a scheme (or a scam), but the result is the same. Promises are seldom kept. The Bosnian government might agree to whatever Smith requested, but they won't honor their agreement. The Serbs seldom do either.

The Bosnian government commander in Gorazde is again demanding notification twenty-four hours in advance before he will allow any movement by UNPROFOR. We will not agree to that demand, Smith said.

There have been incidents in Srebrenica. Both sides are complaining about intrusion by the other side. The Bosnian government has twenty-five hundred troops inside of Srebrenica and will frequently shell and harass Serbian villages on the fringes of the town. The BSA, for its part, frequently lobs shells into the town. We have to devise a strategy, Smith reminded his staff, for what will happen if the BSA attacks and tries to overrun Srebrenica. We still have UNPROFOR soldiers inside the enclave who might be taken hostage. Three hundred lightly armed Dutch soldiers.

Someone at the briefing asked a question about the RRF. The French contingent of the RRF is scheduled to start moving today out of Ploce, Croatia, and into Bosnia. Their intent is to be completely in place within a week. The British contingent of the RRF is scheduled to start arriving in Ploce on 12 July. There are still major problems, however. The Bosnian government is saying that the RRF is not covered under the existing SOFA between itself and UNPROFOR. They refuse to allow RRF elements across the border into Bosnia and to provide sanitation facilities. They want more money, more information, more control. They want to know, among other things, what the RRF's mission is supposed to be. Is it coming to protect UNPROFOR or to protect Bosnia? In other words, will we finally be the Bosnian government's mercenaries, or will the RRF interfere with the Bosnian army's operations and be used against it? Will the RRF secure the road over Mount Igman? And what about supplying Gorazde?

Smith told us that Foreign Minister Muhamed Sacirbey told him recently that if UNPROFOR pushes the Bosnian government too hard on the issue of freedom of movement, then the Bosnian government will lose politically, no matter how many gains its army has made. He appealed for Smith's understanding, but Smith, to his credit, said we should continue to push all the parties for freedom of movement. [The larger questions were, how forcefully should we push, and should we go public with our protests against the Bosnian army and the Croatian army, as we almost always did against the Bosnian Serbs? I could not imagine that we would ever use force against the Bosnian government, although many UN soldiers in the field would have been quite ready to do so in light of the abuse to which they had been subjected by the BiH army.]

Smith is clearly frustrated by what he sees as the disarray in political capitals about the mission of the RRF, and he is right. In the field, at the ground level, one feels isolated and is always resentful about what appears to be the illogicality of policy in the capitals. This lack of clear direction is particularly frustrating to the military, which wants a clear objective and unambiguous orders. Smith wants to use the RRF, principally against the BSA, and sees himself blocked by bureaucrats distant to the daily struggle of life in Sarajevo. The cross purposes of the permanent members of the UN Security Council, together with the tug of their domestic constituencies, add up to disarray, indecisiveness, and confusion.

Nor can greed be underestimated in assessing resistance to the RRF. Both the Bosnian Croats in southwestern Bosnia and the Sarajevo government want more money to host the RRF. [It was bovine politics again: the UN was a cow to be milked. Get as much as you can as often as you can from the UN.]

Finally, there is the matter of attention. The Bosnian Croats feel slighted. Attention is always being focused on the Moslems in Bosnia, they complain.

International dignitaries always visit the Moslems, but seldom the Croats. The press concentrate on the Moslems. But the RRF will have to pass through Bosnian Croat territory in order to deploy in the hills around Sarajevo. Bosnian Croat forces, which supported the Bosnian government army with artillery, want to be treated separately and equally by the international community. The Bosnian Croats have never agreed to be subsumed by the Moslem government in Sarajevo. They have their own ambitions, their own army, and their own roadblocks.

Late this morning, I left for Pale to meet with Professor Koljevic. He was in a somber mood. Republica Srpska is still angry with UNPROFOR and is not yet ready to resume relations with us. At the same time, following a few intermediate steps, it may be willing to talk again to Akashi and Janvier and Smith. But for now, I am the highest official with whom they will speak.

I asked Koljevic if he wants UNPROFOR to remain in Bosnia. He answered in the affirmative, saying that UNPROFOR's presence will lower the intensity of the war. What the Serbs want at this point, he said, is to return to the battle lines of 23 December 1994, when the cease-fire had been agreed upon, prior to the COHA. "If the Moslems want war, they can have war, but we are ready to negotiate." He doesn't want a cease-fire, however; he wants long-term negotiations at the highest level, concerning all the problems of former Yugoslavia, not just a discussion of local issues such as restoring utilities to Sarajevo. He also repeated his mistrust of UNPROFOR. He recalled: "We withdrew from Igman to create an atmosphere for negotiations, then negotiations broke down, and we lost Igman."

[He was right on this point. On more than one occasion, when the UN had been able to convince the BSA to pull back from a position by promising that UNPROFOR would take it over, Bosnian government forces had then seized that position from the UN. It happened in the hills around Gorazde and on portions of Mount Igman. At the end of July 1993, after protracted negotiations, UNPROFOR had convinced the Serbs to give up control of a part of Mount Igman, specifically that part of the road between Tarcin and Butmir. The road led directly to the Sarajevo airport, through Dobrinje. The road remained demilitarized, under UNPROFOR control for a few weeks, but then it was taken over by the Bosnian government army as soon as the government finished building a tunnel (large enough for people, but not vehicles) under the airport runway. By September 1993, the Bosnian army controlled the road, which made possible in some small measure the supply of fruits and vegetables and medicines for Sarajevo, as well as the transport of small arms and munitions. One could then drive over Mount Igman, preferably at night, arrive at the airport runway, unload his vehicle, and auction his goods inside the tunnel. Local merchants, after having bought what they could afford, could then transport their wares into Sarajevo. But the tunnel was a small one (1.2 meters wide, 1.6 meters high, and 760 meters long), and was controlled by corrupt generals who charged exorbitant fees to anyone wanting to use it. It was closed to foreigners, except for highly privileged individuals, including Viktor Jakovic, who was the U.S. ambassador at the time. International photographers unsuccessfully offered up to five thousand German marks to photograph it. Understandably, the tunnel was considered essential to national security.]

So the BSA does not trust turning over any more territory to UNPROFOR. At the same time, there is the sticky issue of sovereignty. It is difficult for the UN to deny a sovereign government recognized by the UN the right to reoccupy its own territory.

Clearly, UNPROFOR is virtually the only one speaking to the Bosnian Serbs at this point, a privilege that both the UN and Pale want to preserve. Others have to go through Milosevic to reach Pale. I myself believe it is important for UNPROFOR to maintain contact with Pale, and that is why I continue to see Koljevic. The Bosnian government, however, resents my contact with Pale. They want Pale completely isolated.

Pale generally sees UNPROFOR as its main channel to the outside world. Karadzic has his feud with Milosevic and doesn't particularly want to rely on Russia either, which is having its own problems with Chechenya. Given the choices, even a hostile UNPROFOR, which just bombed Pale, is preferable to complete isolation. Meanwhile, Koljevic has expressed his anger with Akashi for a recent statement in which Akashi tried to place equal blame on both sides for the current hostilities in Bosnia. The Moslems started the offensive, Koljevic insists. But the Serbs will put an end to it, he adds.

Koljevic says that his first priority is to resume humanitarian convoys to the enclaves and throughout Bosnia, but he will not accept armed UNPROFOR escorts for them. He blames the Bosnian government for interdicting several convoys [he was correct on this one], mentioning specifically the shelling of a UNHCR convoy while it was off-loading in Rajlovac, a Serbian area of Sarajevo. He asserts that on several occasions the Serbs let UNHCR convoys through, only to have them interdicted or shelled by the Bosnian government. He wishes that the international community would make public the harassment of convoys by the Bosnian government. He also argues that the Bosnian government has purposely prevented humanitarian convoys from reaching their own people so that they can retain their image as victims.

On the question of Rajlovac, he is right. After having off-loaded in a government-controlled area of Sarajevo, UNHCR trucks were shelled by Bosnian government forces while in Rajlovac. Of course, I said to Koljevic, the BSA continually pounded Bosnian civilians in Sarajevo, including those standing in line at the water pumps, so the Bosnian government was retaliating. But, Koljevic retorted, such shelling allegedly done by the BSA was in reality being done by the Bosnian government in order to gain international condemnation against the Serbs. [As for the shelling in Rajlovac, when I brought the issue up to the Bosnian government, Muratovic replied that the Serbian police, which had accompanied the UNHCR convoy, as we had agreed, was a hostile element in Sarajevo. It was perfectly logical that the Bosnian government should fire on Serbian police.] Regarding Koljevic's wish to go public with accounts of the Bosnian government's shelling of Serb villages, I reminded him that the Serbs will not allow the international press or our UN monitors (under threat of being taken hostage) to be present in the Serb areas to verify Bosnian government shelling. How can we report what we can't verify? I asked.

Meanwhile, Koljevic proposed a modified strategy for UNHCR convoys. On Srebrenica, he said that Serbian police can escort them to the last Serbian checkpoint and then turn the convoy over to the UNHCR field officer to decide on how to proceed from there. Serbian police can also continue to escort convoys into Sarajevo.

I replied that I could not speak for UNHCR, but that I doubted if his proposal would be acceptable. It has been tried before. One of the reasons why UNPROFOR APC escorts are needed is to provide a haven for drivers when they are being shelled, as they were in Rajlovac. Besides, the presence of Serbian police in Bosnian government areas is a provocation. Finally, UNPROFOR has as part of its mandate the responsibility to assist in the delivery of humanitarian aid. In fact, it has been authorized to use force, if necessary, to assist in the delivery of humanitarian aid. We cannot surrender that obligation.

Koljevic's next point was that following the successful resumption of aid convoys to the people, he will concentrate on the resupply of UNPROFOR. At that point, he will ask for a high-level meeting between UNPROFOR officials and Bosnian Serb authorities to discuss normalization of relations. First, though, he repeated, "we need intermediary steps to create a healthy political atmosphere for negotiations with UNPROFOR. Those steps will be the success of several aid convoys. At the meeting with UNPROFOR, we can then discuss restoration of utilities to Sarajevo and other problems."

[First, the proper political climate, then negotiations. He had his priority list. I was struck at that point, as I constantly was when talking with Balkan officials, not only by the way they tried to manipulate any discussion to their own advantage (that was to be expected) but also by the way they talked *down* to the United Nations. Of the three constituent peoples in Croatia and Bosnia, the Serbs were actually the most polite to UN officials. The Croatians hated us, and the Bosnian government barely tolerated us. Once, in fact, while in Croatia, I lost my temper during a meeting with a small-town Croatian mayor, who was shouting at me, making impossible demands on UNPROFOR and slanderously insulting the UN mission. I reminded him, "You are a small-town mayor in a country of a few million people; the United Nations represents 185 member states, including your own." Blah, blah, blah. I suppose I sounded terribly pompous, but he seemed shocked by my rejoinder.

On the other hand, Koljevic was never directly insulting. He was only condescending, perhaps a more subtle form of insult. He knew or suspected how precarious the Bosnian Serb position was. Their army was being pressed. Their opponents were getting sophisticated military equipment, as well as military training from the West. The Bosnian Serbs had no diplomatic support. They had to make peace, and the UN was their best hope for an impartial interlocutor.

But even Koljevic, or Mladic for that matter, despite all of the Bosnian Serbs' anxieties, did not suspect the terrible magnitude of NATO's fire power. The Serbs saw themselves as some sort of Vietcong, who would stand up to NATO. The comparison was frivolous, however. The Vietcong had had the former Soviet Union, China, and the socialist camp on their side. The Bosnian Serbs had almost nobody. Not even Serbia.

In fact, one of the great miscalculations of Serb military strength in the former Yugoslavia was made by Russian military intelligence (GRU). Out of a wish to strike a blow at NATO hegemony and out of revenge for having lost the Cold War, the GRU constantly overestimated the Serbs' ability, after summer 1994, to withstand Croatian and/or Bosnian offensives. Washington also tended to overestimate the military strength of the Bosnian Serbs, at least publicly, albeit for different reasons. It wanted to portray the Bosnian government as a victim; it wanted to increase pressure for lifting the arms embargo against them; and it wanted to discourage the deployment of American troops against a ruthless Serb army. Of course, it is not unusual to misrepresent the military strength of a warring party. It has always been done. In Bosnia, the result was that the BSA was made to appear one of the great fighting forces of the world, while in reality General Mladic was transporting his troops from one front to another in broken-down school buses, was constantly faced with desertions, and had trouble defending an overextended front line.]

Koljevic then turned to the Contact Group Plan, by which the Bosnian Serbs would retain 49 percent of the territory. He said the RS is prepared to begin negotiations on the basis of the plan, a concession they have never made before, but he added so many qualifications for accepting the plan that it would be virtually impossible to proceed. [This was Balkan diplomacy again. Say *yes* when you mean *no,* say *no* when you mean *maybe,* say *maybe* when you mean *yes*.] "We want to begin negotiations on the basis of viability, on economic issues, and on communications. Then, you proceed to the map. Don't start with the map."

"But that's not what the plan says," I reminded him. "First you accept the plan, and then you have a couple of years to adjust it, to allow for economic viability and so on."

"No. That's just what we're afraid of. If we accept the plan, and the Moslems refuse to allow alterations, then we're stuck with the original version of the plan, and that's unacceptable. It's like this: we're now at point A. If we accept the plan, we go to point B. If the Moslems refuse any changes, then we'll never get to point C, and we won't ever be able to go back to point A. We're stuck at point B."

We spoke of other things. "The Moslem offensive has made the Security Council resolutions null and void," Koljevic said. "We don't recognize the no-fly zone any longer. We'll use air power if we have to."

On the RRF: "The Serbs would like to see humanitarian aid resume because it will mean there is less need to use the RRF. We don't want a bloody war with the British; I know how stubborn they are. They want a fight, but we don't want to give them the opportunity to start one. But if the Moslems don't want the RRF, then why should we accept it?"

"You have no choice," I said.

"I know that," he said surprisingly. "That's why I want to resume humanitarian aid."

Koljevic was nervous during our talk. We were alone. He changed subjects frequently. He sipped scotch, he puffed on a cigar, he talked about his family. He even talked about a book he wanted to write on Shakespeare. "But there are already too many books on Shakespeare. One more isn't needed," he said.

Koljevic's idea for a book (I am oversimplifying it here) was that Shakespeare always placed his heroes in situations where they couldn't operate. That was his way of creating dramatic tension.

[Alas! The more I got to know Nikola Koljevic, the more I was convinced he was unhappy with the inhumane policies of Karadzic and Mladic. He was a nationalist and Milosevic's man, but he was also a humanist. He didn't like ethnic cleansing, he didn't like mass murders, he didn't like war, and he didn't like the war profiteering that was going on. He was sick of it all. He would frequently tell me he was going to leave politics, that he was unable to change Karadzic's policies, but he was unable to leave. Where would he go? He saw the impending doom of NATO intervention. He may not have been of Shakespearean stature, but like one of the Shakespearean heroes that he admired so much, he himself had been placed in a situation in which he couldn't operate effectively. The book he wanted to write was, finally, about a projection of himself. I truly believed that his conscience bothered him for having to be associated with and for having to be a spokesman for this dirty war.]

Finally, Koljevic closed our meeting by telling me that our talk today was a "private" talk, not a formal talk. Perhaps next time we would not even meet in his office as we had today, but rather in a coffee shop, because he wanted to make clear that our meeting does not mean a normalization of relations with UNPROFOR. I said I understood his feelings.

The most unkindest cut of all during our meeting was that he did not offer lunch, a sure sign of disaffection, considering the traditions of Serbian hospitality. In fact, the Serbian security officer who accompanied us back to Lukavica mentioned that fact as soon as we left. Koljevic's bad hospitality, in other words, was not spontaneous. It had been planned and neatly staged, as were so many events in the Balkans.

At the 6:00 P.M. briefing, Smith expressed his concern about the 565 Canadians who are still virtual hostages of Bosnian government forces at Visoko. They cannot leave their camp. Supplies cannot get in. The Bosnian government has again offered to let the Canadians out if they are willing to give up two OPs near the confrontation line. Smith has refused.

I reported on my meeting with Koljevic. He had seemed more conciliatory than usual, I said, even though he had made a show of not wanting to hold "formal" talks. He had expressed the inclination to allow convoys into Sarajevo. UNHCR received a similar message from its talks in Pale. (UNHCR occasionally has contact with Pale.)

If we can get convoys past the BSA into Sarajevo, Smith remarked, it will be a great achievement.

"I think Koljevic is a bit scared at this point," I said.

"Let's not do anything to dispel that feeling," Smith said.

We then heard an analysis from our G-2 (intelligence officer) about the general situation.

1. The COHA had been successful because it had been in place during winter (January–April 1995), when military offensives were difficult because of the snow and mountainous terrain. Since the end of the COHA, however, UNPROFOR has lost control of the Sarajevo airport to the BSA, and has lost freedom of movement through the Sierras. As a result, it has lost all credibility with the Bosnian government.

2. This may be the last year of the war. The populations are tired. The Bosnian government is losing support in the international community, more out of indifference than because of any changes in political policy, and the BSA is weakening militarily.

3. Mladic is in charge in Pale. Karadzic is becoming a figurehead. In order

for Mladic to strengthen his forces, he will have to move against the eastern enclaves. They are a thorn in his back. By taking over Srebrenica he can release ten divisions, which he needs at the front. Also, the enclaves cannot be defended except by air strikes—wide-ranging, disproportionate air strikes for which we have no authority at present.

Does the G-2 think Mladic will try to take over the enclaves? one officer inquired.

"Depends on how strapped he is for troops. He's had no real successes for awhile, and that would be a morale booster."

"It may depend on what price Mladic thinks he has to pay," someone added.

"Problem is," Smith said, "we have very little intelligence on what Mladic's movements are."

"How about satellite intelligence?" I asked naïvely.

"UNPROFOR has no satellite," someone in the back said.

"But NATO does. Do they share it?"

"Afraid not," said the G-2, himself an American.

26 June 1995

The Bosnian government's attempts to liberate Sarajevo continue, albeit with less intensity. There has been sporadic shelling throughout the day. One hears the cracks of rifles from time to time; especially in the early morning hours.

Life goes on in Sarajevo, but with harsh alterations. There are stories of people who went away for a weekend before the war started and have never been able to return. Some people infiltrate every night through mined mountain passes in order to return to their homes or to seek refuge because their villages have been overrun. And scores of men, of all ethnicities, flee Sarajevo in order to avoid the draft. We estimate that 70 percent of the population of Sarajevo is non-Sarajevan.

It is eerie coming over Igman at night, careening in and out through a flurry of clandestine activity on that twisting, rutted mountain road. One always notices the vehicles that have gone over the side. In the darkness they are indefinite masses of iron: wheels askew, doors asunder, windows broken, bodies removed. How ridiculous it is to try to negotiate those sharp curves in an armored vehicle that is too wide and too top-heavy. Really quite stupid.

For nights now, I have been sleeping in my office. Sometimes when a dignitary comes to visit Sarajevo, I have to give up my bed and office, the penultimate sacrifice, and spend the night in my apartment. On such occasions, I usually take a jug of water and a candle with me, but it is difficult carrying water in a bouncing armored car, so I usually take only a small jug, tightly capped. A bucket would be too much. The streets are deeply rutted, whether from mortar shells or disrepair. Not meant for comfortable driving.

People here before me recall the periods of relative "normalcy" in Sarajevo. During the COHA, one could walk the streets. Utilities functioned. Restaurants (which still operate), and even a few movie theaters, were open. Not much hope, but a small respite. Now there is siege. Tension. Death.

The other day we took a wrong turn in downtown Sarajevo, went down the block, and turned around to come back. While we were turning, we were pelted several times by sniper bullets. Thud, thud. Like pebbles they sounded. Very quickly they became more frequent. Within seconds it sounded as if we were being pelted by a barrage of hailstones. "Is that noise what I think it is?" I asked our driver, a young Danish soldier.

"Yes, they're bullets. But don't worry, they're small rounds. They can't penetrate our armor. We don't have to worry unless they use ten-millimeter rounds. Or mortars."

"Is there usually so much sniper activity here?" I asked.

"Not usually. But it's unpredictable. You know, there's no such thing as *one* sniper alley. There are a lot of sniper allies in Sarajevo. You can go someplace downtown for days, and it's okay. Then suddenly you have a storm of bullets. It's crazy."

"Yes, crazy," I said.

At the 8:15 A.M. news reading in my office, we were told that the Bosnian government media reported Serb troop movements around Gorazde. They also reported that Yugoslav troops are coming across the Drina River to support an assault on Srebrenica. We all laugh, even our interpreter, who is a Bosnian Croat and hated by the Sarajevo government. Nobody believes the local news. Nobody believes any news in Sarajevo.

Bosnian government news reports claimed that on 6 July the Security Council in New York is to discuss the issue of sanctions against Yugoslavia. The United States is leading the charge against lifting them.

Next, a comment by the Bosnian foreign minister, Muhamed Sacirbey: Bosnia doesn't need UNPROFOR, he insists, and his government doesn't care if UNPROFOR leaves.

From Croatia, Hovje Sarenic, who is the government minister in charge of cooperation with UNPF, a very important portfolio, has told Akashi that Croatia is prepared to defend itself against Yugoslavia, which is now sending troops, tanks, and helicopters to the Krajina.

None of us believes Sarenic—that Yugoslavia is sending forces to Krajina. Quite to the contrary, it seems Croatia has decided to attack Krajina and is building a case for doing so by saying it is about to be attacked. In fact, the Croatian government has been very effective in employing a combination of

Communist *agitprop* (agitation propaganda) and Washington public relations as an integral part of its war strategy. At the start of the war, the
government hired U.S. public relations firms to promote its cause—as did
the Bosnian government. Thus, modern techniques and technology have
been added to the basic Soviet legacy of disinformation. Control of the
media, especially in the United States, can become a lethal weapon.

[In his book *Balkan Odyssey*, David Owen reports the following:

> Documents filed with the US Justice Department showed that Croatia
> was paying Ruder Finn Global Public Affairs, a Washington-based PR
> firm, $10,000 a month plus expenses to present "a positive Croatian
> image" to members of Congress, administration officials and the news
> media. For their part, the Bosnian government were paying for services
> which included "writing and placing op-ed articles, guest columns and
> letters to the editor." (p. 118)

Owen cites an article in the *Atlanta Journal/Constitution* of 28 February
1993, which notes that between June and December 1992, on behalf of the
Bosnian government, Ruder Finn

> arranged meetings between Bosnian officials and Vice-Presidential
> candidate Al Gore, acting Secretary of State Lawrence Eagleburger and
> 10 influential Senators, including Majority Leader George Mitchell and
> Minority Leader Robert Dole. It made 48 phone calls to members of the
> House, 20 calls to members of the Senate and more than 80 calls to
> newspaper columnists, television anchors and other journalists. (p. 119)

I remember once while I was the UN's chief political officer Sector East
(Eastern Slavonia) in Croatia, the Croatian media began a rumor saying that
a Russian general in UNPROFOR had led Yugoslav tanks and troops across the
Batina Bridge from Serbia into Sector East. It was completely false, but the
story took months to put to rest. I even received a telephone call from a
Washington newspaper asking for details of the story. When I said there was
no truth to the story, I was greeted with disbelief and told that UNPROFOR
headquarters in Zagreb had confirmed the story. Layer upon layer of disinformation. In fact, the Russian contingent commander in Sector East had
allowed, with proper clearance, Serb forces from the southern part of Sector
East to move to the northern part of Sector East. Because there was no
connection between the northern and southern parts of the sector, except
through Serbia, the troops had exited into Serbia and then reentered into the
sector over the Batina Bridge. The procedure had been done with the full
knowledge of everyone concerned, including the Croatian government, and
had been internationally monitored, but the tale of a Russian general leading

Yugoslav troops into Croatian territory was too good for the Croatian/American propaganda machine to miss.

The Bosnian government was almost as bad, or as good, as Croatia when it came to propaganda. The Serbs were notorious too, but because they were seldom given any space in Western media, there was less chance to realize how much they stretched the truth. Moreover, the Serbs didn't care about public relations, much to their detriment. Many times, out of curiosity I would ask the Serbs why they didn't have more of a public relations campaign. Their answer was distressingly stubborn: "The truth will come out." They never appreciated that CNN (*C*ertainly *N*ot *N*eutral) and other media were a major player in the war.

But whenever the Serbs did get involved in propaganda, it was equally primitive and truth slaughtering. They just spent much less time at it, and what effort they made was generally geared to controlling their own people, rather than to influencing others.]

The next item on the Bosnian government news this morning said that French troops are firing at BSA positions on Mount Igman. [That was certainly a possibility because French troops often returned fire when their patrols were targeted. But the spin given to the item suggested that NATO forces were preparing to come to the aid of beleaguered Sarajevo and that the French salvos were the first step. The intent was to give some hope to Sarajevans, but none of us at that point believed NATO was ready to rescue Sarajevo. Not yet.]

Over to Serb radio. The lead item was that a new poll in the United States showed that only 36 percent of the American public supported Clinton's policy on Bosnia. [Ironically, there was probably some truth in that assertion, even though the identity of the pollsters was never mentioned. But the catch was that, of those who comprised the 64 percent, assuming the figures were accurate, most of them probably favored a stronger policy against the Serbs, not a weaker one. They wanted blood. Or, as my friendly neighborhood bartender used to say, "Nuke the goddamn Serbs!"]

At the 8:30 A.M. briefing in the large conference room, Smith voiced his concern once again for finding storage space the RRF will need. If none is found soon, it will be difficult to store equipment for winterizing their quarters.

We went next to the 9:00 A.M. briefing in Smith's office.

Reports from Srebrenica are unclear, but there has been fighting. There seems to have been a BSA attack in response to provocations by Bosnian government troops from inside the enclave.

The Serbs are offering to escort UNHCR convoys into Sarajevo, but they want written guarantees from the Bosnian government that it will not fire while the convoys are unloading in Rajlovac, a Serbian area. Of course, the Bosnian government will not give any such guarantee, and certainly not in writing. They do not want Serbian police coming through Bosnian Sarajevo, whatever the pretext. Besides, the Serbs have fired many times on convoys unloading in Bosnian government territory.

We discussed the options. Should we use armored vehicles to carry the food? Should we accompany the convoys with adequate fire power? Should we be prepared to fight our way through checkpoints? All of the above? None of the above?

Smith said he has been instructed by UNPF headquarters in Zagreb not to accompany UNHCR convoys over Mount Igman, even though the French are willing to take the risk. Apparently, UNHCR still prefers to come through the Sierras, from Kiseljak to Sarajevo, and operate on the principle of consent. Smith wants to use UNPROFOR armed escorts, in accordance with Security Council resolutions. He doesn't like giving in to intimidation. But it is UNHCR's call, and UNHCR wants to disassociate itself from UNPROFOR, which is perceived as a military operation rather than a humanitarian one. Meanwhile, Smith said he expects the situation to become "confrontational."

Rajlovac is, in fact, on the confrontation line, and if the Bosnian government continues to fire at convoys there, it is likely that the Serbs will retaliate by blocking convoys to Sarajevo, Smith said. The agreement made in Pale (on 8 June, when I had gone there as an observer with UNHCR) to bring convoys through the Sierras had been reached prior to the current Bosnian military offensive. Smith is ready, therefore, to make a new push for opening the Igman Logistics Route because UNPROFOR can control that road better than it can control Route Swan through the Sierras and because opening the Igman road will give the Bosnian government less reason to continue its campaign to "liberate" Sarajevo. Smith is planning to send a couple of his officers to Zagreb to lobby Janvier to get permission to force a way through the Igman Road: to open it, to rebuild it, to defend it.

Smith admitted there are good reasons why the Bosnian government will continue to harass UNHCR convoys to Rajlovac. Not only will it deprive the Serbs of much needed international aid but it will force them into making choices they don't want to make. Either they will have to request an armed escort from UNPROFOR, which they will never do, or they will have to retaliate against the Bosnian government by blocking convoys to Sarajevo, in which case the Bosnian government will be able to maintain its image as a victim.

The UNHCR representative then reviewed the choices for supplying Sarajevo. He too favors opening and fortifying the Mount Igman road. He said that UNHCR used to bring in 50 percent of its food by air until the Sarajevo airport was closed. [I doubted this figure; it seemed much too high.] The best route for convoys might be through Hadzici (on Route Swan), but that route is closed because of fighting resulting from the government offensive. At the same time, the slow movement of convoys is inefficient. The route from Metkovic to Sarajevo and back (through the Sierras) used to take less than one day. Now it takes five days, and there is concern that donors will not continue to support aid if they can't get results.

We then turned to a problem we are having with the Bosnian government's harassment of a local employee, who is a Serb (call him "M"). M was drafted on 9 June, more than two weeks ago. We protested to Minister Muratovic, who sent a letter to the municipal and regional secretaries of defense on 13 June. The municipal secretary said he sent a letter to the Third Field Brigade commander on 16 June. On 23 June, M contacted the municipal secretary, who said he had received a letter from the Third Field Brigade saying they would not agree to the request to exempt M from military service.

Meanwhile, M is frightened to death. "They'll put me on the front line. They'll put me right under the gun. I'll be killed," he said. He is in his early forties, has a wife and one child. He came to me after Smith's briefing, very humbly, and asked if I could intervene. I told him I would bring the subject up with Muratovic.

I went to see Muratovic at ten o'clock. When I raised M's case, Muratovic became contemptuous. "Everybody does military service. This is a war! Why should M have special privilege?"

"Because it's part of your signed agreement with UNPROFOR. Its employees do not have to go into military service."

"UNPROFOR! UNPROFOR! You don't do anything for us, and you want privileges."

"Your commanders are ignoring your orders, Mr. Minister. You helped us, as you said you would, and we are thankful for that. But your commanders are not following your instructions, and it makes us wonder about the chain of command. How can we make other agreements if your field commanders won't listen to you?"

"They follow orders. It just takes time. The system is slow."

"I would appreciate it if you would make another call to the commander."

"Take it up with my assistant. I have other things to do." [I did take the matter up with Muratovic's assistant, but to no avail. Moreover, I had no way of knowing if he ever contacted the appropriate commander. In any case, M reported for duty the following day and was sent to the front lines. Ten days later he had a mild heart attack while on duty and was returned to Sarajevo.]

Muratovic then began his daily invective against UNPROFOR. "The Serbs have taken away your jobs. You don't escort convoys any more, you can't open the airport, you can't protect the weapons collection points, and you can't stop the shelling and the snipers. Why don't you go home? You have six thousand troops in Sarajevo, and they're doing nothing. One day the people will begin to resent their presence, and incidents might happen. You should go home. You have no jobs left."

"The Serbs are complaining that you shoot at UNHCR when it tries to unload in Rajlovac."

"Of course we shoot at Serb police. Why not? What are they doing in our area? But we are willing to cooperate. Let them inform us when and where they plan to arrive, and we will arrange to allow them to pass. We will support you in any way you want."

"Thank you. I'll put your proposal to them." [I knew, however, the Bosnian Serbs would never agree to be monitored by the Bosnian government. Thus, Muratovic had been cooperative on an issue he knew the Serbs would never accept.]

Muratovic then moved on to electricity. "If they continue to deny us electricity, we have the capability to destroy the entire transformer station in Raljevo, which supplies Rajlovac and Ilidza [two Serbian areas around Sarajevo]. We could destroy Raljevo in thirty minutes; it's the largest transformer station in former Yugoslavia."

"We're doing our best to restore utilities to Sarajevo," I said.

Muratovic then returned to attacking UNPROFOR. "If you can't do your job, you should leave. Why do you want to see our hospitals? I keep getting requests to see our hospitals. Why don't you do the jobs you're supposed to do instead of snooping around? Do you know, we observed the Danes taking pictures of hidden water sites in Sarajevo. There are several sites where our people take water that are hidden from the general public, and the Serbs shell them. How do the Serbs know where they are? I'll tell you how. They get the information from UNPROFOR. Your observation posts and your patrols collect information and sell it to Pale."

I told him that any proof of espionage would be dealt with severely and urged him to give us any evidence he has.

"We don't need UNPROFOR. NATO will be the judge," he said.

At the 6:00 P.M. briefing Smith reported to us on a conversation he had with Muratovic today. Essentially, he told Muratovic that UNPROFOR has to have freedom of movement. During a war, it needs that freedom even more. As of now, the UN can barely move away from the checkpoints and the OPs. Muratovic promised to cooperate. [I was annoyed that Smith had not invited me to come with him when he visited Muratovic.]

Continuing, Smith told us that he doesn't want to push the issue with the Bosnian government because he doesn't want to have battles with both sides. As of now, Mladic still won't talk to him.

[At times like this, I said nothing because the situation was essentially a military one, but Smith was faced with difficult choices. Of course, he wanted to perform his duty in the best way possible. Yet, he felt he could not push one of the two parties to the conflict. Was this a political bias? Or did he realize that the majority of his forces, including those of us in Sarajevo, were stationed on territory controlled by the Bosnian government and by the Federation? We were all potential hostages of the Bosnian government.

I was sympathetic to Smith's dilemma. He deeply felt his responsibility to his troops: to lead them, to keep their morale high, to set a shining example. He also had a moral sense of wanting to protect the people of Sarajevo and wanting to fulfill his mandate. Then there was his obligation, equally practical, to respect the interests of the government of the United Kingdom (which were rigidly duplicitous), while he was serving the UN. In the best of times, none of these obligations conflicted with any other, but this was not the best of times.

One way out of the dilemma was to concentrate on practicalities: how to maintain freedom of movement, how to escort a convoy, how to guarantee security for one's soldiers. But the moral issues would never go away because they could not be separated from the practical. Resupply of UNPROFOR was immediately measured against resupply of the population and, as such, became a political issue. What message did UNPROFOR send out if it resupplied its own troops, but couldn't resupply the population of Sarajevo? Smith was always aware of the moral and political dimensions of an issue as well as the practical. In fact, his realization that the two could never really be separated was profound and was a part of his character. This admirable awareness, as much as anything else, distinguished him from most men I had met, military or civilian.]

Smith then concluded with some remarks about BSA Colonel Indjic, whom he holds responsible for shelling the Igman road. If Indjic continues this behavior, Smith said, then he, Smith, will put his engineers on the road, improve it, and secure it. He is certain he has the authority to do that. He also has the engineers and the soldiers to protect them. All he needs, he seemed to imply without ever saying so, is the blessing of Janvier to get into a fight with Brother Serb.

27 June 1995

Sent a fax to Akashi this morning. Wrote it last night, but by the time I finished it, around 9:00 P.M., my secretary had gone home for the night, so it didn't go out until this morning.

It is a politically improper and dangerous fax, and I know I shouldn't have sent it because it will be read by the Bosnian government. But I sent it anyway.

I wrote that it was time to use political pressure at the highest level to remove the Bosnian government's restrictions on UNPROFOR's freedom of movement. The longer we wait, the more difficult it will be.

We have seen the gradual encroachment on our FOM by the Serbs. It has almost reached the point of strangulation. We must not let this happen with the Bosnian side.

I suggested we will be faced with several disingenuous arguments by the Bosnian government, and I proposed answers.

1. If the Serbs do it, why can't we? Answer: Because it is against your acceptance of UNPROFOR's presence in Bosnia. Two wrongs don't make a right.

2. If you raise this issue against the Bosnian government at the highest levels, it will undermine the moral high ground of the government. Answer: You are undermining yourselves by harassing UNPROFOR.

3. UNPROFOR is engaged in espionage activities. Its movements must be restricted. Answer: Balkan paranoia is not an acceptable defense for refusing to honor Security Council resolutions.

4. There's a war going on. UNPROFOR can't expect complete FOM during a war. Answer: FOM is even more important during a war because there is an even greater need for the international community to know what is happening.

I also raised the issue of UNPROFOR morale. What we are now experiencing is not a massing of UNPROFOR troops, but a coagulation, and it was bad for morale. We cannot justify the financial burden of having more than twenty-five thousand troops in Bosnia if they can't move about and do their job.

In any case, the daily Sit Reps [situation reports] are replete with examples of restrictions of movement, especially in central Bosnia. I listed a few specific areas where we are restricted: in Zepce, the British cavalry battalion is being asked to notify the Bosnian government twenty-four hours in advance of any intent to move vehicles; in Vares, the Pakistani battalion cannot leave camp without prior notification; in Visoko, the Canadian battalion is allowed out of its barracks only two hours a day and has been told it will not be allowed freedom of movement until it relinquishes two of its observation posts.

If we are going to fight our way over Mount Igman, then we should also be prepared to fight elsewhere, I suggested.

8:15 A.M. reading of local news in my office. Bosnian Serb news said that the Serbs will not allow Bosnian government forces to surround Serb areas and make enclaves out of them. The Bosnian government offensive is still in progress. Mladic is claiming success for his forces in the areas around Mount

Igman. He is also complaining that Bosnian government forces are attacking Serbian villages on the outskirts of Srebrenica and they are receiving support from UNPROFOR, but he did not specify what kind of support. [Perhaps he was trying to justify in advance a planned invasion of Srebrenica.]

Bosnian government news claimed military successes for government forces in various areas of Bosnia, including on Mount Igman. On another item, it claimed that UNPROFOR has finalized its plans for withdrawal from Bosnia and for the arrival of sixty thousand NATO troops.

As usual, one cannot believe anything in the local news. The most valuable news items are reports of speeches given by public officials. Although the content of their speeches may be specious, it is nevertheless helpful to know who is saying what and to which audience.

8:30 A.M. briefing in the large conference room. The logistics officer read out the number of days of supply left for our troops in the three eastern enclaves: in Srebrenica, fifteen; in Zepa, forty; in Gorazde, fifty.

UNHCR convoys turned back before entering Gorazde, after several days of obstruction. Smith thinks this was a mistake. They should have persisted. UNPROFOR finally got through, and it would have been possible to get UNHCR through as well, eventually. This decision sends a bad political message: UNPROFOR can feed itself, but not the people of Gorazde. The world does not distinguish between UNHCR and UNPROFOR. We are all part of the international community.

The two-day meeting of foreign ministers of the European Union has begun in Cannes. Our direction will be set by the decisions taken there, Smith told us. Bildt is expected to be given a mandate to establish a new four-month cease-fire and to open a permanent road to Sarajevo.

Northeast of Gornji Vakuf, in the area between Vitez and Visoko, in Federation territory, our troops are still experiencing serious restrictions of movement. At this point, Smith said, restriction of movement is localized. The various instances are isolated, scattered. "It is not yet time to connect up the dots." He proposes to protest the matter at the local level, but not to bring it to the government in Sarajevo. The infrastructure is so inefficient that raising it to the level of Sarajevo only complicates matters unnecessarily. Besides, there is the question of the relationship between the central government in Sarajevo and the Bosnian-Croat Federation. Most of the restrictions on movement are occurring in territory controlled by the Federation.

The international press is moving out, which suggests a lull in the fighting. They are going to Cannes or to Zagreb. Smith estimates the press corps has diminished by 40 percent in the last two weeks.

A tentative decision has been made in New York, Smith continued, to replace the British in Gorazde and the Dutch in Srebrenica with Ukrainians.

The Bosnian government has not been informed yet. We expect they will protest.

The French ambassador, Henry Jacolin, came to visit me around 10:00 A.M. It was more or less a courtesy call. In the course of his visit, he complained the UNPROFOR did not arrange for Bildt, when he was in Sarajevo, to meet with the ambassadors of the Contact Group (such as himself) who are present in Sarajevo. I replied that Bildt's itinerary was arranged in Geneva. (How ridiculous to blame UNPROFOR for such non-events!)

6:00 P.M. briefing in Smith's office. We have an administrative problem, but it has wider implications. The new chief of mission for Bosnia, Antonio Pedauye, is due to arrive soon, and we must decide where to put him. There is no office space in the main building (known as "The Residence"). We are already cramped, and the Bosnian government does not want to give us more space in the immediate area. They are constantly offering us buildings that have been destroyed, buildings in Sarajevo once used by the JNA, or municipal buildings, all of which would require substantial and expensive renovation. The "Tito Barracks" in downtown Sarajevo, for example, is a massive structure that would take millions of dollars and several months to renovate. It has been offered to us. The game, in other words, is to have UNPROFOR rebuild Sarajevo one way or another.

Pedauye is expected to have a staff of seven or eight, but we are not sure at this point how many of that staff will come with him or how many he will recruit from the present Civil Affairs staff. Such distinctions may sound petty, but the numbers will affect how much office space we must find and how big Pedauye's office will be.

On a more personal note, it is obvious that my own functions will be drastically curtailed, if not made redundant, by Pedauye's arrival. The fact that Pedauye, as chief of mission, will be coming in over Smith is significant, however, in that Smith's staff will be compelled to treat Pedauye with some respect, even though Pedauye will not attempt to interfere in military affairs.

Meanwhile, Smith thinks we should put Pedauye in the main building on the top (third) floor. He will have more security in the building than in an office site halfway across Sarajevo, and it will make for a more efficient operation. Fine, I say, but whom will he displace? "It will have to be Civil Affairs," sayeth the chief of staff. "Oh, no!" says my deputy. And the battle is on. Smith suggested we discuss the matter later.

[In bureaucracies, how near to the boss you sit is important. Smith's bodyguards lived on the third floor, so the issue was where would *they* move? Would they sleep in containers outside the building, like most of the headquarters staff does? Of course not. Would they replace Civil Affairs and move our offices into containers (a kind of house trailer) somewhere outside the main building? Of course. I held out as long as possible against this displacement, but at the last minute I relented because I had no choice. Actually, this issue may seem petty in terms of the larger problems of peace and war that we were in Sarajevo to deal with, but, in fact, I never doubted that it was one more example of how Civil Affairs was to be diminished at every opportunity and, by implication, how diplomacy was to be scuttled for military presence wherever possible. "Are you telling me that we have to surrender working office space to make room for a dormitory for the commander's bodyguards?" I asked the chief of staff. "That's not the way to look at it," he replied. But those were the facts.]

On to greater issues. The early news from Cannes is disappointing. It appears to say that Bildt will be given a mandate by the European Union to try to do whatever everyone else has been trying to do before him. No new wrinkles. He will not be permitted to speak to Pale, and he has a time limit. Six weeks. Then back to Sweden.

Meanwhile, Sacirbey has gone public, saying UNPROFOR should leave Bosnia, and the Bosnian Serbs have said we can leave through the Sierras if we want to.

Once again, the Balkan ballet is becoming a war dance.

28 June 1995

Saint Vitus Day today. The Serbs consider Saint Vitus one of their saints. We expect a lot of celebratory shooting. Yesterday was the anniversary of the death of Tsar Lazar, who died in 1389 at Kosovo Polje, fighting the Turks. A sacred day for the Serbs. They are one of those unusual peoples who preserve the memory of great losses even more than great victories.

At the 8:15 A.M. press reading our interpreter told us that Sacirbey is bleating again to the media, the same song. If UNPROFOR cannot combat Serbian terrorism (i.e., the shelling of civilian populations) and fulfill its mandate, then it should leave, he has said.

How stupid the Serbs are. With the whole world watching them, they persist in shelling civilians. This is more than cruelty; this is stupidity. On the other hand, the Bosnian government has mounted a military offensive against them. The Serbs feel they must respond.

At the 8:30 A.M. briefing, we heard about the next VIP who will come to visit Sarajevo. It is difficult not to be a bit cynical about our visitors. Generals, diplomats, and UN officials—they all come with their cameras, looking for ways to record their experiences. Some are quite serious about their duties, some are frivolous, and all are awed. Sarajevo is unforgettable. Our protocol officer is the busiest officer of all.

Tomorrow the chief of staff of UNPF in Zagreb will arrive. Another British general. (He will not ask for a political briefing, I am sure. And if he asks for one, Smith or Baxter will brief him. Civil Affairs will be ignored.)

The G-2 reported confirmation of two Bosnian government attacks out of Srebrenica against Serb villages. We can expect retaliation by the BSA. The only question is how severe it will be.

Following the morning briefings, I went to see Muratovic. He began by expressing his strong dissatisfaction with a letter that Boutros Boutros-Ghali sent to the Secretary-General of NATO, Willy Claes. I had never seen the letter, dated 23 June. Muratovic showed it to me. (I told him I had seen the letter before, but would like to glance at it again. Meanwhile, I fumed at the procedure of an organization that didn't bother to let its field officers know what was going on at headquarters.)

In his letter Boutros-Ghali essentially told Claes not to take any action to try to demilitarize Sarajevo, that UNPROFOR would do it in accordance with Security Council resolution 998. Muratovic was derisive. "Why should we give up our weapons to the UN or to anyone else? We would be killed." Then he added: "You can't do the jobs you're supposed to do, and now you want to disarm us so we can be slaughtered." I assumed that Boutros-Ghali's letter had the objective of not wanting to cede UNPROFOR's responsibility to NATO. Only the Security Council can give the UN responsibility, and only the Security Council can take it away. I fully understood Muratovic's position, however. I would say exactly what he said if I were sitting where he is sitting.

Next, Muratovic noted that Haris Siladzic, the prime minister, would be traveling in coming days and would not be in Sarajevo. [I assumed that meant that Siladzic would be trying to rally international support and raise money. Siladzic was seen in Western capitals as the member of the Bosnian presidency who most believed in a multiethnic, multicultural Bosnia. Ironically, by schooling, he was the most Islamic of all the Bosnian government officials. He had done Islamic studies in Cairo, spoke fluent Arabic, and was a bit of a Koranic scholar, but he was regarded as pro-European. In general, Siladzic dealt with Europe; Eyup Ganic, who was vice president of the shaky Bosnian-Croat Federation, dealt with the Croats; and Sacirbey dealt with the West, which was why he was based in New York rather than in Sarajevo, even though he was the foreign minister. Sacirbey was basically an American of Bosnian parentage.]

Muratovic is still strongly against the RRF, a heavy irony because the RRF is being deployed, in effect, to attack the BSA. "We will try to convince America not to pay for it," he said. It is useless, he said, unless it will be used to open roads, forcibly if necessary. [The press was already joking about the RRF, calling it PROFOR-UNPROFOR—protection force for UNPROFOR.]

"UNPROFOR should be thinned out. They can remain to support the

Federation, to escort convoys, and to protect the safe areas. Otherwise, let them leave. Our people are tired of them." [If I had to fix a date when the Bosnian government officially lost faith in UNPROFOR, I would say it was around 7 May of this year, when Serb mortar shells killed eleven people in Butmir, which was near the entrance to the tunnel that runs under the Sarajevo airport and links Sarajevo to the outside world. (There were many other instances of civilian massacres, but somehow this one was the straw that broke the camel's back—or, as the French say, *la dernière goutte qui fait déborder la vase* [the last drop that made the vase overflow].) The Bosnian government demanded that UNPROFOR call for NATO air strikes at that point, but those strikes never came. Ever since then, the government stepped up its campaign to evict UNPROFOR.]

I raised the issue of Visoko, where 565 Canadian soldiers were being blocked from entering or leaving their barracks. Muratovic said: "They can leave for home anytime they want. They have no jobs now. They are sup-posed to guard the WCPS, but they don't do that any more. They can go back to Canada." Of course, this statement begged the issue. The point is they are being blocked, in effect are being held hostage while the Bosnian govern-ment conducts military operations in the area. Muratovic, not wanting to address the issue of restriction of movement, simply turned my complaint into a condemnation of UNPROFOR.

This evening I sent Akashi a fax that eventually caused me a lot of trouble. Yesterday the Bosnian Serbs rocketed the TV building in downtown Sarajevo, right across the street from the UN's Sector Sarajevo Command, and caused terrible destruction. Early reports said one person was killed and more than fifty wounded. Offices were destroyed, including CNN's studios. In my fax I said there is reason to believe that the Serbian attack on the TV building was provoked by Bosnian government attacks upon two Serbian areas near Sara-jevo: Nedarici and Rajlovac. Moreover, the type of rocket employed, appar-ently an improvised rocket, is notoriously inaccurate, so the Serbs may not even have intended to hit the TV building.

I wrote that I had spoken to several people about the meanness of the BSA's attacks on Sarajevo, not only yesterday's but all of them. I had spoken with the chief of staff of UNPROFOR, the G-2 (intelligence), a representative of the French general who headed Sarajevo Command (and who was sta-tioned across from the TV building), and a high-ranking UN military ob-server. The common conclusion of these four experts is that the Bosnian government is increasingly using the cover of UN facilities to provoke BSA attacks. Thus, I wrote, reports from our military suggest that the Bosnian government is using UNPROFOR facilities as a shield for their mobile mor-tars. In the past, I went on, they had used hospitals, schools, and other sensitive facilities as shields. All is fair in war, as the saying goes, and the BSA needs no special reason to continue its outrageous attacks upon civilian areas, but a provocation is a provocation, and should be exposed.

I wrote that the Bosnian government is now waging a battle to change UNPROFOR's mandate. It wants to reduce UNPROFOR's presence and have the arms embargo against Bosnia lifted. One way to do that is to provoke BSA attacks upon UNPROFOR, attacks to which UNPROFOR cannot effectively respond. It might then be said that UNPROFOR must either respond robustly to those attacks or leave and let NATO respond. Although UNPROFOR seems indifferent to attacks upon Bosnians, perhaps it would not be indifferent to attacks upon UNPROFOR, that argument goes. Though I am more a believer in logic than in conspiracy, even in the Balkans, it doesn't really matter whether the sequence of recent events is coincidental or conspiratorial; the political effects are the same: to undermine UNPROFOR's withering credibility so that its mandate might be altered. This tactic was used very successfully in Croatia by the Croatian government.

I concluded that UNPROFOR's response in this situation should be to gather information about the use of our facilities as a shield and then protest it as soon and as strongly as possible. In no way should this protest mitigate our condemnation of BSA attacks upon UNPROFOR and against the civilian populations of Bosnia, but we must be honest.

[The next morning I received a call from UNPF headquarters in Zagreb questioning my sources and my recommendations. I insisted that my sources were high, reliable military sources. "If so, then why doesn't the military report them itself?" I was asked.

"They do, and they're ignored," I replied. "More people read my reports." My interlocutor was very pro–Bosnian government.

He asked further questions. "I'm here, and you're there. What's the problem?" I asked. "Are you telling me what I see and hear?"

"Just checking."

"Grab a flak jacket, and come down here and check," I said.

But the most flagrant opposition came from one of my own staff, who sent an angry, bitter memo of protest to Akashi and the force commander, my superiors, saying I had no grounds for my suggestion that the attack on the TV building had been provoked by Bosnian government shelling. He had seen a copy of my fax. He said that he had been present in the building across the street and that there had been no provocation. I called him, and we had a shouting match. I asked him how he could justify writing over my head to Zagreb and how he could dispute the integrity of my report when he didn't even know who my sources were. But he righteously stood his ground.

That same day I got a call from Reuters, asking me about my fax. The reporter had heard (without disclosing his sources) that I was going to approach delegations in Sarajevo to protest that the Bosnian government was using UN facilities as shields. "What fax are you talking about?" I asked. "All communications between myself and Zagreb are confidential. I have no idea what you're talking about." But he knew. Clearly, he knew.

In fact, I could never prove that anyone had intentionally leaked my fax to the pro-Bosnian press, but the sequence of events seemed more than coincidental.

I also suspected that the Bosnian government was treated to a copy of that particular fax—and never forgave me for it.]

Thoughts:

Good ol' boy Willie Jeff, on the horns of a dilemma, seems certain that the Bosnian people are prepared to make whatever sacrifice is necessary in order to achieve his ultimate goal of reelection. And because he does not want to seem a wimp to Bob Dole's corrosive macho, Clinton has promised to send U.S. troops to Bosnia—once there is peace. Because he does not really want to send U.S. troops to Bosnia under any condition, however, he needs UN troops to stay where they are.

This is not good for UNPROFOR. UN troops do not have sufficient fire power to do the job, and the U.S. Congress will not give the necessary financial and military resources to any organization that it cannot control. The result is that the UN will never get adequate resources, but that it cannot leave until Clinton is sure its leaving will help his reelection.

Meanwhile, Congressional hawks from both parties, conscious of the fact that U.S. companies hold thirty billion dollars in defense contracts with Saudi Arabia (the great mosque builders), are not yet ready to make peace in Bosnia. They want more favorable terms for the Bosnian government (there are a lot of defense contacts to be had in the Persian Gulf), so they keep advising Izetbegovic to hang tough until the United States can lift the arms embargo. We'll get you more air strikes, they are promising. Don't worry. Lift and strike will one day become a reality: lift the arms embargo against the Bosnian government and air strike the Bosnian Serbs.

But for now there are no air strikes, no NATO offensive, no lifting of the arms embargo, and no peace. Most thinkers in the mission, wrongly or rightly, believe that if the United States wants peace, there will be peace.

As far back as February 1992, *before* the referendum on Bosnian independence, at a meeting of Serb, Croat, and Moslem leaders in Lisbon, under the auspices of Portuguese diplomat José Cutileiro, whose country was at the time president of the European Community, President Izetbegovic had agreed to a proposal for dividing Bosnia, a proposal that might have prevented war in Bosnia. When he returned to Sarajevo, however, his Parliament told him it would refuse to endorse the deal to which he had agreed.

They said he had given away too much. The United States, for its part, gently encouraged Izetbegovic to abide by the understanding he had made in Lisbon because it thought it would prevent a war, not because it was taking sides. Had the United States been more insistent, say some critics, Izetbegovic might have gone along with the Lisbon understanding (it was not a formal agreement). [I think this speculation is unfair, however. Although U.S. pressure might have swayed Izetbegovic, the United States at that point was not involved and was not ready to take on the responsibilities inherent in strongly promoting the conclusions of the Lisbon meeting. In fact, the United States still considered Bosnia to be a European problem.]

But by October 1992, when the Vance-Owen Peace Plan came along, and there was a real opportunity to settle a war that had already started, the United States had become an enthusiastic supporter of the Bosnian government and was not about to endorse compromise. [This time the United States *did* bear much of the responsibility for preventing a settlement. In his book *Origins of a Catastrophe*, published in 1996, Warren Zimmerman, the U.S. ambassador to Yugoslavia at the time, describes American indifference (which was actually opposition) to the Vance-Owen Plan this way:

> I had been in Vance's office in Geneva a few weeks before, when Vance and Owen received the Bosnian government's reaction to the plan. It was not only positive, but enthusiastic; the Muslims said they were ready to announce support immediately. Vance urged them to delay; he was afraid a quick Muslim acceptance would cause the Serbs to raise the price. With that background, I gave Christopher my view that any current Muslim objections were likely to be tactical and that in the end they would probably accept the plan. Unfortunately, the administration delayed in its support for the plan, thus missing a chance to get it launched. (p. 222)

By now, summer 1995, U.S. resistance to a peaceful settlement is even stronger, and pretty much out in the open. As John Menzies told me only weeks ago: "The Bosnians are going to deal from a position of strength; they're not ready to make peace yet. They can get better terms."

Another story circulated in diplomatic circles about how Clinton became such an enthusiastic supporter of the Sarajevo government, a story I strongly believe, goes like this. Clinton, with no interest in and little knowledge of foreign affairs, was told by his advisors during the presidential campaign in 1992 that he had to find a foreign policy issue on which he could hammer away at Bush and the Republicans. Bush was clearly more knowledgeable on foreign affairs. Up popped Bosnia, and Clinton's advisors told him to seize on it in order to embarrass Bush. If Clinton supported the Bosnian Moslems, he would be able to reap several benefits. He could capitalize on being a friend of the Moslems, after decades of pro-Israel sentiment (and he could still support Israel because Israel was not involved in the Balkans). He could support the anti-fundamentalist Moslems against the fundamentalist Moslems and exploit the split in the Arab world between the "conservative" Good Arabs (Saudi Arabia and other anti-democratic medievalists) and the "radical" Bad Arabs (such as Iraq and Libya). One did not have to be monolithic, in other words, when dealing with Islam. Just as it was possible to dislike Jews in the United States and like them in Israel, it was possible to oppose Moslem interests in the Middle East, and to support them in Europe. It was even possible to be elected president of the world's only superpower and be uninterested in and ignorant of foreign affairs.

William Jefferson Clinton took the advice of his campaign strategists, became a supporter of the Bosnian Moslems, and as a bonus was elected president of the United States.

Richard Holbrooke later discussed this 1991 campaign strategy of Clinton's, a strategy so successful that he never backed away from it:

> The Clinton campaign message was, famously, focused on the economy. Still, it was not wise to leave Bush's leadership in foreign policy unchallenged. . . . The issue that presented itself most starkly . . . was Bosnia. Governor Clinton attacked. Criticizing the Bush Administration for "turning its back on violations of basic human rights" and "being slow on the uptake," he called on President Bush to show "real leadership" and urged air strikes, supported by the United States if necessary, against the Serbs if they continued to block the delivery of humanitarian goods to the people trapped in Sarajevo. (pp. 41–42)]

Today there has been a lot of shooting. We are virtually unable to move, even in armored cars. Not only can we *not* enter or leave Sarajevo but we can barely move *inside* Sarajevo. Even armored cars are not particularly safe because they will resist only bullets, not mortars, and they will not even resist heavy explosive rounds, only lighter rounds.

Meanwhile, Smith is due to leave for Split on Friday and then go back to England for home leave. He will meet Alvaro de Soto (Assistant Secretary-General in the Department for Political Affairs at UN headquarters in New York) in Split before de Soto comes to Sarajevo. I will meet de Soto in Sarajevo, and we will meet with Vice President Ganic and perhaps President Izetbegovic before going to Mostar the following day to see Kresimir Zubak (a Bosnian Croat and president of the Federation) and others. At least, that is the plan, but one never knows because of the shelling. Roads are always being closed at the last minute, even for dignitaries.

The plan is for de Soto and me to go to Mostar by road over Mount Igman in the early morning (leaving Sarajevo barracks at around 5:00 A.M.) in an armored vehicle. I will return alone two days later from Split in an armored vehicle that will be sent from Kiseljak.

Of course, there is always danger, armored vehicle or not, because even armored vehicles are not resistant to heavy shelling and are always in danger of going over the side and down the mountain if they should miss one of the hairpin turns while traveling at high speed. If one travels over Igman during the day, one tries to transit at hours when, according to previous patterns, there is less likely to be heavy shelling. There is almost a recognizable schedule for shelling. But just when one gets accustomed to the "schedule," it is changed. Thus, there is clear and present danger anytime one transits by road over Mount Igman, but relatively less if one leaves in the dark, around 5:00 A.M.

29 June 1995

Usually in the morning, before breakfast and just after having tapped away at my word processor, I wander down the hall to the press area to read the latest news. This morning, the press summaries described the mandate that Bildt received from the meeting of EU foreign ministers just concluded at Cannes. He has been given five objectives.

1. To lift the siege of Sarajevo and establish an access route to the city all the way from the Dalmatian coast [where goods that arrived by ship and were destined for Sarajevo were usually offloaded].

2. To renew a dialogue with all sides in Bosnia on the basis of the Contact Group Plan.

3. To renew a dialogue between Croatian authorities and Serbian secessionists.

4. To renew negotiations with Milosevic, with the objective of achieving mutual recognition between Bosnia and rump Yugoslavia (Serbia and Montenegro) as the first phase in mutual recognition among all the former Yugoslav republics. [Ironically, Milosevic was not even president of Yugoslavia; he was only president of Serbia. Zoran Lilic was president of Yugoslavia, but negotiations with "the Serbs" always addressed Milosevic.]

5. To establish a four-month moratorium on all military activities in the theater.

Good luck, we all say skeptically. In the Balkans, history is always on the side of the pessimists.

Smith made several points at the 8:00 A.M. briefing.

1. We must secure the Igman road. The airport was "a snare and a delusion." It could be closed easily, simply by threats, and it was more difficult to

defend than a road. We needed a secure road, all the way to the Dalmatian coast.

Those of us who doubted the wisdom of trying to secure the Igman road used the following arguments:

—It will take an extensive and expensive amount of improvement to make it worthy of heavy traffic.

—It will be unusable in winter when the heavy snows come.

—It will be difficult to defend because the terrain is not suitable to emplacing heavy artillery.

—It will be seen as escalatory by the BSA, and unless UNPROFOR is willing to deal with the escalation, as Smith himself always maintains, then we should not force our way over Igman.

—The route through the Sierras (Route Swan) is preferable, more suited to heavy traffic, and generally usable in winter.

2. Until we have freedom of movement in the entire theater, we will remain part of the problem rather than part of the answer because we must constantly resupply ourselves. Also, the larger our force grows, the more often and extensively we will have to resupply.

(I agree with Smith on this second point, and that was why I believe we should cut the size of our forces in Bosnia. In the anteroom to the general's office, for example, four soldiers sit and play games on the computer virtually the entire day. Nothing to do. The soldiers who used to guard the weapons collection points are now secure in their barracks. As Muratovic says, send them home. Instead, we are getting another ten thousand troops. A Rabid [*sic!*] Reaction Force.)

3. To open the Igman road we must be prepared to fire back and, in the second phase, to improve the road. We can use the RRF to fire back or use Smith's own Task Force Alpha to accompany convoys. To improve the road, we must first shore it up, then erect an antisniper barrier. [The second action would put us openly on the side of the Bosnian government, which would use the road, but that was the reality. During the day, the road would be used by UNPROFOR (a "blue route"), and at night it would be used by the Bosnian government for troop movements and to resupply Sarajevo.]

4. The eastern enclaves are indefensible by force on the ground. Their security will have to be negotiated. Only wide-ranging and massive air strikes can defend the enclaves. NATO will have to bomb command and control centers far from the eastern enclaves to defend them.

5. Our convoys are still blocked by government forces at checkpoints at Gornji Vakuf and Zenica. They have been held up for more than a week now. We must deal with local commanders on this issue; otherwise, we will have generals and government ministers dealing with convoys, and the infrastructure does not allow for that. Messages from Sarajevo rarely get through

to field commanders, and when they do, it is not certain those messages will be obeyed.

Other business at the morning briefing:

A French soldier was killed by a tank mine in the Dobrinja area.

Convoys to Srebrenica and Zepa are still being blocked by the BSA.

Foreign Minister Sacirbey wrote a letter to Boutros-Ghali saying that the Bosnian government intends to review the extension of its sovereign consent to allow UNPROFOR to remain in Bosnia. It is prepared to consider all relevant contingencies.

At the 9:00 A.M. briefing in his office Smith told us he has been given some slack by Janvier to move convoys into Sarajevo over the Mount Igman road. Smith has been saying for weeks that aid convoys should move across Igman—with prior notice to the Serbs—and that we should be prepared to defend those convoys with force against BSA shelling. That is one aspect of what is known as "robust" response. Janvier has resisted, in part because UNHCR has told him it does not want to be associated with the use of force. They would still prefer to travel through the Sierras with the consent of all the parties. Janvier himself agrees with this approach. At the same time, Foreign Minister Alain Juppé of France has come out in support of robust response, apparently contradicting Janvier. Thus, the French have maintained their traditional attitude in foreign policy of coming down firmly on both sides. Juppé talks tough, and Janvier talks about "consent." In some circles, such an approach would be called duplicitious—perfidious Albion, for instance, and all that—but when the French do it, it is called diplomacy. Myself, I have always respected French diplomacy. Also, now that Mitterrand, an unapologetic protector of the Serbs, has gone, the new French government can make pro-Bosnian noises.

In any case, Smith plans to start moving convoys across Mount Igman immediately. He wants to move about ten UNHCR trucks every night, with military drivers and UNPROFOR military escort. They will make every attempt to avoid provoking the BSA, because they know full well that the BSA routinely shells convoys coming across Mount Igman. For the past forty-eight hours, the shelling has stopped, although individual cars have been targeted. Apparently, the Serbs are ready to make a deal. The convoys will start tonight.

We are facing a complex attitude among the Serbs. Though they dislike and distrust UNPROFOR, and particularly Smith, they prefer UNPROFOR to NATO, the Contact Group, or any other international actor. We are the best they have and always have been, partly because we are the only interlocutor speaking to all the parties.

The Serbs are willing to make a deal to allow convoys into Sarajevo because they do not want a wider war, particularly against the French and the British. At the same time, they have a certain residual anger against UNPROFOR for having allowed the Bosnian government to take over some of the high ground around Sarajevo that the Serbs once controlled and relinquished to UNPROFOR, specifically the stretch between Tarcin and Butmir, which leads to the Sarajevo airport.

[Regarding this dispute, here is a passage from a report by the Secretary-General to the Security Council, dated 22 March 1995 (document S/1995/222), just three months ago. Paragraph 17 of that document reads:

> During the period from 1 October 1994 to 18 December 1994, the urban area of Sarajevo remained largely free from fighting. Shelling, sniping and military engagements were all at low levels and the heavy weapons exclusion zone was generally respected. Elsewhere in the Sarajevo area, however, there was more activity. Bosnian Government forces launched a series of attacks on Bosnian Serb–controlled territory in the area of Mount Igman and Mount Bjelasnica, gaining approximately 100 square kilometres of territory. To prosecute their offensive, Bosnian Army troops transited the "Igman demilitarized zone," which represented a clear violation of the agreement of 14 August 1993. UNPROFOR obtained numerous undertakings from the Bosnian authorities indicating that they would return to compliance with the agreement. Despite this, the Bosnian Army continued to use the zone for military purposes, and UNPROFOR's apparent failure to stop them was the cause of considerable friction between UNPROFOR and the Bosnian Serb side.

The facts here are clear, but they have rarely been publicized to the outside world. After the Serbs pulled back from a strategic area on Mount Igman, allowing UNPROFOR to take control, the Bosnian government violated its part of the agreement and moved in. The Serbs retaliated against UNPROFOR. When an UNPROFOR soldier was seriously injured, UNPROFOR responded with close air support (in self-defense). The Serbs then retaliated against the use of close air support by shutting down the Sarajevo airport. The world public, however, thanks to the voluntary censorship of the international press, believed simply that the Serbs had shelled UNPROFOR and then closed down the Sarajevo airport.

Moreover, the UN was then blamed for not using force to open the airport. It was also blamed for responding with air power only when *its own* soldiers were wounded, but ignoring retaliation when Bosnian soldiers and civilians were wounded—even though UNPROFOR's mandate, which had been negotiated and approved by all the major powers, including the United States, made clear that close air support was only to be used in self-defense.

On the other hand, anytime that the Bosnian government went on the offensive, it could say it was trying to put down a (Serbian) secessionist movement. It had a point, except that in 1991, when the JNA moved against Croatian secessionists, before Croatia was internationally recognized, the JNA said the same thing—namely, that it was moving against secession. Then it was called an aggressor.]

At 2:00 P.M. this afternoon we had a strategy session. Smith is scheduled to depart for a few days of leave time, and he wants to anticipate what might happen during his absence, even though he will always be reachable by telephone.

He estimates that it will probably take about a week to organize a convoy over Igman with the type of escort he wants, the type that will be prepared to fight back.

We then discussed the question of "effectiveness." In spite of the BSA's continual firing at convoys coming over Igman, one has to ask whether their harassment has been effective. The fact is, the convoys are still coming. We should not allow the BSA's harassment to become effective by stopping our convoys. If the BSA firing *does* become effective, then we will have to commit Task Force Alpha, which Smith has just formed, to accompany convoys.

Phase two of opening Igman, Smith went on, will be to rebuild the road. We have discussed this problem before. It will put us clearly on the side of the Bosnian government, and there might be political fallout from it, but we must rebuild the road.

The main concern about returning mortar fire is the danger of collateral damage, but Smith added, "I see no harm in being thoroughly assertive if someone shoots at us."

We brought up again the problem of defending the safe areas. The RRF, Smith said, will be used to defend convoys. It has nothing to do with the safe areas. Besides, we cannot defend the entire road network leading into the safe areas in order to ensure that convoys will reach those areas. We can provide escorts, but we cannot control the entire territory. Only air strikes can protect the safe areas; not even close air support is enough. Meanwhile, the Security Council has never defined the boundaries of the safe areas.

We also raised the question of civilian protests. Suppose the local Sarajevans should decide to march into the Serbian-controlled areas around Sarajevo to protest being under siege. Should UNPROFOR stop them? Protect them? Negotiate with their leaders? Best to leave them alone, is the general feeling. We doubt they will do it.

Meanwhile, five French convoys to supply the RRF crossed into Tomislav-grad (in Federation territory) from Ploce (on the Dalmatian coast, in Croatia). But the president of the Federation, Kresimir Zubak (a Bosnian Croat closely allied with Croatian President Tudjman), has said that if the RRF's mission were not clarified, it will have to leave within thirty days. He stated his position in a letter to General Janvier, the force commander.

It is clear that none of the warring parties in Bosnia wants the RRF.

30 June 1995

The pressure is building. One can feel it in the air. Not only this morning but every morning. It is palpable, the type of pressure a runner feels when the air is humid and heavy with water, and each stride is a swimstroke. The air *is* heavy and humid. It rains a lot during June, but that is not the heaviness one feels, not the real heaviness.

The real heaviness is dread, the wet weight of a run-up to disaster, the gathering of a terrible storm, the imminence of wanton slaughter. The government military offensive has bogged down; it has taken heavy casualties. Morale is poor. The young boys do not want to fight; their mothers do not want them to fight; the fathers do not want either their sons or themselves to fight.

But the war goes on, and it may get worse. (It is politicians who start wars, not generals, and the politicians in Bosnia and in the metropolitan capitals have not had enough yet.)

The Bosnian government army is suffering from political corruption. The top generals are political appointments; the best soldiers are not necessarily the ones promoted. The party faithful, those belonging to Izetbegovic's party (the Party of Democratic Action, or SDA), are promoted. The ruling political party controls the military, as it did during the Communist era.

The war will continue for a while. The West will not be cheated from defining its new identity now that it has won the Cold War. Clinton and Major and Juppé and Kohl have their careers to consider. They will have their war for the glory of Bosnia until domestic political considerations force them to do otherwise.

Then there is Smith with his charming tenacity. He wants a fight—not necessarily a full-scale war, but a good fight. He wants to show Brother Serb who is boss, and his officers want a fight, even the twentysomething female officers with blue eyes. "The people of England," one distaff captain said to me, "would be happy to make whatever sacrifices were necessary if they only knew how bad Serbian atrocities were, if they could only see those concentration camps. I used to interview Bosnian survivors. The stories they told would make your hair stand on end."

"It would make my hair fall out," I said. [I am bald.]

She was not amused. She is a bulldogette; applications for humor had to be submitted in triplicate. Her commander wants a fight, so she wants a fight. Not necessarily a full-blown war, but a good fight.

As I took my difficult shower from the chest-high faucet across the hall this morning, I thought about the indignities of war. Not the bloodletting, but the discomfort, the indignities. With a full-scale war there might be no water at all for the barracks. Electric generators might go out. Meanwhile, the people of Sarajevo have been without utilities for almost two months now, and negotiations for restoring utilities have broken down completely.

Inevitably, in the modern era there is a relation between water and personal dignity, as well as between water supply and the will to fight. Whatever that relation is, the Serbs calculated it, and that is one of the reasons they cut off the water supply to Sarajevo.

At the 8:30 A.M. briefing, it was announced that there would be a ceremony this afternoon at 4:00 P.M. for the French soldier killed yesterday by a mine. I decided I would attend.

Three more shells landed on the PTT (Post Office and Telecommunications) building in downtown Sarajevo. Our intelligence sources say that the shells were in response to outgoing Bosnian government mortars.

UNHCR convoys are still being blocked by the Bosnian government at Gornji Vakuf, and the government wants twenty-four-hour advance notice on all convoys.

Gorazde is in desperate need of humanitarian aid. Smith asked me to mention this to Koljevic the next time I see him. The BSA is also blocking convoys to Zepa.

Meanwhile, Minister Muratovic called and asked for a helicopter to take him to Split. Our air operations officer said that the government army itself would give clearance for air traffic only as far as Zenica, not all the way through Federation territory to Split. If Muratovic wants a UN helicopter to fly to Split, he will have to intervene with the Bosnian army. (I grumbled about not wanting to be Muratovic's personal taxi service, but I acceded to his request.)

At the 9:00 A.M. briefing in Smith's office we had a discussion about the Bosnian government's continuing provocations against the BSA. I stood virtually alone in saying these provocations should be protested. The apologists—led by UNHCR—said yes, there may be occasional provocations, but it's a small city, and almost anywhere the Bosnian government sets up its weapons systems will be near an UNPROFOR facility. Or, if we protest, the press will say we are pro-Serb. Or, the government will say they have no choice but to attack the enemy from advantageous positions, whatever the consequences, so long as the siege of Sarajevo continues, and so on.

[The local UNHCR team were clearly part of the politically correct pro-Bosnian government juggernaut. To their credit, when it came to human-itarian activity, they were impartial, and courageous, but at the local level, whenever they dabbled in politics, they were in Muratovic's stable. As in UNPROFOR, there was a divergence of views in UNHCR between those in Sarajevo and those in Zagreb. Although we in Sarajevo may have been closer to the real situation on the ground, we were also the potential hostages of the Bosnian government. Anything less than full support for the Bosnian government was met with restrictions on our movement and with harass-ment. Understandably, the Bosnian government wanted all UN-related oper-ations dealing with Bosnia to be headquartered in Sarajevo, not because local personnel had a better understanding of the situation in Sarajevo, but because then the government could better control and intimidate that personnel.

In any case, I retained the highest respect for the judgment and dedication of Anne-Willem Bijleveld, UNHCR's special representative for all of former Yugoslavia, who worked out of Zagreb. He balanced, as well as anyone I have ever met in international life, the qualities of compassion and reason. One frequently meets people in the humanitarian agencies who are extremists in compassion. Their high idealism is at times totally unrealistic. They think with their hearts and not with their heads, but Bijleveld was able to do both.

In fact, if those in Sarajevo were closer to battlefield realities, those in Zagreb were closer to the realities of international politics; they had a better idea of what was possible politically. They may not have felt the pressure of everyday life in Sarajevo, but they felt the extreme and often contradictory pressures of NATO, Washington, London, Paris, Moscow, and so on.]

The discussion on government provocations continued. Whatever the Bosnian government's reasons for its actions, I argued, they are putting our soldiers at risk, and we must protest. How can we fail to protest attacks against our own soldiers? A provocation is a provocation is a provocation, and if one wants to search for origins to the present conflict, for whatever reason, one can flirt with absurdity by going back to the Turkish invasion six centuries ago in order to explain the behavior of Pale. But that is all frivolous, and the point is that there is no justification for provoking the shelling against UNPROFOR. We are supposed to be a peacekeeping force.

I couldn't believe what I was hearing: that even when UN troops are targeted, a room full of UNPROFOR officers (*not* Smith) are rolling over, ready to apologize for the Bosnian government. One British army major even admitted at that point that on most mornings a Bosnian government soldier will set up a mobile mortar just on the other side of the fence surrounding the barracks, next to his sleeping area, lob a few shells at BSA positions, and then run.

"Is that being reported in our daily Sit Reps?" I asked.

Silence.

1 July 1995

8:15 A.M. press reading in my office. Bosnian government news reported that the government offensive is continuing on several fronts. An attack had just been launched from Visoko on BSA positions around Sarajevo. (Hence, we cannot expect freedom of movement for our Canadian soldiers in the Visoko area, in spite of Bosnian government assurances that the problem has been solved.)

Meanwhile, Fikret Abdic's forces are attacking Bosnian government forces in Bihac. [Abdic was an entrepreneurial Moslem businessman who had Serbian support for seceding from Bosnia and setting up his own state in the northwest of the country, just across the border from the Serbian-controlled Krajina area in Croatia. In 1991, Abdic had run for president of Bosnia against Alija Izetbegovic and actually won more votes, though not a majority. He could not win the presidency, however, largely because he lacked party organization. After Izetbegovic's election, the international community buried Abdic. It wanted no more fracturing of the Bosnian political scene, no more secessionist movements in Bosnia, and no Bosnian politicians who were sympathetic to the Serbs. As for Abdic, supported by the Krajina Serbs, he had never been able to conquer the Bihac pocket, largely because the Bosnian government V Corps stationed there was constantly being resupplied with weapons and other vital materials by air from Zagreb. The weapons resupply was, of course, contrary to the arms embargo against all the republics of former Yugoslavia, but no matter. NATO would have its way. Serbian interest in capturing the pocket was strategic in that it would unite Serb-controlled territory in western Bosnia, already linked to Serbia through the Posavina corridor, with Serb-controlled territory in Croatia and, in effect, create Greater Serbia.]

Otherwise, another item on the morning news carried a pledge by the British defense minister, Malcolm Rifkind, who said that the RRF will never be used to force open humanitarian routes; it will only be used to protect UNPROFOR. [I wondered how popular that policy would be with the Bosnian people. With the imminent arrival of the RRF, such disavowals had become more and more common. Those of us in theater suspected such statements to be outright lies, but another body of opinion, especially among the warring parties, took such statements to be true. Both the Sarajevo government and the Federation kept demanding a clear definition of the RRF's mandate, as did the Bosnian Serbs, though for different reasons. The former two feared the RRF would *not* be used against the Serbs, whereas the BSA feared it *would* be. Perhaps at that point a decision had not yet been made, and Rifkind was being honest, but, for me, the role of the RRF was a foregone conclusion.]

At the 8:30 A.M. briefing, our sources reported a decrease in shelling yesterday on the city of Sarajevo. At the same time, it was confirmed by our sources that the attack on the PTT building a couple of days ago was concurrent with attacks on three other UN facilities around Sarajevo. This pattern seems to suggest a deliberate targeting of UNPROFOR facilities. Meanwhile, convoys to Srebrenica, Zepa, and Gorazde, the eastern enclaves, are still being blocked by the BSA.

After the morning briefings, I went to see Minister Muratovic. Sometime in the last few days, Eyup Ganic, a member of the Bosnian presidency and a vice president of the Federation, was seriously injured in a car accident. It was not an assassination attempt; it was an accident, but his incapacitation has led to several questions. What will happen to the Federation administration? President Zubak, a Bosnian Croat, is due to be succeeded by Ganic at some point. Will Zubak continue on indefinitely as president of the Federation? Will a new Moslem official be named to replace Ganic?

Muratovic said there is a large presidency in the Federation. At least six others will be able to share Ganic's duties. Zubak is not scheduled to step down for awhile anyhow. He will remain as president until voting in each of the cantons of the Federation has been completed. Elections are now being prepared for. Not to worry.

I noted that Muratovic was quoted in the Sarajevan press as having said that Akashi was persona non grata in Bosnia. Was that true? Muratovic answered that only the parliament of the city of Sarajevo had asked the Bosnian government to declare Akashi PNG, but the Bosnian government had not done it yet.

[Was it possible, I wondered, for a city council to ask federal authorities to declare an international diplomat PNG? More than likely, Muratovic was simply lying. He had made one of his frequent threats and was trying, perhaps under pressure, to recant. The Bosnian government was constantly threatening to declare people PNG or to kill them; it was their way of doing business. At one point, Muratovic even held a press conference and declared, "Akashi is dead!" He meant that the Bosnian government would never speak to him again. Meanwhile, I had to wonder what such hostility to Akashi would mean for me, his delegate to Bosnia.]

We then returned to the question of having UNPROFOR separated completely from UNPF headquarters in Zagreb. The Bosnian government wants to deal directly with UNPROFOR without having to go through Zagreb.

"We don't want the decision makers to be in Zagreb," Muratovic said as he has before. He was angry. "Janvier has met with Mladic three times recently without informing us, and those meetings involved our country. If Janvier doesn't need us, we don't need him. He has meetings in Belgrade and Pale, and we are not informed. That is unacceptable." [On this point, I agreed with Muratovic. Janvier was more secretive than he should have been on such occasions. I was told by friends in Zagreb that Janvier kept no written notes and made no reports on his meetings with Mladic. Thus, there was no official record of representations he might have made to Mladic.]

"We would like to establish a direct line to Mladic, and I can tell you that the Croatian government feels the same way. We don't need the UN to interfere. Why do you keep talking about 'former Yugoslavia'? We are Bosnia and Herzegovina, not former Yugoslavia. We cannot accept a UN mission here unless there is an independent force for Bosnia."

Muratovic then turned to the issue of weapons. When the Serbs had recently overrun a French camp, in the course of taking hostages, they had also captured vehicles and weapons. UNPROFOR has never retrieved those weapons.

"The French simply gave fifty tanks and APCs to the Serbs. It was a *delivery*. It was a business deal," Muratovic asserted.

I expressed disbelief.

"Then why doesn't the UN demand them back? You asked for the hostages but not for the weapons. Those weapons will be used against our people."

"We *have* demanded them back!"

"And why didn't the French fight?" Muratovic continued. "Why did they just surrender their weapons? What kind of soldiers are they? We don't need soldiers who won't even defend themselves and who sell weapons to our enemy."

"They were overwhelmed," I said.

Muratovic scoffed. "The French are here to protect the Serbs. That was a *deal!* They made money on it." [Everything had a money value for Muratovic.]

"But the French have lost several soldiers in this war, killed by the Serbs. Only this week I attended the funeral of a French soldier."

"That shows how stupid they are. If they had been tougher with the Serbs from the beginning, they wouldn't have had so many casualties. The only thing the Serbs understand is force."

[After sending a fax to Akashi about my meeting with Muratovic, I permitted myself to speculate in my journal. Here is what I wrote.]

In addition to the main conflict between the Serbs and the Moslems there is another conflict, and that is between using force and not using force, between a military solution to the conflict and a negotiated solution, between traditional peacekeeping and peace enforcement. Then there is a further distinction between those who want to use force to bring the other party to the negotiating table and those who want to use force to conquer, humiliate, and defeat.

What interests me at this point is the division within UNPROFOR, particularly between Smith and Janvier, a divergence that is very complex, not merely strategic, and reflects their personalities, military experiences, and national origins, not simply their politics. Smith, on the ground here in Sarajevo, sensing the popular sentiment and encouraged by the international press, is in favor of "robust" response to the Serbian shelling and restriction of movement. He has been influenced by his experiences in the Gulf War and in the Falklands, where the use of force against an inferior opponent proved successful. I also suspect his views are influencing the foreign office in London, rather than vice versa, which is the usual pattern.

Janvier, on the other hand, based in Zagreb, sees the situation as being wider than Sarajevo, feels the pressures of international involvement, is more suspicious of American "cowboy" diplomacy, and is mindful of the ignominious French defeat at Dienbienphu. He, in turn, is influenced *by* his foreign office.

The reference to Dienbienphu is not frivolous. While looking at a map of Sarajevo, General André Soubirou, commander of the French Brigade of the RRF and a former French commander of Sector Sarajevo, once reportedly commented on the similarity between Sarajevo and Dienbienphu. Both were in valleys, virtually indefensible. His point was that the UN should not get itself locked into a war to defend Sarajevo. To make this reference, however, is not in any way to suggest a lack of professionalism or bravery on the part of the French military. It is simply to acknowledge that the French command is more capable of envisioning the possibility of a military debacle than is Smith, with his string of successes. At the same time, both generals are quite aware of the relative inadequacy of UN forces if faced with a BSA assault. Whereas Janvier wants to avoid that assault, conscious that the UN might be defeated, Smith wants the resources to deal with that potential assault and is willing even to provoke it.

Coincidentally, all the eastern enclaves—Sarajevo, Gorazde, Srebrenica, and Zepa—are in valleys, surrounded by mountains. In each case, the Serbs control the high ground. If UNPROFOR is to resist a Serb attack on the enclaves, therefore, it will have to respond with air power against Serb military targets *outside* the enclaves, such as command and control centers in Banja Luka and Han Plesak.

My differences with Smith have nothing to do with Serbs versus Moslems. It is a question of my preferring traditional peacekeeping principles to peace enforcement. Whereas it is generally acknowledged that military capacity is a necessary component of political policy, it must also be noted that it is a danger. Ill-timed military usage can undermine the political process. Although Smith might be genuinely guided by his analysis of the situation on the ground in Sarajevo, he is also, coincidentally, satisfying those elements in the international community, particularly U.S. hawks, who believe in "robustness." Though he is guided by a sense of duty and personal pride, he is also acutely aware of political correctness.

This conflict between the use of force and the non-use of force is the major conflict within the international community at this time, and how it is resolved will ultimately become one of the most important lessons learned from the war in former Yugoslavia.

2 July 1995

Alvaro de Soto arrived yesterday. He came by armored vehicle over Mount Igman. Our drivers gave him a quick tour of Sarajevo en route to the office. While he was passing by the presidential palace in downtown Sarajevo, a soldier in front of the palace was hit by a sniper. De Soto's driver and another soldier in his car got out and helped load the wounded soldier into an ambulance that came by moments later. It was a nice welcome for de Soto. In fact, thirteen people were killed yesterday in Sarajevo.

Usually when a high-ranking official comes to visit Sarajevo, I have to give up my office with the big bed—that is where dignitaries stay. Accordingly, I moved to my apartment last night. I rode home in an armored car and retired to my candles and water buckets.

The weather is steamy, muggy. For days it has been raining or preparing to rain. There is temperature inversion. As I look out toward the surrounding mountains, I think how very beautiful they are, how Olympic the city's aspirations are, and how unspeakably criminal and disgraceful this war is.

On Sundays we hold our briefings an hour later in deference to the Christian Sabbath. Some people attend church in Sarajevo.

This morning at the 9:30 A.M. briefing, our logistics officer reported that convoys are still being prevented from entering Srebrenica, Gorazde, and Zepa, the eastern enclaves, but we gained entry to Bihac with 103 tons of food. Finally, our Bangladeshi troops will be resupplied.

There has been a dramatic increase in casualties within Sarajevo during the last few days. The snipers are active, the shelling more frequent. Meanwhile, the government offensive is continuing in central Bosnia.

One UNHCR convoy came over Igman last night and made it into Sarajevo. Another is due tonight. There has been no firing from the BSA. Perhaps the Serbs are keeping to their part of the bargain to allow Sarajevo to be resupplied. The UNHCR representative wants to go public with UNHCR's plans to run regular convoys into Sarajevo. He wants to announce to the world that UNHCR will not be stopped by the Serbs, that it will feed Sarajevo one way or another. Smith and I, however, think it best to keep these small successes private. No need to call attention to the sudden Serbian compliance. I wrote a note to Akashi recommending that we be "judicious" about the temporary success of our convoys. He agreed.

The question of command has come up. What if there is a conflict in policy between UNPROFOR and UNHCR? During a meeting with Smith, which I attended, de Soto said that the UN Secretary-General has made it clear that his special representative in the theater, Akashi, is in charge. Akashi will have the final say, but we anticipate no disagreement.

The UNHCR representative, however, still wants to go public with his successes. [He was a young, ambitious Brit who came from a clerical background and whose girlfriend was a journalist based in Sarajevo. As it was, those two influences combined to make him a Christian crusader for the Bosnian government, as all of the UNHCR staff in Sarajevo were, but he also had an eye to making a name for himself, in the press if possible. His pretty girlfriend was just as committed to the cause of the Bosnian government. They were both members of that altruistic international elite who considered themselves "Sarajevans"—in effect, expatriate Christian soldiers who could, by the by, at a moment's notice fly off to Paris or London while their flock remained mired in Sarajevo. I found their sanctimony appalling.] On this occasion, Smith suggested to the UNHCR representative that he should share some of the flour coming in over Igman with the Serbian area of Sarajevo, notably Grbavica. It could be shared on a three to one basis, with the Moslems getting three out of every four tons because the Moslem population of Sarajevo was about three times that of the Serb population. The UNHCR representative refused, however; he doesn't believe the Serbs deserve any assistance. Meanwhile, the Serbs want supplies shared on a fifty-fifty basis.

Around 12:30 P.M. this afternoon, while I was eating lunch, a large mortar shell landed in the compound. It landed just on our side of the fence that separated the UNPROFOR compound from the U.S. embassy compound. It was deflected by a tree but was still strong enough to shatter glass in the immediate vicinity, including the window in my office. It also injured four people and scared the hell out of all of us.

De Soto was in my office at the time. He was sitting at the large desk in the center of the room, perusing some papers. A serious jogger, de Soto had jogged through a sheltered area of Sarajevo that morning with my driver, Bruno Chaubert, a Corsican Warrant Officer, as his guide. De Soto had left his jogging gear near the terrace window, and the window open, to allow his gear to air out. The explosion deposited shards of glass in his gear. Thus, within forty-eight hours, not only had he witnessed a sniper attack, but he had almost been blown up while sitting quietly in his office. I was sure that such experiences were more instructive than all the official reports he had read about the security situation in Sarajevo.

I had never been that close to the explosion of a large artillery shell, and the sound was terrifying. At first, those of us in the dining room just looked at one another in shock and disbelief. The soldiers knew what had happened and also knew how close we had just come to being killed. I didn't even think about the latter until much later today. But it was not courage that made me ignore the proximity of death. Quite the opposite. I simply didn't want to imagine such a grisly reality except in retrospect, with some intellectual distance. I was in a state of shock.

I went outside to see how much damage had been done. There were four casualties, all soldiers who had been sitting at a picnic table near the impact site. They had been scratched superficially by shrapnel. One, who had taken a few shards of glass in the face, was in shock.

A few more feet in the wrong direction and the shell might have hit the headquarters building where we were having lunch. Many of us might have been killed; certainly, several of us would have been seriously wounded.

When a shell lands that close, one never knows whether another is on the way. Clearly, our barracks are within range of Serb artillery, but was this detonation merely a misfire? How accurate are such shells? And how long will it take to locate where they came from? There are no answers to such questions.

Meanwhile, we put on our helmets and flak jackets, evacuated corridors, and took whatever measures were demanded by a higher state of alert.

As luck would have it, I had planned to visit Pale that afternoon, and now I would have a very particular grievance to discuss. I grabbed my gear and my driver, and we left for Pale immediately.

While we were on the road to Pale, I was contacted on the radio. Two more shells had landed near the compound. One had landed across the street in front of the compound, and a second had landed next to the front gate. Two international photographers standing just outside the gate had been injured by the second one.

I brought the matter to Koljevic's attention as soon as I arrived in Pale.

At first he played dumb. "What street is the barracks on? What part of the city is it in?" he asked.

"You know Sarajevo better than I do, Professor. You know very well where it is, next to the U.S. embassy. For God's sake, you have to stop the shelling and tell me what the hell is going on."

"You know these shells are not always accurate. It may have been a mistake."

"Once might be a mistake. Three times is deliberate."

He reached for his Scotch in the bottom drawer. I declined a drink. He ordered food for us both, and I asked he would also have food prepared for my two drivers, one of whom was a bodyguard. I feared it would be a long afternoon.

Koljevic came at me from several angles at once. He was either groping or dodging or obfuscating. Or all three. He mentioned one possible explanation for the shelling, then withdrew it, broached another, and so on. He may not have known about this particular incident, but he was putting a spin on it as he talked. Koljevic can be as sincere as Anthony or as wily as Cassius. This afternoon he was in his Cassius mode.

"I wouldn't be surprised if it *was* the BSA," he confided after his third Scotch. "They're angry at you for bringing convoys over Igman without getting prior clearance. Next time they might even shoot at the convoy."

I recalled the morning meeting that very day and how Smith and UNHCR had boasted of having brought a convoy over Igman the night before without having asked for clearance from the BSA. But the BSA had not been asleep. They knew very well what had been happening, and often the BSA's responses to what they considered provocations are calculated, rather than spontaneous. At the same time, that explanation didn't really fit. It just didn't sound right to me.

"Look! You have to stop shelling UN headquarters! There's no justification for that," I insisted. "For God's sake, if I had been sitting outside, I might have been killed. We had four injured. What the hell is going on?"

Koljevic shifted gears. "Thousands of shells fall on Serbian villages and suburbs of Sarajevo, and you never protest. Not a word. The Security Council never passes resolutions when Serbs are killed." He then mentioned mortar rounds that had allegedly fallen in Serbian areas the day before—in Ilidza, Grbavica, and Rajlovac.

"You won't let us in to verify the shelling," I retorted. "You won't let the press in, and you won't let our military observers in. How can we report what we can't verify?"

I didn't believe that today's actions were a response to the shelling of Serb suburbs. It was something else.

We sparred a while. I insisted that the Serbs should stop shelling UN headquarters, as well as the civilian populations everywhere.

Koljevic shifted again. "The battle for Sarajevo has begun. It's the final countdown."

I fought off a smile. Then I thought about Muratovic. Inevitably, Koljevic is as theatrical as Muratovic, and as paranoid, though with a different manner. Koljevic is anxious, cautious, wily; Muratovic is brazen. But both are performers. Theater is an essential ingredient of Balkan politics.

"The battle for Sarajevo has been going on for three years. What we are talking about now is shelling of the UN compound. There's no strategic or political or humanitarian value to attacking the UN. It's stupid! You have to stop!"

"I have to admit, it could have been Mladic. Sometimes he's uncontrollable. I saw him in church this morning. He's very depressed. You know his daughter recently committed suicide."

Or was murdered, I thought. In the Balkans, whenever a prominent political figure or a member of his family dies unexpectedly, the official explanation is suicide, but in many cases it is murder.

This was Koljevic's fourth explanation: uncleared convoys; retaliation for shelling Serb suburbs; the apocalyptic battle for Sarajevo; and now, Mladic's emotional instability. I didn't believe any of them. It was possible that they were each parts of a greater picture or that, taken together, they had a cumulative effect. But I didn't believe any of his explanations, and I even began to think that Koljevic might not himself have known why UN headquarters had been targeted that day.

Perhaps Mladic didn't know what his local commanders were doing. That was the "rogue element" defense, often used by all sides. Koljevic hadn't tried that yet, but it was always a possibility. Perhaps there were other factors none of us knew about. Illogic, deception, machination, disorder, rogue elements—those were the components of negotiation in the Balkans.

Then Koljevic offered still another explanation, perhaps the most credible of all. "The only way to stop the shelling is for Bildt to come to Pale as soon as possible. As soon as he comes here, the international conference begins, the shelling stops, and the humanitarian convoys resume. All we need is for Bildt to come to Pale."

[I knew, however, that the United States, Germany, and the Bosnian government did not want another international conference on the Balkans. Not yet. They wanted the Bosnian Serbs to accept the Contact Group Plan first, and to be represented by Milosevic. Besides, the European Union had not given Bildt permission to visit Pale.

In one or two of my faxes, I had recommended to UNPF in Zagreb that I thought it would be a good idea for Bildt to spend an hour with the Bosnian Serb leadership, but there was no sympathy in the international community for such a suggestion. The Bosnian government, which intercepted all my faxes, was bitterly opposed to my position. I was more inclined to believe this last explanation for the shelling of the UNPROFOR compound than any other one, however. The point is that one never knew what to believe when talking to politicians in the Balkans. It was smoke and mirrors and bloodshed; that was the Balkans.]

"If you really want to help," Koljevic said, "you can convince Bildt to come here. Then the artillery will stop."

"I'll pass your offer up the line," I said.

Koljevic was still sipping Scotch. The food arrived.

"I'll tell you something," Koljevic said in his best Iago-like tone. "I wanted to let the convoys through immediately. I said it would show Bildt that we have good will, but Karadzic said *no*. He wants to have something to reward Bildt with when he comes to Pale. If we give him something too soon, then we won't have anything to give him when he comes to Pale."

I decided at that point that I needed a drink. Koljevic was happy to oblige me. "I see," I said.

As he poured me a drink, he repeated: "I'm telling you, as soon as Bildt comes to Pale, the international conference begins, the shelling stops, and the humanitarian convoys resume."

"Don't you realize that you're only encouraging the RRF to get involved?" I warned. "If you keep blocking humanitarian aid, you're asking for the RRF."

Koljevic sighed. "I know. I know the British," he said, shaking his finger. "They're stubborn. If they say they'll fight, they'll fight, and I don't want to have a fight with the British."

"Then let the convoys through."

Koljevic thought for a moment. "I think you're right, but Karadzic doesn't agree."

So we were back to Good Serb, Bad Serb. It was a game, a tale told by an idiot, full of sound and fury and scotch.

"Did you know that Karadzic wrote Clinton a letter last week proposing an international conference? A Camp David–style conference?"

"No, I didn't know."

Koljevic asked an assistant to bring him a copy of the letter. I read it quickly. I had never seen it before, had never seen any reference to it in the press. I asked if he could make a copy for me so that I might show it to Smith. Koljevic pondered melodramatically for a moment and then agreed. He had a copy made for me. (How quintessential it is these days, I thought, for every military headquarters to have a photocopy machine. One can't fight a modern war without a photocopy machine.)

Koljevic then asked me about the RRF. What is its mission? I gave him the standard answer—that it has been dispatched to improve UNPROFOR's self-defense capabilities and to help it fulfill its mandate of escorting humanitarian aid convoys.

Koljevic reiterated his fear of having a battle with the British. "It would be bloody," he said. "We're not looking for a fight with the British."

We then chatted for awhile about a range of topics, from Shakespeare to the inevitable tour of Serbian history. Koljevic presented me with a thick anthology of Serbian literature, written completely in Serbian. "Maybe one day you'll learn our language," he said.

I arrived back in Sarajevo after dark, around 8:00 P.M. I briefed Smith, then wrote a fax to Akashi. Smith listened closely to everything I said. He is a good listener; that is one of his many attributes. Meanwhile, shelling on the compound had stopped.

I told Smith about Koljevic's concern regarding the RRF. Smith doesn't mind that. He rather likes the thought that Koljevic is afraid of a battle with the Brits. However, at this point Smith feels that one of the big problems with the RRF is its lack of communication with the Bosnian Croats. Both England and France have been pushing the RRF without properly clearing the way with the Bosnian Croats, and the latter are offended at being slighted. There is also the inevitable question of command and control. Who will be in charge? There can be either a unified command at the top in Zagreb, a local command, or an intermediate command between the RRF and the force commander in Zagreb. The French want the RRF to report directly to Zagreb; Smith favors an intermediate command.

The devil is in the details, as always, but the main point is not to be lost. The RRF is arriving to declare war on the Bosnian Serbs. UNPROFOR is now taking the giant step of changing the mission from one of peacekeeping to one of peace enforcement. There will be no turning back.

3 July 1995

De Soto and I left Sarajevo at 5:30 A.M. and drove over Mount Igman. We had to cancel two or three air transport requests. We wanted to fly to Mostar from the French helipad at Veliko Polje on top of Igman, or fly from Kiseljak to Mostar if Igman-Mostar were not possible, but each time, either the weather or security arrangements broke down. So we drove.

Driving through eastern Bosnia is always a thrill, at any time of year, snipers be damned. It is an unmanicured Switzerland, replete with mountains, valleys, forests, lakes, twisting mountain roads with picturesque views, and tiny tile-roofed villages with legendary hospitality. One might as well expect war in the Land of Oz, as expect to find here Europe's bloodiest conflagration in five decades, but there is no explaining political hatreds. The kind of cruel and murderous devastation in Bosnia cannot be solely understood either in terms of class antagonism, religious rivalry, psychological perversity, or malevolent leadership. All of those factors are parts of the puzzle, but they all exist in dormant form in every society. What has catalyzed the madness in Bosnia? I have my own theories, but they seem academic at this point. Instead, I recall a Chinese saying that a friend, a female friend, used to quote to me: the more beautiful the woman, the more danger involved. Bosnia is the same.

We arrived at Mostar around 11:00 A.M. after a bumpy, uneventful ride. The city is generally divided between the Moslems on the east bank of the river and the Croats on the west bank. There is a small Serbian population, less than 5 percent. Before the war, the demographic breakdown had been: Moslems, 34.8 percent; Croats, 33.8 percent; Serbs, 19 percent; and others, 12.4 percent.

The BSA controls the hills above the city, and every once in awhile, in their tradition of shelling civilian populations, they lob a few shells into Mostar. But for the most part the shelling has stopped. There had once been a historic old bridge across the river dividing the city, a bridge that dated back to the Turkish occupation, but it had been destroyed early in the war during the fighting between the Moslems and the Croats. Mostar is in the Spanish battalion's area of responsibility. [Officially, we were supposed to refer to Bosnian Croats as *Croats*, to distinguish them from *Croatians*, who lived in Croatia.]

Though it might apply anywhere in the Balkans, I recalled Rebecca West's comment about Mostar when she arrived there: "There was immanent the Balkan feeling of a shiftless yet just doom."

Meanwhile, much of the Croat side of Mostar is placid now and beautiful: trees on the boulevards; gardens and orchards behind the beautiful houses; cafés; a few tourist hotels; and a lazy style of life. The Bosnian Croats use Croatian currency, the Kuna. The Bosnian Croat *policija* wear the same uniforms as the *policija* in Croatia, and there are Bosnian Croat soldiers in Mostar. [We referred to Bosnian Croat soldiers as the HVO to distinguish them from Croatian soldiers, known as the HV.] There is also a nationalist Croatian mayor. Moslems have been cleansed from the Croatian side of the city.

The word in the international community is that Mostar is run by gangsters on both sides of the river—not simply by nationalist politicians but by organized crime, with ties to the military. The war and the economic embargo have raised smuggling and black marketeering to the level of high patriotism. Gangsters have become paramilitary formations in the service of nationalism. It is true all through former Yugoslavia, but it is truest in Mostar.

The first briefing we had today was from the UNHCR liaison officer, Chris Jacobs. He noted that both Bosnian government and Bosnian Croat forces are present inside Mostar, in violation of the agreement on demilitarization of the city. Some of those soldiers are men returning from duty or preparing to go on duty because many soldiers have their homes in Mostar, but there are more soldiers—and weapons systems—than can be explained by residential necessities. Jacobs estimated about thirty-five hundred Bosnian Croat soldiers and one thousand Bosnian government soldiers are in Mostar on a regular basis. When there is shelling by the Serbs, about 80 percent of the time it is against the Bosnian Croats.

We went immediately to the Croat part of the city to a meeting chaired by Hans Koschnick, the European Union's administrator for Mostar. Koschnick, formerly a mayor of Dresden, was appointed by the European Union to help with the reconstruction of Mostar. The European Union is investing in rebuilding Mostar, hoping that its actions here will set an example for all of Bosnia.

[I was very favorably impressed with Koschnick, whom I had met over dinner in May during my familiarization tour of Sarajevo. He was impartial, well informed, energetic, charming, and dedicated. He knew about running cities, and he knew about international organizations. I almost couldn't believe he was German because every other German I met in former Yugoslavia was so biased and so obviously promoted the German government's political agenda. Koschnick, however, seemed to know that all three warring parties were unreasonable, all culpable in one way or another, and all generally corrupt and uncooperative. What he was dealing with were gangsters, not simply politicians on the take, and he knew it.]

Koschnick chaired the meeting, which was attended by the three mayors of Mostar: a Croat, a Moslem, and a Serb. De Soto was introduced at the start, and he made a brief statement saying he was in Mostar to gather information, not to institute any policy. When asked about the RRF, he gave the official line, that it is meant to strengthen the UN on the ground and enable it to carry out its mandate.

Mijo Brajkovic, the Bosnian Croat mayor, then spoke. He was a large man, big shouldered and assertive, and looked like a professional wrestler. He started slowly, with a few facts, and then drew a completely illogical conclusion. [He was quintessentially Balkan in that sense, reinforcing my thesis that in the Balkans the shortest distance between two points was a parabola.]

Mostar is better than it was two years ago, he began. There are no mass killings now, and there were no dead babies. There is peace in the Federation area. But Mostar is not an island. It is part of the Federation, and it should reflect the realities of the Federation. What are those realities? "We now have separate police, separate armies, and separate finances, but we should have a united city."

Right on, I thought.

"What are the choices for the Croatian people?" the mayor continued. "The fact is that this city is made of two peoples who have fought each other and spilled each other's blood. If we try to unite now, there will be more bloodshed, so let us begin with two separate municipalities that will eventually make one. Each municipality will retain its own culture, religion, educational system, and so on, but we can share public utilities—gas, electricity, and water—and the use of an airport."

Astonishing, I thought. Apartheid revisited. Also, incidentally, no mention of the Serbs, who were originally almost 20 percent of the population.

"There are many DPs. When the war is finally over, and the DPs are ready to return, then Croatian DPs will come home. In the Herzeg Bosna region, there will be 250,000 Croats. Those people need a center for their culture. The Serbs have Banja Luka. The Moslems have Zenica, Tuzla, and Sarajevo. The Croats have nowhere. They should have Mostar. It should be the center of Bosnian-Croat culture."

Koschnick was poker faced. He had heard this before, but it was a wonderful introduction for de Soto.

Then Janic, the Moslem mayor, spoke. He said that he had lived on the Croatian side of the city before the war, but his former apartment and property had been seized. He had not been able to retrieve it. At one time, fifteen thousand Moslems had lived in west Mostar. They had been expelled. Much of the eastern part of the city had been destroyed. For twenty-two months, the Moslem population had been without utilities.

Janic said he appreciates the efforts of the European administrator, who has undertaken many projects, but the administrator has not been very successful in the field of human rights.

Eighteen months after the Washington Agreement was signed (establishing the Federation), Mostar is not functioning as it should under the agreement. It is the worst city in all the Federation in terms of freedom of movement. Human rights are being violated. Security is inadequate. Crime is high. The police force should be unified. There should not be two separate police forces, and police should be recruited in proportion to the ethnic composition of the prewar population.

The Moslem side, he continued, does not believe in divided cities. It wants complete freedom of movement. As it stands now, the Moslems cannot cross freely over the bridge to the Croatian side of the city. They cannot return to their prewar dwellings. They are severely restricted in their movements.

He insisted that Moslems are still being expelled from the western side of the city, but that Croats can return to their homes on the eastern side of the city. All people should be allowed to return to their homes. Before the war, Mostar had a Moslem plurality. Why should it become a center for Croatian culture?

The Croatian mayor replied that expulsion is a criminal act, not an official policy of his administration. He does not support expulsion. As of now, nine thousand Moslems and two thousand Serbs live in the western part of Mostar. Fifty percent of the Moslems and Serbs who had lived in west Mostar before the war still live there, but only 1 percent of the Croats who had lived in east Mostar live there now.

[Lies, damned lies, and statistics, said Mark Twain, were three voices of a politician. But in this case, I suspected that even the statistics were lies. There are true statistics that can be given a spin, depending on the intent of the speaker. Here, however, I suspected the worst—not that the statistics were stacked, but that they were simply invented. How can one refer to population figures during a war when no census is possible?]

We stayed for about an hour in the meeting room. It seemed that everyone except de Soto and myself was smoking. It was very warm. Regrettably, the Serb mayor did not have a chance to speak. Koschnick apologized for that at the close, as the Serb futilely raised his hand for permission to take the floor.

Finally, as we were leaving, the Serb, quite shyly, put in a sentence or two condemning the policies of Karadzic and affirming his belief in a multi-ethnic city and society.

One could tell from the complaining tone of the Moslem mayor that his side had lost the most from the war; from the haughty, openly racist attitude of the Croat that he had the advantage and was not about to relinquish it; and from the hesitant approach of the Serb that he was basically irrelevant in Mostar and threatened.

After we left the mayors, we went to meet the Federation president, Kresimir Zubak. He had been handpicked by President Tudjman of Croatia. It would not be making a moral judgment one way or the other to say that Zubak considers himself first, a Croatian; second, a Bosnian Croat; third, a citizen of the Federation; and fourth, a citizen of Bosnia and Herzegovina.

Zubak was both buttressed and censored at our meeting. Local officials were present who from time to time added supportive material to whatever he said, but also present was the deputy foreign minister, a rather stern-looking, dark-suited, middle-aged member of the thought police who occasionally barked instructions to the interpreter, telling her what to leave out, what to put in, and how to render particularly sensitive political terms. He spoke very good English, even better than the official interpreter. [As I often said while in the former Yugoslavia, you can take the Communist out of the system, but you can't take the system out of the Communist. This was the KGB revisited—or continued.]

After we exchanged pleasantries and suspicious glances, Zubak turned to the subject of the RRF. [The RRF was having troubles obtaining permission to cross into Federation territory. It was due to arrive at Ploce, on the Croatian coast, and then cross into Federation territory, to bivouac at Tomislavgrad, but the Bosnian Croats were refusing to let it through the checkpoints. Meanwhile, the French were vowing to force their way through.]

Zubak assured us that basically the Federation approves of UNPROFOR, so it also approves of the RRF, but it mistrusts the British and French, who are providing the main components of the RRF. That mistrust is increasing as the forward elements of the RRF arrive because of the way they have entered "our country." They have entered without prior approval. The Federation has not been a party to negotiations on the RRF. It was been notified only at the end.

[I smiled to myself. The Federation was clearly not a "country." The "country" we were in was Bosnia and Herzegovina, and the Federation was only a part of that country, less than 50 percent at this point. Meanwhile, Zubak still made a distinction between the "Federation" and the government in Sarajevo. It was as though the Sarajevo government were in Washington, D.C., and the Federation were a union of 25 western states. As for the UN's obtaining prior permission, we had brought with us a copy of a letter sent by Muhamed Sacirbey, the foreign minister of Bosnia, to the president of the Security Council, accepting the presence of the RRF in Bosnia and Herzegovina.]

Zubak continued. The RRF has entered without UN emblems, without blue helmets, without white vehicles, and they are deploying in areas already under Bosnian-Croat control. How can that be explained? And it is not even clear who their commander is.

[Zubak had some valid points here, and I took note in my journal of his objections, determined to raise them with Akashi and Janvier. The question of command and control was still being worked out, although in theory all forces reported to Janvier and, through him, to the Secretary-General of the United Nations or to his representative in the mission area, Akashi. But theory and practice were often poles apart. On the question of uniforms, Zubak again had a point. Were these peacekeeping forces or not? And if they were not wearing blue helmets, then were they under command of their national capitals, namely Paris and London? Moreover, was it possible that Paris and London might turn the RRF against the Bosnian Croats? Otherwise, the concern about permission reflected the sensitivities of the Bosnian Croat community. Sarajevo, which was far away and didn't even control its own territory, was always consulted; the Bosnian Croats were not. All of these points presented themselves by implication rather than direct expression, but I made certain to brief de Soto on my views of the situation. He was always very appreciative.]

De Soto replied to Zubak that the RRF is intended to strengthen the capacity of UNPROFOR to implement its mandate in the mission area. That goal has been clarified many times. If there are further questions, they will be answered in due course, but he himself has not come to negotiate on the RRF or on any other issue. He has come on a fact-finding mission. He then asked Zubak about the Federation. Is there widespread support for it?

Zubak replied that the Croats have the political will to support the Federation. The Moslems also have the will. There are some obstacles, but they are not insurmountable.

Where are the obstacles to the Federation coming from? de Soto asked. From all sides?

Zubak then refined his earlier statement. The Croats believe in the Federation, he said, but the Moslems and others resist it. The Moslems are divided. The highest Moslem military officials want to continue the war until they have liberated all of Bosnia, whereas Moslem political officials support the Federation and accept its boundaries. There is confusion on the Moslem side, but the real problem is the Serbs. Military and political leaders on the Bosnian side can be convinced to enter the Federation. The Croats have already accepted it. The problem is with the Serbs.

[Zubak's comments were particularly interesting if, once again, one read between the lines. When he said that the Serbs were the main problem, and the Moslem military were another problem, he was being realistic from a military viewpoint, but he was also reflecting Croat anxieties. The Bosnian Croats had joined the Federation for two reasons: to form a common front against the Bosnian Serbs and to protect Croatian minorities in Moslem-held territory. They didn't give a damn about multiculturalism or the eventual composition of Bosnia and Herzegovina. Like the other ethnic groups, they were concerned exclusively about their own people. Once the Bosnian Serbs had been neutralized, their fears were that Bosnian government forces might turn against the Bosnian Croats. Therefore, they were wary of the Bosnian government military's opposition to the Federation (as well as of that military's being rearmed). They also were suspicious that the RRF might come to the aid of the Bosnian government against the interests of the Bosnian Croats.]

De Soto then expressed his hope that Bildt and Stoltenberg, now both in the region, will be successful in their efforts to end the war and arrive at a peaceful solution, but the process is slow, and the parties will have to cooperate. A solution cannot be imposed on the parties. It will be best if the parties themselves come to an agreement.

Zubak disagreed that the full responsibility is with the parties themselves. There are Security Council resolutions and norms of international law, and the international community should enforce those resolutions. They should not leave it to the parties themselves.

[When I returned to Sarajevo three days later, I sent a fax to Akashi about our meetings in Mostar and added my own analysis of the situation. I emphasized the following points:

1. There was a lack of a clear constitutional relationship between the Federation in Mostar and the Bosnian government in Sarajevo.

2. The use of non-UN uniforms generated suspicion among the Croats. They feared the RRF might be used against them to roll back their military gains. They suspected the British and French of being pro-Serb.

3. The Federation wanted more money. More troops meant more facilities, which meant more MONEY. That was part of the reason they were resisting.

4. The Federation feared the RRF might be there to lead NATO soldiers out of Bosnia. The Croats want NATO to remain in Bosnia and whack the Serbs.

5. The Bosnians and the Croats felt they were winning, and that the RRF would freeze the situation. Worse, they might interfere by gathering intelligence, by setting the stage for political pressure, or by actual interposition between the Bosnian Croat army and the BSA at a time when Bosnian Croat forces were making important advances, especially in the Livno Valley, in preparation for an assault on the Krajina.

Anecdotally, I also recounted what our interpreter had told us following our meeting with Zubak. We had all gone to a local cafe to have coffee, and she volunteered the information that the deputy foreign minister had told her not to interpret a brief intervention by Zubak denouncing the British and the French for being pro-Serb. Minutes later, our same lovely young interpreter, upon seeing in a store window a photo of President Tudjman next to the pope, said: "Look at that: my president with the pope." *My* president? But your president is President Izetbegovic, I thought. But for once I had the good sense not to articulate my irreverent ponderings. So much for the Federation.]

We left Mostar by road for Kiseljak at around one o'clock. From Kiseljak we were able to fly to Split, Croatia, on the Dalmatian coast. I stayed overnight in Split, prior to returning to Sarajevo. De Soto departed by air for Zagreb. He had had a full visit, both in Sarajevo and in Mostar. He has a first-rate political mind, and I appreciated his presence.

While here in Split I tried to visit Eyup Ganic, the Bosniak vice president of the Federation, who had recently been seriously injured in a car accident. He was in a hospital. I found the hospital, but I could not get in to see him. He was too heavily sedated and was not accepting visitors. I left a note with my condolences and wishes for a speedy recovery. Akashi had already done the same.

I made extensive notes about the RRF, notes that I eventually incorporated into a fax that I sent to Akashi. Here were my thoughts:

Before the operation becomes irreversible, it is time to reconsider the wisdom of deploying the RRF. I offer a balance sheet: arguments in favor versus arguments against. I have two arguments in favor and at least ten against.

Arguments in favor.

1. The European Union wants it and believes it will assist UNPROFOR in implementing its mandate.

2. It may break the siege of Sarajevo and thereby prevent a major military battle for control of Sarajevo.

Arguments against.

1. *None* of the parties to conflict wants the RRF. The Federation and the BiH government fear it will be used to protect the Serbs, to freeze the present battle lines. Worse (for them), it may be used against Bosnian government forces and Bosnian Croat forces at a time when they are winning. Even if it is used to freeze the current situation, they consider this approach to be against the best interests of the Bosnian Moslems and the Bosnian Croats. They don't want the RRF to interfere unless they can be guaranteed that the RRF will be used against the Serbs. Meanwhile, the Serbs are certain the RRF will be used against them.

2. The RRF has and will continue to have major funding problems.

3. The RRF has and will continue to have major command and control problems.

4. The RRF will cause serious strategic and logistic problems. It has to be fed, billeted, supported. The troops's quarters will have to be winterized, which, with the current restrictions on movement, will be a nightmare.

5. The RRF base in Tomislavgrad is on the wrong side of the mountain chain if troops are to be flown *rapidly* to the Mount Igman area. Given fog or rain, they will be immobilized. On the other hand, installing them on or near Igman involves a entirely different set of problems—political, logistical, financial, and even military.

6. Arrival of the RRF is undeniably escalatory. In retrospect, the use of air strikes against Pale on 26–27 May has had several negative consequences. As a result of those bombings, we lost the exclusion zone around Sarajevo; we lost the WCPs; we lost communication with Mladic; we have all but lost the ability to use air strikes while UNPROFOR troops are on Bosnian Serb territory; we have more difficulty in delivering humanitarian aid; and we have encouraged a Bosnian government offensive. If we cannot deal with the consequences of escalation, we should not escalate, as General Smith has often said.

7. Bureaucracies begin with idealism and end in self-perpetuation. We are bloating like a slug filled with beer. Instead of concentrating on diplomacy, we are desperately trying to justify our presence through marginal military activity. It would be far more sensible to send Bildt to Pale than to bring in twelve thousand RRF troops. Two hours in Pale would be more productive than twelve thousand troops in Tomislavgrad and Visoko.

8. The RRF is politically embarrassing. Their stated mission is to protect UNPROFOR, although the Bosnian people remain unprotected and vulnerable to continued shelling and strangulation. The RRF is a reaction to attacks upon UNPROFOR, which was a reaction by the BSA to air strikes, which was a reaction to violation by the Serbs of the Total Exclusion Zone, which was a reaction by the Serbs to offensives out of safe areas by the Bosnian government, which was a reaction to . . . We are reacting against elements of the situation, rather than taking creative diplomatic initiatives. The calculated use of force does not show determination; it shows desperation.

9. There is no doubt that the RRF will be used against the Serbs. The governments want a bang for their buck. Once the RRF is deployed, it will be used, and given the current political climate, there is no doubt against whom it will be used. By entering into a combat role against the Serbs, we have finally destroyed the UN as a peacekeeping mechanism in this conflict. There is no way to remain an impartial interlocutor when one is militarily aligned with one side.

10. The final transition from a peacekeeping force to a peace-enforcement operation will place at risk all military and civilian personnel in the region. This transition is being done without the clear consent of the governments whose personnel are in the region. If those governments had known from the start that their personnel were being sent to war, either they would not have sent them, or they would have trained them differently and sent them with different equipment.

6 July 1995

8:30 A.M. Smith's briefing. Another UNHCR convoy made it into Sarajevo last night. Contents of the last three UNHCR convoys have all gone to the Moslem population, none to the Serbs. On another matter, our military intelligence confirmed SAMS [surface to air missiles] being installed in Serb-controlled areas around Bihac, in northwestern Bosnia, on the border with the Krajina area in Croatia.

Meanwhile, Bildt is back in Sarajevo.

At the 11:30 briefing, General Hervé Gobilliard, the French commander of Sector Sarajevo, made a statement about the situation in Sarajevo: it is tense and dangerous. [I had great respect for Gobilliard, whose balanced, well-informed approach to the situation in Sarajevo walked a wiggly line between Serbs and Moslems, French and British, Sarajevo and Zagreb, and the political and the military poles of the conflict.]

While Smith is the commander for all of Bosnia, Gobilliard is in charge of Sector Sarajevo and has the daily responsibilities for implementing the policies of the international community regarding Sarajevo. There are also Egyptian, Russian, and Ukrainian contingents in Sarajevo, but the French have 95 percent of the responsibility here.

[There was an inevitable rivalry between the French and the British forces in Bosnia, and although it didn't obstruct UNPROFOR's operation, it caused some friction. It was the Brits and the French, in fact, who had been fighting for a millennium, not the Serbs and the Croats and the Moslems. It was common and politically correct in the world community to say that the peoples of Bosnia had been fighting one another for hundreds of years, but several historical studies contradict that assumption. The internecine fighting among Serbs, Croats, and Moslems did not really start earnestly until after the Congress of Berlin in 1878 and it reached its zenith only under the Nazis, about sixty years ago. It was the Nazis who decided their puppet fascist state of Croatia, which included Bosnia under its wing, was the outpost of Western civilization and that the Serbs throughout Yugoslavia were *Untermenschen*, like the Russians. Before that, much of the fighting in Bosnia had been either anticolonialist (against the Turks and the Austrians) or class oriented—Moslem and Serbian and Croatian peasants rising against their landowners, who were largely Moslem. In defense of the Croatians, however, it must be said that they were willing to bond with anyone, even Nazis, if it would free them from Serbian domination. The ones who had really been quarreling and warring with each other for hundreds of years as stated, were the French and the British. That rivalry continued even in Bosnia for several reasons.

For one thing, there was a difference of opinion at the top, between Paris and London. President Mitterrand had said early on during the conflict that France would never go to war with the Serbs, whereas Smith, who reflected Washington's attitudes and influenced London's policies, was eager for a scrap with "Johnny Serb."

Another reason for the difference in approach was the situation on the ground. The French were the implementing force in Sarajevo and thus were continually harassed, shot at, blocked, and threatened by Bosnian government forces, as well as by the BSA. Hence, they were more critical of the Bosnian government. It was the French who frequently pointed out that the Bosnian government was placing weapons systems next to UN facilities in order to draw fire from Serb artillery onto civilian and UN targets, and thus to provoke international outrage against the Serbs; it was the French who manned the checkpoints entering and leaving Sarajevo; it was the French who were responsible for the Sarajevo airport; it was the French who accompanied convoys over Mount Igman and were targeted by *both* Serbian and Bosnian government gunners; and it was the French who guarded most of the weapons collection points around Sarajevo until they were overrun by the BSA.

The French also took the heaviest casualties in the Sarajevo area. By summer 1995, the French had already suffered about fifty dead and five times as many wounded.

Finally, there was the rivalry between military traditions. Off the record, the British (never Smith himself, who was too much the diplomat), ridiculed French military defeats in World War II, Vietnam, Algeria, and elsewhere. The French, on the other hand, disliked what they saw as the arrogance and cultural hegemony of the Anglos. By disliking the British, the French could also dislike the Americans, a side benefit.]

In his briefing to Bildt, Smith noted that he has no contact with General Mladic, which he regrets. Otherwise, the Bosnian government offensive is continuing, and the Bosnian government is doing a good job of maintaining its status as victim, even while it continues to attack. He feels that UNPROFOR must react carefully to any provocations and limit itself to proportionate response because it is still only mandated to protect humanitarian convoys, nothing more.

Over the last few weeks, Smith continued, we have lost our credibility with the Bosnian government, largely because of the resumed shelling of Sarajevo, to which UNPROFOR has been unable to respond. We had long since lost our credibility with the Serbs. UNPROFOR is being marginalized and faces increasing hostility.

The BSA is behaving like terrorists, and there is nothing we can do about it under our present mandate.

On another point, Smith thinks it will be "quite dangerous" to have Ukrainian troops in the eastern enclaves, where there are Bosnian government troops, because the government troops hate the Ukrainians. Reportedly, UN headquarters in New York is considering withdrawing British troops from Gorazde and Dutch troops from Srebrenica, and replacing them with Ukrainians. Smith thinks that will be a bad idea. So does the Bosnian government.

Finally, a second tunnel under the airport in Sarajevo is being built and is expected to be ready within a month. This tunnel will be high and wide enough to handle vehicles. The present one is only for people.

We then chatted briefly about the RRF: who will be in charge, where it will be stationed, what exactly will be its mission. I voiced my concerns about its deployment. Bildt listened and took notes, but the decision has been made. It is bigger than both of us. The RRF is a fact of life.

At lunch I informed Bildt of how eager the Serbs in Pale are to speak to him, but of course I didn't proffer advice. He has his mandate, and I am not about to question it. I merely informed him how the Serbs are thinking.

He said he feels that the major key for resolving the conflict is in Belgrade, and he will pursue his contacts with Milosevic. If he talks with the Bosnian Serbs, he will not go to Pale. Perhaps he might meet them in Zvornik, but not in Pale. He believes that Milosevic is the one who can make things happen.

On 24 June, a couple of weeks earlier, Koljevic and company actually had a secret meeting in Zvornik with members of Bildt's entourage: General de la Presle (a former force commander, and a French national); General Christopher Elliot, a British national; and two U.S. military advisors, but Bildt and Karadzic had not been present.

My impression in speaking to Bildt is that he is interested in the end game, not in details such as opening Route Swan or the road over Mount Igman. He wants a comprehensive peace settlement, but is limited by the mandate he holds. The matter of approach was discussed at the Cannes Summit of European foreign ministers on 26–27 June, and the Germans won—no Pale, no Karadzic, no concessions. At the least, Bildt will have to be guaranteed a positive result before he will meet with the Bosnian Serbs, and even then, he cannot meet in Pale.

After lunch, I heard one of the young British officers, a woman, talking to a colleague. "If only everyone, on the political side as well, would get behind the commander, then we would be able to take action. If only the governments would back us, then the people would back us, even if it meant losing a few lives. Force is the only thing the Serbs respect."

Another British officer said to me. "You have to understand. It's very difficult to be shot at and harassed, and not to be able to respond. That's not our training. We're soldiers. We fight."

"But this is a peacekeeping mission," I said.

Scowl. Wimpy intellectual.

I pulled out my old line: "What about the letters home to the parents of young men and women that would have to be written by the commander? Think on it. 'I regret to inform you that your son or daughter died defending the Igman road into Sarajevo.' Or how about 'defending the principle of freedom of movement in Bosnia.' Are you willing to pay that price?"

"The British people would accept it," Wonder Woman replied.

[I wanted to say: "If you want to play your rotten war games, then go rent yourself an island off the Adriatic and have your fun. The escalation of this conflict will cause greater casualties to all concerned than the attempt at a peaceful resolution. The ripple effect of escalation will not be restricted to Sarajevo. Everyone, soldier and civilian alike, will be placed in jeopardy. The dustbins of history are filled with the names of leaders who overestimated their military capabilities, and the cemeteries are cluttered with their soldiers and innocent civilians. What is wanted is a political solution, not a military disaster." I wanted to say all that, but did not. "Oh," I merely said and walked away. I depended on the Brits and had to live in Sarajevo for a while. Besides, I would never attempt to undermine Smith, especially to his own soldiers.

But I had probably made another enemy.]

7 July 1995

8:15 A.M. local press reading in my office. Bosnian government news was reporting air attacks on Srebrenica by the BSA. Our own sources have not confirmed such attacks.

The government press spoke disparagingly about Bildt because he wants a political solution to the conflict, and he opposes lifting the arms embargo on Bosnia. Otherwise, they insisted that Milosevic is the only one with whom to speak on the Serb side; Bildt should not go to Pale.

Prime Minister Haris Siladzic went to a meeting of Islamic states in Morocco to seek political support from those countries. [He was, of course, also seeking military support.] The Islamic countries are calling for a special session of the UN General Assembly on Bosnia. They feel they will have wider representation in the General Assembly than in the Security Council. Siladzic, who speaks perfect French (as well as Arabic and English) will also be going to Paris, to seek French support for opening a corridor from Sarajevo all the way to the Adriatic coast. He is likely to get political support for this idea from the French, but unlikely to get military support from them.

Bosnian Serb news reported fighting in Bihac. The Serbs say they now have the means to respond to NATO air attacks, and they will do so. They cannot remain passive to such attacks, and they cannot allow themselves to be humiliated.

[When I heard this comment on Serb radio, I had two thoughts. First, I doubted if the BSA really understood the awesome magnitude of NATO's military capacity. From cruise missiles to Cobra helicopters, NATO could destroy whatever military arsenals the Serbs had, including SAMs. It was sheer stupidity, egotism, and masochism for the Serbs to think they could stand up to NATO, but I was fearful that the Serb rhetoric was serious. They really believed they could deter NATO, and they were dead wrong.

The other thought that entered my mind was a strategic one. Mladic had apparently made up his mind to concentrate on Bihac, believing that if he captured Bihac, he could have one contiguous Serbian nation, from Belgrade in Serbia, through Republika Srpska in Bosnia, all the way to the Krajina in Croatia. If he could capture Bihac, he could protect the Krajina, deepen his defense perimeters, and be in a much better bargaining position when it came to peace talks. However, he did not have the troops to fight on two major fronts at once, and by concentrating on Bihac, he was sacrificing southwest Bosnia, where Bosnian Croat forces, assisted by Croatian army regulars, were working their way slowly up the Livno Valley, the back door to Knin, which was the rebel Serb capital in Croatia. If Knin fell, then all of Serb-controlled western Bosnia, up to the gates of Banja Luka, would be endangered. In Mladic's mind, however, Bihac was more important than Knin, partly because it would be easier to defend. Mladic's supply lines were already overextended. He would never be able to reach all the way to Livno.]

At the 8:30 A.M. briefing, we heard of a protest staged by Moslem women in the town of Bugojno. Yesterday, they sat down in the road to protest their sons being drafted into the Bosnian government army. They blocked a group of recruits marching out of town, about to be taken to Sarajevo to fight in the current government offensive. We took this move as a sign that the battle for Sarajevo is not going well for the government side, that it is taking heavy casualties.

Another aspect of the situation should also be considered. Bugojno is a placid village in Federation territory, relatively unthreatened, with a factory and some light industry. If the boys go off to war, there will be a severe labor shortage, and as poor as the wages are in Bugojno, they are still better than they are in the army. And factories are safer than battlefronts.

We have confirmed reports that Srebrenica is being shelled and that the Dutch battalion there is being shelled. They are being shelled by artillery, not by air attacks (which would be a violation of the no-fly zone), as was claimed on Bosnian government radio. Either way, it is another violation of the safe area concept, and the Dutch are not equipped to fight back. Not only can they not defend Srebrenica, they cannot even defend themselves. Only air strikes will protect them.

On a local matter, our transport office is now trying to lay on a shuttle between Sarajevo and Split, on Mondays, Wednesdays, and Fridays. It will be over Mount Igman, and one will have to book two days in advance. People have been cooped up in Sarajevo for some time now, and there is a need to be able to get out, not simply for rest and recuperation but also for troop rotation and for business in Zagreb.

Finally, at the 9:30 A.M. meeting in Smith's office, I volunteered that the new chief of mission, Antonio Pedauye, is due to arrive in Sarajevo around midmonth, between 16 and 19 July. The problem continues to be where to put him. Since office space in Sarajevo is at a premium, Smith and I agreed it will be best to put him in the main building at headquarters, for purposes of security as well as efficiency. However, if we put him on the top floor, that means Smith's bodyguards, who sleep there, will be displaced. If the bodyguards have to be moved, then office space on one of the other floors will have to be sacrificed. The British army thereupon glanced at the Civil Affairs representatives. I vowed to resist, even though I know that I can expect no support from anywhere. Our offices are destined to be turned into dormitories.

This afternoon I went to Pale to see Koljevic. He was in a garrulous mood—very eager to see Bildt and concerned that the situation is deteriorating rapidly, especially with regard to humanitarian aid. A meeting with Bildt might be able to rescue it, he believed. [In fact, although the BSA had been able to frustrate the Bosnian government offensive, the Serbs were deeply concerned about their long-term military future. Not only were they at a military peak now, with nowhere to go but down, but they sensed that the international community was preparing to intervene militarily on the side of the Bosnian government.]

I told Koljevic that Bildt cannot meet with the Bosnian Serbs because it is not within his mandate and that if anyone from his party meets with the Bosnian Serbs, it will not be in Pale because that will be too much like formal recognition. Perhaps in Zvornik, where Koljevic previously met with members of Bildt's team, but not in Pale.

Koljevic seemed surprised that I know about the meeting in Zvornik, but he repeated that the Bosnian Serb leadership should meet with Bildt himself, even if it will not be in Pale. The important thing is to meet. However, if it is not to be in Pale, then Karadzic will not attend. The Serb delegation will comprise himself, Foreign Minister Alex Buha, and Jovan Zametica, a political advisor to Karadzic.

Koljevic said he cannot understand why Bildt refuses to come to Pale. I said again that the EU has given Bildt a very specific window within which to operate. He has to stay within that window.

We moved next to discuss an agenda. [All negotiations begin with questions of venue and agenda. In international negotiations, substance is frequently debated in terms of protocol: where a meeting will take place, who will attend, who speaks first, what the topics will be, and so on. In such situations, form *is* substance; the two merge, but at the same time they remain distinct. In a way, it is like looking at Jasper Johns's U.S. flag paintings. One wonders: am I looking at a flag or at the representation of a flag? Am I responding to the flag or to what the flag represents? Is the meeting the message, or is the message what is discussed at the meeting?]

In any case, Koljevic didn't want to discuss a possible agenda, saying that the holding of the meeting itself will transcend any agenda. At the same time, the BSA might offer to open Route Swan through the Sierras, leaving only one checkpoint in place. (The Serbs promised this a month earlier at the meeting I attended in Pale between Koljevic and Bijleveld of UNHCR. At that time, Koljevic was much haughtier because the Serbs were holding UNPROFOR hostages.) Koljevic added, as before, that he is still not eager to have UNPROFOR escorts for UNHCR convoys. I replied that I am not competent to discuss that issue; he will have to take it up with UNHCR.

He then confided to me, in his most melodramatic tone, a recent incident that occurred in Gorazde and that would explain why the Serbs can't trust the international community and have to remain vigilant. The BSA confiscated thirty thousand German Marks from the convoy of a nongovernmental organization attempting to enter Gorazde. No doubt the money was to be used to buy weapons for the Moslems, he said. While on the subject of Gorazde, he added that members of the French organization, Médecins Sans Frontières, who are presently being detained by the BSA outside of Gorazde, would soon be released. He reminded me that a UNHCR convoy was allowed to enter Gorazde yesterday, showing that the Serbs were willing to allow humanitarian aid into the enclaves. Meanwhile, the munitions factory run by the Bosnian government in Gorazde is still operating. It is a provocation. What sort of safe area permits an arms factory to continue operating?

He then veered off to Srebrenica, complaining that armed Moslem marauders are going out on raids into Serbian villages and stealing livestock— sheep and goats—from local Serb farmers. That, too, is a provocation against the Serbs.

"The Moslems have no food. They have to steal. You won't allow aid convoys to reach Srebrenica," I said.

"They have an army inside Srebrenica: thirty-five hundred soldiers. You know that. We are not talking about feeding civilians. If their army gives up their weapons and leaves, they can have all the food they want."

"They're afraid that if they give up their weapons, the whole town will be cleansed, and that you will slaughter them." [I remember a comment once made to me by Muratovic when I asked him why government forces simply didn't surrender in situations when they had no hope of winning. "We can't surrender. They kill us!" he said.]

"And what about the Serbs who have been cleansed from the area? Where have they gone? Where can they go?" He didn't respond to my concern that the BSA would slaughter the Moslems if they surrendered, that the BSA would take no male prisoners between the ages of six and sixty.

I told him I was not authorized to negotiate the future status of Srebrenica. It was a military matter, but said I would pass his views on up the line to my superiors.

I returned then to the problems of supplying Sarajevo. Why, I asked, as I had in the past, if he is willing to open the Sierras, doesn't he just do it? Why all this maneuvering? Why all these feints? Why wait for Bildt, who may never come and who may be more encouraged to come *after* the Serbs have opened the Sierras?

He answered, as he had before, that the Serbs want to save something to offer Bildt.

I suggested that he may not be able to entice anyone in Bildt's party without first agreeing on an agenda. Moreover, he should indicate that he is willing to make a concession to Bildt. He should not be so rigid. "If 'twere done, then 'twere well it were done quickly," I Shakespeared him, well aware that the quote from *Macbeth* referred to a political assassination. He smiled. He said that the Serbs are willing to agree not to meet in Pale and will guarantee that one agenda item could be how to end the humanitarian aid crisis in Sarajevo. Those are his concessions.

Once again, I had the distinct impression that the Serbs want to cut a deal. (The same message was recently conveyed separately to UNHCR and to General Gobilliard by their interlocutors in the Serb community.) Moreover, I had the suspicion that Koljevic's anxieties concern not only the possible intervention of the RRF but also the possible response of the Bosnian Serb army to the RRF. Whether genuine or feigned, Koljevic has more than once conceded to me how ruthless the Serb military can be. He is not happy that he and Karadzic have lost power to the military; Mladic is uncontrollable.

Finally, as I was about to leave, Koljevic expressed his belief that UNPROFOR should stay in Bosnia. Its presence will prevent a wider war, he said. I thanked him for his support of UNPROFOR, but wondered to myself about the irony of the Serbs wanting UNPROFOR to stay in Bosnia even after UNPROFOR bombed them and after the Serbs themselves just antagonized UNPROFOR by taking its troops hostage. Or perhaps he believes that NATO will never start a war against the Serbs as long as UNPROFOR is still in the theater. Besides, UNPROFOR is still his only contact with the outside world.

Better to bear those ills he has than fly to others that he knows not of.

At the 6:00 P.M. briefing, Smith announced that Belgium has said it will contribute 180 paratroopers to the RRF.

On another matter, the BSA has given permission for a Danish convoy to enter Sarajevo through the Sierras. This new flexibility is probably in order to discourage use of the Mount Igman road, which the BSA does not control. We are all aware, however, that the Serbs can easily reverse themselves at any time and close the Sierras again. This is why Smith wants to open the Igman road—because he feels it will be easier for UNPROFOR to control.

Apparently, French President Chirac has been pushing the Serbs to open the Sierras. The French are once again playing the double card. They are taking a hard line by urging forward deployment of the French component of the RRF, and they are using political pressure behind the scenes to convince the Serbs to make concessions so that the French will not have to use force. The threat to use force is public; the political pressure is private.

Smith expressed his approval that convoys may be moving into Sarajevo. However, he mentioned a few key conditions that have to be satisfied: permission should be extended to both UNPROFOR and UNHCR convoys; we, not the Serbs, should decide on the content of the convoys; and UNHCR convoys should be accompanied by an UNPROFOR escort.

On another matter, one of our press spokesmen mentioned the continuing furor in Washington over Akashi's letter to Karadzic. The storm was started by a Roger Cohen article in the *New York Times,* which implied that in his letter Akashi reassured the Bosnian Serbs that the RRF will not be used against them. The U.S. permanent representative to the UN, Madeleine Albright, made one of her Serb-hating, UN-bashing statements, demanding a copy of Akashi's letter and implying that Akashi should be recalled.

[UN headquarters in New York refused to release the letter, but the vilification of Akashi continued for another week or two, and the incident eventually became part of the mythology of the UN's shameful performance in Bosnia; soon, it was routinely included in the so-called summaries that the Reptile Kingdom produced in their capsule histories of Bosnia.

The UN's refusal to release the letter was not merely based on the principle that UN internal correspondence must remain internal but also reflected the concern of the Secretary-General that, once released, the letter would have a life of its own. It would become even more of a rallying point for anti-UN activists, and it would divert attention from more substantive problems.

As for the letter itself, which I had personally delivered to Pale, it was, as stated earlier, completely proper. It recounted phrases from Security Council resolutions and paragraphs from letters by the Secretary-General. For example, Akashi referred to the following statement by the Secretary-General:

> As the Security Council has recognized, UNPROFOR's ability to carry out the tasks given to it by the Council depends to a very large extent on the readiness of the parties to cooperate with it. This would remain the case. In this connection, the three Governments [contributing to the RRF—namely, France, England, and the Netherlands] have made it clear that their intention is that the reinforced UNPROFOR would continue to be a peacekeeping mission.

Akashi was simply too professional a diplomat to make an error in a case like this. His letter was intended to maintain calm and state the facts. Officially, the Security Council had said that the RRF was being deployed to protect UNPROFOR's mission to assist in the delivery of humanitarian aid. The RRF had never been given a mandate to be used aggressively against the Serbs, but Karadzic was, understandably, suspicious and had asked for clarification. Akashi had quoted to him the official line. There was nothing unusual about such behavior.

But Roger Cohen had a different agenda; he was determined to skewer the UN. In May, when the Croatian army had retaken Western Slavonia from rebel Serbs, Cohen had been given a tour of the area and had lyrically defended the "professional" nature of the operation, denying any persecution of Serb civilians and stating that no proof existed for claims by the Serbs of human rights abuses, including the existence of mass graves. Later information, specifically regarding a mass grave at Pakrac, would prove him dead wrong, but his reports had confirmed him as a reliable Serb basher, a man to be trusted by the international community's policymakers.

As for Akashi, he didn't flinch. He made no public statements, no denials, no defenses; he kept his cool. I myself would not have had his patience.]

8 July 1995

8:15 A.M. press reading in my office. Serb radio was reporting Bosnian government attacks against Serb areas. Bosnian government radio was reporting BSA attacks against Moslem areas. [They were both correct in this case.]

The French wire services were reporting that the French contingent to the RRF (i.e., the French battalion in the multinational brigade) will act on its own, without asking approval from UNPF headquarters in Zagreb. The French battalion is composed of the famous French Foreign Legion. France is determined to open a route to Sarajevo one way or another and to use force if necessary.

[This public bellicosity by French military spokespersons, which contrasted with Boutros-Ghali's and the French government's own quiet diplomacy, had probably been aggravated by the recent death of another French soldier on Mount Igman. It was also motivated, some believed, by France's wish to recapture some of the weapons market in the Arab Gulf states, a market taken over by the United States after the Gulf War and then strengthened by the continuing support of the United States for the Bosnian government. France, a traditional ally of the Serbs, was looking to assuage the Moslem world and build bridges to the Gulf Arabs.]

The command structure of the RRF is still being discussed. At this stage, Smith told us, the decision to use it will have to be taken at UNPF headquarters in Zagreb, but once that decision is taken, Smith will be able to use it however he wishes.

8:30 A.M. briefing. Bildt departed the theater yesterday afternoon by helicopter from Konjic. As his helicopter was preparing to depart, it was shelled. No hits, just harassment. We are not certain where the shelling originated. We know that Bosnian government forces shelled Bildt on the Igman road the day before, when he had arrived by armored vehicle. They might also have shelled the helipad, but we can't be certain yet, and will await an investigation. Usually, though not always, we can be reasonably sure who is doing the shelling, since we know which forces control which ground, and we know the distance that various shells can travel. Certainly, the Bosnian government knew Bildt's schedule, and certainly they dislike him. In fact, the Bosnian government communicated to us only yesterday their deep resentment that we are only *notifying* them of our helicopter flights, rather than asking them in advance for clearance. Meanwhile, we were sure that the world press, which also disliked Bildt, would never report that the Bosnian government had tried to kill him.

On the matter of convoys, one reached Bihac yesterday without any problem. Today, convoys are scheduled to go to Gorazde and Srebrenica. The next convoy for Sarajevo is several days away.

So, it appears there is some loosening of the noose by the BSA with regard to convoys, but there is no way we can be certain how long their cooperation will last. And it certainly will not discourage deployment of the RRF.

At the 9:00 A.M. briefing in Smith's office the chief of the UN military observers asked me if, on my next trip to Pale, I would raise with the Serb authorities the question of allowing UN military observers back into Bosnian Serb territory. I said I would. He himself can't go to Pale because the Serbs won't let him in.

I decided to go to Gornji Vakuf as soon as possible to visit my staff there and to take a quick tour of the area. Gornji Vakuf is the subheadquarters for Sector Southwest. Since arriving in Sarajevo, I have tried three times to go to Gornji Vakuf, but each time I have been prevented from doing so because of ongoing fighting or political developments. Roads or helipads were closed, or VIPs were coming to Sarajevo and needed a briefing. There were always reasons not to leave Sarajevo. There is really too much to do, especially with a small staff and someone always on leave or stuck somewhere and unable to return to duty. But this time I would go to Sector Southwest because I had an additional incentive. Smith asked me if I would speak with General Andrew Pringle, the British commander for the sector, about problems associated with accommodating the RRF.

Plans are to have the RRF accommodated initially at Tomislavgrad, which is in Sector Southwest, but there are several problems so far: where exactly in Tomislavgrad will the RRF be accommodated; who will pay for it; will we deal with the Federation (Tomislavgrad is in Federation territory) or with the central government in Sarajevo; and will the RRF be allowed freedom of movement in Federation territory? Questions about the military chain of command will be handled by Smith, but they need coordination with the civilian side. I suspect that each of the issues Smith mentioned will have to be resolved at higher levels, at the level of Akashi and Janvier, but I welcomed the opportunity to speak with General Pringle as a way of augmenting my knowledge of the situation. British generals are always very articulate.

6:00 P.M. briefing. The bad news began to trickle in from Srebrenica. The BSA has been very active there.

At 2:00 P.M. this afternoon, a Dutch observation post was overrun by the BSA. The Dutch soldiers were at first taken captive, then released. In the course of maneuvering to take a better defensive position against the BSA, one of the Dutch soldiers was shot and killed—by Bosnian government forces who did not want him to leave.

Meanwhile, Smith requested and got "air presence" over Srebrenica in the form of two British Jaguar jets. Air presence is a warning and a possible prelude to the use of air power, but the weather was poor over Srebrenica and precluded at this point the use of air power.

Close air support would have been justified, in Smith's opinion, because the Dutch were directly attacked. The UN compound there was shelled, but we are also in a potential hostage situation again. When the Dutch commander in Srebrenica, Colonel Tom Karremans, warned Mladic that NATO air power was imminent if the BSA did not halt its offensive, the BSA responded by taking Dutch peacekeepers hostage. When there was no use of air power, both because of the bad weather and out of concern for the safety of the hostages, the Dutch were released. Once UNPROFOR soldiers were released, there was no justification for using close air support in self-defense.

There are about twenty-five hundred Bosnian government soldiers in Srebrenica, but after months of deprivation and with only light arms, they are not about to fight against the overwhelming force of the Bosnian Serb army should a battle ensue.

Meanwhile, our intelligence sources are saying that they do not anticipate that the BSA is preparing to overrun the entire safe area of Srebrenica. The BSA action is still considered to be a "probing" attack, with limited objectives. One intelligence officer told me that if the BSA is preparing to overrun Srebrenica, it will be using a pincer movement, attacking from the north as well as the south. There are no attacks from the north.

[The tragedy of Srebrenica, then unfolding, was to become a tragedy of massive proportions, but few of us in the international community, even those of us familiar with the numerous atrocities already perpetrated in this war, were prepared for what would happen. We didn't want to believe it—not those of us at UNPROFOR headquarters in Sarajevo, not the Dutch in Srebrenica, not UNPF in Zagreb, and not the many international negotiators who had paraded through Bosnia. Perhaps the only ones who anticipated the merciless carnage that would take place were the Moslems themselves, from Hasan Muratovic, who had told me that Bosnian government forces could never surrender because they would be massacred, on down to the many common people throughout Bosnia, who had themselves been terrorized and tortured and expelled from their homes. They knew it could all happen again as long as the war continued. So did those Bosnian Serbs who did not support Karadzic and Mladic (and there were many of them, especially from Sarajevo). They knew how murderous their own military could be. So did Nikola Koljevic.

Perhaps what was most surprising of all to international observers like myself was the arrantly stupid indifference of Serb leaders to world opinion. Atrocities and mass executions are indefensible under any circumstances, but the fact that the Serbs would do what they did when they knew that the whole world was watching them, that they would commit mass slaughter in the light of day, *that* was not only inhuman, it was stupid!

At the same time, we were aware of the history of Srebrenica and the penchant, indeed the passion, for revenge in this part of the world. Laura Silber and Allan Little, among others, make mention of the massacre perpetrated by the infamous Bosnian commander Naser Oric in Serb villages around Srebrenica some thirty months earlier: "On January 7, 1993 (the Orthodox Christmas), Oric's forces launched a surprise attack on Serb positions to the north, killing Serb civilians and burning their villages."* Serb sources claim Oric massacred as many as twenty-five hundred Serbs on this occasion. While the actual number may have been less, and while Serb forces more than compensated in other areas of Bosnia, this particular defeat and atrocity was never forgotten by Serbian commanders.

Tales of the Srebrenica massacre by Serbian forces in 1995 have been documented elsewhere, and there is no need to repeat them here, but one small paragraph from a report by the UN Secretary-General published four and one-half months later, on 27 November 1995, in a section subtitled "Statements by Witnesses of Executions," is worth noting in this context:

> Statements were collected from 10 to 12 men by United Nations personnel, human rights organizations and journalists, in which they describe mass executions that they survived or witnessed from a distance. The statements of these men describe executions at no fewer than six sites in

*Op. cit., 265–66.

the Srebrenica area, namely Nova Kasaba-Konjevic Polje (Kaldrumica), Kravica, Rasica Gai, Zabrde and two sites in Karakaj. One organization, Human Rights Watch/Helsinki, has collected indirect evidence that points to a possible additional site in Bratunac. There is also both direct and circumstantial evidence of executions in Potocari. (S/1995/988, para. 10)

How could Mladic's forces have believed these executions would not be recorded, reported, discovered? Might as well perform them on satellite television. In fact, one of the Serb tactics during the early months of the war had been to use their own TV broadcasts to publicize atrocities committed against the Moslems as a way of encouraging all non-Serbs to flee their homes and villages. Terror had a psychological dimension as well as a strategic one. The standard rationalization (of which there can be none) for the use of military terror, whether in Bosnia or Hitler's Germany or in Cambodia, has been that it would break the spirit of the enemy. Killing entire families would not only prevent revenge by a future generation, not only prevent young men from becoming enemy soldiers, not only avoid the responsibility of having to feed and guard prisoners but it would also discourage resistance among survivors. Rape one woman and televise the tale, and all the women would flee. That was the theory, and so long as there was an opportunity to flee, the tactic was measurably successful.

Srebrenica was virtually in a ravine. It had only one main road. Air strikes inside Srebrenica (where there were mostly Moslem refugees) or immediately around Srebrenica (where there were few, if any, stationary targets), were useless. The Dutch compound, at the head of the main road entering Srebrenica, could not stop a tank assault and could not even defend itself against heavy infantry. Moreover, without the presence on the ground of tactical air control parties (TACPs) or special forces to direct air strikes, aerial bombardments would not have been likely to hit tanks moving along the road, unless those tanks were foolish enough to be in a straight line and contiguous. No, the use of close air support in or around Srebrenica was never a realistic possibility. If air power were to be used at all, it would have had to be wide ranging, against the major command and control centers of the Bosnian Serbs, far from Srebrenica. The practical answer to an attack on Srebrenica would have been to bomb Banja Luka, Pale, and Han Plesak, *but at that point UNPROFOR did not have the mandate to take that step.*

And it is not a good idea to ignore mandates. The same member states that had not yet given UNPROFOR the authority to widen the war and take it to the Bosnian Serbs were the same ones responsible for not having given UNPROFOR an adequate troop component. If blame *were* to be assigned, then it must be placed on the member states, basically the European states, for not acting in a more forthright manner from the very beginning of the war in Bosnia. One can understand the hesitation of European nations to confer authority on an international force that no single nation can completely control, given the potential domestic backlash, not to mention shifting alliances. The fall of Srebrenica, however, and the inability of the United Nations to prevent it were the result of decisions made by the member states of the Security Council. UNPROFOR was only the agent for those feckless decisions.

To be specific: the Secretary-General had originally asked for thirty-four thousand troops to protect the six "safe areas." The member states had authorized up to seventy-six hundred, what was called a "light option," but those same member states had delivered less than five thousand by the summer of 1995. At Srebrenica there were around three hundred Dutch soldiers, lightly armed with defensive weapons only.

In their book *Srebrenica: Record of a War Crime*, Jan Willem Honig and Norbert Both report the dangerous inconsistency of the Security Council in establishing Srebrenica as a "safe area":

> On 16 April 1993, the Security Council adopted Resolution 819, which declared Srebrenica a safe area. The resolution was dangerously inconsistent. . . . In the rushed decision-making necessitated by the town's imminent fall, the Council agreed on creating a safe area without specifying what the "area" was and how its safety could be achieved. The resolution masked, but did not resolve, any of the fundamental differences of opinion regarding the establishment of safe areas.
>
> Still, resolution 819 created high expectations. Many, both in Bosnia and elsewhere, believed that the United Nations from now on would protect Srebrenica against the Serbs. In reality, the resolution carefully avoided creating new military obligations for UNPROFOR either to establish or even to protect the safe area. The Council firmly placed the onus on the Serbs and the Muslims to make Srebrenica safe. UNPROFOR's role would simply be to "monitor" the humanitarian situations.*]

9 July 1995

9:15 A.M. Sunday. Morning press reading in my office. BSA radio announced that UNHCR convoys will be allowed to take Route Swan through the Sierra checkpoints starting on Saturday, six days from now, accompanied by Serb police. I suspect that if this is true, Bosnian government forces will shell the

*Jan Willem Honig and Norbert Both, *Srebrenica: Record of a War Crime* (New York: Penguin Books, 1997), 103–4.

convoys in order to force UNHCR to take the Mount Igman road. The Bosnian government does not want UNPROFOR or UNHCR to use Route Swan, even though it is the most direct route, because the Serbs have four checkpoints along the way and can control the road. [Part of that road was controlled by the Bosnian Croats.] The Bosnian government, meanwhile, wants to secure the Mount Igman road so that they can use it for military and commercial transport.

Bosnian government radio was reporting that close air support was requested yesterday in Srebrenica, but that NATO had not responded. The government this time did not blame Janvier or Akashi; it also did not mention that the weather made it impossible for air strikes.

At the 9:30 A.M. briefing in Smith's office, we learned that the Bosnian government is massing troops in the northwest area of Sarajevo. Apparently, another offensive is being planned. We doubt it will be successful.

On another matter, we are still experiencing severe restrictions of movement in Sector Southwest, which is in Federation territory, especially in areas controlled by the Bosnian government, but also in areas controlled by Bosnian Croat forces.

The situation in Srebrenica is continuing to deteriorate. Last night, two more observation posts were overrun by the BSA. The Dutch soldiers were given the choice of returning to their base, but they opted not to travel on unlit roads in the dark. They preferred to return to base this morning. Some stayed the night in their OP, under BSA guard, and some were taken to a nearby town, where they were quartered in a hotel. They were not considered hostages, not even detainees at this point. We all believe they will be returned safely to base today.

It seems the BSA is preparing a larger military offensive, but we are still not sure if they are planning to overrun the entire enclave or just a few OPs at the southern tip. There is an important road network in the region where they are conducting operations. If they take over that network, it will cut their resupply routes from Belgrade by about sixty kilometers, which will save a lot of fuel. There are also other assets in the area: a furniture factory and an aluminum mine. Our military intelligence still does not project a full-scale attack on Srebrenica.

[I recall again a little known fact about Srebrenica: it had never been delimited, which is to say that neither the Security Council nor anyone else had ever defined the boundaries of the safe area of Srebrenica. To begin with, there was the town of Srebrenica, which was generally considered to be within the safe area, but from the town outward, there was a large region comprising villages, forests, and hills, which were not considered part of the safe area. Technically, if those areas were attacked, the UN had no right to defend them *unless the attack was against UN soldiers stationed there at OPs.*

When UNPROFOR observation posts were overrun, the UN had the right to call for close air support, but if the BSA and Bosnian government forces wanted to fight it out between themselves, the UN had dubious, if any, authority to intervene. Most of the fighting in the Srebrenica area to this point was outside anybody's conception of the safe area. Besides, as noted, Security Council resolution 819 had essentially relegated UNPROFOR's role to that of a monitor.

This lack of definition of Srebrenica's boundaries as a safe area was conveniently overlooked by the laptop bombardiers, who were constantly calling for air strikes. But if military action were to be taken without proper authorization, then what was the point of having authorization for anything? The international community was fond of insisting that UN resolutions be implemented to protect the safe areas. If so, then the member states should have first defined the safe areas. Once again, it was the conflicting attitudes of the governments that prevented vigorous action by UNPROFOR. Clearly, some governments, with forces on the ground, wanted strong limitations placed upon NATO's authority to bomb.

Meanwhile, certain political factors also had to be taken into account regarding the use of NATO air power in Srebrenica. Because Carl Bildt was on a diplomatic mission in the region, there was concern in European capitals that the use of NATO air power at this point might diminish his capacity to negotiate. Conflicting messages also emanated from The Hague, which had to be concerned about the domestic impact of Dutch soldiers being taken hostage and possibly killed, either by air strikes or by BSA retaliation. Dutch soldiers had already been taken hostage in Srebrenica on at least two previous occasions. Honig and Both recount the first of those occasions this way:

> In November 1994, NATO aircraft attacked a Serb airbase in Udbina and, a few days later, a number of Serb anti-aircraft missile batteries. In retaliation, seventy Dutch soldiers who were on their way home were taken hostage by the Serbs. Forbidden to use their radio communications, the outside world lost all contact with them. On the fourth day of their forced stopover, they were visited by General Mladic, who arrived in a resprayed Mercedes jeep that the Serbs had confiscated from one of the previous Dutch convoys. . . . After more than six days, and interventions on the highest diplomatic level, the seventy Dutch soldiers were released. (*op. cit.*, 128–29)

Interestingly, Udbina was not even in Bosnia, but in the Serb-controlled Krajina area of Croatia, across the border.

A second occasion on which Dutch soldiers were taken hostage occurred in January 1995. This time their captors were the Bosnian government army.

One hundred Dutch soldiers had been investigating fighting that had broken out in the southwestern part of Srebrenica, in an area known as the Bandera triangle, from which the Bosnian government frequently launched attacks upon neighboring Serbian villages. The Dutch troops were taken hostage and then released, unharmed, after a few days. From then on they avoided entering the Bandera triangle area.]

The situation in Srebrenica is not a simple one by any means. But then again, war situations never are.

On another item this morning, Smith said he has agreed to a long-standing request from the Bosnian government to allow it to fortify the Igman road. I was astonished.

"Do you mean that we are going to provide the Bosnian government with materials and protection so that they can fortify a blue route for their own military use?" I asked.

"Yes," one of the British engineers answered.

"That's a political decision. I wish I had been consulted."

Silence. Embarrassment. Haughty disbelief. How could a civilian like myself challenge the commander? Only my deputy and staunch ally, John Ryan, who was taking notes, smiled at my irreverence.

[As soon as the briefing was over, I drafted a fax to Akashi. One should never send faxes that are written while one is steaming. Drafting them is one thing; but sending them is another. Yet, to this day, I am not sorry I sent it. One of the fires that drove me was the posture of Smith, who was constantly complaining to Zagreb, New York, Washington, and London, that he needed a political officer to take on his unwanted political responsibilities. He lamented that he barely had time to attend to his military obligations because of all the time he spent doing political work. The truth was, however, that he *loved* the political side, and he guarded his involvement there very preciously. He would never think of asking Izetbegovic or Siladzic or Sacirbey to talk to me instead of him about a political matter, or even of allowing me to be present if they had requested to speak to him. He alone handled most of the political discussions with the Bosnian government, and he loved it.

The Bosnian government knew it had a friend in Smith. UN political officers in Sarajevo rarely had the confidence of the Bosnian government, long before I appeared on the scene. Viktor Andreyev, a Russian national, one of my predecessors in Sarajevo, was instinctively mistrusted by the Bosnian government because of his nationality. My immediate predecessor, Enrique Aguilar, a Mexican national, was not in Sarajevo very long, and in fact was there during the COHA when the situation was relatively calm. Because he was a good diplomat, he had gotten on well in the diplomatic

community and had been able to obtain, through that community, information about the Bosnian government that he could not get from Smith. But
he, too, was blocked out by Smith. As for myself, I was kept out of the loop
not because of anything I did, but because the Bosnian government saw the
conflict primarily as a military one and resented Akashi and all his civilian
representatives. In fact, it despised the UN with an intensity that was as
palpable as it was irrational.

When Smith talked about wanting a political officer, what he meant was
that he wanted someone to deal with marginal civilian matters that had little
military import. For instance, if a nongovernmental organization in Greece
wanted to hold a sporting event in Sarajevo, they had to be told with diplomatic propriety that they could not, or that they could. Or if a report had to
be written that the military didn't want to bother with, Smith would prefer
that it be written by the political office.

But when it came to negotiating the passage of convoys or speaking to
Carl Bildt or fortifying a blue route for use by the Bosnian military, Smith
was not about to relinquish that prerogative or even share it with civilians.]

I faxed Akashi after the briefing. I wrote that I was concerned about the
political implications of UNPROFOR's decision to allow the Bosnian government to fortify the road over Mount Igman. Road repairs are one thing, but
barrier building is another. "Apparently, UNPROFOR has decided to accede to
the demands of the Bosnian government and give it fifty thousand sandbags
to do the necessary protection work," I wrote. I felt that because UNPROFOR
is not doing the work itself, it is openly siding with the Bosnian government.

If UNPROFOR does the work, it might well say that, in accordance with Security Council resolution 836, which authorizes it to take "all necessary measures" to assist in the delivery of humanitarian aid, it is taking those measures. Sandbagging an aid route might come under that category, but to turn
over fifty thousand sandbags to one of the parties to the conflict is tantamount to an alliance. Also, I was never consulted. Although the Igman road
is a blue route, there is no doubt it will be used by the Bosnian government
for military movements, especially during its ongoing military campaign
around Sarajevo. It already is. What are we saying then: if we can't give you
close air support, then at least we can give you material and logistic support?

Furthermore, I doubt that fifty thousand sandbags will actually deter the
BSA. On the contrary, it will antagonize them. It will be yet another escalatory step and provide another reason for the RRF to become involved in
protecting the Igman road (so that the Bosnian military can utilize it).

There is not very much to do in Sarajevo on a Sunday afternoon in July 1995.
There is a war going on in the city's environs, the weather is oppressively hot,
and we are restricted from moving around downtown Sarajevo.

In every environment there is always a need to get away from one's workplace, to take a walk, a drive, a vacation, whatever. But in Sarajevo, such escape is very difficult, though nonetheless imperative. Of course, there is some movement in the city during daylight hours. The local population goes about its business with courageous indifference, our patrols circulate in their armored vehicles, and some of us go jogging or out to a shop or a restaurant, but during daylight hours there is always risk whenever one moves about in Sarajevo, and in summer it is daylight until 9:00 P.M. The oppressive feeling that one can never move about with impunity in Sarajevo is just what the BSA wants, and it is that which requires the most courage to oppose. Moreover, getting out of Sarajevo, whether on leave or on duty, is a terrible hassle: there are roadblocks, snipers, bad weather, a shortage of vehicles, conflicting transport schedules, and sundry bureaucratic bumbles. Usually one has to wait several days before receiving permission to enter or leave Sarajevo.

Of course, we in UNPROFOR have more protection than the local citizens because we have a number of armored vehicles, bulletproof vests and flak jackets, and a relatively safe compound to work in. Indeed, for the Sarajevans it is always more discouraging and more restrictive—which is why so many in the world have come to identify with them and laud their courage.

As for myself, I sometimes think: should I go for a drive today and taunt the snipers in my thick-skinned vehicle? Or take a wary walk among the high buildings, sweating in my flak jacket? Or go to a nearby cafe and have a cup of smuggled coffee that might take twenty minutes to brew because of the limited electrical power? Or should I sit in my dark apartment or my unprivate office and write letters? Or read a book? Or drink? In every environment there are choices, and there are limits, but when those choices are limited under penalty of death or permanent injury, the feeling is very different. A curtain of dread always hangs over one's daily life in Sarajevo, an invisible but palpable cloud that threatens to darken one's spirit, if not claim one's life.

This afternoon I have decided to write in my journal, to record some irreverent thoughts about humanitarian aid beyond the generally agreed point that food is a political weapon during a war.

First of all, humanitarian aid of the magnitude involved in Bosnia is big business. Certain parties are making millions from the provision, transportation, storage, and distribution of humanitarian aid, and their interests are frequently less than altruistic. I am referring to private companies and to war profiteering. Other parties, meanwhile, want to limit the provision of aid by international organizations so that the price of smuggled goods will remain as high as possible. I am talking about Bosnian government military officials, who control the black market in Bosnia.

Then there is the image factor that governments want to cultivate with their people. To suffer is human; to donate, divine. The contribution of foreign aid to a popular cause diverts attention from the inability to take military action.

There is also the bléssèd media, seeking megabucks in advertising. Lurid pictures of suffering generates massive business for the humanitarian aid industry in all its aspects and concurrent advertizing revenues for media conglomerates. Nothing sells ad space like misery.

Finally, in dealing with aid, one has to allow for a "skim factor." Whether talking about guns or butter, there are always those who will skim from the top. One has to set a limit. Perhaps 20 percent is OK, but 25 percent is not OK. Whatever. One cannot expect 100 percent efficiency when dealing with aid, but one cannot give carte blanche to the gangsters. Regrettably, the provision of massive international humanitarian aid encourages illegal gangs and discourages legitimate individual initiative.

There is also the issue of economic sanctions.

1. One has to reflect on their consequences. They *do* have political impact. Witness how they have hurt Serbia. Milosevic is obsessed with having them lifted, and has had to change his policies accordingly. At the same time, in the long term, economic sanctions destroy the social fabric of a culture. They encourage black marketeering and the growth of a gangster class. They create a welfare mentality. They destroy any movement toward democracy by creating conditions in which warlords and gang bosses thrive, and they aggravate and bring to a critical level the true need for humanitarian aid. In the long term, economic sanctions put at risk the welfare and the futures of the very people they are trying to save. They victimize the old, the very young, and the infirm. They jeopardize and virtually destroy the economies of neighboring nations that depend on trade with the sanctioned nation. The theory that the people will pressure their economically sanctioned government to change its policies, or that they will even rise up and overthrow it in the hope of ending economic sanctions, is a cruel hoax. It is a ruse perpetuated by governments seeking popular support from their domestic constituencies. These governments can act tough by imposing sanctions and then appear humane by offering international aid. But the common people under sanctions, as well as contiguous nations and trading partners, suffer cruel and inhuman punishment.

2. Economic sanctions create political problems by necessitating the installation of a complex distribution mechanism that undermines sovereignty. If an international force such as the UN takes over distribution of food aid, it becomes an occupying army. Local authorities want to have the power to distribute aid. If local authorities have that power, then they cheat. They "skim," and they turn over much of the aid to the army.

3. The urgency of humanitarian aid encroaches on peacekeeping. At the level of the UN Security Council, the need for humanitarian aid has become a component of peacekeeping. The needs of humanitarian aid are written into Security Council resolutions on peacekeeping missions. The primary responsibility of UNPROFOR, in fact, is to facilitate the delivery of humanitarian aid. What is the UN to do when that delivery is blocked? Can the international community allow gangs of thugs to block the delivery of humanitarian aid? Should we fight our way through? Should we negotiate? Or should we consider doing away with economic sanctions?

Late this afternoon, I left for Gornji Vakuf, the administrative capital of Sector Southwest, by armored car over Mount Igman. We had arranged for clearance at least forty-eight hours in advance. I took with me Merrick Fall, a veteran peacekeeper who served in Namibia and Cambodia, and has just joined our staff in Sarajevo. Fall has been in Bosnia several months, but is new to Sarajevo. He is an outstanding political officer: a polyglot, a perceptive observer and reporter with good political sense and a knowledge of military weaponry, and singularly inconspicuous.

Our journey to Gornji Vakuf this time was uneventful. We passed through territory controlled by each of the three warring parties without significant incident or delay, which is unusual because traveling through Bosnia is more often than not like negotiating an obstacle course. It is full of dangers and surprises. One can suddenly come upon a UN civilian or soldier walking along the road trying to flag down a UN vehicle because his own has just been hijacked, or because there is an incident to be reported, but his radio has broken down. On some occasions, one encounters a refugee family straggling along with a few battered suitcases and plastic bags, looking for a ride, and dragging or carrying small children. Though it is against UN rules to give rides to locals (they are not covered by insurance), we often do. And there is always a local driver begging fuel for his car, which is stalled at the roadside. He wants no more, he will tell you, than a soda bottle full of petrol, only enough to get him to the next town (where the service stations have no fuel).

Then there is the culture of tobacco. There are times when one is flagged down by someone waving frantically at the side of the road because he wants a cigarette. Not money, not food, not fuel, but a cigarette. At the checkpoints, the guards frequently ask us for cigarettes. In fact, we have learned to travel through Bosnia always carrying cigarettes, usually two kinds: a local brand that serves as cheap currency and a few packs of Marlboros, which are like gold. We use them for bribes and to promote goodwill. It seems that everyone in former Yugoslavia above the age of ten smokes incessantly, relentlessly, and incorrigibly. But at issue is more than simple addiction; tobacco is a convertible currency. For a pack of Marlboros, the preferred brand, one can barter for almost anything. I will never forget that in Gorazde many of the refugee families I met grew tobacco in the window boxes of their devastated apartments. Not herbs or vegetables, but tobacco. They grew vegetables in their gardens and sometimes planted mines there to protect their crop. If the vegetables were stolen, they would go hungry, but they would survive. But the most important crop, tobacco, was grown in window boxes, which were more secure. Food could only be eaten and could spoil, but tobacco could be used for currency. Although home-grown tobacco was not as valuable as Marlboros, it could still be traded for bread or sugar. There were even stories that women would offer sex for cigarettes.

10 July 1995

My first briefing at Gornji Vakuf was from a political officer, but it concerned staffing needs, an administrative problem. The Civil Affairs component often requests more staff because they want to do fuller coverage. The administration, on the other hand, is always trying to save money, which means trying to reduce staff or hold it to current levels. Inevitably, the administration has to report to governments, which are paying the bills, and that is why they try to keep costs down, without regard to the quality of the operation.

The first message I got in Gornji Vakuf was that Civil Affairs needs at least four more officers there: one to handle administrative matters within Civil Affairs and at least three political officers to staff various locations within the sector: Zepce, Zenica, and Visoko. As of now, the few officers in Gornji Vakuf are responsible for all those cities, and it takes hours every day to drive back and forth. Phone or fax connections are not enough. The officers have to be able to talk to local officials and to the population. The question is whether those cities are important enough to merit a full-time political officer. Can't an officer go there one day each week? I asked. And so on.

A more substantive problem is posed by the movements of the French Foreign Legion within Federation territory. The French contingent of the RRF has crossed into Bosnia and is currently at Tomislavgrad, but its commander, General Soubirou, wants to move them to Knesevo, across the mountain, from where they will be better placed to defend Mount Igman. Tactically, he is correct. The problem is a political one. Federation officials don't want the French to move to Knesevo yet. Meanwhile, Soubirou is concerned about winterizing the quarters of his troops, which will take a couple of months. It is already July. He needs winterized accommodations for as many as six thousand troops.

The RRF is made up of three brigades, totaling about 12,500 soldiers. One brigade is a French brigade, on stand-by in France. One brigade is British, an

air mobile brigade; the British troops are on stand-by in the United Kingdom, but their equipment is already in theater, in Ploce, Croatia, where
about seven hundred soldiers are busy polishing and maintaining helicopters. The third component of the RRF, a multinational brigade (MNB), is the
brigade that General Soubirou commands. The MNB has two battalions:
Alpha, which is British and now in Vitez, and Bravo, which is French and
now in Tomislavgrad. The French are about twenty minutes by helicopter
from Igman, and the British are about forty minutes away by helicopter. But
in winter helicopters are almost useless because of snow and fog. Even in
summer, frequent rainstorms may prevent their movement.

The deputy military commander of Sector Southwest, Colonel Abdullah,
a Malaysian, told me that UNPROFOR's movement has become even more
restricted since the arrival of the French battalion—mainly, he said, because
of the way in which the French arrived, pushing their way across the border
into Bosnia, ignoring local officials, and showing indifference to the local
population. I listened. [I had met General Soubirou at least once before. He
was a tempestuous, black-gloved, ramrod straight, career officer who expected compliance and not debate when he gave orders. A very difficult
man. In his defense, however, I knew that he had an unswerving dedication
to duty, that the Foreign Legion troops he commanded were fearless, and
that he had little patience with harassment by stubborn pig farmers and
petty political officials who were always grubbing for money. He had a job to
do, and he was determined to do it. From what I could gather, he had the
allegiance and support of his troops. I never forgot that the French took
more casualties than any other contingent during UNPROFOR's stay in Bosnia
and that they felt minimized and stifled by the Anglo-American command
structure. Soubirou deserved to be taken seriously.]

After the briefings we took a drive. We passed first through Gornji Vakuf,
which is a divided city, like Mostar, except that this time the money and the
rebuilding are on the Moslem side. The word is that Saudi Arabia has been
pouring money into Gornji Vakuf, just as the Croatian government has been
putting money into Mostar.

We took what is called the Triangle Road, a scenic, winding mountain
road that made me conscious once again of the dramatic beauty of Bosnia.
We passed by the town of Prozor, which Croats have cleansed of Moslems,
and then past Jablanica, which Moslems have cleansed of Croats. Minorities
still live in most of the villages in Federation territory, but they are not
secure. [I suspected that in the next couple of years, whether there was peace
or not, those minorities would leak out into their own areas of control, and
the majority of those movements would be permanent unless another war
reversed them.]

I could see from my tour that there is more need for engineers in Sector

Southwest than for infantry. The territory is so vast and so mountainous that UNPROFOR infantry will hardly be able to defend itself or the local population if war resumes. UNPROFOR's presence is a deterrent, but it cannot prevent a war. In Sector Southwest, as in other parts of Bosnia, the real good UNPROFOR could do was to repair bridges and roads, and to improve or restore water systems. These small services were essential and did not take large influxes of capital. Most of the villages in this region did not even need humanitarian aid; they were agricultural communities and were self-sufficient in food. What they needed was the restoration of essential public services.

As for Zenica, where a Turkish battalion is stationed, I was told that the situation is calm. One of the military officers in our party told me: "TurkBat (Turkish battalion) runs Zenica, so the Moslem men in town can go to war." Since I have no way of knowing if that is true, I must get a briefing from the Turkish commander, not only on that question but on the general situation in his area of command. The Turks are always very hospitable and cooperative, but I am concerned that such stories are circulating.

In Visoko, where our 585 Canadian peacekeepers are barracked, our Bosnian hosts offered us a "window," now between 10:00 A.M. and 4:00 P.M. every day, to enter and leave the premises, if we give them twenty-four hours notice. Otherwise, the Canadians are restricted to base—in other words, held hostage. Two of our OPs in the area—one with six men, the other with thirteen men—have not been resupplied with food and water for three weeks now. Observation post CV2, with six men, has only three days of drinking water left and no fresh rations; they are on hard rations. CV4, which has thirteen men, has two days of water left, no fresh rations, and only two days of hard rations. The siege began about a month ago, when the Bosnian government demanded that the two OPs and their accompanying checkpoints be withdrawn. Eyup Ganic, the Federation vice president, an extremist Moslem originally from the province of Sandjak in Serbia, went to see the Canadian commander in Visoko and demanded the removal of the two OPs. He said they were collecting intelligence and had to be shut down. UNPROFOR refused. We agreed to close two checkpoints in the area, but not the OPs, so the Bosnian government began its siege.

Smith is aware of the situation. He has refused to close the OPs, and he has protested at the local level, but he will not go public about the dilemma. He is not about to confront the Bosnian government while so many of his men are vulnerable in territory controlled by them.

In any case, I wrote a fax to Akashi from Gornji Vakuf about the outrageous condition of the Canadians at Visoko. I know that the deputy force commander in Zagreb is Canadian. I sent Smith a copy of my fax. I noted that the main restrictions on freedom of movement are at checkpoints Bravo

One (near Gornji Vakuf) and Bravo Five (near Vitez), and I asked if the RRF is to be used only to unblock the Mount Igman road, or if it can also be used to unblock checkpoints in Federation-controlled territory.

[I knew in advance what the answer would be; in fact, I knew that my question would go unanswered, and I was also sure that my indiscreet query would not endear me to the Bosnian government, which pirated or was surreptitiously supplied with copies of all my correspondence. I was indignant, however, at the abandonment of the Canadians.

The UN was often pilloried because it could not protect the Moslems or other threatened ethnic groups in Bosnia. Would that it had had the resources and the mandate to do so. In the meantime, however, it was imperative, I believed, for us to protect ourselves; self-defense must begin at home. It was imperative for good morale, and it was imperative so that the troop-contributing governments could be assured that their men and women would not be abandoned once they became part of a UN force.

Using force to feed Sarajevo was perfectly justified under Security Council resolution 836, but so was protecting the Canadian contingent at Visoko, I was convinced, and protecting the Bangladeshi contingent in Bihac, which was blockaded by the Serbs.]

At a military briefing I had later today, a Canadian colonel explained to me how the Bosnian government is improving its capabilities and what its tactics are. Their strategy is to nibble and consolidate, nibble and consolidate. Government forces know that the Serbs are stretched out across a long frontier. Therefore, the Bosnian government continues to attack on several fronts simultaneously. Their objectives are limited: a feature here, a feature there, always going after the high ground. They have been slowly successful. They have also been improving their command structure under the tutelage of retired U.S. generals. They have been able to replace local fighters with professional soldiers, and they have been able to make an administrative division between brigade level and corps level. The Serbs still have superiority in heavy weapons, but the Serb command structure is weakening, partly because of internal political squabbling and partly because of the losses they have suffered in the past year. Their morale is in decline.

[At some point in the future, historians will write about the true nature of the BSA. The common perception of it as a ruthless and efficient military machine, much like the Nazis of World War II, was hardly accurate. Ruthless, yes, but efficient and well trained, not necessarily. Many of their soldiers were part-time citizen soldiers—reservists, not even professionals. They were undisciplined, fun-loving farmers who preferred brandy and women to war. During the whole of the Bosnian conflict there were very few examples of hand-to-hand combat, guerrilla operations, or sabotage behind the lines. Bayonets and other paraphernalia of close combat were almost unknown.

The Serbs set up their artillery on mountain tops and shelled villages until the civilians decided to leave. Then the BSA swooped in, "cleansed" the village by massacring enough of the locals still present to convince the rest to leave, and occupied the city by moving in their own displaced persons from other parts of Bosnia. This war was one of artillery and massacre. The BSA did not want an infantry war because it was outnumbered and did not have the morale to fight such a war. They preferred long-distance shelling to hand-to-hand combat.

At this particular time, government forces were becoming more mobile, a crucial capability. A year before, the only mobile force the Bosnian government army had was the Mujahadeen, which were roughly 2–3 percent of the entire BiH army. They were mercenaries from Afghanistan, Iran, and other extremist Islamic countries, who were never integrated into the government army and were in some ways as much a problem for the Moslems as for the Serbs. They were shock troops and terrorists, militant fanatics who were much disappointed by the type of Islam they encountered in Bosnia. Bosnian Moslems were Europeans. Some were religious, but most were not. After fifty years of Communism, many did not even know how to pray. They drank, smoked, danced, ate pork, and lived like their Serb and Croat neighbors. They wanted nothing to do with Middle Eastern culture. As the Bosnian government army developed more mobility, the strategic value of the Mujahadeen lessened.

From the start, almost everyone, especially the United States, overestimated the importance of the Mujahadeen. Because the Mujahadeen were never accepted by the local population, however, they were doomed to irrelevance as soon as government forces could develop the capability to defend themselves.]

The situation in Srebrenica has deteriorated drastically. The real assault has begun. Mladic needs a victory to improve Serb morale. He needs to release the eight to ten divisions deployed in and around the eastern enclaves so that he can send them to fight in western Bosnia. He needs to plug the hole in his back in eastern Bosnia. From the viewpoint of the BSA, the eastern enclaves have to go: Srebrenica, Zepa, Gorazde.

As the reports about Srebrenica filter in, it is clear that our intelligence has been faulty, our defensive capacities are inadequate, and our resolve is divided. We expected an action with limited objectives; we were dead wrong. Three hundred lightly armed peacekeepers facing approximately five thousand Serb soldiers, fifty artillery pieces, and fifteen tanks. A credible defense is inconceivable without air strikes. Also, conflicting instructions from the metropolitan capitals have made it difficult for Janvier to make a clear military commitment.

[Though it was convenient to blame the UN for the disaster at Srebrenica, we were once again the victim of indecision among the big powers, as well as of manipulation by the Bosnian government. As stated, the troop-contributing governments never gave us the troop level we had requested to be able to defend the six safe areas. Nor were the major governments willing to share their intelligence-gathering capacities with us or to give us the necessary funding to set up our own intelligence network. It was a common joke that the UN had no intelligence in Bosnia. In fact, it was true. UNPROFOR had no significant intelligence-gathering capacity all the time we were in Bosnia.

Pro-Bosnian journalists (were there any other kind?) were also fond of skewering Janvier and Akashi for not ordering massive air strikes against the BSA on that fateful day in July when the Serb offensive began. Once again, however, signals from the capitals were conflicting. The Dutch were hostages during the siege of Srebrenica. The French in and around Sarajevo were potential targets. When the Croatians had overrun Western Slavonia a couple of months earlier and in the process had overrun UN troops, the UN did nothing. Would air power in this case, therefore, have been inequitable and set a precedent? Would any future attack against a United Nations Protected Area (UNPA) in Croatia or against a safe area in Bosnia automatically have called for the use of air power?

Any use of NATO air power around Srebrenica would have risked serious collateral damage, as well as the lives of the Dutch peacekeepers, who were now virtual prisoners. To respond properly to the BSA assault on Srebrenica, NATO would have had to target Serb command and control centers elsewhere in Bosnia, such as Pale and Han Plesak, acts that would have raised the conflict to a new level, with serious political implications.

But there was another element. The Dutch had very poor relations with local Moslem leaders in Srebrenica and were unable to coordinate any meaningful action with them. Here, for example, is a comment by Honig and Both, a year after the events in Srebrenica:

> The Dutch were blamed for the perceived failure of the UN to do enough for the people of Srebrenica. Matters were not helped by the character and behaviour of the dominant personalities in the enclave. Naser Oric, the overall military commander, and his two main "brigade" commanders, Zulfo Tursunovic and Hakija Meholjic, appeared to the Dutch to be little more than gangsters, who terrorized the refugee population and profited greatly from the war. These men jealously protected their own fiefdoms. As the refugees were not represented in the local government, international aid agencies suggested in the second half of 1993 that the refugees should elect their own representative to assist in the distribution of food. The man was found murdered the day after his election.

Oric and his cronies were also responsible for much of the trouble with the Serbs, which stemmed from Muslim raids on Serb communities just outside the enclave. Also, Oric's men had the disconcerting habit of taking up positions close to the Dutch and then opening fire on the Serbs, hoping to entice them and the Dutch into a firefight. At times, when the Presidency found the Dutch insufficiently accommodating at supplying them with desired items, they would turn off the water supply to the Dutch compounds. Local commanders would stop Dutch patrols when it suited them. (*op. cit.*, 132–33)

Minister Muratovic harassed UNPROFOR similarly in Sarajevo. Once, a day after I refused to send an UNPROFOR car to pick him up on Mount Igman on his return from a shopping trip in Split, his soldiers held a French UNPROFOR patrol at a checkpoint for four hours.

But such corruption on the part of the Bosnian government was seldom, *if ever*, reported by the world press. And they knew about it. Oh, yes, they knew about it, and they knew about the harassment at Srebrenica.]

11 July 1995

At the 8:00 A.M. briefing in Gornji Vakuf, we received reports about the imminent fall of Srebrenica. It was clear the BSA would take Srebrenica, probably today. The city that French General Philippe Morillon once protected by refusing to leave until the BSA stopped its shelling will finally fall to the Serbs. There is still talk of using air power against the BSA around Srebrenica, but the weather is not good for flying, and the Dutch troops in Srebrenica are intermingled with the Serbs and the Moslems. Collateral damage is a clear and present danger. [Later on this date, in fact, NATO did use air power once against the BSA, but it was too late by then to have any influence on the outcome of the battle. Two more strikes were called off because of the weather.] Most of all, we are concerned about the fate of the Moslem civilians in Srebrenica. Many of them are draft-age men who for months have been prevented from leaving by Moslem officials. The Sarajevo government has not wanted to abandon Srebrenica and leave it to the Serbs.

The other major topic of the day was the disposition of the RRF, which is still having trouble moving into position. Negotiations are continuing with the Federation. Though the troops can provide their own accommodations, they need land, waste disposal services, and secure access routes to and from their camp. Once again, the relationships between the Federation and the Bosnian government in Sarajevo, and within the Bosnian government itself, given its internal rivalries and legendary inefficiencies, come into question. [Obtaining official permission for anything in the Balkans was like negotiating with carnivorous ghosts. First of all, one had to identify where the authority lay. Usually, there were several authorities, each of whom was fighting bitterly with every other. Obstinacy and treachery were endemic to the region. If a signature were finally obtained, the local official or soldier who had to implement the decision on the ground was either uninformed or so corrupt that he wanted a bribe to do what he was supposed to do as part of his duty. Most of the time, agreements were ignored. After awhile, one tried to deal with the system as it was, but those Westerners who arrived in the Balkans self-righteously, even imperiously, expecting sincerity and openness soon became frustrated and angry. Eventually they either learned to dance the Balkan ballet or they went home, but once they learned to dance the Balkan ballet, they soon realized it was a war dance.

One of the oldest folk tales in Bosnia is about an old Serb who passed up and back between Turkish-controlled Bosnia and Serb territory every day with a wheelbarrow full of hay. The Turkish guard at the border crossing would poke at the hay, expecting to find contraband, but never found anything. When the occupation ended and the Turks were about to leave, the border guard asked the old man what he had been smuggling. The old man replied: "I wasn't smuggling anything; I was trading wheelbarrows."]

In negotiating the disposition of the RRF, the Bosnian government wants a guarantee that the RRF will not interfere with Bosnian military objectives— in other words, that the RRF will neither be used against government forces, nor prevent them from making further military gains against the BSA, nor take over areas the Bosnian government already controls. [Ultimately, a confidential agreement between UNPROFOR and the Federation was concluded that contained a paragraph essentially agreeing to those demands. I was astonished when I saw it.

There was no longer any question in my mind that Smith was fighting a war with Mladic and that Smith would win, but I was also convinced that the UN had never given Smith any *clear* authorization to fight that war. I am not in any way suggesting that Smith was taking powers not authorized to him. The operative word here is *clear*. Smith was working in a gray area, and when the language of Security Council resolutions was in any way dubious, he would ask for interpretation from the UN and from the U.K. government. Once he was assured that he could legally pursue his aggressive stance against Mladic, he would proceed. But it was Smith who took the initiative.

Mladic may have deserved no better, but what irritated me was that Smith was operating under a UN flag. "If you want to fight a war with Mladic, then fight it under a U.K. flag or a NATO flag, not under a UN flag," I would say to Smith, and Smith, perfectly honorable soldier and aspiring statesman that he was, would agree. He wanted a fight, and he wanted a NATO flag, but lacking the preferred flag, he carefully obtained the proper authorization and pursued his war.]

This morning at the briefing we also talked about the "Maglai finger," a finger of land in Federation territory bounded on three sides by the confrontation line (CL). Not since the UNPROFOR mission began has the Bosnian government allowed us any closer than three to five kilometers to the confrontation line. Clearly, government troops do not want us to have intelligence about their fortifications along the CL. Understandable. But the result is that we have no intelligence information at all about the CL in that area. The BSA will not allow us on their side of the line, and the Bosnian government will not allow us on their side. Meanwhile, the ethnic complexity of the area and the shifting allegiances are representative of the illogicality of the war. The "finger" is predominantly Moslem, with a significant Croat minority in the north, but during the war before the Federation was formed, the Moslems in the southern part of the "finger" fought alongside the Serbs against Bosnian government forces, whereas Moslems in the northern part fought alongside the Bosnian Croats against the Serbs. Since the formation of the Federation sixteen months ago, the area has been pacified, but should the war resume, it is unpredictable who will fight against whom.

In general, I was told, the Moslem communities in the region fear the BSA and want a UN presence to protect them. They feel a UN presence will deter the Serbs. Meanwhile, the Bosnian government in Sarajevo wants the UN out of the Moslem region so that the BIH can attempt to take it by force.

I shall always remember 11 July 1995 because it was the day that Srebrenica fell and the day that I was almost killed by a Bosnian sniper.

I decided to return to Sarajevo this afternoon rather than wait until dark, as I was advised. It is usually safer to cross over Mount Igman at night. But I had a lot of work to do back in Sarajevo, and I was eager to return. I wanted to go to Srebrenica.

Several stretches along the Igman road are exposed—no natural cover, no rocks or trees or bushes, no turns, just simple straightaways in full view of anyone who chooses to shoot, from almost any direction. Four of us were traveling along one of those stretches when we were targeted. We were in an armored vehicle, a Landrover.

Our driver was Bruno Chaubert, a French warrant officer from Corsica, who functioned as chauffeur and bodyguard. I was sitting next to Chaubert in the front seat. In the back were Private P. Kristensen (from the Danish headquarters company), who functioned as a backup driver and bodyguard, and my colleague, Merrick Fall, a Civil Affairs officer.

When I travel any considerable distance, I try always to have two drivers, one of whom can act as bodyguard. Usually, but not always, I also have a colleague with me.

P. Kristensen is about twenty years old, well disciplined, slightly built, and pleasant. We call him P. K. Chaubert is in his thirties, a robust bodybuilder and jogger, tireless, and with a wonderful sense of humor. Fall is a British national, a polyglot with degrees in Romance languages, a former headmaster at a Swiss boarding school, and a veteran peacekeeper who has been in Namibia and Cambodia, and has recently come to Sarajevo. He is a very fine writer and a good political analyst, and he has a sound knowledge of weaponry from the days when he used to translate military pamphlets in order to earn a few extra francs.

When we passed the last Bosnian government checkpoint at the top of the Igman road, before beginning our descent toward Sarajevo, Bruno informed the French post at Tarcin (lower down on Mount Igman) that we were en route by giving them our radio call sign. It was about 6:00 P.M. Bruno told us, "This is a dangerous part. It's fully exposed. We are going to move quickly."

"Mais pas trop vite," I said. The road was lumpy and tortuous, a kind of narrow goat path, and the armor-plated Landrover was not really that maneuverable. It had a high center of gravity, particularly unsuitable for that terrain. But Bruno ignored my anxiety and floored the gas pedal.

We raced along at high speed, bouncing, virtually soaring. Then at a point where the road followed a slight spur, an explosive round hit the metal plate just above where the windscreen joins the roof, in direct line with Bruno's eyes. We heard a loud bang and felt a muffled impact. Ka-boom! The shot was no doubt aimed at the driver and was devilishly accurate. Fortunately, Bruno held fast to the wheel, unfazed. If he had lost control, even for a few seconds, the car would undoubtedly have gone over the edge, killing everyone.

Going over the side is the real danger when taking the road over Mount Igman. Being shot at, even being hit, may not necessarily be fatal, but going over the precipitous mountainside is certain to be fatal.

In fact, the shooting, the explosion against the metal, the bouncing, and the race for cover all happened so fast that I couldn't really comprehend what was going on, and I didn't, until afterward, genuinely realize how close we had all been to death, how stubbornly and instinctively courageous Bruno had been, and how many other vehicles may have had a similar experience traveling along the ILR. I also tried to imagine myself driving the Landrover and being shot at while going maximum speed down a bumpy mountain road, but I could not. Bruno was amazing to hold on as he did. He saved our lives.

We stopped at the last French outpost on the downhill before going on to the BiH checkpoint at the bottom of the mountain. We looked at the Landrover and concluded that we had been hit by a 7.62-millimeter explosive round. The metal and corner of the windscreen were covered with a large smoky stain, and there were traces of powder on the glass. I asked the French where they thought the shot might have come from, and they agreed unanimously it was highly unlikely that a 7.62-millimeter round could have been fired with such accuracy from Serb-held territory, which was at least eighteen hundred to two thousand meters away. The shot had to have come from BiH-held territory.

Although the French were equipped with a light tank and a mortar, and were authorized to respond immediately to any fire from hostile elements, they had not done so this time because it had been impossible to identify exactly where the shot came from. It might well have been fired by a sniper hiding behind a tree. [Even in the days before the RRF arrived, our units were authorized to return fire anytime they were targeted by enemy forces, but they were limited to firing at specific targets in self-defense; only after the RRF arrived were UN forces authorized to respond disproportionately and randomly.]

After a few deep breaths and some excited conversation with our French colleagues, we continued on down to the bottom of the Igman road, to the BiH checkpoint, where Bruno handed over our clearance document to the two guards. The two Bosnian soldiers examined the document and handed it back, saying nothing.

Bruno remarked to us that whoever the gunman was, he must have been a sharpshooter to have hit a moving target at considerable range, even though we were coming right at him rather than at right angles or on a diagonal. Bruno was furious, but still in control. He snarled something in French at the Bosnian guards, but they did not respond.

[I had to believe that it was one of the functions of the upper BiH checkpoint to inform the lower one about the vehicles coming down. And they had our names. Certainly, they had my name. Was it only my imagination then to think that the two unsmiling, poker-faced BiH soldiers at the bottom checkpoint, who saw the black stain on the windscreen, ignored it because they knew already what had happened and were not the least surprised? Or perhaps they were disappointed. Bruno and the French soldiers at Tarcin, however, had no doubts about which side had targeted us.]

In my report on the incident to Zagreb, I remarked that this was by no means the first time that the BiH has fired at the UN. In previous cases where soft-skinned vehicles have been accompanied by APCs, shots have always been fired at the APCs, as if to make a political point—that we are in their gunsights and vulnerable anytime they choose to go after us. This time they went after us. From now on, we will have to be prepared for the worst.

It is clear that this shot was aimed at the driver, not at the radiator. The intent was to kill the passengers, not to disable the vehicle. Perhaps the BSA attack on Srebrenica, for which UNPROFOR has been scapegoated, has incited the BIH against us more than usual. Or perhaps this particular marksman is what all sides call "a rogue element." Whatever the reason, I don't believe our being targeted was an accident, and I don't believe it was a "renegade" soldier acting on his own. Our white vehicles are clearly identifiable. Besides, next time a more powerful weapon may be used. The armor plating of the Land-rover can resist 7.62-millimeter rounds, but probably it will not be able to stop a 12.7-millimeter round or anything of larger calibers. We have to consider whether it is still safe to use Landrovers on Mount Igman at all during daylight.

At the end of my report, I recommended that, in future, Landrovers should be accompanied by an APC traveling in front of them so that the Landrover will be protected to some extent while it is traveling enfilade.

[Srebrenica fell during our trip back from Gornji Vakuf. Forty thousand Moslems were trapped there. The Dutch troops were in Potocari, their base in the enclave, but they were powerless. My first instinct was to go to Sre-brenica to survey the situation, perhaps make arrangements for a human rights team to go there. In fact, Akashi had already appointed a task force of three or four to go. They would be coming from Tuzla and from Zagreb, but I knew that it would be difficult for them to get into Srebrenica and that I might have a better chance than anyone else. I wanted to go there with General Kees Nikolai, a Dutch national who was the chief of staff of UNPROFOR and stationed in Sarajevo. I resolved to contact both sides as soon as I got back to Sarajevo, to ask permission to travel to Srebrenica. If I got in, I would make arrangements for the task force.]

The BSA has already begun its preparations to "cleanse" Srebrenica. It is going to transport Moslem civilians to Kakanj, and they can make their own way from there to Tuzla. The Bosnian government, however, does not want its people to leave Srebrenica. They feel it is unsafe for them to be transferred through Serb territory all the way to Tuzla, where there are already tens of thousands of Moslem refugees. Tuzla has no facilities for more refugees, and the Bosnian government is insisting it is the responsibility of the UN to feed, shelter, and protect the Moslems of Srebrenica. The Bosnian government is refusing any responsibility for them.

A UN civilian presence in Srebrenica is urgent at this point. We have to get to Mladic and impress on him the unacceptability, the crime, and the terri-ble consequences of "cleansing" or abusing forty thousand Moslems. It is imperative that their lives be spared, their dignity respected. Not only will Mladic face military retaliation by NATO but he will lose heavily again in the court of world opinion. He has to be made to understand the awesome power of NATO waiting to descend upon him given the right provocation. And this will be the right provocation. The world is watching him. He is on camera. Taking territory is one thing, but massacring civilians is impermissible. Perhaps there is some ground for rational discussion. Even with Mladic.

12 July 1995

Bosnian Serb TV is showing General Mladic handing out lollipops to children. He is assuring everyone there will be no slaughter.

I began the day by speaking to Minister Muratovic, at his request. At 7:45 A.M. He was understandably furious about the fall of Srebrenica. He discounted statements being made by Moslem officials in Srebrenica about the exodus of the Moslem population. Local officials are not authorized to speak about the movement of the population there, he insisted. Only the central government in Sarajevo has the authority to discuss the fate of the Moslem population of Srebrenica.

At this point, he continued, Sarajevo authorities have not agreed that the Moslem population should be moved to Tuzla. They should remain in Srebrenica. The international community should bring tents there to house them. The international community should take responsibility to shelter, feed, and protect them. A helicopter bridge should be used to supply the people of Srebrenica if roads are blocked. The international community should not allow the Moslem population to be "cleansed" from Srebrenica.

"No movement is acceptable to us," he said. "Srebrenica is a UN safe area. The UN should protect the people there."

He was on his way to Tuzla this very morning, he told me, to discuss the logistical problems of supplying Srebrenica by air from Tuzla.

I listened carefully and took notes. I went alone to see Minister Muratovic. He always speaks more freely when we are alone.

I assured him I would pass his thoughts on up the line to my superiors.

[When I left his office, I reflected on how adept he was at politicizing crises. Good Communist training. The Moslems of Srebrenica were political capital to the Bosnian government. As long as they remained in Srebrenica, they were a strategic asset. The Moslem mayor of Srebrenica had refused for months to allow Moslems to leave Srebrenica, even though their safety there was dubious, and they could not be consistently supplied with food. Muratovic knew very well that UNPROFOR did not have the fire power to protect the Moslem population of Srebrenica, and he knew the international community did not have the assets to set up a helicopter bridge between Tuzla and Srebrenica and care for forty thousand refugees. Who would supply the helicopters? The fuel? The tents and blankets? How would their providers fight their way through the BSA? Of course, we were concerned about the fate of the forty thousand Moslems in Srebrenica, but proposing unrealistic courses of action was no help. In fact, in spite of our inability to use the force that was necessary, we cared more about the Moslem population of Srebrenica than the Sarajevo government did.]

At the 8:30 A.M. briefing, I reported on my conversation with Minister Muratovic. Heads nodded glumly. The mood was grim. Although we could have done precious little to protect Srebrenica, we felt a sense of failure. Although we are continually telling the world that we lack the necessary resources, that we are not meant to be a fighting force, that we have chalked up several small successes in Bosnia, in our hearts at that moment we felt a sense of failure, of frustration, of anger, of impotence. Even a desire for revenge.

But we had to think practically. We decided that one of our primary concerns is for the future of Zepa and Gorazde. We suspect Mladic will go after them next. Srebrenica is lost, and Zepa will fall within the next few days, but Gorazde might be defendable. Plans have to be made.

We are also concerned about getting our unarmed military observers out of Srebrenica. The Dutch commander in the region has spoken with Mladic about that and other issues. Fifteen thousand Moslem civilians are outside the UNPROFOR compound at Potocari seeking protection. Mladic has informed the Dutch commander that he wants to begin immediately the evacuation of the Moslem population—first, the wounded, then women and children. He says he will guarantee the safety of all civilians.

Not a single one of us believes that the Moslem population of Srebrenica will be safe. The pattern is all too familiar, and it is a pattern used by Croats and Moslems as well. The draft-age men will be separated from their families, then tortured, imprisoned, executed. Women will be raped. Mass graves will be hurriedly dug to hide the evidence. And local Serb television will try to "cleanse" the facts. The Bosnian government (and the international press, which is at its service) will blame UNPROFOR, and any attempt we make to analyze the situation rationally will be considered cowardly.

As soon as the round of morning meetings ended, I called Koljevic in Pale. Communications were difficult, but I got through to him. I asked for clearance for myself and General Nikolai to go to Srebrenica. He said he would get back to me. He would talk to Mladic directly about my going there, but he was doubtful about allowing Nikolai or a team from Zagreb to go there, and he will want to accompany me.

13 July 1995

At breakfast this morning I had a conversation with one of our engineers, a Spaniard. He was very informative and forthcoming, much to the apparent disapproval of the British officers at our table, who rarely share information with Civil Affairs.

We spoke about the enormity of the concept of withdrawing UNPROFOR and replacing it with NATO troops. It is assumed that most of the UNPROFOR troops—about twenty thousand from Western European nations—will simply switch helmets, from blue to green, and become part of the NATO force. The rest, about seven thousand, will leave Bosnia. Another forty thousand, including twenty thousand Americans, will come in. The exchange will probably not occur before this winter, when the roads and rivers are virtually impassable because of snow, stalled farm vehicles, aid convoys, and local resistance. Weather conditions are a major factor in any military deployment, and they are the most unpredictable of all.

To withdraw completely, whether it is UNPROFOR being withdrawn or NATO being withdrawn after it had replaced UNPROFOR, will require a minimum of three thousand convoys of twenty trucks each for a duration of at least six months. This estimate is based on a force of about twenty-seven thousand troops now in theater. That size will be more than doubled if NATO's projections hold.

Eight thousand containers, at a cost of five thousand dollars each, for a total forty million dollars, will probably be left behind. It will require two thousand trucks to move only the containers. It will take four men, six hours each, just to fold one container and place it on a truck.

Planning for the withdrawal is taking an increasing amount of time, and taking valuable time away from the operation itself. Our engineer reported, "We are bringing in additional troops to plan for withdrawing other troops. The troops coming in will themselves have to be withdrawn and fed and housed while they are here. Their quarters will have to be winterized, and that winterizing will have to begin soon because it takes a few months to do and winter comes early to the Balkans. It will be a nightmare, an expensive nightmare."

8:15 A.M. press reading in my office. Serb radio was saying that the BSA had liberated Srebrenica in response to attacks by BIH troops against Serbian villages out of the safe area. The safe area was being used as a staging ground, the Serbs alleged. Zepa, another safe area, was expected to surrender soon. Karadzic went on Serb radio to say that his troops could no longer tolerate attacks against Serbs out of the safe areas. He pledged that the BSA will not kill Moslems, as the Croatians killed Serbs when they overran Western Slavonia in May.

Bosnian radio expressed the government's bitterness against UNPROFOR for not protecting the safe areas. UNPROFOR will be allowed to finish out its mandate in Bosnia, the government said, but it will not be allowed to renew its mandate when it expires on 31 November.

8:30 A.M. briefing. Sarajevo is stable; Zepa is tense; Srebrenica is in disarray.

We are all waiting to see what will happen to the Moslems of Srebrenica. We fear mass executions.

The Bosnian government offensive is continuing on several fronts throughout Bosnia, but our reports are that government forces have taken heavy casualties and are not making much, if any, progress. There is no question that the BSA's capture of Srebrenica and Zepa is a morale booster; they have been taking losses in the field for almost a year now without much response. Mladic needed a morale booster as much as he needed a tactical victory, and he needed to free up his troops around Srebrenica to use them against the Bosnian government's current offensive.

The BSA has requested the withdrawal of UNPROFOR's Ukrainian battalion in Gorazde. Smith is of two minds on that. He does not want to cave in to Serb demands. On the other hand, by withdrawing UNPROFOR soldiers from BSA-controlled territory, he can protect his troops from being taken hostage if NATO were to use air power. In fact, Ukrainian troops have been leaking out of Gorazde for weeks now.

Sixteen hundred Bosnians expelled from Srebrenica are already at Tuzla. Another one thousand are being processed at Kladanj.

We are concerned for the fate of UNPROFOR's local employees at Potocari. They are Moslems, and we want to protect them, but we've already heard stories of the male population between sixteen and sixty being separated from the general population and moved for interrogation to Bratanac.

There are reports that a convoy of lightly wounded Moslems coming from Srebrenica were denied access to Kladanj; they returned to Srebrenica but were denied reentrance because of continued fighting. We are making plans for the medical evacuation of casualties by helicopter, but it is difficult to obtain clearance for flights in and out of Srebrenica.

Forty-eight Dutch soldiers are reported to be in custody in Srebrenica, but we are uncertain of their condition. Are they confined to barracks? Are they being interrogated?

Meanwhile, here in Sarajevo, the Danish headquarters company have not been resupplied with fuel for seven weeks. From 10:30 P.M. tonight until 6:00 A.M. tomorrow morning there will be no power in "nonessential" offices. There are still no utilities in all of Sarajevo.

All civilian staff, excepting myself, have been told they can no longer eat in the barracks. They will have to provide for their own meals. The remaining rations are for the soldiers (and, of course, the restaurants have no food or gas to cook what food they have, and the markets are essentially closed).

UNHCR is estimating that four thousand Moslems have already left Srebrenica. All Dutch OPs there, except for two, have been abandoned.

At Visoko, in Federation territory, two OPs with nineteen Canadians have run out of water. We will probably have to abandon those posts. The Bosnian government army will not allow them to be supplied.

9:00 A.M. briefing in Smith's office. Bosnian authorities are refusing to make space in the town of Tuzla for incoming refugees from Srebrenica. UNHCR estimates that there is room in the town for about ten thousand more refugees, but the Bosnian government is trying to make a political point. If the Srebrenica refugees go to Tuzla, the Bosnian government insists, they will have to be accommodated at the air base outside the city. There will have to be international pressure at the highest levels to convince the Bosnian government to help accommodate refugees arriving in Tuzla.

I have tried to imagine what I might do to help protect the Moslem population of Srebrenica. At this point, contact with the Bosnian government in Sarajevo, except with Muratovic, is useless. They will either avoid speaking to me or will attack UNPROFOR for not assuming responsibilities for which it has neither a mandate nor material resources. The Sarajevo government is powerless now anyway. I am convinced that the only way I can help the Moslem refugees in Srebrenica, if at all, will be to get to Mladic and convince him it is in his own best interests not to mistreat them. If I can get permission from Koljevic to visit Srebrenica, then I will also have to get permission from the Bosnian government to leave Sarajevo.

At the same time, I am not deluding myself. I realize I will have little chance as an individual to convince a general with overwhelming superiority on the ground to pursue humanitarian policies that he has not pursued throughout the entire war. Very little chance. Mladic already knows about NATO's threats and about UNPROFOR's weaknesses, and he knows what it will mean to have to feed several thousand refugees when his own troops do not have fuel and food and are being squeezed by an international embargo. Clearly, he wants the Moslems out of Srebrenica, for both strategic and logistical reasons, and he fears the recruitment of the younger men into the BiH army once they reach Tuzla. But (how naïvely self-evident this sounds) there is no justification for mass murder.

There is also another risk in my going to Srebrenica. There is the danger that Mladic may try to exploit me to legitimize his actions—UNPROFOR official seen (on television) accompanying General Mladic as they view orderly evacuation of Moslem population, the headlines will read. And so on. My presence there may be exploited as an endorsement of Mladic's actions.

On the other hand, how can I *not* try to save thousands of lives? And if I can have any influence at all, it will have to be from inside Srebrenica. I cannot do anything from Sarajevo.

Finally, there is Zepa, which will fall imminently. We have between six hundred and one thousand British troops there. The local Moslem population is approximately ten thousand anxious, battered souls, most of whom were expelled from other villages and sought refuge in Zepa.

[The frustration at a time like this is indescribable. One's value system goes topsy-turvy. Suddenly, the mass expulsion of forty thousand people, about 75 percent of whom are already displaced persons from other areas of Bosnia overrun by the BSA, becomes a desirable alternative. One thinks, "If it were certain that forty thousand human beings will *only* be expelled from Srebrenica, that will be tolerable." *Tolerable* because the alternative is mass slaughter. The possibility of their remaining safely in Srebrenica is zero.

What sort of a world is it, what are one's values, when one is willing to accept the expulsion of forty thousand people as a preferable alternative?]

I called Muratovic and asked for a meeting this morning. I wanted to inform him that I hope to go to Srebrenica and that eventually Akashi will be sending a civil rights team there to monitor the situation. I was set to listen to his tirades so that I might report to Zagreb on the mood in Sarajevo. He agreed to see me, we talked, and then at the end of our meeting, quite matter-of-factly, looking straight into my eyes, he threatened my life. He informed me that I have twenty-four hours to leave Bosnia or the Bosnian government will publicly declare me persona non grata, in which case it will no longer be able to guarantee my safety. In other words, get out of town by sunrise or face assassination.

[Four days later I sent a memo to Akashi summarizing my meeting with Minister Muratovic. Here is the essence (not the literal text) of the memo I sent to Akashi:

On Thursday, 13 July, Bosnian government Minister Hasan Muratovic demanded that I leave Bosnia immediately and made a veiled threat on my life. This intimidation is part of a campaign to render inoperative the civilian component of UNPROFOR. Neither the Bosnian government nor the BSA is interested in peace talks at this point. They are only interested in a military solution.

It is a serious matter when a government minister from a member state of the United Nations threatens the life of a United Nations official. Such behavior must be protested at the highest level.

I told Minister Muratovic that UNPROFOR intended to send a human rights team to Srebrenica to make an assessment of the situation on the ground there. I said I intended to go to Pale to gain permission for this team to enter Srebrenica. His response was contemptuous and angry. As expected, he blamed UNPROFOR for the fall of Srebrenica and said, "Why go there now? It is useless."

When we finished our discussion on Srebrenica, he said: "Mr. Corwin, you have twenty-four hours to leave Bosnia. If you do not leave the country within forty-eight hours, we will go public with our demand and declare you persona non grata, and then something unpleasant might happen to you. You know this is a war, and we cannot always control our people. During a war accidents can happen."

I replied that I was shocked by his ultimatum and asked what reason he had for issuing it. He said such matters were handled by the Ministry of the Interior, and he didn't know the reason.

I said I would have to consult my superiors for instructions. I did not work for him, I worked for UNPROFOR.

When I pressed Minister Muratovic further for the reasons for his government's action against me, he said; "Perhaps you go to Pale too much." I responded that it was my job to go to Pale in order to maintain a line of communication, that I usually informed him before I went and reported to him when I returned. Besides, during our first meeting, he had urged me to visit Pale so that he might know their thinking. At the time, Civil Affairs was the *only* office in Sarajevo that went to Pale on a regular basis.

I added that I was not upset at the prospect of being declared PNG because I would then join a distinguished group that had been either declared PNG or threatened with it, including Akashi; former UNPROFOR commander, General Sir Michael Rose; Carl Bildt, the European Union's envoy; General Lewis MacKenzie, a former UNPROFOR chief of staff; and General Philippe Morillon, a commander in Sarajevo.

I believe there are several reasons for the government's action against me, the least of which is personal:

—To end all civilian contact with Pale in order to isolate it even further.

—To embarrass the Secretary-General's special representative, Mr. Akashi, by intimidating his staff.

—To make clear that the Bosnian government is not interested in political negotiation at this point. They are seeking a military solution, and they want to expel UNPROFOR in the hopes of having the arms embargo against Bosnia lifted and of having NATO intervene to protect them.

—To scapegoat the UN.

A protest must be made at the highest level, to President Izetbegovic, that it is unacceptable for the government of a member state of the United Nations to threaten the lives of United Nations officials. For the moment, it may be inadvisable for me to travel to Pale from Sarajevo, but in the long run we cannot and must not accept that our contacts with the Bosnian Serbs be annulled by terrorist intimidation.

There were other elements to my discussion with Muratovic that I did not include in my fax to Akashi, but which are worth noting here.

To begin with, such intimidation of UN personnel was not limited to the Bosnian government. The Serbs did it, and the Croats did it. It was almost a normal way of doing business in the Balkans. As far as Sarajevo was concerned, if you were not in lockstep with the Bosnian government, then they tried to eliminate you one way or another. It was no small coincidence that our vehicle had been shot at coming over Mount Igman only two days before. The Bosnian government didn't want any of Akashi's political representatives around. No peaceniks.

During our meeting Muratovic had become particularly bitter when I mentioned my wish to go to Srebrenica. "Last week you went to Pale, and this week Srebrenica falls. Now you want to go to Pale again. What's next? Zepa?"

Did he really believe I was carrying military secrets to Pale, that I or anyone on my staff was an intelligence courier working for the Bosnian Serbs? Of course not. But such delusions served well Muratovic's purpose of cutting UNPROFOR's contact with Pale. Smith could still not speak to Mladic.

At another point Muratovic said to me: "Perhaps the Interior Ministry has a report on something you did in Eastern Slavonia, your previous assignment." Yes, perhaps they found out I ate pork, I thought.]

When I returned to the barracks, I told Smith about Muratoric's ultimatum. He was surprised. I told him I intended to hang tough, but perhaps he could find out what was going on. He said he would be talking to Vice President Ganic later in the day and would inquire. He did, but got the same evasiveness. Ganic said that such decisions are made by the Ministry of the Interior. He professed to know nothing.

Then I called UNPF headquarters in Zagreb. [In the next couple of days I called Zagreb several times and spoke to different people to seek advice. In the near term, I realized, the decision was mine to make, whether to stay or to leave Sarajevo, but several points emerged during my discussions.

1. There was general agreement that one of the intentions of the threat against me was to discourage contact with Pale. The Bosnian government was furious that Carl Bildt had sent envoys to Zvornik to speak with Karadzic's representatives and that I went to Pale so often.

2. I did not need to leave Sarajevo immediately. I might wait at least until the new chief of mission, Antonio Pedauye, arrived. He was due within ten days.

3. I should cancel any plans to go to Srebrenica.

4. John Almstrom, a former military man who was Akashi's top assistant—always serious, conscientious, and reliable—said to me: "You'd better be careful. People in that part of the world can be pretty nasty. And remember, you were shot at only two days ago. If you want to come back, we'll find something for you here." I told Almstrom that I preferred to stay in Sarajevo.]

I had only taken one suitcase with me from Zagreb, and I quickly went to my residence this afternoon, packed it, and moved completely into the barracks. If I decided to leave, I would be able to leave immediately.

I fought hard to control my anger. After a day of reflection I have decided that I will leave for Zagreb within a day or two, for consultations, take my belongings with me, and postpone a final decision until after I discuss the matter in Zagreb, even though I know that once I leave Sarajevo, it will be extremely difficult to return until the war is over.

The main reason for my deciding to leave is not Muratovic's threat. It is the new structure of the UN mission, which will create the post of chief of mission for Bosnia and Herzegovina.

Antonio Pedauye, the new chief, who is scheduled to arrive within a week to ten days, will assume all of my primary functions. It will be he who deals with the Bosnian government, who goes to Pale, who works with Smith, and who reports to Akashi. He will also have his own staff. That is what the Security Council has decided. I will be effectively marginalized. Meanwhile, until Pedauye arrives, the Bosnian government will block me from going to Pale or Srebrenica or Tuzla or anywhere else that is considered sensitive. It will be like being under house arrest. Under such conditions, there is no point remaining in Sarajevo. If I cannot be effective, if I cannot be involved, then why stay? There are more comfortable places to be.

[A development occurred on 15 July that relates to the threat made against me by Minister Muratovic.

Because it was not safe for me to go to Pale, my deputy John Ryan went there on 15 July. He was accompanied by Merrick Fall, the same man who had been with me when we were shot at going over Mount Igman on 11 July.

On his return from Pale, while passing through the Bosnian government checkpoint at Dobrinje, Ryan was arrested by the Bosnian police, interrogated, threatened with a pistol, and verbally abused. Following are excerpts from the IncRep (incident report) filed with UNPF headquarters in Zagreb:

While returning from a discussion in Pale with Professor N. Koljevic, Mr. Ryan's car was stopped by Bosnian police at the Dobrinje checkpoint after the airport, at about 17:15 hours. After waiting for 25 minutes, the passengers were taken out of their vehicle and obliged to follow another car, to what appeared to be a police station. Upon arriving at the police station, Mr. Fall instructed the driver, Private P. Kristiansen, to radio to Sarajevo HQ, but Pvt. Kristiansen was physically prevented from leaving the building. The police were very aggressive, and forced Mr. Ryan into an interrogation room while Mr. Fall was forcibly kept in another office, under armed guard. During interrogation a gun was brandished at Mr. Ryan when he attempted to leave the room. After some time, the UNPROFOR detainees were asked to move to a different, undisclosed location. When they refused, the tone of the police became even more hostile: "Will you come quietly or not? We are prepared to use force if necessary." The UNPROFOR party then left the police station. On arrival at a further, fifth-floor office some distance away, Mr. Ryan was interrogated by the same police officer, now in civilian clothes. No reason was given for the move, but it may have been to frustrate any attempt by UNPROFOR colleagues to locate the suspects.

At first, the purpose of the questions put to Mr. Ryan was not explicitly stated. The interrogating officer kept repeating: "We must unreveal [*sic!*] some things. Mr. Ryan, you know what I am talking about." Mr. Ryan clearly stated the nature of Civil Affairs, and said that he had nothing to say to the officer. Eventually, it emerged that Mr. Ryan was alleged to be pro-Serb: in the course of his conversations with Mr. Koljevic—both on the previous occasion he had met with Mr. Koljevic, and in the meeting that had just taken place—it was alleged that Mr. Ryan had passed on sensitive military information to the Serbs. Apparently, the Bosnian police had an intelligence source in Pale, who was informed of the content of the conversations between Mr. Ryan and Mr. Koljevic. The question of Zepa, the interrogating officer claimed, had been on the agenda of today's meeting. "You went to Pale, the next day Srebrenica fell; now you go to Pale again: what about Zepa?"

The focus of the interrogation was only on Mr. Ryan, not Mr. Fall. Throughout the interrogation, the manner used by the officer was increasingly aggressive, threatening, and unpleasant. For example: "In war many mistakes are made. What is one more?" These words were intended to suggest that if Mr. Ryan were to disappear, nobody would be any the wiser. Mr. Ryan had Mr. Muratovic's telephone numbers, at work and at home, but throughout the interrogation, at all three locations, the interrogator systematically denied Mr. Ryan to right to use the telephone to reach either Mr. Muratovic or UNPROFOR Headquarters.

At one point, in the face of Mr. Ryan's determined refusal to supply any information, Mr. Fall was again separated to an adjoining room. The mood then changed, and became somewhat more conciliatory. The police then demanded to see the notes of the meeting Mr. Ryan had held with Mr. Koljevic. Given the condition of duress, and since the victim had nothing to hide, it was decided to acquiesce to this demand. The police officers copied some of the points recorded in Mr. Ryan's rough notes, and seemed to be satisfied.

In conclusion, though a case of mistaken identity is unlikely, this incident should perhaps not be seen in isolation, but rather as part of an elaborate plot to undermine and intimidate UNPROFOR, and is most probably connected to the recent threats against Mr. P. Corwin.

As the suspects were released, the police officer commented: "We do what we can to defend our country."

When I spoke to John Ryan after the event, he also told me, though it was not reflected in the incident report, that the interrogator had asked him several times: "Where's Corwin? Is he still in Bosnia?"

I was particularly struck by the fact that the same phrase—about going to Pale before Srebrenica fell and now going again to prepare for the attack on Zepa—that had been used on me was used on Ryan. I didn't doubt that the Bosnian government had a "mole" in Pale, but the lies, the paranoia, and the death threats were all legacies of the Communist system. Totalitarianism had never left Bosnia. After Communism comes Communism.

Some days later, a high UNPROFOR official in Zagreb sent a letter of protest to Muratovic, noting that the Bosnian government's treatment of Mr. Ryan violated Article V, Section 18a of the Convention on Privileges and Immunities of the United Nations (1946), to which the Bosnian government was a party. In that convention it is stated that "officials of the United Nations shall be immune from legal process in respect of words spoken or written and all acts performed by them in their official capacity."

Blah, blah, blah. I doubt if Muratovic ever responded to this letter, although I was pleased it was sent.

No such protest, however, was made on my behalf. It was thought best to sweep that incident under the rug.]

6:00 P.M. briefing in Smith's office. We spoke again about one of the components of the RRF, the multinational brigade (MNB). The MNB is now composed of a British battalion and a French battalion, each with artillery, and a Dutch mortar company. Its need to be in the Sarajevo area is greater than ever before. The ripples from Srebrenica are already being felt. In the immortal words of Star Wars, "There has been a tremor in the force." A mass of humanity has been violated, and priorities are being reassessed. The MNB wants to be in Knesevo within three days.

UNHCR estimates that fourteen thousand people have already been bused out of Srebrenica. Five thousand are at Tuzla air base, another four thousand are at Kladanj. The rest are unaccounted for.

Meanwhile, I have been receiving constant telephonic updates from one of my civil affairs officers in Tuzla, a daring and tireless Ethiopian woman, Hannah Yilma. The situation in Tuzla is chaotic, shifting, dangerous.

The Bosnian government is complaining that the Dutch battalion is not accompanying convoys out of Srebrenica, as it promised to do. In fact, our information is that the Dutch *have* been accompanying convoys that leave from Potocari, where the barracks of the Dutch battalion are, but they have not been able to accompany convoys that leave from elsewhere. Quite simply, three hundred troops are not enough to monitor the fate of forty thousand distressed and desperate souls.

Otherwise, the Bosnian government is still insisting that all refugees from Srebrenica be accommodated at the air base in Tuzla. They do not want to release any space in the town of Tuzla. They want Zepa to be reinforced, but we cannot reinforce Zepa. It would be a major battle to try to get into Zepa with troops, and we have no extra troops. On the contrary, we have been trying to withdraw our troops from Zepa to make them less vulnerable to being taken hostage.

The Bosnian government is understandably frantic. In its frustration it is lashing out at UNPROFOR. The most effective course of action it has, short of surrender, is to be uncooperative. Meanwhile, it is trying to retain what little influence it has outside of Sarajevo, in the eastern enclaves and in Federation territory. When a government suffers a military setback, it comes unglued. Its survival is threatened. Bosnian government politicians are at this point as concerned about their own survival as a government as they are about the forty thousand souls in Srebrenica. In fact, more concerned.

[Here are some additional thoughts I recorded on the evening of 13 July:]
The BSA has staged a Tet Offensive. Srebrenica has fallen, and Zepa is next. The eastern enclaves will fall to the BSA, and thousands of people will be "cleansed." Not too long ago Western pundits were predicting the imminent collapse of the BSA: the BSA is stretched crust thin, it cannot withstand the improved assaults of the BiH, it is on the defensive, and so on. The BSA is not as strong as it once was, but it is not yet ready to roll over.

If there are to be NATO air strikes, they will have to be massive. And immediate. And beyond any existing mandate.

President Chirac, newly elected, reasonably secure, and trying to divert attention from economic problems at home, offered to have the French liberate Srebrenica, if only the UN will allow him to do so. Chirac knows very well the Secretary-General cannot grant him permission. It will take a Security Council decision, which is unlikely, and France will not act on its own. It is an empty offer, calculated to generate support in the international community and to assert France's "independence." Disgraceful how political leaders will exploit human tragedy to advance their own ambitions, to promote their own image. The fact is that until the world community is ready to commit infantry against the Serbs, it will not defeat them. Air strikes will weaken but not defeat them.

Srebrenica fell on 11 July. Last night, buses with Moslem refugees were being offloaded just before the confrontation line at Kladanj. The refugees walked across the line and were picked up by Bosnian government buses, which brought them to the Tuzla air base. It is now the responsibility of UNHCR to feed, house, and provide for them. The magnitude of this tragedy is almost indescribable. The repercussions will be cataclysmic because the world is watching the tragedy closely. It will not be obscured, and there will be retaliation.

At first the government in Sarajevo said it would not allow the refugees to leave Srebrenica. It called on the few hundred Dutch UNPROFOR troops to prevent the refugees from leaving. When it became clear the Moslems would be "cleansed" and in many cases wanted to leave because they feared Serbian administration, the Bosnian government refused to assist. When the refugees—about five thousand already as of midnight last night—arrived at Kladanj, the Moslem governor of Tuzla sent buses to pick them up and drop them at the Tuzla air base. He then organized demonstrations and blockades of the Norwegian Medical Company and Norwegian Battalion in the Tuzla area as a way of protesting UNPROFOR's inability to protect the Moslems (thus denying his own people medical aid). We expect increasing harassment, perhaps even shootings, against UNPROFOR personnel and facilities by the Bosnian government and by Bosnian civilians.

The Bosnian government has suffered a military defeat and is in disarray. If there were an opposition party, the government would fall, but there is no significant opposition party, so the government is looking to divert attention from its unpopularity by shifting the blame to UNPROFOR, which has itself suffered a military defeat and may at last be replaced by *its* opposition party, NATO. The message has gone out: Srebrenica has fallen; it is time for UNPROFOR to fall.

The Sarajevo government is virtually irrelevant in Federation territory. It is like a government in exile. It is not even contiguous to Federation territory. The only ties it has to Federation territory are through the ruling political party, the SDA. The Sarajevo government's main constituency is NATO, not the Moslem people of Bosnia and certainly not the non-Moslem people.

14 July 95

9:00 A.M. briefing. We have reports that there are twenty-seven severely wounded persons in Bratunac. They need to be evacuated. We need medical helicopters, but they cannot get clearance from the BSA.

Srebrenica is virtually "cleansed." In three days, forty thousand people have been uprooted and expelled, many of them possibly murdered. Meanwhile, Dutch soldiers are still being held at Potocari. The Dutch commander there is asking Mladic to release his soldiers.

UNHCR reports eleven thousand refugees at Tuzla now: three thousand at the airport, eight thousand in surrounding areas. Reports are circulating about missing persons, but we have no way of confirming anything at this point.

We are trying to get clearance for a convoy of Norwegian ambulances to go to Srebrenica from Tuzla.

The Moslem mayor of Zenica has said he will accept five thousand to six thousand Moslem refugees. There is a need to press the Bosnian government in Sarajevo to help with the problem.

Smith says he has told Prime Minister Siladzic that UNPROFOR has no orders to reinforce Zepa. It is impossible to do so at this point anyway. How would we move the troops? Roads are closed. And where would we find the troops to move?

I brought up again the issue of our nineteen Canadians at two OPs outside Visoko. They have not been resupplied for almost three weeks. They have one day of water and one day of hard rations left. Why have we not gone public with the fact that the BIH is holding our soldiers hostage?

"No, we can't criticize the Bosnian government," said Alex Ivanko, UNPROFOR's civilian spokesman in Sarajevo. Smith concurred.

"Ever?" I asked. I was furious that Ivanko was continually acting as the spokesman for the Bosnian government and that Smith protected him.

Smith said: "The way to handle this is to speak quietly to the Bosnian government, and have our troops simply stay put."

"Without supplies?" I asked.

"The Canadian issue will pale when placed alongside the situation in Srebrenica," Ivanko said.

"Yes, of course," I said. "But these are UNPROFOR troops we're talking about. They are being blockaded, held hostage, harassed, and starved, and yet we refuse to say so publicly. Please, Alex, you do not make policy here."

Smith interceded. "I shall talk to Siladzic again, chaps. I take the situation seriously." There were a few Canadians at the briefing. They were supportive of me, but didn't utter a word; they wouldn't dare contradict the commander.

Then Ivanko said to Smith: "The Bosnian government has instructed the

Bosnian press not to criticize you for the fall of Srebrenica. They were told they could attack Janvier if necessary. Or Akashi. Anyone in Zagreb. But they are to leave you alone."

"That might not be so good, actually," Smith said. He was embarrassed.

Because the world press takes its lead from the Bosnian government, we can expect they will also focus on Janvier and Akashi in Zagreb and on Boutros-Ghali in New York. No such thing as objective reporting. Advocacy journalism is the name of the dirty game in Sarajevo. The only possible advantage of this policy for us is that it may discourage harassment of UNPROFOR by the locals. The local population marches to the drumbeats of official policy. They may shoot less at us, stone our vehicles less, if the government tells them the responsibility for Srebrenica lies with UNPF in Zagreb. On the other hand, the locals never make such intellectual distinctions. They will continue to stone us, I suspect.

[One more word on the Canadians. In an article that was to appear in the *Globe Mail* of Toronto on 30 October 1995, correspondent Bill Schiller, reporting from Croatia, spoke with Canadian troops as they were leaving Bosnia and returning to Canada. He wrote:

The tour was marked by the hostage-taking of some of their members by the Bosnian Serbs—as insurance against further NATO air strikes—and another incident in which the mainly Muslim Bosnian army blocked the camp's entrance with land mines.

Despite making significant contributions to the humanitarian effort in Bosnia, the aggressive actions of the Bosnians left them bruised.

"There was a lot of frustration," said Lt. Paul D'Orsonnens, a liaison officer with the Fusiliers du Mont-Royal.

"From June, when the Bosnian army launched its major offensive, our movements were restricted and there was a frustration with what I'd call a certain arrogance in the Bosnian command."]

15 July 95

7:00 P.M. Have decided to go to Zagreb for consultations. Said goodbye yesterday to Smith and my staff in Sarajevo.

Have had the usual difficulties in leaving Sarajevo. Was scheduled to leave at 6:00 A.M. this morning by armored vehicle over Mount Igman, but the BiH is blocking all traffic at the foot of Igman, so I never left the compound. Might have been able to leave this afternoon and catch a helicopter from Kiseljak to Split, but if I reached Split this evening, I would not be able to go to Zagreb until Monday, which would mean spending the summer weekend in the resort town of Split. But I decided to stay in Sarajevo. Such are the attractions of war.

Smith left headquarters at 5:00 A.M. this morning, intending to go over Igman to Kiseljak, then by helicopter to Split and on to Belgrade. As of 7:00 A.M., he was still at the bottom of Igman waiting to get clearance. He was supposed to go to Belgrade to meet with Stoltenberg, Bildt, Akashi, Milosevic, perhaps even Mladic. I have not followed his progress, but I am sure he got through. Siladzic would see to that.

Yesterday evening a Norwegian convoy bringing flour to Sarajevo was targeted by the BSA while it crossed Igman. One truck was disabled, and two soldiers were injured, not seriously. French artillery returned fire. Don't know if they hit anything. Serbs are playing hardball everywhere.

Yesterday afternoon I received permission from Koljevic to go to Srebrenica, via Pale, but I doubt if the Bosnian government will let me out of Sarajevo. I told Koljevic I couldn't go.

Last night as we drove through Sarajevo, young punks threw large rocks at our armored vehicle. The windscreen of John Ryan's vehicle was shattered during the night while it was parked outside his apartment. Vandalism against UNPROFOR is increasing. We are being blamed for the fall of Srebrenica.

[I left Sarajevo that weekend for Zagreb. During the next few weeks, before I was sent to the Krajina on 4 August, the night before the Croatian army began its "Operation Storm" offensive there, I continued to follow the situation in Bosnia. I was in daily contact with Sarajevo.

On 19 July, the chief administrative officer in Sarajevo, Peter Jones, a retired British general and an articulate, conscientious man with a wonderful sense of humor, asked me if I would liaise with the RRF contingent due to arrive the following week at Ploce, Croatia. There were problems: with the Croatian government, with Federation authorities, and within the RRF structure. What was needed was a political assessment of the situation. I agreed to go. In a way, it was an acceptance that I would not return to Sarajevo until the war was over.]

26 July 1995

Today I began my discussions in Ploce. Mayor Joshko Damic expressed his concern that the arrival of the RRF will be a psychological shock to the small community there. Five thousand troops will be landing in a town of five thousand people. The mayor is concerned about sewage, water, and roads, as well as about the intermingling of foreign troops with the local population.

Port Ploce is particularly important because it is the port that will be used to supply Bosnia.

Ivan Pavlovic, the general manager of Port Ploce, was quite direct in telling me his concerns: "Our main concern is that the RRF can be turned against Croatia because its mandate is unclear. Why is the RRF being deployed in Bosnia in areas that are already under Croatian control?" (I noted that he said *Croatian*, not *Bosnian Croat* or *Federation* control.) I told him that this matter is to be discussed at higher levels and that I would pass on his concerns to my superiors in Zagreb.

While I was in Ploce, Croatian officials from Zagreb came to discuss customs fees. Of course, the UN is not supposed to pay customs duties associated with a peacekeeping operation, but the Croatian government is not about to miss the opportunity to milk the UN cow. Croatian Admiral Letica also arrived in Ploce. He wants to see the port improved to allow for better use by the Croatian navy. He also wants to see the airstrip at Ploce improved so that the Croatian air force might get better use of that facility as well.

Finally, Mr. Pavlovic expressed to me his concern that the RRF might actually be used to protect the Serbs and limit the military activities of the Croatian army.

[I waxed sentimental about the natural environment for a moment, but I was also aware of the legitimate concerns of the Croatian government and of many Third World governments that become hosts for international peacekeeping operations. On the one hand, I thought of the sleepy beauty of the Dalmatian coast and how it was about to be transformed into a military camp by the arrival of thousands of foreign combat soldiers. A pity. Yet, this impending metamorphosis also made me understand the resentment of many governments in developing countries, not simply Croatia, where the UN had set up mega–peacekeeping operations. Sometimes the sovereign government felt it had lost control of its own country. (In Somalia, there had not even been a government when the UN arrived.)

The UN would come in with its trucks and Landrovers and car radios and elaborate communications paraphernalia to a country where most citizens could not afford automobiles or even telephones and would one day go home leaving nothing behind. Perhaps they would leave peace behind, but that was not enough to assuage the hunger of a population that had little access to consumer goods. There was, in other words, a dimension of cultural relativity to what Westerners viewed simply as greed, as a wish to milk the UN cow. Eventually, I was sure, this topic would become one of ideological debate in future peacekeeping operations. As for the military concerns of the Croatian government, they were of another order and could also be understood, especially since the Croatian army and the Bosnian Croat army were making steady advances in southwest Bosnia, up the Livno Valley, and did not want to be deterred.

The arrival of the RRF, more than any other single action, was what transformed UNPROFOR from a peacekeeping to a peace-enforcement mission. Once the decision had been made to deploy the RRF, we had passed the point of no return.

Moreover, once the RRF was deployed, governments would want a bang for their buck. The laptop bombardiers had won their war to go to war against the Bosnian Serbs, and they would win their war against the Bosnian Serbs. Perhaps that was only just, but it would seriously damage UN peacekeeping operations in the immediate future.

Politicians begin wars and leave it to generals to end them.]

Afterword

I returned to Bosnia at the end of April 1997, almost exactly two years from the day I first arrived in Sarajevo to take up my duties as the UN's chief political officer in the country, the date on which I began the journal that is now *Dubious Mandate*. This time, however, I was working for the Organization for Security and Cooperation in Europe (OSCE), which was charged with supervising elections in Bosnia. I remained for six months in a diplomatic post as OSCE's political officer in Banja Luka. In northwest Bosnia, Banja Luka was a Bosnian Serb stronghold that eventually became the capital of the Bosnian Serb Republic (Republika Srpska).

The changes in Sarajevo and throughout all of Bosnia since I had left were dramatic. The General Framework for Peace in Bosnia and Herzegovina (the "Dayton Agreement")—initialed in Dayton, Ohio, on 12 November 1995, and signed a month later in Paris—had officially ended the war. Bosnia was from then on considered to be one country with two entities: the Federation (composed mainly of Moslems and Croats), which controlled 51 percent of the country's territory, and Republika Srpska (composed mainly of Serbs), which comprised 49 percent of the country's territory. OSCE was authorized by the Dayton Agreement to carry out several rounds of elections in order to put a democratic structure in place. As a political officer in Republika Srpska, my main task was to maintain contact with the numerous Bosnian Serb political parties, so that I might monitor, advise, and report on them as the municipal election campaign progressed.

In accordance with Annex 3 of the Dayton Agreement, OSCE had already supervised six levels of elections on 14 September 1996: for the House of Representatives of Bosnia and Herzegovina (comprising representatives from each of the two entities), the presidency of Bosnia and Herzegovina (three representatives—one each from the Moslem, Serb, and Croat communities), the House of Representatives of the Federation, the National Assembly of Republika Srpska, the presidency of Republika Srpska, and cantonal legislatures in the Federation. The one election that had not taken place was for municipal authorities in Republika Srpska. That election, for mayors and city councils, had not taken place because, in the opinion of OSCE, the proper conditions for holding them had not existed. Republika

Srpska municipal elections were twice postponed and finally took place on 14–15 September 1997.

Municipal elections are the most basic elections in any country because they determine who runs the daily life of the community. They are the foundations for higher levels of government and frequently reflect a community's approval or disapproval with the way the entire country is being governed. In Germany after World War II, the Allied troops held elections first at the municipal level and worked their way up. In Bosnia and Herzegovina it was done the opposite, and perhaps wrong, way.

Municipal elections in Republika Srpska were intended to restore, as much as possible, the same proportional representation that had existed before the conflict, according to the 1991 census. In other words, they were intended to reverse the results of ethnic cleansing. People were allowed to vote in their prewar residences. Of course, many people had either died or found new homes in another part of Bosnia or in third countries. They would not return to their original communities, and in many cases they had no homes to return to anyway because their homes had been destroyed. They could vote in their home towns, however, either in person or by absentee ballot, subject to very strict regulations. A Moslem who had been expelled from Zepa could vote for a Moslem mayoral candidate in Zepa, even if he did not want to return there to live.

Meanwhile, there was the postelection problem of implementing the results of the municipal elections. Would a duly elected Moslem mayor be able to assume his functions in Srebrenica, for example? Even so, the elections were mandated and went forward quite effectively.

When the OSCE remarked that proper conditions for carrying out the elections in 1996 had not existed, what it had meant was that the elaborate structure was not yet in place that would be needed to prevent fraud and intimidation. All sides attempted to do both. That much was assumed and confirmed. The most OSCE could do was to minimize those tendencies, and it did. Of all the operations, civilian and military, that I witnessed in Bosnia, none was carried out with more professionalism than the municipal voting exercise.

Though I was stationed in Banja Luka, I went to Sarajevo many times, and because I had spent most of my previous tour of duty there, I noticed the changes there more readily than in other areas. After eighteen months of peace, Sarajevo was once more a bustling, active, international city. It may seem a cliché to praise the Sarajevans for having been so indomitable, brave, and proud, but I could sense that pride almost like the fragrance of a flower. It was everywhere in the air. It was not a boastfulness; it was a quiet affirmation.

The various markets in downtown Sarajevo, repeatedly devastated by Serb shelling, were all functioning. There were fresh fruits and vegetables, trucked in daily from the countryside. People shuffled about with purposeful abandon. Foreign uniforms were everywhere, but the city indubitably belonged to the Sarajevans. Actually, it seemed strange to be able to drive around the city without having to go through checkpoints and roadblocks, and without being sealed inside an armored car. The ability to stroll without having to worry about snipers was perhaps the greatest luxury of all.

At the same time, life was certainly not back to the relative comfort of the prewar level. Electricity and water had still not been completely restored. (The flush toilets at OSCE headquarters, for example, were not working and had to be activated by hand-pouring water down them.) Unemployment was high, and there was a shortage of livable housing. Large ruins—on the main boulevards, in back streets, in the squares—stood as dramatic monuments to the cruelty of the war. Apartment buildings were pockmarked from the firing of automatic weapons; on the far bank of the Miljachka River that ran through the city, the Jewish cemetery was still mined; and there were war wounded everywhere.

The demographics in Sarajevo, as throughout most of Bosnia, were also different—different from what they had been before the war and different from what they had been in 1995 just before the Dayton Agreement. There were tens of thousands of Moslem refugees in the city, many of whom had sought refuge during the war after they had been "cleansed" from their villages, as well as many Sarajevan Moslems who had not been there in 1995 and had come back once the war ended. Postwar Sarajevo was also without the many Serbs and Croats who had fled *after* the war had ended. Many of the Serbs had fled voluntarily, encouraged by their leaders in Pale, who warned them that they would be persecuted by the Bosnian government if they stayed. And many Sarajevan Serbs who tried to stay were, in fact, "cleansed" by the vindictive actions of Bosnian government police. As government police established their control over Sarajevo suburbs where Serbs lived, Serbs were turned out unceremoniously and vengefully, and they left "with a howl." They burned the houses they lived in, mostly houses that once belonged to Moslems who had themselves been "cleansed," dug up the coffins of their dead from Serbian cemeteries, loaded them into carts along with their farm animals, and fled to Republika Srpska or to Serbia.

One can understand the anger of Bosnian government police officers, many of whom were themselves Sarajevan refugees. One can also understand the guilt and fear of the many Sarajevan Serbs who anticipated retaliation after the crimes their leadership had perpetrated. But the exodus of thousands of Serbs from Sarajevo was an inauspicious beginning to the implementation of a peace agreement that envisioned reintegration of the country's three main ethnic groups, and it was a sign that ethnic antagonism had not ended, that revenge was in the air.

At the same time, most of those very Sarajevan Moslems who had endured the ugliest of onslaughts were amazingly magnanimous. In September 1997 I went to Sarajevo along with two Bosnian Serb women to attend a rock concert by U2. We stayed overnight in the private home of a Moslem family. At breakfast the next morning, the two Serbs and the Moslem woman of the house chatted away comfortably, even speaking about the war. The two Serbs certainly were not ready to move to Sarajevo (they were originally from Banja Luka, and one of them had sat out the war in Italy), and they were afraid to walk the streets of Sarajevo at night, but both said they would like to return to Sarajevo. They liked Sarajevo, and, appropriately enough, they despised Radovan Karadzic and Momcilo Krajisnik and the rest of the Bosnian Serb "leadership" in Pale.

What was most memorable, however, was the magnanimity of the Moslem family, a married couple and the woman's brother, who breakfasted with us the next morning. It was like nothing I had ever expected. They had a son who had been in the war and survived. Their apartment had been shelled. They still had no water between 10:00 P.M. and 6:00 A.M. But they were gracious. And it was not an act.

Yet the scars were there for everyone, and it would be naïve to pretend otherwise. Every family that lived in Sarajevo during the siege suffered—if not in blood, then in extreme discomfort, in anguish and uncertainty.

I remember speaking to a Moslem woman in her thirties who worked for OSCE as an interpreter. She was a lovely woman, bright and intense, married with two children. "What people here have to do is forgive," I said to her once. "It is impossible to forget. And besides, a nation should not forget its past. To forgive is more important than to forget."

"Oh, no," she said to me immediately. "I would *love* to forget. Problem is that I can't. One day my four-year-old daughter and I and my father were sitting at the dinner table, and a Serb shell came through the window and blew my father's head off. My daughter and I were unharmed, but we saw it all happen. For four years my daughter was able to put it out of her mind, but then one night, in the middle of the night, she woke up crying. She had remembered. And I still remember. No, I would love to forget."

Since the war ended in Bosnia, the general view in the U.S. media has been that: (1) NATO's bombing of the Bosnian Serbs, from 30 August through 14 September, was what effectively brought an end to the war; (2) it should have been done sooner; and (3) the arms embargo (which had been imposed against *all* of former Yugoslavia) should have been lifted early on in order to allow the Bosnian government to be able to defend itself (the Bosnian Serbs had superiority in heavy weapons throughout the war). In other words, the "lift and strike" policy (lift the arms embargo against Bosnia and hit the Bosnian Serbs with air strikes) had been the correct policy all along. U.S. diplomacy, led by Serbophobe Richard Holbrooke during the negotiations at Dayton, Ohio, had finally saved the day after the Europeans had been fumbling for four years.

This view is what I call the "B.C. to A.D." view: Before Clinton to After Dayton. It's the official, politically correct line. But it is terribly distorted.

First, there is the question of timing. I remember speaking to a retired U.S. diplomat a few months after the Dayton Agreement was signed. He had come to UN headquarters in New York, and he kept asking me and Shashi Tharoor, who was in charge of the Yugoslav desk in the Department of Peacekeeping Operations, exactly *when* did we think the bombing should have begun. Obviously, he thought it should have been done months, perhaps years, earlier. He kept pressing us to give him an exact date when it should have started. Why had we waited until 30 August 1995?

I asked him if the invasion of Normandy by the Allies shouldn't have been earlier, or if the atomic bomb shouldn't have been dropped on Berlin? The point is that it is idle speculation to imagine that a particular policy might have been successful at a different point in time. A policy worked when it worked because the time was right, and it might not have worked if that same policy had been tried earlier.

More important, the emphasis by Washington on air strikes obscured at least two significant issues: that the air strikes were not what brought about an end to the war and that military action veiled the failures of diplomacy—failures largely due to U.S. opposition, failures twisted by the press and Washington spin doctors into looking like heroic gambits, like profiles in courage.

What broke the back of the Bosnian Serb military machine in the summer of 1995 was the strength of the Croatian and Bosnian Croat forces in the western part of Bosnia and in the Krajina area of Croatia. The movement of the Croatian and Bosnian-Croat forces up through the Livno Valley, their capture of Knin, and the coordinated movement of the Bosnian army's valiant V Corps, coming south out of Bihac, as well as the fire power of the RRF in breaking the siege of Sarajevo—*these* were what brought the Serbs to their knees. As long as there is gravity, territory will have to be taken by infantry, and air strikes alone will not do the trick. Most military analysts I spoke with did not think that air strikes would have been successful earlier in the war, not to mention the fact that they were politically impossible any earlier.

In this regard, at the end of their book, *Srebrenica,* Honig and Both comment in a footnote:

Air attacks, which the Clinton administration so favored and executed, proved relatively ineffective in September 1995. The NATO air forces quickly ran out of targets, and in 750 attack missions, bombed the same fifty-six ground targets over and over again. The Serbs were not so susceptible to air power because their "pain barrier" had risen after they had achieved their territorial objectives in eastern Bosnia. By this stage, they could cope with air strikes by sitting tight. It was the other ground operations—by the Croats, Bosnians, and RRF—that forced them to seek an end to the war. (186)

Indeed, the history of U.S. policy during the war in former Yugoslavia made Washington's ultimate claim to diplomatic success seem quite cynical. To begin with, *the United States had no troops on the ground until the war ended.* The reason that European countries resisted calls for air-strike diplomacy was that their troops were potential hostages and targets for retaliation. In fact, on several occasions UNPROFOR troops had been taken hostage, and on many other occasions they had been shot at, blockaded, harassed, and abused. Even in Serb-occupied Croatia, where I was stationed during the early stages of the war in Bosnia, there were retaliations against UNPROFOR whenever NATO conducted air strikes in neighboring Bosnia. Clinton knew the U.S. Congress would be extremely resistant to sending American ground troops to Bosnia until the fighting ended. A few bombs were all right, but no ground troops. Of course, the European countries had parliaments also, and those parliaments didn't want to see their men and women being killed and taken hostage. *That* was the main reason the Europeans opposed air strikes, not because they were politically dysfunctional. In fact, the NATO bombing of September 1995 took place only after the last UNPROFOR troops had been withdrawn from Serb-controlled territory.

There were also, as already mentioned in the course of this book, occasions when Washington's support, or even passive compliance, might have brought a settlement along the lines of one of the earlier peace proposals: the Cutileiro initiative in spring 1992, the Vance-Owen Peace Plan in early 1993, or the Contact Group Plan later in 1993. Washington had resisted each time, however, insisting that it could get *more* for the Bosnian government.

Indeed, Washington even resisted withdrawing UNPROFOR troops from Bosnian Serb enclaves so that NATO could bomb without endangering them. In the words of Honig and Both:

> As for the Clinton administration, it pursued a high moralistic policy for which it was totally unwilling to accept responsibility. . . . When Generals Smith and Janvier tried to create the preconditions on the ground which, in actual fact, might have made tougher action possible, the US ambassador to the UN strongly opposed their proposal to with-

draw UNPROFOR units from the eastern enclaves. Such statements undoubtedly also stiffened the resolve of the Bosnian government to hang on to them, by creating the false hope that the US might fight politically, if not militarily, to prevent the Serbs from obtaining the enclaves at a low price. That was a pipe dream. (186)

In short, it seemed inexcusably cynical to those of us mired in Bosnia that Washington, having no troops on the ground and refusing to pay its dues either to the United Nations regular budget or to the budget for UN peacekeeping operations (two separate budgets), should demand the right to call the tune in Bosnia and should claim credit for ultimate success after long nonparticipation, even obstruction. It was one of those situations in which Americans like myself, who consider themselves vigorously patriotic, had to issue political disclaimers. The Europeans were particularly resentful. The final irony was that in the eyes of most observers, the Bosnian government ended up getting precious little more territory than it might have under earlier proposals, and suffered more casualties.

With regard to lifting the arms embargo, I have heard numerous American critics say it should have been done early on in the war and that it would have allowed Bosnian government forces to defend themselves. But this approach belies several facts and is another example of politics by sound bite rather than reason.

It is necessary, first of all, to ask *who* first imposed the weapons ban on all of former Yugoslavia and who refused to lift it. The answer to both questions is the UN Security Council, led by its five permanent members. The United States, which voted in favor of the original ban, later reversed itself and lobbied for repealing it, but the other four permanent members (the United Kingdom, France, Russia, and China) did not want to see the ban lifted. Once again, the United Kingdom and France knew their troops on the ground would be placed at risk. They were already taking casualties and didn't want to see the war widen. The Russians were not happy with the prospect of a wider war, orchestrated by NATO in an area once under their control and arching up toward Hungary, which was aspiring to NATO membership. The Chinese, for their part, were against all foreign interference, which included NATO intervention in the Balkans. (There were also questions raised during this debate on how Bosnia could even have been admitted to the United Nations and how it could invoke claims to sovereignty when it had no control over more than half of its territory at the time it was admitted. There were no territorial maps submitted to the United Nations with Bosnia's application for membership. But that was another issue.)

There were also practical concerns involved in supplying arms to Bosnian government forces. Weapons would have to be offloaded at Croatian ports and transit through Croatia and the Bosnian Croat portion of Bosnia. (There were too many to be transported by air.) Croatian and Bosnian Croat forces would probably skim off up to 35 percent of those weapons, so whatever budget was being allowed for supplying weapons to the Bosnian army would have to be doubled. (Good for the arms manufacturers, but bad for the taxpayers of the world.) Croatia would be fearful that the Bosnian government army might use those weapons against the Bosnian Croats to recapture areas from which they had been cleansed by the Croats. Significantly, both Croatian and Bosnian Croat leadership (which were virtually one and the same) were strongly against the lifting of the arms embargo, just as they had opposed the arrival and deployment of the RRF.

Secondly, weapons *were* coming into Bosnia. They were being smuggled in, not in the quantities the Bosnian government wanted, but the embargo was being violated by many of the same countries that had voted for it, including the United States. The flagrant violation of the arms embargo by the United States with regard to Croatia was later to come out in the newspapers, but the United States also encouraged violations of the arms embargo in Bosnia, if only to minimize the influence of Iran, which was the Bosnian government's main supplier.

As Udovicki and Stitkovac say in an essay on this topic:

> In part, the import of weapons for the Croatian side was conducted as an offshoot of the smuggling route that Iran, assisted by Turkey, opened in 1992, to supply the Bosnian government. Of the total amount of weapons designated for Bosnia, Croatia kept about one-third. The supply route involved Saudi Arabia, Pakistan, Brunei, and Malaysia, as well as Hungary and Argentina. (*Op. cit.*, 190)

Most important, the Serbs would have tried to interdict any arms shipments. To bring heavy weapons into Bosnia would have meant the need to secure and defend roads on which to transport them (there was very little freedom of movement at the time), to provide and secure storage sites, and to construct and protect ammunition dumps. Government soldiers would also have had to be trained because many weapons systems today are highly technical. As in all operations, trainers would first have had to be trained so that they could teach others how to use weapons. And there was the problem with language. A minimum of English is required to operate such weapons. Moreover, existing weapons systems had to be replaced almost in their entirety because the weapons being used by the government forces were made in the former Soviet Union or in former Yugoslavia. One can't simply substitute U.S.-made shells for Russian shells. U.S. shells fit U.S.-made tanks. And so on. All these operations take time. When I returned to Bosnia in May

1997, about eighteen months after the ban on weapons had been lifted, the Bosnian army was still learning to use the new weapons systems.

Even much of the Pentagon opposed lifting the arms embargo, because it meant a wider war and danger to U.S. pilots and naval personnel that might be involved in the operation. It was politicians such as Senate majority leader Bob Dole and vice president Al Gore, not Pentagon brass, who favored lifting the embargo.

Finally, as noted, the Bosnian Serbs would not have liked it if the weapons ban had been lifted, and they would have translated their dissatisfaction quite quickly and quite ruthlessly into action. Every UNPROFOR soldier and civilian, as well as everyone who worked for the various international agencies, would have become a potential target, hostage, victim. In other words, four out of five permanent members of the Security Council did not want to see the arms embargo lifted, and two of the three signers of the Dayton Agreement (Croatia and rump Yugoslavia) did not want to see the arms embargo lifted. Those were realities, based on practicalities, but long after the war ended some elements in Washington still persisted in their view that the arms embargo against all of former Yugoslavia should have been lifted earlier.

Voting in Bosnia became an industry after the Dayton Agreement. During the first year, elections for six levels in that fractured country took place on the same day. On 14 September 1997, a seventh group of officials was elected, municipal officials. On 22–23 November that same year, yet another election took place, for representatives to the Republika Srpska Assembly, and in spring 1998 another Republika Srpska presidential election was held. Elections for the Assembly and for the presidency had already taken place, but internal developments within Republika Srpska necessitated that a second election for those posts be held. Oh yes, in autumn 1998, another round of elections took place for the same six levels as in 1996, as well as for the municipal level, the latter of which should have taken place in 1996, but only took place in 1997.

Now, if such doings sound confusing, that is because they are. Moreover, imagine a farmer (70 percent of Bosnia is rural), who for the past fifty years simply voted for the only party (Communist) on the ballot, trying to decipher this newly imposed conundrum of democracy. Yet, skeptical though I was, I myself eventually became a believer, as much in the *process* as in the results. I emphasize *process* because at times the process itself was as important as the results. The process was dazzling, especially for the voters, even more dazzling than confusing.

On 14 September 1997, it was raining. Yet the voters lined up quietly in the rain to wait their turn to vote. Many of them had come long distances. Many of them had never voted. But they came, they saw, and they conquered. It was quite a moving experience. It was incredible, for instance, how many people could not believe that their ballot would be secret.

Of course, the so-called democratization process carried with it the important benefit of legitimization in the eyes of the world community. In plain terms, a democratically elected government could borrow money from the World Bank, could attract private and bilateral investment, and could take a seat in the world's international organizations. Democracy has its merits. It promotes stability, and stability attracts investors.

Although every historical experience is unique (history *never* repeats itself exactly), there were, nonetheless, important lessons to be learned from the elections experience in Bosnia, lessons that might be applied in other so-called emerging democracies—that is, countries that do not have a democratic tradition. The most important lesson was that voting itself would not resolve deep conflicts. Deep conflicts must be resolved *before* an election so that an election can then confirm what has already been agreed to. This is not a matter of "fixing" the election. It is a way of assuring that the results of the election will be respected by the loser because if agreement on controversial issues has not been reached prior to voting, then the loser will not accept the results of the elections. We have already seen this pattern in Angola, Algeria, Sierra Leone, and Georgia, among other countries. It is one of the reasons that elections in Western Sahara were postponed for so long: there was no agreement between the conflicting parties on essential issues. The decision to hold elections sets a time frame for resolving conflict, and in that sense it is useful, but it will not resolve the conflict. Diplomacy and sometimes more forceful methods are needed before an effective election can take place.

Within the Republika Srpska entity, for example, two of the most serious conflicts involved control of the police and the press. Once that entity was recognized by the Dayton Agreement, Bosnian Serb leaders in Pale attempted to subdue all internal opposition, in good totalitarian tradition. The Serbian Democratic Party (SDS) was the majority party in Republika Srpska after the war. It was interested neither in democracy nor in change, and, in fact, it was not even interested in Communism. It was interested in power and all the privileges that accrued to it.

SDS luminaries included such figures as Radovan Karadzic, Momcilo Krajisnik, Foreign Minister Alex Buha, Interior Minister Dragan Kijac, Parliamentary Speaker Dragan Kalinic, and Prime Minister Gojko Klickovic. Krajisnik was one of the three rotating members of the presidency of Bosnia and Herzegovina, and one of the most powerful figures in Republika Srpska.

These were the men who had led the republic into war, had led it during the war, and were clinging to power after the war. They treated every voice of dissent as a threat to the survival of the republic.

A strong dissenter to this dark conspiracy of power emerged, however, and appropriately enough in this male-dominated society, that person was a woman: Biljana Plavsic, once a vice president of SDS, a good and loyal Serb nationalist, a cohort of Karadzic during the war, and the newly elected president (in September 1996) of the entity of Republika Srpska. She blew the whistle on corruption. (On most other issues, particularly ethnic nationalism, her views were consistent with those of the Pale leadership.)

In most countries that worked through the process of burying Communism and building democratic societies to replace them, the transition phase was a painful one. Many former Communist leaders simply changed uniforms, became nationalists, and fought to retain power. Moreover, because it was these leaders who had hoarded the country's resources during the Communist period, they were the ones able to purchase the ownership of privatized industries. Often, former secret police officers became private security guards in the service of new entrepreneurs (they ended up working for many of the same people), and demobilized soldiers became police officers, still in the service of the state. In this atmosphere, organized crime flourished. Enterprises and individuals who had been living on government subsidies were suddenly cut loose. There was widespread resentment and disaffection, fueled by unrealistic expectations. As consumer goods became scarce, smuggling increased. Services once provided by the state became unaffordable to private citizens and had to be obtained through the underworld. The underworld was either tolerated or controlled by government officials (often democratically elected). Throughout Eastern Europe, the former Soviet Union, and most of former Yugoslavia, new leaders were frequently little more than gangsters wearing jackets and ties.

The West, meanwhile, which did not want to establish protectorates over former Communist countries, searched for dissenting voices within those countries to challenge government gangsters. It was far more sensible to support indigenous democratic leadership than to become trustees of bankrupt economies. Biljana Plavsic, with strong Western backing, became an honorable dissenter.

There were those cynics (myself not among them) who believed that Plavsic objected to government corruption only because she was not getting her fair cut. If that were true, however, then one had to ask *why* she was not getting her fair cut, and the answer had to have something to do with the fact that she was a woman and that she was expected to be a figurehead and leave the spoils to the men. In any case, Plavsic, a professor of biology now in her sixties, had always opposed corruption, even while she had served as a delegate to the Serb parliament in Pale during the war. Once the war ended, she decided that she had had enough of it. The Karadzic-Krajisnik leadership in Pale was skimming off millions of German Marks every month in smuggling, extortion, and diversion of tax revenues, while the people of Republika Srpska, particularly the refugees and displaced persons in Banja Luka, were getting nothing. Enough was enough. The best way for Republika Srpska to survive, she realized, would be for it to accept the Dayton Agreement and establish respect for the rule of law. She moved the seat of the presidency to Banja Luka, and one fine day in June 1997 announced she was removing Interior Minister Kijac from his post for his involvement in smuggling and for refusing to make reforms in the police, reforms that had been mandated by the Dayton Agreement. However, Kijac—who had been appointed by an Assembly that was controlled by the ruling SDS party (still led by Karadzic, despite a signed statement that he would step down)— refused to be removed. A few weeks later, President Plavsic dismissed the Assembly and called for new elections, believing that the Assembly would never enact the necessary reforms unless the SDS lost its majority (forty-six seats out of eighty-three), but the Assembly refused to be dismissed and continued to meet. (The Assembly met in Pale, whereas Plavsic remained in Banja Luka.) There was a full-blown constitutional crisis.

OSCE then became openly involved in the internal politics of Republika Srpska, an involvement for which it had, arguably, no mandate under the Dayton Agreement. (The Dayton Agreement had been sculpted to deal with interentity politics, not with the politics within one of the entities.) OSCE and the rest of the international community threw its full weight behind Plavsic.

That brought up the issues of the press and the police, as well as the need to resolve those issues *before* the parliamentary elections called for by Plavsic. There was a stand-off between Plavsic and Pale for several weeks while the Constitutional Court decided whether Plavsic had the right to dissolve parliament. The arguments were elaborate and self-serving. Plavsic argued that a president had the right to dissolve parliament and call for new elections. Her legal advisor cited appropriate passages from the Constitution. SDS in Pale argued that parliamentary elections in Republika Srpska had already been held, in accordance with the Dayton Agreement, and there was no need to hold them again. It also argued that Plavsic's dismissal of Interior Minister Kijac was unconstitutional because that power devolved to the prime minister alone. (The prime minister, Gojko Klickovic, was an SDS stalwart and was not about to dismiss his fellow traveler, Dragan Kijac.) The Constitutional Court, which sat in Pale and was controlled by Karadzic-Krajisnik forces there, delayed its decision. Finally, the court handed down a decision that owed more to intimidation and politics than to justice (one of the judges who threatened to vote against Pale was severely beaten). The court said Plavsic had no authority to dismiss the Assembly. That decision was promptly overturned by the Office of the High Representative, which had supreme authority in Bosnia under the Dayton Agreement. Elections, to be supervised by OSCE, were set for 23 November, and the battle for power moved to the elections arena.

By the summer of 1997, there were thirty-two thousand police in Republika Srpska (about twice the number of soldiers in the army). Once the split between Plavsic and Pale occurred, one of the key questions became, To whom would the police declare their allegiance? To Pale or Plavsic? To the ruling party, SDS, or to the president of the republic? As the split deepened, it became evident that this problem would have to be resolved *before* Assembly elections, not *through* the elections, because without the cooperation of the police, the political campaign would be severely hampered. There would be no guarantees on freedom of movement or on the safety of public rallies and demonstrations, and there would be intimidation of opposition political parties and leaders, even voters. If the international community were determined to proceed with elections, then the elections would take place, but without the full cooperation of the local police the whole process would lose credibility, take on the appearance of an imposed settlement, and not receive the endorsement of the loser. During the summer of 1997, there were two interior ministers—one appointed by Plavsic to replace Kijac and Kijac himself, who refused to resign. Moreover, the dismissed Assembly continued to meet in Pale and continued to adopt legislation.

The second issue was that of the press. Pale controlled the main radio and TV transmitters throughout all of Republika Srpska, and consistently broadcast the worst filth, slander, and distortion imaginable—against the international community, against Plavsic, and against anyone deemed to be challenging the hegemony of the ruling party. The media needed to be freed up so that more than one opinion could be heard and so that there could be an open political campaign.

In both cases, remedial action was taken by the international community, with the assistance of NATO peacekeeping troops. Special police forces were disarmed, radio and TV transmitters were seized, and freedom of movement was enhanced. The details are too extensive to mention here, and besides, that is not the purpose of this discussion. The purpose is to emphasize that issues of deep conflict in countries with no democratic tradition must be resolved prior to election day so that the final vote will confirm agreements that have already been made. Otherwise, campaigns will be disrupted, rhetoric will inflame passions, and the losers will not accept the results of the election.

Unwisely, one of the main priorities for Washington and the West, ever since the end of the war, has been the issue of indicted war criminals. Placed in a global context, however, the urgency of this issue seems blown out of all proportion. In a world where Yasir Arafat can win the Nobel Peace Prize, where seventy-five years or more of racist brutality in South Africa can be assuaged by a Truth and Reconciliation Commission, where the three signatories of the Dayton Agreement (Milosevic, Tudjman, and Izetbegovic) can be granted virtual immunity from prosecution, and where major international actors speak about the need to forgive and forget, one has to wonder why the arrests of Radovan Karadzic and Ratko Mladic are considered to be the sine qua non for peace in Bosnia.

I am not referring to the need for justice; I am referring to priorities. Take Radovan Karadzic. Perhaps he *is* a war criminal, thoroughly reprehensible, a sociopathic exploiter who led his own people into a senseless war that will stigmatize all Serbs for generations to come. Let him eventually be arrested, tried in a fair court, and given just punishment if convicted. To pretend, however, that the democratic process in Republika Srpska cannot go forward without his arrest is illogical and simplistic, and it gives rise to the most preposterous fantasies, including one that appeared in 1997 in a European newspaper asserting that he had been planning to build an atomic bomb and must be removed before Republika Srpska became a nuclear power! No, the arrest of Karadzic is not the most important issue in bringing a durable peace to Bosnia. On the contrary, his immediate arrest might be destabilizing (and bloody, because he is heavily guarded), his trial would be even more disruptive, and his conviction would be a contributing factor to a war of revenge, a rallying point for revanchists. It would make him a martyr.

Ironically, when I was last in Bosnia, what Karadzic feared most was not prosecution at The Hague. Thespian that he is, he might even welcome the opportunity to present to the world the case for the Serbs. What he feared most was assassination by Milosevic's forces. He feared that if arrested, he would never be allowed to come to trial. He knew (pardon the image) where the bodies were buried. He could, and most probably would, implicate Milosevic in the slaughters in Bosnia. Moreover, if Karadzic were arrested, then the pressure would increase to arrest high-ranking indictees in the Federation, an act that neither Tudjman nor Izetbegovic wanted. (When, in October 1997, ten indicted Bosnian Croats voluntarily surrendered to The Hague, the rumor was that Tudjman had agreed to release them in exchange for a guarantee that neither he nor anyone close to him would be indicted.)

Finally, the pressure exerted by the world community to prosecute indicted Bosnian Serb leaders had an effect on the Serbs directly opposite to that which was intended. The theory behind prosecuting war criminals is that it will exonerate an entire people by punishing only those few who were responsible for mass crimes, but the pressure of the War Crimes Tribunal to seize Bosnian Serbs made every Serb feel threatened. Virtually every Bosnian Serb family had relatives who had been in the war. All eligible men between sixteen and sixty had been soldiers at one point during the war. When the War Crimes Tribunal in The Hague began the practice of issuing *sealed indictments*, it recalled the worst traditions of totalitarianism. Insecurity was increased and credibility decreased. The use of secret lists, secret forces, and secret agendas, which was construed by Washington as a sign of determination, was actually a sign of desperation. Credibility—which is necessary if there is to be any cooperation between local people, including officials, and the international community—depends on transparency. The War Crimes Tribunal, however, believed that public lists would allow indicted war criminals to go into hiding, so it began compiling secret lists, or *sealed indictments*. To local Serbs, even those who disliked their leadership, it was little more than a form of terrorism. Instead of exonerating the innocent, it intimidated them. As one political leader in Banja Luka said to me, "We have military officers at high levels in our party. Are they war criminals? How do we know? Who is safe? We had enough of these secret lists during the Communist era."

Finally, I was sure that, given the proper amount of time, the Bosnian Serbs would deal with their own criminals. There were precedents in that part of the world for taking care of deposed dictators.

On the issue of the return of refugees, I again had my doubts about the emphasis being placed on it. To begin with, the pressures to accomplish this extremely difficult task were disingenuous. Foreign governments were not primarily interested in the comfort of the hundreds of thousands of Bosnian refugees and displaced persons, nor were the leaders of the nationalist parties inside Bosnia. The Europeans, in particular, simply didn't want any more refugees; they didn't even want the ones they had. That was understandable. Refugees are very expensive to maintain, and in economies with high unemployment, there is little chance to put them to work. They are a drain. Better to return them from whence they came.

Impure motives on the part of host countries, however, did not erase the basic human need of displaced persons and refugees to return to their homes if they wished to. The distinction to be made here involves two points: the first is again the question of priority, and the second is the question of preconditions.

Many refugees and displaced persons want to return home, *but that does not mean they want to live together with other ethnic groups or live under the governance of other ethnic leaders.* Most people who want to return home want to return en masse, with the proper security (which means their own police or at least an integrated police force), and they want the freedom to practice their own culture (their own churches, schools, currency). As many historians will affirm, except in the major cities, the three major ethnic groups in Bosnia (or in other regions of former Yugoslavia) did *not* always live together. They frequently lived peacefully and often contiguously, but not necessarily together. Throughout Bosnia, there were Serb villages, Croat villages, and Moslem villages. In many villages, and even in cities, there were Serb, Croat, or Moslem neighborhoods. Yes, there were intermarriages, but there was also a great deal of separation, including in cemeteries. Except for the elderly, few people wanted to return alone to a village where they would be a minority of one or two families. They wanted to return in large groups, which would help their security, and they wanted a high degree of cultural autonomy.

Time and again, as international agencies tried to resettle families, the houses of returnees would be blown up shortly before they were scheduled to return. The majority of Serbs and Croats did not want to integrate, either with the Moslems or with anyone else. The reason they gave was not simply cultural; it was also demographic. As the Serb mayor of Prnjavor once said to me, "The Turks [i.e., the Moslems] have one child for themselves, and another nine for Allah. If we allow a minority to come in, within twenty-five years they will be a majority. And then what happens to Serb culture? No, there have to be separate states."

Moslem leaders, on the other hand, officially favored a multiethnic state. For one thing, this position was politically correct, which translated into financial and military backing from the international community. Equally as important, though, it was an insurance policy for the future. An isolated, exclusively Moslem state within Europe was much more vulnerable to attack than a multiethnic state. One recalls the cynical joke about how to deal with a racial minority: move them all into one area, and then blow up that area. The Moslems of Bosnia did not want that to happen to them.

Meanwhile, there *were* examples of successful repatriation. In many cases, villagers actually preferred to have their expelled neighbors return rather than have strangers resettled. Some Serbs in Banja Luka would much have preferred to have their former Croatian and Moslem neighbors living there rather than displaced Serbs from faraway Sarajevo or from the mountains around Knin in Croatia. But repatriation is a long and slow process, and my own belief is that more attention should be given to resettling people in the locations to which they fled, instead of promising them they will one day return to their prewar residences. Why not build a home for a displaced Serb family in Banja Luka instead of promising them they will one day return to Sarajevo? Why not encourage legal exchanges of property? Why not have a

Serb now living in a Moslem's former home in Prijedor legally exchange his former home with a Moslem now living in a former Serb home in Tuzla? But such ideas were politically incorrect. Of course, there should be a continuing effort at repatriation and return, but more emphasis should also be given to practical alternatives.

The third priority of the international community during 1997 was the need to defeat SDS, the Bosnian Serb majority political party. The way to do this, went the conventional wisdom, was to build a multiparty democracy and thereby break the hegemony of the ruling party. The first problem with this approach was that it flew in the face of tradition in that part of the world. Political change in Eastern Europe for decades had almost always came from within the ruling party, not from opposition parties. Mikhail Gorbachev was the secretary-general of the Communist Party of the Soviet Union; he was not the leader of an opposition party. Building a multiparty democracy takes time. More specifically, it requires within a society a level of economic development that allows for the representation of separate economic interests. Political parties represent economic interests. In Republika Srpska there was as much as 80 percent unemployment. *There were no diverse economic interests; there was no economy.* To place political development ahead of economic reality, to desynchronize the two, is a recipe for instability, not for "multiparty democracy."

Another problem with the rush to undermine SDS was that the more the international community pressurized the Bosnian Serbs to desert SDS, the more recalcitrant the Bosnian Serb people would become and the more they would rally to support those who, they believed, had fought to found Republika Srpska and were still being persecuted by the world community (led by the United States and Germany). Even the Serbs themselves will admit to being stubborn, and the more they are pushed, the more they will resist. Even the charges of massive corruption against Karadzic and Krajisnik (which I believed to be true) were potentially less serious than the charges of betrayal against Plavsic. The Serbs have lived for centuries with corruption. They don't like it, but they accept it as the normal way of running a government. They do not, however, take kindly to betrayal. In a contest between a dirty nationalist and a clean foreign puppet, they will vote for the dirty nationalist every time, especially right after a civil war. Rather than try to achieve total victory over SDS, the international community should have tried more to promote reform within SDS. To say that Pale was not willing to compromise is only to admit that international diplomacy was unimaginative. When diplomacy fails, it is always convenient to blame the other side for being "hardliners," but in this particular case, there were many hardliners in the international community. On occasions when they became more flexible, they were able to achieve concessions and even successes—and with less resentment.

At 1:45 A.M. on Monday, 14 July 1997, my apartment in Banja Luka was bombed. I was asleep there at the time. I had no doubt the bomb was intended for me and that it was intended to be nonlethal.

A plastic explosive had been placed just under my ground-floor bedroom window. The blast shattered two large windows, spraying glass over the room and into the corridor beyond. Fortunately, I had had the plastic shutters down and was sleeping under a blanket, so the impact of the bomb was muted, and I was protected from flying glass. I received no injuries. My head was about one meter from the window, off to the left and facing it, partially protected by a headboard. There were shards of glass on top of my blanket.

I had been sleeping deeply. The sound of the bomb awoke me (it was a small plastic device, not a grenade). At first I thought a car had crashed into the building. I was aware of the sound of shattering glass. Even in the dark I could see the outline of broken glass in the window frames, and the sparkle of glass shards on the floor.

I got out of bed slowly and in my bare feet edged toward the light switch at the rear of the bedroom, aware that the floor was covered with broken glass. I flipped the light on and off very quickly, just long enough to see what had happened. I checked the front door; it was still double locked. There were bars on the windows. Nobody else was in the apartment.

Next, I put on my sneakers, which were in the outside corridor behind a wall and had been shielded from the explosion. Able to walk about, I went back to the bedroom to find my blue jeans, shook them in case they had collected any glass, came back into the hall corridor, took off my sneakers, put on my jeans, then put my sneakers back on again. All in the dark. I wanted to be prepared to flee.

I heard a siren, but ignored it. I telephoned the OSCE duty officer, told him what happened, and asked him to call the local police. Then I decided (how ridiculous these details seem now) that I needed underwear, so I returned to the bedroom and took some clean underwear out of a closed suitcase that had been lying on the floor. Back in the hall corridor, I undressed and dressed again. It was too hot to put on a shirt. I tied my sneakers, took a deep breath, and called the OSCE duty officer again. I needed to get from him the home telephone number of the Regional Center director, my colleague Roger Bryant. I told him what had happened and that I needed an interpreter to be able to speak with the police. It was not worth waking up a local interpreter in the middle of the night, so I suggested that he call our human rights officer, Victor Ullom, who had his own car and could speak the local language.

About fifteen minutes after the explosion, the local police *milicija* arrived. I don't know if they arrived on their own or in response to our duty officer's call. Roger and Vic arrived soon after, as did my landlord, who lived two floors above. He spoke very little English, but expressed his sympathies and asked if I had any idea why this had happened. I replied: "NATO, Prijedor, American, political."

Four days earlier, on 10 July, a U.K. detachment of NATO special forces in Prijedor had moved against two Bosnian Serb indicted war criminals: Simo Drljaca, a former police chief, and Dr. Mico Kovacevic, the head of a local hospital. Two separate operations had been carried out during the morning hours. Drljaca had been out fishing with his son and another individual, while Kovacevic had been at work in his office. The soldiers had been able to arrest Kovacevic and spirit him off quickly to The Hague, but Drljaca had resisted and fired at the soldiers, who had returned fire and killed him. Neither Serb had been on published lists of alleged war criminals; they had been cited on sealed indictments.

The immediate reaction of all Serbs had been one of outrage, without regard to the personalities involved. Drljaca was commonly thought of as being a gangster. He had been a gangster during the war, and he had been a gangster since the war ended. He drove large German cars, lived in a big house, and always had plenty of cash. He was alleged to be in charge of a large smuggling operation. The local people hated and feared him. His death, however, became a political issue. As one of our local drivers said to me, "He was a pig, but he was a Serb pig." Kovacevic, in addition to having been the chief physician during the war at the infamous Omarska prison camp, near to Prijedor, had also been allegedly profiteering from medicines and drugs he sold on the black market; he had done that during the war, and he had been doing it since the war ended.

Usually, whenever international agents used force against the Serbs, the Americans were blamed. Even though the soldiers in this case had been British, the Americans were still deemed responsible. Thus, my first thoughts that night were that the bombing had been directed against me as an American, not as Phillip Corwin, and that I had been an easy target because I foolishly had been living on the ground floor in an unprotected apartment house. The bombing was a form of political retaliation against NATO, and I was a convenient symbol.

The local police arrived, asked a few questions, and said they would return again at 8:00 A.M. with a proper investigating team. Windows in the stairwell had also been shattered.

We walked outside in the light rain and saw that a piece of concrete sidewalk had been blown away directly under my window. The perpetrator (or more than likely, his driver) had probably parked in the street outside, walked along the concrete path that went under my window, detonated the explosive, and then run back to his car and fled. All within seconds.

At about 3:00 A.M. a member of the United Nations civilian police called me, asking if he could come over and look at the situation. He was Ukrainian. I asked if he could return at 8:00 A.M. because I was tired and wanted some sleep. The local police placed a guard outside my door for the rest of the night.

At 7:30 A.M., Stabilization Force military police arrived. The Serb police returned about 8:30 A.M., this time with an investigating team. They all remained until about 9:30 A.M. They asked questions and took photos. It was raining heavily.

I decided to stay in my apartment a few days before looking to move in order to have time to consider my options, but two days after the bombing, my landlord's wife came, apologetically, to tell me her neighbors had complained about my presence in the building. I told her that I understood, that I did not want to jeopardize the safety of families in the apartment complex, and that I would move as soon as possible. I did and stayed another three and one-half months in Banja Luka, until my contract expired. Then I came back to New York to complete this book.

At first, as noted, I thought the attack against me had been impersonal, simply because I was an American, and that the Serbs wanted to show that they could and would retaliate against the international community for any attempt to arrest their leaders. I even thought that the bombing might have been done by neighborhood punks—referred to as "rogue elements" in official jargon—that it might have been a "thrill" bombing, not even a politically motivated act. Everyone knew where I lived. I was an easy target. Eventually, however, I changed my mind. I came to believe the bomb had been directed against me personally and that the local police either had done it themselves or knew very well who had.

What changed my mind was that about a month later, I was having a discussion with Ostoja Knezevic, who was then still a vice president in the Banja Luka chapter of SDS, the ruling party. (Not too long afterward, Knesevic became a first vice president in Biljana Plavsic's new SNS political party, which she formed when SDS in Pale expelled her from the party.) I met regularly with Knezevic. We had a cordial relationship. Though he was an important official in SDS, he was flexible and was willing to consider reforms to the party's antagonistic attitudes toward the international community and the Dayton Agreement.

During one of our meetings in August, he told me that he hadn't known the last time we spoke that I had been the target of the bombing, although he had known about the bombing. He expressed his condolences and volunteered that he had argued vehemently against the bombing (post facto, of course) during a recent discussion. He did not volunteer with whom he had had the discussion, but he emphasized that the debate had been very heated. He raised the issue two or three times that morning, each time apologizing for the incident and reassuring me of his sympathies and how he had taken my side during the debate. I thanked him for his support and assured him I would continue to maintain good relations with SDS and all other political parties. The incident was behind us. Besides, next time it would be someone else's turn, I said.

I believed that Knezevic had been having a dispute with the Pale-oriented faction of SDS, which were Karadzic supporters, as opposed to the Banja Luka faction, which Knezevic represented and were Plavsic supporters. Following the NATO action against Drljaca and Kovacevic, the SDS main board in Pale had decided to undertake what a party newspaper in Pale had called "nonlethal acts" of reprisal against the international community. The bombing of my apartment had been one of those acts. Knezevic had not been consulted about specific targets; he may not have even agreed with the overall policy. Terrorist actions were probably under the control of some subcommittee that took its orders directly from Pale. What Knezevic was angry about, I guessed, was not the bombing itself, but that it was I who was bombed. A distinction had to be made between the act itself and the person targeted. Perhaps he would not have protested so vehemently if it had been someone else.

It was not, however, simply diplomatic protocol that had made him take my side. Basically, he agreed with specific ideas I had broached during our discussions, ideas that he had subsequently proposed to other party members. Those ideas had antagonized Pale, and the retaliation against me had been a warning to him as well. Dissent was not allowed.

There was no question in my mind that all the offices of SDS were bugged. Knezevic knew it, I knew it, everybody knew it. Precisely because I knew it, I ignored it and spoke my mind. I didn't believe OSCE was a secret organization, and I had no secrets to keep. Quite possibly, SDS recorded what I had said and was antagonized by it; more likely, they mistrusted what they felt was my influence, through Knezevic, and decided to take action against me.

For weeks during my discussions with Knezevic, I had been urging him to make compromises with the SDS leadership in Pale, to propose certain reforms that would simultaneously comply with the Dayton Agreement and help his own people; they might even strengthen his party. I suggested, among other things, that SDS should remove several high officials, including Interior Minister Kijac, that it should kick them upstairs to titled but powerless posts, and then undertake essential reforms. I said the party should oust those I called the "Three Ks": Prime Minister Gojko Klickovic, Speaker of the Parliament Dragan Kalinic, and Interior Minister Kijac. Replace them and go on with business. But apparently that suggestion and others were repugnant to Pale leaders. I was considered a provocateur, a meddler, an agent of U.S. policy, a spy. Blah, blah, blah. Actually, I was none of the foregoing. What I had been trying to do, in fact, was what many of the internationals who worked among the Bosnian Serb people were constantly trying to do: save the Serbs from their own leaders.

Finally, there is one more point to note. It concerns anxiety. There are realistic anxieties, and there are unrealistic anxieties. The Serbs, the Balkans, Eastern Europe—they are all fertile ground for anxieties, suspicions, and conspiratorial thinking. An effective political analyst must try, however, to distinguish between realistic anxieties based on facts and unrealistic anxieties *not* based on facts. Unfortunately, during a civil war, the two sometimes overlap, even merge.

At the beginning of the war, the Bosnian Serbs feared that, as a minority, they would be subordinated to Moslem culture if they lived in a multiethnic state. In fact, that anxiety was one of the reasons they decided to secede from Bosnia. After the war ended, they feared that the Bosnian government, supported by NATO, eventually would try to achieve a military victory over them and negate what they had fought for. Neither of these anxieties (which were actually one and the same, fear of subjugation by the Moslems) was completely unrealistic.

Here is an excerpt, for example, from an article by Mike O'Connor, dateline Sarajevo, published in the *New York Times* on 1 January 1997 (a day, coincidentally, on which circulation is traditionally lower than on other days):

> On Sarajevo's main street, named Marshal Tito after the Communist leader, a photograph of Ayatollah Ruhollah Khomeini peers from the wall of the Iranian Cultural Center at the bright Christmas decorations in the *Benetton* clothing store across the way. . . .
>
> From what is visible, it would be hard to find evidence to support the feeling among many Sarajevans that they are being subtly but very clearly told by the governing Muslim political party that public Christmas celebrations represent an influence of Western culture that is no longer acceptable. . . .
>
> Many are not only concerned about losing a community holiday celebration, but they also think that the authorities are creating divisions between Muslims and others and they feel a heavy lid coming down on them from a Government that wants to tell even Muslims what to hold valuable.

"We supported these leaders in the war because they protected us against an aggressor," said Alma Hodzic, 29, a waitress. "But now, they want to impose their personal views on the whole country." . . .

Those who are suspicious point out that there is a reason to believe that a campaign against Grandfather Frost is being directed at the highest levels. Last January, President Alija Izetbegovic, a Muslim, wrote an open letter calling Grandfather Frost a symbol that was foreign to his people. Mr. Izetbegovic said he would see to it that people rejected the false culture that he said Grandfather Frost represented.

Two months later, on 11 March, Chris Hedges of the *New York Times* wrote:

> NATO strategists say that the Bosnian Government increasingly sees the Serb zone as an easy military objective. These commanders say that if the peacekeeping forces withdraw it will be difficult to hold the Muslim-led Government back.
>
> "At least this war would probably be swift," said a senior Western diplomat. "And frankly there would be little sympathy for the Bosnian Serbs, given their role in the war, their refusal to cooperate with the joint Government institutions and their refusal to let displaced people go home. War, in fact, might be the best solution."

Now that the war is over, the danger of the international community's continued Serb bashing is that it will promote instability in Republika Srpska. If there is instability in Republika Srpska, there will be instability in Bosnia, in all of former Yugoslavia, and potentially throughout central Europe. There will be refugee flows. There will be repercussions in European and even in North American electoral campaigns. There will be chaos. The two *New York Times* articles quoted above are not meant to prove anything except that the Bosnian Serbs have legitimate reason to fear a Bosnian government military takeover, supported (more than simply tolerated) by NATO. The goal of international policy, therefore, must be to promote a solution that is consistent with both the Dayton Agreement and at the same time with the cultural and political needs of each of the parties to the conflict. Unless that is done, the specter of another war in the Balkans will remain distressingly real.

Driving toward Sarajevo across Mount Igman at Night, 1995

Even with nightlights whitening the dark
and funneling the blackness into cones
that we could tunnel through, the road itself
was still unsafe; rutted and narrow
with sharp switchbacks and pointed rocks,
it crumbled like a biscuit at the curves.
No hearse could ever make a U-turn there.
Bikers walked their wobbly rims with caution.
We crawled and lurched, mechanized pilgrims
on a trail for goats and wooden wheels,
like armadillos in formation, past
carcasses of APCs, vehicles
gone off the edge and caught in trees,
rusting shells of ruined caravans;
were pushed aside by buses fat with troops,
by tubercular trucks and stoned police,
by convoys dodging rockslides.
The air above buzzed with death
while stray dogs snapped at our tires.
We steamed, sealed in armor in summer,
polyglot and wordless as the wind;
and as night retreated into dawn
we prayed to our weapons systems
for protection and deliverance,
knowing we were going nowhere
we had ever been or dreamt of being.
—Phillip Corwin, *Binoculars* (Catnip Press, 1997)

Selected Bibliography

Andric, Ivo. *The Damned Yard and Other Stories.* Edited by Celia Hawkesworth. London: Forest Books, 1992.

Boyd, Charles G. "Making Peace with the Guilty," *Foreign Affairs,* September–October 1995.

—— "Making Bosnia Work," *Foreign Affairs,* January–February 1998.

Donia, Robert J. and John V. A. Fine, Jr. *Bosnia and Hercegovina: A Tradition Betrayed.* New York: Columbia University Press, 1994.

Glenny, Misha. *The Fall of Yugoslavia: The Third Balkan War.* Third rev. ed. New York: Penguin Books, 1996.

Handke, Peter. *A Journey To The Rivers: Justice For Serbia.* English translation by Scott Abbott. New York: Viking Penguin, 1997.

Holbrooke, Richard. *To End A War.* New York: Random House, 1998.

Honig, Jan Willem, and Norbert Both. *Srebrenica: Record of a War Crime.* New York: Penguin, 1997.

Kaplan, Robert. *Balkan Ghosts: A Journey through History.* New York: Vintage Books, 1993.

Kumer, Radha. *Divide and Fall? Bosnia in the Annals of Partition.* London: Verso, 1997.

Maas, Peter. *Love Thy Neighbor: A Story of War.* New York: Vintage Books, 1997.

Owen, David. *Balkan Odyssey.* New York: Harcourt Brace & Co., 1995.

Pavic, Milorad. *Dictionary of the Khazars.* English translation by Christina Pribicevic-Zoric. New York: Alfred A. Knopf, 1989.

Phillips, John. *Yugoslav Story.* Belgrade: Jugoslovenska Revija, 1980.

Ramet, Sabrina Petra. *Balkan Babel: The Disintegration of Yugoslavia from the Death of Tito to Ethnic War.* Boulder: Westview Press, 1996.

Rose, Gideon. "The Exit Strategy Delusion," *Foreign Affairs,* January–February 1998.

Selimovic, Mesa. *Death And The Dervish.* English translation by Bogdan Rakic and Stephen M. Dickey. Evanston: Northwestern University Press, 1996.

Silber, Laura, and Allan Little. *Yugoslavia: Death of a Nation.* Rev. ed. New York: Penguin Books, 1997.

Singleton, Fred. *A Short History of the Yugoslav Peoples.* Cambridge: Cambridge University Press, 1989.

Udovicki, Jasminka, and James Ridgeway, editors. *Burn This House: The Making and Unmaking of Yugoslavia.* Durham and London: Duke University Press, 1997.

West, Rebecca. *Black Lamb and Grey Falcon.* New York: Penguin Books, 1982.

Woodward, Susan L. "Avoiding Another Cyprus or Israel," *The Brookings Review,* Winter 1998.

—— *Balkan Tragedy.* Washington, D.C.: Brookings Institution, 1995.

Zimmermann, Warren. *Origins of a Catastrophe: Yugoslavia and Its Destroyers.* New York: Times Books, 1996.

commander, (*see* Mladic, Ratko); atrocities committed by, 65, 99, 153, 178, 188–89, 211, 215; Bosnian government attacks on, 69, 113, 122, 126, 138–39, 141, 142, 154–56, 177–78, 186, 194, 213; civilians targeted by, 19, 25, 75, 90–91, 95, 125–26, 141, 143–44, 168; and confrontation line, 207; and Contact Group Plan, 9, 52, 119, 127–28, 165; and Dayton Agreement, 229; Dutch soldiers attacked by, 188; effectiveness of, 152; and elections, 229; and end of war, 233–34; and escalation of war, 19–20, 151, 180, 226; ethnic cleansing by, 25, 26, 28, 210–11, 222; ethnic cleansing of, 231; and Federation, 173; and freedom of movement, 76, 113, 117, 123, 129, 138, 150; hostages taken by, 18, 19–20, 21, 31, 33, 50, 57, 65, 67–68, 69, 83, 100, 106, 113, 183, 184, 193; and humanitarian aid, 32, 38, 95, 97, 128, 133–34, 150, 154, 162, 183, 187; international recognition of, 13, 40, 68, 148; media bias against, 8, 38, 42, 69, 87, 186, 251; military officers, 27–28; military strength of, 127, 160, 184, 202, 214, 222, 232–33; as minority group, 22, 25, 26, 65, 70; money as motivation for, 49; NATO air strikes against, 18, 31, 35, 47, 58, 105–6, 120, 145, 176, 180, 193; and no-fly zones, 128, 181; propaganda of, 133, 180, 211, 213; retaliations of, 11, 151, 164, 176, 189, 195, 231; roads controlled by, 32, 35–38, 57, 58–59, 64, 67, 78, 116, 117, 124, 129, 150, 152, 154, 178, 183, 184, 191–92; RRF against, 50–51, 97, 123, 142, 158, 176, 184, 185, 228; and safe areas, 41, 181, 191; sanctions against, 29, 51–52; and SDS, 238–41, 245, 248–50; and self-determination, 25–26; and siege of Sarajevo, 74–75, 143–44, 163–67; and Srebrenica massacre and fall, 188–91, 192, 203–7, 209, 213; statelessness of, 25, 40, 87, 91, 127, 150; true nature of, 202–3; UN as link to, 20, 90, 124, 125, 127, 150, 165, 184, 217; and UNPROFOR staff, 13, 150, 218; UN staff bias against, 17–18, 72, 117, 224; UN troop withdrawal requested by, 214; utilities shut down by, 71, 84, 92, 154; and War Crimes Tribunal, 242–43; weakening of, 51–52, 58, 64, 66, 113, 114, 120, 121, 127, 129, 182, 202; and weapons collection points, 19, 75, 178; world bias against, 92,

189, 210–11. *See also* Republika Srpska; Serbs

Both, Norbert, 191, 193, 204, 233–34

Boutros-Ghali, Boutros: media bias against, 102, 225; and RRF, 116, 186; and UN-PROFOR mandate, 142, 150. *See also* Secretary-General

Boyd, Gen. Charles G., 39, 73

Brajkovic, Mijo, 169–70

Bratunac: medical helicopters needed in, 224; Moslem males moved to, 214

Britain: anti-Americanism of, 54; APCs as escorts from, 37; and arms embargo, 121, 235; army bias of, 38; Civil Affairs belittled by, 102, 118; and Contact Group Plan, 9; French rivalry with, 111, 177, 178; ground troops from, 21, 24, 50, 80, 117, 138, 139, 178, 216, 235; journalists from, 101–2; and RRF, 50, 123, 166, 172, 174, 185, 199–200, 221; and Smith, 160, 206; and use of force, 25, 70, 179–80

Brunei, 236

Bugojno: factories in, 181

Buha, Alex, 182, 238–39

Bush, George, 146, 147

Butmir: Serb attack on, 143; Serbian loss of, 151

CACs (Civil Affairs coordinators), 60; AORs of, 6; and chiefs of mission, 55; functions of, 5, 6–7, 11

Cambodia: parallel case of, 45–46

Canadian troops: as hostages, 115–16, 129, 138, 143, 157, 201–2, 215, 224, 225

Cannes: European ministers in, 121, 139, 141, 148, 179

Carter, Jimmy, 74

Cessation of Hostilities Agreement (COHA), 102, 113, 124, 129, 131

Chaubert, Bruno, 163, 207–9

China: and arms embargo, 235; and use of force, 25

Chirac, Jacques, 184, 222–23

Christian Science Monitor, 100–101

Christopher, Warren, 74, 146

Civil Affairs: attitudes of combatants toward, 102, 118–19, 142, 216; Coordinators of (CACs), 5, 6–7, 11, 55, 60; communication with, 142, 194; press briefings of, 98–102; space allotment for, 140–41, 182; staff ambition in, 55; staffing needs in, 199

Claes, Willy, 115, 142
Clinton, Bill, 22, 35, 51, 52, 85, 89, 145, 146–47,
153, 166, 234
CNN, 101, 109, 111, 143
COHA (Cessation of Hostilities Agreement),
102, 113, 124, 129, 131
Cohen, Roger, 86–87, 116, 185–86
Congress of Berlin (1878), 177
Contact Group: name of, 52; in negotiation
process, 111, 140, 150
Contact Group Plan, 9–10, 40, 43, 52, 53, 68,
80, 89, 119, 127–28, 148, 165, 234
Coward, Col. Gary, 98, 117–18
Croatia, 5; and arms supplies, 53, 54, 236, 237;
and Bosnian Croats, 52, 54, 109, 139, 168,
173; chief of mission in, 55–56; Croatians
vs. Croats in, 168; and Dayton Agreement,
229; diplomatic recognition of, 9, 26, 148;
and end of war, 233–34; and Federation,
53, 76, 80, 104, 109, 139, 158, 173–74, 229;
and freedom of movement, 123; humanitarian aid to, 68–69, 109; impact of UN
action on, 41; independence of, 27; and
Serbian secessionists, 148; Mount Dinara
shelled in, 106, 113; Nazis and, 177; political
aims of, 53; public image of, 132–33; and
RRF, 51, 158, 227; and Serbian communication, 159; and Serbian domination, 177;
Serbs as minority in, 26, 27; threats from,
109; UNCRO in, 121; UN hated in, 45, 126–
27, 218; as UN member, 40, 126; UN-
PROFOR in, 6, 121–22; Vance Plan for, 111;
vs. Western Slavonia, 11, 14, 33, 35, 45, 48,
83, 90–91, 121, 186, 204, 213; vs. Yugoslavia,
131–32, 152
Cutileiro, José, 145
Cutileiro initiative (1992), 234

Damic, Joshko, 226
Dayton Agreement, 229, 233, 237, 238, 240,
241, 242, 248, 249, 251
Dayton talks, 100–101, 233
de la Presle, Bernard, 119, 120, 179
Democratization process, 238–41, 245
de Soto, Alvaro, 147–48, 161, 162–63, 167–74
Dienbienphu: as parallel case, 160
Dinara, Mount, 106, 113
Diplomacy: blame placed for failure of, 245–
46; and confidence building, 20; and elec-

tions, 238–41; vs. military action, 20, 41,
148, 150, 160, 173–74, 176, 180, 233–35; and
sovereignty, 40. See also UN; UNPROFOR
Dole, Robert, 52, 85, 132, 237
D'Orsonnens, Lt. Paul, 225
Drljaca, Simo, 247
Dutch troops: as hostages, 188, 193–94, 204,
212, 224; and refugee convoys, 222, 223; in
RRF, 50, 185, 221; in safe areas, 81; in
Srebrenica, 122, 139, 178, 181, 188–94, 204–
5, 210, 214

Eagleburger, Lawrence, 132
Eagleton, Bill, 38–39, 70
Eastern Slavonia, Croatian control of, 46, 132
Egyptian troops, 177
Elliot, Gen. Christopher, 119, 179
England. See Britain
EU (European Union), 84, 97, 106, Bildt as
representative of, 47; and Contact Group,
52; and continuation of war, 153; cross pur-
poses within, 111; meeting in Cannes of,
121, 139, 141, 148, 179; Mostar administered
by, 169; in negotiation process, 111, 112, 165;
political responsibilities in Yugoslavia of,
110, 119, 120; reconstruction of, 169; and
RRF, 175
Evans, Rowland, 21–22

Fairweather, Dianne, 3
Falkland Islands: as parallel case, 70, 160
Fall, Merrick, 198, 207–8, 219–21
Fawcett, John, 70, 71, 84
Federation, 76, 80, 109, 169, 223; confrontation line in, 207; and Dayton Agreement,
229; and elections, 229; establishment of,
53, 170; and freedom of movement, 139,
192; Maglaj finger of, 207; money sought
by, 174; purposes of, 53, 173–74; and RRF,
104, 158, 171–72, 174, 187–88, 205–6; Zubak
as president of, 171
Foreign Affairs, 39
France: and Arab world, 186; and arms embargo, 121, 235; British rivalry with, 111, 177,
178; casualties of, 54, 57, 63, 150, 154, 159,
178, 186; and Contact Group Plan, 9; and
Dienbienphu, 160; ground troops from, 21,
24, 50, 54, 58, 80, 117, 177, 204, 235; and
hostages, 49, 65, 67–68, 159, 183; and re-

taliation, 209; and road openings, 134,
184–85, 186; and RRF, 50, 123, 152, 172, 174,
185, 186, 199–200, 221; Sarajevo administered by, 176–78; and use of force, 25, 117,
133, 150, 177, 180, 222–23
FYROM (Macedonia), 5, 6, 55–56

Galbraith, Peter, 9
Ganic, Ejup, 73, 74, 122, 142, 147, 158, 174, 201,
218
Geneva conventions: on humanitarian aid, 13
Genscher, Hans-Dietrich, 26
Germany: anti-Serbian bias of, 245; and
Contact Group Plan, 9, 165; and diplo-
matic recognition of Yugoslav states, 26; in
negotiation process, 111, 179
Glavas, Branimir, 46
Gobilliard, Hervé, 176–77, 184
Gorazde: defense of, 160; heavy-weapon ex-
clusion zones around, 24; humanitarian
aid to, 183; munitions factory in, 183; roads
blocked to, 63, 69, 116, 122, 139, 154, 161, 183;
as safe area, 13, 24–25, 41, 80; Serbian
threats to, 13, 62, 203, 212; shelling of, 64;
troops in, 41, 139, 178, 214
Gorbachev, Mikhail, 245
Gore, Al, 132, 237
Gornji Vakuf: briefings in, 198, 199–203, 205–
7; rebuilding of, 200; roads closed to, 97,
122, 139, 149–50, 154, 187; and Sector
Southwest, 187, 198; UNPROFOR suboffices in, 6, 199
Grabavac, Nikola, 108–10
Great Britain. See Britain
Greece: and Macedonia, 5
Gulf War, 160, 186

Hadziomeragic, Amir, 70, 71
Hannay, Sir David, 82
Han Plesak: attacks on, 190, 204
Harland, David, 72
Hedges, Chris, 86, 251
Helms, Jesse, 66
Herzeg-Bosna, 109, 170
Hodes, Matthew, 31, 37
Hodzic, Alma, 251
Holbrooke, Richard, 77, 100, 147, 233
Honig, Jan Willem, 191, 193, 204, 233–34
Humanitarian aid: APC escorts for, 35–37;

coordination of, 11–12; Corwin's thoughts
on, 196–98; deteriorating situation of, 182;
economic sanctions and, 197–98; Geneva
conventions on, 13; and hostages, 225;
limits on distribution of, 13, 103, 117, 154;
for Moslems, 38, 92, 176; and peacekeeping, 80, 198; profitability of, 196–97; protection of convoys with, 97, 125, 126, 133–
35, 149, 150, 152, 183, 198; and RRF, 128, 166,
186; and siege of Sarajevo, 164; skim factor
in, 197; and UNHCR, 29, 139; UNPROFOR
distribution of, 29, 107, 109, 126, 161, 175,
186, 187, 195, 198
Human Rights Watch/Helsinki, 190
Hungary, 235, 236
HV. See Croatia
HVO. See Bosnian Croats

ICFY (International Conference on the Former Yugoslavia), 43, 47–48, 110–11
ILR (Igman Logistics Route), 31, 32, 147–49,
167–68, 181, 198; Bosnian government control of, 78, 124, 184, 192, 194–95, 225; Bosnian Serb control of, 58–59, 78, 124, 150,
151, 152, 162, 164; Corwin's vehicle hit by
sniper on, 207–10, 218, 219; dangers of, 4,
15, 103, 148, 186, 207; French platoon on,
58–59, 133, 178; as humanitarian aid route,
80, 134–35, 150, 152, 162, 164, 192; rebuilding of, 152; RRF and, 116, 149, 202; and
Sarajevo airport tunnels, 124, 151; as UN-
PROFOR blue route, 149, 194–95
Indjic, Col. Milenko, 89–93, 137
International Committee of the Red Cross
(ICRC), 13
International press. See Media
Iran, 23, 52, 203, 236
Iraq, 147
Israel, 147
Italy, and Contact Group Plan, 9
Ivanko, Alex, 17–18, 98, 117–18, 224–25
Izetbegovic, Alija, 65, 77, 101, 106–7, 108, 109,
147, 174; and Akashi, 47; on continuation
of the war, 92, 145; and Dayton Agreement,
242; and division of Bosnia, 145–46; elec-
tion of, 157; and Grandfather Frost, 251; on
international conferences, 68; protests to,
217–18; and SDA, 153; on siege of Sarajevo,
68, 74; on UNPROFOR autonomy, 107

road access, 92, 138–39; and safe areas, 13; and Serbian shelling, 7, 58, 165; and Serbian territories, 79; and Srebrenica massacre and fall, 130, 190, 203, 210–12, 215; and use of force, 69, 113–14, 127, 130, 180–81, 184, 206; weakening force of, 64, 114, 127

MNB (multinational brigade), in RRF, 50, 200, 221–22

Montenegro, 5, 9, 148

Morillon, Gen. Philippe, 205, 217

Moslems: and anticolonialism, 177; in Arab world, 147; in Bosnian cities, 26, 82; Bosnian Croats vs., 123–24; and Dayton Agreement, 229; and elections, 229; and Federation, 53, 173, 229; and Ganic's accident, 158; "good" vs. "bad," 30, 147, 203; in Gornji Vakuf, 200; humanitarian aid to, 38, 92, 176; in Mostar, 170–71; multiethnic state favored by, 244; protest by women, 181; and RRF, 51, 123, 175; in Sarajevo, 231, 232; secession of, 157; Serbian, 33, 34; Serbian animosity toward, 22–23, 25, 28, 70, 80, 92, 124, 125, 160, 183, 186, 189–90, 205; Serbian villages raided by, 183, 205; Serbs killed by, 91; shelling by, 39, 157; and siege of Sarajevo, 92, 95; and Srebrenica massacre and fall, 189, 205, 210–12, 214, 215, 223, 224; in UN troops, 115; U.S. support of, 146–47; in Zepa, 216

Mostar, 168–74, 200; criminal element in, 168, 169, 170; demilitarization of, 169; and Federation, 169, 170, 174; and freedom of movement, 170–71; mayors of, 169–71; roads to, 147–48; shelling of, 168

Mount Igman road. See ILR

Muratovic, Hasan, 68, 70, 78–85, 93, 126, 155, 183; and Akashi, 46, 67, 72, 158; on Contact Group Plan, 80, 89; Corwin threatened by, 216–18, 219; on demilitarization, 83–84; favors requested by, 79, 95–96, 154, 205; and Federation, 158; on origins of war in Bosnia, 79–80; personal attributes of, 78–79, 107–8; and restriction of movement, 143; on RRF, 82, 142; and Ryan's arrest, 220, 221; on safe areas, 80–81; on Sarajevo utilities, 84, 88, 136; on Serbian refugees, 83; and Srebrenica massacre and fall, 189, 211–12, 215; on UNPROFOR, 80–81, 84–85, 97–

98, 102, 104–5, 108, 135–36, 149, 158–59, 205; on weapons confiscation, 83, 142, 159

NATO: air strikes by, (see Air strikes); air superiority lost by, 113; and arms embargo, 157; and Bosnian protection, 217, 250; destructive potential of, 35, 127, 128, 180, 222; diplomacy vs. use of force by, 47, 82, 97, 174, 193; and dual key concept, 21, 44; and hostile retreat, 48–49; and no-fly zones, 24; and nuclear deterrence, 30; peacekeeping troops of, 241, 251; post-Cold War identity of, 30, 44, 48; pressure for intervention by, 39, 41–42, 43, 51, 58, 70, 193; propaganda about, 133; retaliation for attacks of, 106, 113, 234; and safe areas, 80, 193; and Sarajevo government, 223; support from Bosnian government for, 119, 121, 250; and UN mandate, 44, 49, 115, 142, 193; and UNPROFOR jurisdiction, 142, 150, 184; and UNPROFOR replacement, 213; and war criminals, 247; and weapons confiscation, 142

Nazis, and ethnic rivalry, 34, 177

Nedarici, attacks on, 143

Nikolai, Gen. Kees, 119, 210, 212

Norwegian battalion, 223, 224

Norwegian Medical Company, 223

Novak, Bob, 21–22

O'Connor, Mike, 86, 250–51

O'Grady, Scott, 21, 22, 24, 25, 33

Oric, Naser, 189, 204–5

Origins of a Catastrophe (Zimmerman), 146

OSCE (Organization for Security and Cooperation in Europe), 229, 240, 241, 249

Ottoman Empire, records lacking from, 34

Owen, Lord David, 10, 47, 110, 132; and Vance-Owen Peace Plan, 40, 111, 146

Pakistan, 236

Pakistani battalion, 138

Pakrac, mass grave at, 186

Pale: and Bildt, 84, 112, 120, 165, 166, 176, 179, 182, 184; and Bosnian government attacks, 69, 84; as Bosnian Serb capital, 20, 120, 124, 125, 232; and elections, 238–39; isolation of, 84, 90, 125, 165–66, 217, 218; NATO air strikes in, 18–19, 36, 48, 58, 93, 96–97, 113,

nels in airport area of, 124–25, 143, 178; UNPROFOR delegates in, 6, 155, 182; UNPROFOR harassed in, 205, 226; UN unpopularity in, 7; utilities lacking in, 7, 12, 31, 56, 61–62, 66–67, 70–73, 84, 88, 92, 98–100, 103, 104, 109–10, 136, 154, 214, 231; weapons collection points in, 18–19

Sarajevo Agreement (1994), 18

Sarenic, Hovje, 131

Saudi Arabia, 52, 145, 147, 236

Schiller, Bill, 225

Schwarz, Delmore, 121

SCS (Special Coordinator for the Reconstruction of Sarajevo), 12

SDS (Serbian Democratic Party), 238–41, 245, 248–50

Secretary-General, UN: on air strikes, 18–19; CACs and, 5; and internal correspondence, 185; media bias against, 102, 225; on peacekeeping vs. peace enforcement, 50, 191; reports to Security Council, 6; on RRF, 82–83, 116, 172, 185, 186; and safe areas, 81, 82, 151, 191; on SOFA, 105; on Srebrenica massacre, 189–91; on UNPROFOR jurisdiction, 142, 150, 162

Security Council: and arms embargo, 53, 121, 235–37; CAC reports to, 6; chiefs of mission from, 55–56; and domestic constituencies, 6, 81, 85, 123; and freedom of movement, 115; and heavy-weapon exclusion zones, 24; and humanitarian aid, 42, 44, 134, 195, 198; implementation of resolutions from, 29, 81, 142, 173, 185–86, 191, 193, 195, 206; and member responsibilities, 24, 39–40, 54, 111, 138, 191, 235; and NATO air strikes, 25, 44; in negotiation process, 111, 123; and no-fly zones, 24; political consensus required in, 81; and RRF, 123, 185–86; and safe areas, 80, 81–82, 152; and sanctions against Serbs, 33, 63, 197; and sanctions against Yugoslavia, 131; and troop-supplying nations, 111; and UNPROFOR mandate, 43–44, 142; and use of force, 29, 42, 51; and Vance Plan/Vance-Owen Plan, 111; veto power in, 111, 121

Selimovic, Mesa, 27

Serbia, 5, 177; and Contact Group Plan, 9; Greater, 157; military strength of, 127; military threats from, 13; president of, (see

Milosevic, Slobodan); in rump Yugoslavia, 148; sanctions against, 63, 197; Sarajevan refugees in, 231; settlement needed with, 122, 148

Serbs: in Bosnia, (see Bosnian Serbs); hospitality of, 91, 129; in JNA, 27, 28; Krajina, 90, 106, 157; linked territories of, 28; vs. Moslems, 160; in Mostar, 170, 171; Nazis vs., 177; refugees, 83, 91; retaliation against, 27; sanctions against, 33; U.S. distrusted by, 95; in World War II, 32

Sierras: Bosnian Serb checkpoints along, 32, 38, 92, 95, 103, 129, 183, 184, 191; and principle of consent, 134, 150; Route Swan through, 31, 103, 134–35, 149, 183, 184, 191

Siladzic, Haris, 121, 142, 180, 224

Silber, Laura, 101, 189

Skopje, UNPROFOR delegates in, 6

Slobodanka (Boba), 112

Slovenia, 5, 26, 27

Smith, Adm. Leighton, 50–51

Smith, Gen. Rupert, 41–44; and air presence, 188; and air strikes, 7, 18, 58, 96–97, 120; briefings held by, 5, 12–13, 56–57, 62–64, 68, 69–70, 75–76, 78, 103–4, 105–6, 112–18, 121–24, 129–30, 133–35, 140–41, 148–53, 176–77, 215, 221–22; as commander of Bosnia, 177, 206, 224–25; and freedom of movement, 42, 44, 57, 64, 69, 75–76, 95, 103–4, 115, 116–17, 122, 123, 129, 136–37, 139, 149, 160, 201–2; and humanitarian aid, 134, 150, 152, 154, 164; and Janvier, 41–42, 56, 69, 137, 150, 160; mandate as seen by, 42, 43–44, 57, 160, 206; and media, 98, 102, 224–25; and Pedauye, 106; personal qualities of, 10, 167; and political responsibilities, 194–95, 201; and road closings, 78, 93, 134, 194; on "robust response," 43–44, 57, 150, 160–61; and RRF, 50, 50–51, 55, 69, 97, 104, 105, 122, 123, 133, 184, 186, 188, 206; and Sarajevo utilities, 73; and Serbian communication, 90, 124, 166, 178; on staff housing, 182; statements approved by, 17; Task Force Alpha of, 149, 152, 200; and troop morale, 42, 55, 57, 76; and troop security, 57–58, 64, 104; on UN hostages, 63, 95; use of force supported by, 43–44, 57, 69–70, 75–76, 96, 97, 114–15, 137, 150, 153–54, 160–61, 175, 177, 206; and U.S. political intervention, 234–35; and withdrawal of troops, 214

Vance Plan, 111
Vietnam War, analogies to, 33–34, 87, 127, 160
Visoko: administration in, 199; Canadian
  troops in, 115–16, 129, 138, 143, 157, 201–2,
  215, 224, 225; resupply of, 201, 215
Vitus, Saint, 141
Vladusic, Lyubisa, 35, 36–37

War Crimes Tribunal, 65, 241–43, 247
Washington. *See* United States
Washington Agreement, signing of, 170
Weapons: and arms embargo, 53–54, 157,
  235–37; confiscation of, 142, 159; and siege
  of Sarajevo, 74–75; smuggling of, 236;
  technical, 236–37; in TEZ, (*see* TEZ)
Weapons collection points (WCPs), 18–19;
  abandonment of, 113, 117, 135, 143, 149;
  French as guardians of, 178; hostages in,
  29; and siege of Sarajevo, 74, 76; UN protection of, 30, 57, 63, 83, 96–97
West, Rebecca, 88, 168
Western Slavonia: Croatian attacks on, 11, 33,
  45, 90–91, 121, 204; Croatian takeover of,
  14, 48, 83, 186, 213; Serbs expelled from, 11,
  33, 35, 83
WHO (World Health Organization), 11, 80
World Bank, 238
World press. *See* Media
World War II: Balkan civil wars in, 34; concentration camps in, 22; and ethnic rivalry,
  34, 177; Serbs harassed in, 32

Yeltsin, Boris, 34
Yilma, Hannah, 222
Yugoslavia (former): anxieties in, 250–51;
  arms embargo in, 23, 53–54, 75, 157, 232–
  33, 235–37; arms smuggling in, 40, 53, 75;
  and BiH, 159; CACs in, 5; COHA in, 102,
  113; criminal element in, 48, 168, 245;
  Dayton talks on, 100–101, 233; democratization process in, 238–41, 245; economic

sanctions against, 9–10, 45, 53, 131; ethnic
  rivalry in, 34, 160, 177, 244, 250–51; European involvement in, 110–11, 190–91, 234;
  ICFY and, 43, 47–48, 110–11; inertia in, 88–
  89; international conferences on, 68, 148,
  165, 180; Lilic as president of, 148; military
  vs. negotiated solution in, 148, 160, 173–74;
  misinformation in, 45, 48; as multiethnic
  society, 101, 250; mutual recognition
  within, 148; and nationhood, 34, 48; negotiations in, 111, 119; refugees from, 30, 85,
  94, 146; republics of, 5, 26–27; return of
  refugees in, 243–45; revenge in, 189–90,
  232; rump, 148; self-contained war in, 29–
  30, 114; tobacco as currency in, 198–99; use
  of term, 159; war criminals in, 241–43, 247;
  war for territory in, 80; in World War II,
  22, 32, 34, 177
Yugoslav National Army (JNA), 27, 28, 74,
  152

Zagreb, Croatia: Akashi based in, 5; Janvier
  based in, 160; and RRF, 167; Serbian shelling of, 90–91; UNHCR in, 155; UNPF in,
  121, 122, 134, 144, 159, 165, 189, 218; UN-
  PROFOR headquarters in, 42, 84–85, 109,
  111, 114, 120, 121
Zametica, Jovan, 182
Zenica: administration in, 199; refugees to,
  224; road blocks at, 149–50; Turkish battalion in, 201
Zepa: defense of, 160, 222, 224; fall of, 214,
  216; roads blocked to, 69, 150, 161, 224; as
  safe area, 13, 41, 80; Serbian threats to, 13,
  203, 212, 213, 220; troops in, 41, 139, 222
Zepce: administration in, 199; movement restricted in, 138
Zimmermann, Warren, 35, 146
Zubak, Kresimir, 147, 152–53, 158, 171–74
Zvornik: meetings in, 179, 182, 218; police
  units in, 28

During his twenty-seven years of service with the United
Nations, Phillip Corwin held a number of posts, including that
of a speech writer for former UN Secretary-General Javier Perez
de Cuellar. During the 1990s, he served on peacekeeping
missions to Haiti, Afghanistan, and Western Sahara, as well as
the former Yugoslavia. He is also a widely published poet and
short story writer.

Library of Congress Cataloging-in-Publication Data
Corwin, Phillip.
Dubious mandate : a memoir of the UN in Bosnia, summer
1995 / Phillip Corwin.
Includes index.
ISBN 0-8223-2126-2 (cloth : alk. paper)
1. Yugoslav War, 1991–1995—Bosnia and Hercegovina.
2. United Nations Protection Force—History.   3. United
Nations—Bosnia and Hercegovina.   4. Bosnia and
Hercegovina—History—1992–   I. Title.
DR1313.3.C67   1999   949.703—dc21   98-39289 CIP